DB2® Univ

Database

Certification

Exams 701

and 706

Study Guide

ON DEMAND COMPUTING BOOKS

On Demand Computing: Technology and Strategy Perspectives
Fellenstein

Grid Computing
Joseph and Fellenstein

Autonomic Computing
Murch

Business Intelligence for the Enterprise
Biere

DB2 BOOKS

DB2 Universal Database v8.1 Certification Exams 701 and 706 Study Guide
Sanders

DB2 for Solaris: The Official Guide
Bauch and Wilding

DB2 Universal Database v8.1 Certification Exam 700 Study Guide
Sanders

DB2 Universal Database v8 for Linux, UNIX, and Windows Database Administration Certification Guide, Fifth Edition
Baklarz and Wong

Advanced DBA Certification Guide and Reference for DB2 Universal Database v8 for Linux, UNIX, and Windows
Snow and Phan

DB2 Universal Database v8 Application Development Certification Guide, Second Edition
Martineau, Sanyal, Gashyna, and Kyprianou

DB2 Version 8: The Official Guide
Zikopoulos, Baklarz, deRoos, and Melnyk

Teach Yourself DB2 Universal Database in 21 Days
Visser and Wong

DB2 UDB for OS/390 v7.1 Application Certification Guide
Lawson

DB2 SQL Procedural Language for Linux, UNIX, and Windows
Yip, Bradstock, Curtis, Gao, Janmohamed, Liu, and McArthur

DB2 Universal Database v8 Handbook for Windows, UNIX, and Linux
Gunning

Integrated Solutions with DB2
Cutlip and Medicke

DB2 Universal Database for OS/390 Version 7.1 Certification Guide
Lawson and Yevich

DB2 Universal Database v7.1 for UNIX, Linux, Windows and OS/2— Database Administration Certification Guide, Fourth Edition
Baklarz and Wong

DB2 Universal Database v7.1 Application Development Certification Guide
Sanyal, Martineau, Gashyna, and Kyprianou

DB2 UDB for OS/390: An Introduction to DB2 OS/390
Sloan and Hernandez

IBM Press™

DB2® Universal Database™ V8.1 Certification Exams 701 and 706 Study Guide

DB2® Information Management Software

Roger E. Sanders

PRENTICE HALL
Professional Technical Reference
Upper Saddle River, New Jersey 07458
www.phptr.com

Editorial/production supervision: *MetroVoice Publishing Services*
Cover design director: *Jerry Votta*
Cover design: *IBM Corporation*
Manufacturing manager: *Alexis Heydt-Long*
Publisher: *Jeffrey Pepper*
Editorial assistant: *Linda Ramagnano*
Marketing manager: *Debby vanDijk*
IBM Consulting Editor: *Susan Visser*

Published by Pearson Education, Inc.
Publishing as Prentice Hall Professional Technical Reference
Upper Saddle River, NJ 07458

Prentice Hall PTR offers excellent discounts on this book when ordered in quantity for bulk purchases or special sales. For more information, please contact: U.S. Corporate and Government Sales, 1-800-382-3419, corpsales@pearsontechgroup.com. For sales outside of the U.S., please contact: International Sales, 1-317-581-3793, international@pearsontechgroup.com.

Printed in the United States of America

First Printing

ISBN   0-13-184048-7

Pearson Education LTD.
Pearson Education Australia PTY, Limited
Pearson Education Singapore, Pte. Ltd.
Pearson Education North Asia Ltd.
Pearson Education Canada, Ltd.
Pearson Educación de Mexico, S.A. de C.V.
Pearson Education — Japan
Pearson Education Malaysia, Pte. Ltd.

To Bob Jancer and Mark Hayakawa

About Prentice Hall Professional Technical Reference

With origins reaching back to the industry's first computer science publishing program in the 1960s, and formally launched as its own imprint in 1986, Prentice Hall Professional Technical Reference (PH PTR) has developed into the leading provider of technical books in the world today. Our editors now publish over 200 books annually, authored by leaders in the fields of computing, engineering, and business.

Our roots are firmly planted in the soil that gave rise to the technical revolution. Our bookshelf contains many of the industry's computing and engineering classics: Kernighan and Ritchie's *C Programming Language*, Nemeth's *UNIX System Administration Handbook*, Horstmann's *Core Java*, and Johnson's *High-Speed Digital Design*.

PH PTR acknowledges its auspicious beginnings while it looks to the future for inspiration. We continue to evolve and break new ground in publishing by providing today's professionals with tomorrow's solutions.

PRENTICE
HALL
PTR

Contents

. . . .

Foreword

Administering a database can either be lots of fun or a dreadful struggle. Database Administrator (DBA) is a job nobody will notice as long as everything runs smoothly; when not, it is all your fault (you being the DBA). This book teaches you basic DB2 version 8 database administration—not necessarily the most easy tasks but certainly the most frequent ones. These tasks are collected in IBM's Basic Database Administration Exam and, after having read this book, you will be well prepared for both basic database administration and the exam.

Your needs are simple enough to state: usefulness (the topics you need most) and didactics (compellingly written). A lot of sources attempt to help with learning to use and administer DB2, and many are technically worthy but many come up short through their choice of topics and their presentation. "Limited resource management" is one of today's opportunities and banes and your time is the scarcest of the lot: getting it done by last week (and knowing how to!) is barely acceptable. "Getting it done" in the case of a DBA implies that you not only master the tools to manage a database and the strategies to use them effectively, but that you also do this within the context of complex, unstructured, and non-deterministic problems caused by what users want, what the hardware can do, what the company can afford, what the business rules require, management demands, and how much time you have to satisfy everybody (not least of it yourself—after all, you want to get satisfaction out of what you do).

It is normal that when learning a trade there is a certain amount of data to be absorbed about what you need to do and how to do it. There is no substitute for putting your nose to the grindstone and acquiring some experience, and this book does not pretend to avoid that. But some road maps are better than others and this, in my opinion, is the best. Roger is gifted with a rare combination of knowledge and the capacity to pass it on. This finds its expression in a balance between the tasks you will face, the tools DB2 has to accomplish them, insight about which choice to make, and essential understanding on how things work under the covers. With this you will end up with a well-balanced network of knowledge and how to apply it to a DBA's diverse tasks—

including the constraints they come with, instead of unconnected islands of data you do not necessarily understand how to apply to your needs. But best of all (in my opinion) is the understanding Roger imparts of how the parts fit together: your understanding will help you remember things much more easily, your decisions will be more informed, and you will also be better equipped for tasks outside of the scope of basic database administration.

Before this book hit the press I had already had a good look at it. It was fascinating, it was fun, and to me it has (already) proven to be very useful.

—Jan Kritter
Database Specialist,
IBM SAP Integration and Support Center,
Toronto

SAP

Preface

. . . .

One of the biggest challenges computer professionals face today is keeping their skill sets current with the latest changes in technology. When the computing industry was in its infancy, it was possible to become an expert in several different areas, because the scope of the field was relatively small. Today, our industry is both widespread and fast paced, and the skills needed to master a single software package can be quite complex. Because of this complexity, many application and hardware vendors have initiated certification programs to evaluate and validate an individual's knowledge of their technology. Businesses benefit from these programs, because professional certification gives them confidence that an individual has the expertise needed to perform a specific job. Computer professionals benefit, because professional certification allows them to deliver high levels of service and technical expertise, and more importantly, professional certification can lead to advancement and/or new job opportunities within the computer industry.

If you've bought this book (or if you are thinking about buying this book), chances are you have already decided you want to acquire one or more of the IBM DB2 Universal Database (UDB) V8.1 Professional Certifications available. As an individual who holds eight IBM DB2 UDB professional certifications, let me assure you that the exams you must pass in order to become a certified DB2 UDB professional are not easy. IBM prides itself on designing comprehensive certification exams that are relevant to the work environment an individual holding a particular certification will have had some exposure to. As a result, all of IBM's certification exams are designed with the following items in mind:

> ➤ What are the critical tasks that must be performed by an individual who holds a particular professional certification?

> ➤ What skills must an individual possess in order to perform each critical task?

> ➤ What is the frequency with which each critical task must be performed?

You will find that to pass a DB2 UDB certification exam, you must possess a solid understanding of DB2 Universal Database (and for some of the more advanced certifications, you must understand many of its nuances as well).

Now for the good news. You are holding in your hands what I consider to be the best tool you can use to prepare for the DB2 UDB V8.1 for Linux, UNIX, and Windows Database Administration certification exam (Exam 701) or the DB2 UDB V8.1 for Linux, UNIX, and Windows Database Administration certification upgrade exam (Exam 706). When IBM learned that I was planning to write a series of study guides for the DB2 UDB V8.1 certification exams, they invited me to participate in the exam development process. Among other things, I had the opportunity to evaluate several of the beta DB2 UDB V8.1 exams before they went into production. Consequently, I have seen every exam question you are likely to encounter, and I know what concepts you will be tested on when you take the DB2 UDB V8.1 for Linux, UNIX, and Windows Database Administration certification exam (Exam 701). (I did not participate in the development of the DB2 UDB V8.1 for Linux, UNIX, and Windows Database Administration certification upgrade exam (Exam 706); however, IBM provided me with detailed information on the types of test questions a candidate might encounter when taking that exam.) Using this knowledge, along with copies of the beta 701 exams, I developed this study guide, which not only covers every DB2 UDB concept you must know in order to pass the DB2 UDB V8.1 for Linux, UNIX, and Windows Database Administration certification exam (Exam 701) or the DB2 UDB V8.1 for Linux, UNIX, and Windows Database Administration certification upgrade exam (Exam 706), but also covers the exam process itself and the requirements for each available DB2 UDB V8.1 certification role. In addition, you will find at the end of each chapter, sample questions that are worded just like the actual exam questions. In short, if you see it in this book, count on seeing it on the exam; if you don't see it in this book, chances are it won't be on the exam.

About This Book

This book is divided into two parts:

➤ Part 1—DB2 UDB Certification (Chapter 1)

This section consists of one chapter (Chapter 1), which is designed to introduce you to the DB2 UDB Professional Certification Program that is available from IBM. In this chapter, you will learn about the different certification roles available, along with the basic prerequisites and requirements for each role. This chapter also explains what's involved in the certification process, and it includes a tutorial on the IBM Certification Exam testing software, which you will encounter when you go to take a DB2 UDB V8.1 certification exam.

➤ Part 2—DB2 UDB Linux, UNIX, and Windows Database Administration (Chapters 2–7)

This section consists of six chapters (Chapters 2 through 7), which are designed to provide you with the concepts you will need to master before you can pass the DB2 UDB V8.1 for Linux, UNIX, and Windows Database Administration certification exam (Exam 701) or the DB2 UDB V8.1 for Linux, UNIX, and Windows Database Administration certification upgrade exam (Exam 706).

Chapter 2 is designed to introduce you to the various aspects of server management and to the authorization levels and privileges that are supported by DB2 UDB V8.1. In this chapter, you will learn how and where users are authenticated, how authorities and privileges determine what a user can and cannot do while working with a database, and how authorities and privileges are given to and taken away from individual users and/or groups of individual users. You will also learn how to configure client/server connectivity and you will learn how to obtain detailed information that can be used to resolve problems when they occur.

Chapter 3 is designed to provide you with everything you need to know about how data in a DB2 UDB database is physically stored. In this chapter, you will learn how to create a DB2 UDB database and you will see what a DB2 UDB database's underlying structure looks like, as well as how that structure is physically mapped to directories, files, and raw devices. You will also learn how buffer pools and tablespaces are used and you will find out how to obtain information about a database's tablespaces without having to query the system catalog.

Chapter 4 is designed to provide you with everything you need to know about tables, indexes, and views. In this chapter, you will learn how to create tables, indexes, and views, and you will learn when and how NOT NULL constraints, default constraints, check constraints, unique constraints, referential integrity constraints, and informational constraints should be used. You will also learn how to automate routine maintenance operations using the Task Center.

Chapter 5 is designed to introduce you to the various tools that are available for monitoring a database's performance. In this chapter, you will learn how to configure and use the snapshot monitor, event monitors, the Health Center, and the Explain facility. You will also learn how to analyze the information produced by these tools to locate weaknesses in database and/or application design.

Chapter 6 is designed to provide you with everything you need to know about DB2 UDB's data movement and data management utilities. In this chapter, you will learn how to use the Export utility to extract data from a database and store it to an external file and you will learn how to use the Import and Load utilities to move data stored in external files into database tables. You will also learn how to reorganize database tables, update statistics that are used by the DB2 Optimizer, and rebind existing applications once statistics have been updated.

Chapter 7 is designed to introduce you to the concept of database recovery and to the various tools that can be used with DB2 UDB V8.1 to return a damaged or corrupted database to a useable state. In this chapter, you will learn what transaction logging is, how transaction logging is performed, and how log files are used to restore a damaged database. You will also learn how to back up a database using the Backup utility, restore a database using the Restore utility, and reapply transaction records stored in log files by performing a roll-forward recovery operation.

The book is written primarily for IT professionals who have already taken and passed the DB2 UDB V8.1 Family Fundamentals exam (Exam 700) and want to take (and pass) the DB2 UDB V8.1 for Linux, UNIX, and Windows Database Administration certification exam (Exam 701). IT professionals who possess DB2 UDB Version 7.2 Database Administration certification and wish to upgrade their certification by taking (and passing) the DB2 UDB V8.1 for Linux, UNIX, and Windows Database Administration certification upgrade exam (Exam 706) will also benefit from this book. Additionally, any individual who would like to learn the basics of DB2 UDB V8.1 for Linux, UNIX, and Windows database administration will benefit from the information found in this book.

Conventions Used

Many examples of DB2 UDB administrative commands and SQL statements can be found throughout this book. The following conventions are used whenever a DB2 command or SQL statement is presented:

[ ]   Parameters or items shown inside of brackets are required and must be provided.

< >   Parameters or items shown inside of angle brackets are optional and do not have to be provided.

| Vertical bars are used to indicate that one (and only one) item in the list of items presented can be specified

,...   A comma followed by three periods (ellipsis) indicate that multiple instances of the preceding parameter or item can be included in the DB2 command or SQL statement

The following examples illustrate each of these conventions.

Example 1

```
REFRESH TABLE [TableName ,...]
<INCREMENTAL | NON INCREMENTAL>
```

In this example, at least one *TableName* value must be provided, as indicated by the brackets ([ ]), and more than one *TableName* value can be provided, as indicated by the comma-ellipsis (, . . .) characters that follow the *TableName* parameter. INCREMENTAL and NON INCREMENTAL are optional, as indicated by the angle brackets (< >), and either one or the other can be specified, but not both, as indicated by the vertical bar (|).

Example 2

```
CREATE SEQUENCE [SequenceName]
<AS [SMALLINT | INTEGER | BIGINT | DECIMAL]>
<START WITH [StartingNumber]>
<INCREMENT BY [1 | Increment]>
<NO MINVALUE | MINVALUE [MinValue]>
<NO MAXVALUE | MAXVALUE [MaxValue]>
<NO CYCLE | CYCLE>
<NO CACHE | CACHE 20 | CACHE [CacheValue]>
<NO ORDER | ORDER>
```

In this example, a *SequenceName* value must be provided, as indicated by the brackets ([ ]). However, everything else is optional, as indicated by the angle brackets (< >), and in many cases, a list of available option values is provided (for example, NO CYCLE and CYCLE); however, only one can be specified, as indicated by the vertical bar (|). In addition, when some options are provided (for example, START WITH, INCREMENT BY, MINVALUE, MAXVALUE, and CACHE), a corresponding value must be provided, as indicated by the brackets ([ ]) that follow the option.

SQL is not a case-sensitive language, so even though most of the examples provided are shown in uppercase, they can be entered in any case.

Acknowledgments

A project of this magnitude requires both a great deal of time and the support of many different individuals. I would like to express my gratitude to the following people for their contributions:

Susan Visser—IBM Press, Data Management Program Manager, IBM Toronto Lab

Once again, Susan's help was invaluable—without her help, this book would not have been written. Susan paved the way for my participation in the DB2 UDB V8.1 exam development process, providing me with both the exam objectives and beta copies of the DB2 UDB V8.1 certification exams. More importantly, Susan helped me make the migration from Osborne/McGraw-Hill to IBM Press. Susan also reviewed many of the chapters as they were written, and she made sure the appropriate subject-matter experts at the IBM Toronto Lab reviewed portions of the manuscript as well.

Jan Kritter—Database Specialist, IBM SAP Integration and Support Center, Toronto SAP

Jan did a superb job of reviewing the manuscript and providing me with feedback. Jan pointed out where I assumed the reader was already familiar with a topic (that they might not be familiar with), and he kept me honest. Because of Jan's efforts, some of the finer points you will find throughout this book were clarified or edited before the manuscript went into production. Jan also provided me with the Foreword for this book.

Melissa Montoya—Certification Program Manager, DB2 Information Management Software, IBM Menlo Park

Melissa provided me with detailed information about the DB2 UDB V8.1 for Linux, UNIX, and Windows Database Administration certification upgrade exam (Exam 706) and she arranged for Hana and Darrin to review the manuscript for clarity and accuracy.

Hana Curtis—Advisory Development Analyst, DB2 Integration, IBM Toronto Lab

Hana did an excellent job of reviewing the manuscript and providing me with feedback. Because of Hana's efforts, some mistakes in the manuscript were corrected or clarified before the book went into production.

Darrin Woodard—DB2 UDB Development, DB2 UDB Release Team, IBM Toronto Lab

Darrin also did an excellent job of reviewing the manuscript and providing me with feedback. Like Hana, Darrin pointed out some mistakes in the manuscript and recommended changes, which were incorporated before the book went into production.

Rick Swagerman—Sr. Technical Manager, DB2 SQL and Catalog Development, IBM Toronto Lab

Rick provided me with detailed examples illustrating how the UPDATE/ DELETE NO ACTION and UPDATE/DELETE RESTRICT rules of referential constraints work. His examples were converted into some of the illustrations you see in Chapter 4, and Rick reviewed the final draft of many of these drawings for accuracy and completeness.

Dale McInnis—Sr. Technical Manager, DB2 / LUW Backup, Data Protection and Recovery, IBM Toronto Lab

Dale provided me with detailed information on how DB2 UDB performs transaction logging and he reviewed the sections on transaction logging in Chapter 7 for accuracy and completeness.

Paul Rivot—Director of Database Servers for Software Group (Vera Patterson, Secretary)

Paul and Vera provided me with a copy of the *DB2 Universal Developer's Edition, Version 8.1*, software. This software, in turn, was used to produce the screen captures found throughout the book. The online documentation that comes with the DB2 Universal Developer's Edition was used extensively as well.

I would also like to thank my wife, Beth, for her help and encouragement, and for once again overlooking all of the things that did not get done while I worked on yet another book.

About the Author

Roger E. Sanders is a Database Performance Engineer with Network Appliance, Inc. He has been designing and developing database applications for more than 18 years, and he has worked with DB2 Universal Database and its predecessors since it was first introduced on the IBM PC (as part of OS/2 Extended Edition). He has written several articles for publications such as *DB2 Magazine* and *IDUG Solutions Journal*, authored a tutorial titled "Database Concurrency: DB2 Version 8.1 Family Fundamentals Certification Preparation" for IBM's DeveloperWorks Web site, presented at three International DB2 User's Group (IDUG) conferences, and is the author of the following books:

➤ *DB2 UDB V8.1 Certification Exam 700 Study Guide*

➤ *DB2 UDB Exploitation of NAS Technology* (IBM RedBook; coauthor)

➤ *All-In-One DB2 Administration Exam Guide*

➤ *DB2 Universal Database SQL Developer's Guide*

➤ *DB2 Universal Database API Developer's Guide*

➤ *DB2 Universal Database Call Level Interface Developer's Guide*

➤ *ODBC 3.5 Developer's Guide*

➤ *The Developer's Handbook to DB2 for Common Servers*

In addition, Roger holds the following professional certifications:

➤ IBM Certified Advanced Database Administrator—DB2 Universal Database V8.1 for Linux, UNIX, and Windows

➤ IBM Certified Database Administrator—DB2 Universal Database V8.1 for Linux, UNIX, and Windows

➤ IBM Certified Developer—DB2 Universal Database V8.1 Family

➤ IBM Certified Database Associate—DB2 Universal Database V8.1 Family

➤ IBM Certified Advanced Technical Expert—DB2 for Clusters

➤ IBM Certified Solutions Expert—DB2 UDB V7.1 Database Administration for UNIX, Windows, and OS/2

➤ IBM Certified Solutions Expert—DB2 UDB V6.1 Application Development for UNIX, Windows, and OS/2

➤ IBM Certified Specialist—DB2 UDB V6/V7 User

PART 1
DB2 UDB Certification

IBM DB2 Universal Database Certification

The Professional Certification Program from IBM is recognized the world over and offers a range of certification options for IT professionals. This chapter is designed to introduce you to the various paths you can take to obtain DB2 Universal Database Certification from IBM and to let you know what you can expect when you sit down to take your first DB2 UDB certification exam.

DB2 Universal Database Certification Roles

One of the biggest trends in the IT industry today is certification. Many application/software vendors now have in place certification programs designed to evaluate and validate an individual's proficiency with their latest product release. In fact, one of the reasons the Professional Certification Program from IBM was developed was to provide a way for skilled technical professionals to demonstrate their knowledge and expertise with a particular version of an IBM product.

The Professional Certification Program from IBM is comprised of several distinct certification roles designed to guide you in your professional development. You simply select the role that's right for you, then you begin the certification process by choosing the role you wish to pursue and familiarizing yourself with the requirements for that role. The following sections are designed to help get you started by providing you with the prerequisites and requirements associated with each DB2 UDB Version 8.1 certification available.

IBM Certified Database Associate— DB2 Universal Database V8.1 Family

The *IBM Certified Database Associate—DB2 Universal Database V8.1 Family* certification is intended for entry-level DB2 UDB users who are knowledgeable about the fundamental concepts of DB2 UDB, Version 8.1, or DB2 UDB for iSeries (AS/400), V5R2. In addition to having some hands-on experience with and/or some formal training on DB2 UDB, Version 8.1, and/or DB2 UDB for iSeries (AS/400), V5R2, individuals seeking this certification should:

➤ Know what DB2 UDB products are available and be familiar with the various ways DB2 UDB is packaged.

➤ Know what DB2 UDB products must be installed in order to create a desired environment.

➤ Possess a strong knowledge about the mechanisms DB2 UDB uses to protect data and database objects against unauthorized access and/or modification.

➤ Know how to create, access, and manipulate basic DB2 UDB objects, such as tables, views, and indexes.

➤ Be familiar with the different types of constraints that are available and know how each is used.

➤ Possess an in-depth knowledge of the Structured Query Language (SQL), Data Definition Language (DDL), Data Manipulation Language (DML), and Data Control Language (DCL) statements that are available.

➤ Have a basic understanding of the methods used to isolate transactions from each other in a multiuser environment.

➤ Be familiar with the methods used to control whether a transaction acquires row-level or table-level locks.

In order to acquire the IBM Certified Database Associate—DB2 Universal Database V8.1 Family certification, candidates must take and pass one exam: the **DB2 UDB V8.1 Family Fundamentals** exam (Exam 700). The roadmap for acquiring the IBM Certified Database Associate—DB2 Universal Database V8.1 Family certification can be seen in Figure 1–1.

Certified for **DB2.**
IBM® e-business software

Professional Certification Program from IBM
IBM Exam 700
IBM DB2 UDB V8.1 Family Fundamentals
Examination Score Report

CANDIDATE: Ian Blair

CANDIDATE ID: vuea77536   **DATE:** 04-Jul-2006

REGISTRATION NUMBER: 216203240   **SITE:** 51217

VALIDATION NUMBER: 368620925

EXAM: IBM DB2 UDB V8.1 Family Fundamentals

EXAM SERIES: 700

PASSING SCORE: 61% (23 out of 54) **YOUR SCORE:** 94% (51 out of 54) **GRADE:** Pass

Your order is finished!

This page is your receipt.

- To print your receipt, click **Print Confirmation**. We will also send an email **PRINT CONFIRMATION** containing this information to ianblair@btopenworld.com.

Candidate:	Ian Blair
Exam:	700: IBM DB2 UDB V8.1 Family Fundamentals
Test Center:	Pitman Training (Gloucester) Eastgate House 121-131 Eastgate Street GLOUCESTER GL1 1PX GBR +44 (0)1452 504509
Appointment:	Tue, 4 Jul 2006 / Start Time: 18:30
Appointment Number:	216203240
Date/Time Appointment Created:	Thu, 29 Jun 2006, at 07:39 GMT
Exam Total:	GBP 96.00
VAT:	GBP 16.80
Amount Paid:	**GBP 112.80** **** ****** ***** 2090
Order Number:	0000-4216-4929

Check-in Policy:

Please arrive at the test center 15 minutes before your scheduled appointment. This will allow required to show two (2) forms of personal identification. Both forms must contain your signature, and at least one form must contain your photo. If you arrive more than 15 minutes after your appointment time and are refused admission, the exam and delivery fees are not refundable.

You will not be allowed to take any personal items with you into the testing room. This includes all bags, books not authorized by the testing program, notes, cell phones, pagers, watches and wallets.

Cancellation Policy:

To cancel or reschedule your exam appointment and receive a full refund, you must notify Pearson VUE at least one business day before your appointment. Otherwise, your exam fee is not refundable. Your exam fee is also not refundable if you do not arrive at the test center for your scheduled appointment. (There is no liability for any fees if your exam is free.) Please contact a Pearson VUE agent if you have questions about this policy.

In case of a failure to deliver the exam, Pearson VUE will not be held responsible for expenses you incur beyond the cost of the exam, including but not limited to travel expenses and lost wages on the day of the exam.

All policies are subject to change without notice. Please check your email confirmation letter for the current policy for this program.

Pearson VUE's goal is to make your testing experience a pleasant one. We thank you for selecting Pearson VUE as your testing service provider, and look forward to serving you again. Please feel free to contact us with your comments or questions.

Directions to Pitman Training (Gloucester)

Directions and a location map can be found on our website at http://www.pitman-

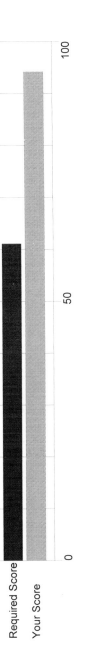

Required Score

Your Score

0   50   100

The following shows the percentage weighting of each section/category and your related score.

Section/Category	Test Info	Your Score
1. Planning	8 out of 54	8 out of 8
2. Security	5 out of 54	5 out of 5
3. Accessing DB2 UDB Data	8 out of 54	7 out of 8
4. Working with DB2 UDB Data	17 out of 54	17 out of 17
5. Working with DB2 UDB Objects	10 out of 54	9 out of 10
6. Data Concurrency	6 out of 54	5 out of 6

Information on all certifications offered through the Professional Certification Program from IBM can be found at **www.ibm.com/certify**. Questions and concerns should be addressed to **certify@us.ibm.com**.

IBM is a registered trademark of IBM Corporation.

YOU CAN AUTHENTICATE THIS SCORE REPORT USING A DIGITAL EMBOSSER!

Digital embossing maintains the integrity of this testing program and the value of your certification. Digital embossing

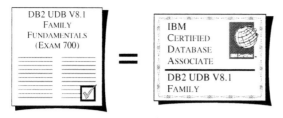

Figure 1–1   IBM Certified Database Associate—DB2 Universal Database V8.1 Family certification roadmap.

IBM Certified Database Administrator— DB2 Universal Database V8.1 for Linux, UNIX, and Windows

The *IBM Certified Database Administrator—DB2 Universal Database V8.1 for Linux, UNIX, and Windows* certification is intended for experienced DB2 UDB users who possess the knowledge and skills necessary to perform the day-to-day administration of DB2 UDB, Version 8.1 instances and databases residing on Linux, UNIX, or Windows platforms. In addition to being knowledgeable about the fundamental concepts of DB2 UDB, Version 8.1, and having significant hands-on experience as a DB2 UDB Database Administrator (DBA), individuals seeking this certification should:

➤ Know how to configure and manage DB2 UDB instances.

➤ Know how to configure client/server connectivity.

➤ Know how to create DB2 UDB databases.

➤ Possess a strong knowledge about SMS and DMS tablespaces, as well as be familiar with the management requirements of each.

➤ Know how to create, access, modify, and manage the various DB2 UDB objects available.

➤ Be able to create constraints on and between table objects.

➤ Possess a strong knowledge about the mechanisms DB2 UDB uses to protect data and database objects against unauthorized access and/or modification.

➤ Be able to obtain and modify the values of environment/registry variables.

➤ Be able to obtain and modify DB2 Database Manager and database configuration file parameter values.

➤ Know how to capture and analyze Explain information.

➤ Know how to use the DB2 UDB Control Center and other GUI tools available to manage instances and databases, create and access objects, create tasks, schedule jobs, and view Explain information.

➤ Be familiar with the functions of the DB2 Governor and the Query Patroller.

➤ Know how to capture and interpret snapshot monitor data.

➤ Know how to create and activate event monitors, as well as interpret event monitor data.

➤ Possess an in-depth knowledge of the EXPORT, IMPORT, and LOAD utilities.

➤ Know how to use the REORGCHK, REORG, REBIND, RUNSTATS, db2look, and db2move utilities.

➤ Know how to perform database-level and tablespace-level backup, restore, and roll-forward recovery operations.

➤ Have a basic understanding of transaction logging.

➤ Be able to interpret information stored in the administration notification log.

Candidates who have either taken and passed the **DB2 UDB V7.1 Family Fundamentals** exam (Exam 512) or acquired the IBM Certified Solutions Expert—DB2 UDB V7.1 Database Administration for UNIX, Windows, and OS/2 certification must take and pass the **DB2 UDB V8.1 for Linux, UNIX, and Windows Database Administration** exam (Exam 701) to acquire the IBM Certified Database Administrator—DB2 Universal Database V8.1 for Linux, UNIX, and Windows certification. All other candidates must take and pass both the **DB2 UDB V8.1 Family Fundamentals** exam (Exam 700) and the **DB2 UDB V8.1 for Linux, UNIX, and Windows Database Administration** exam (Exam 701). The roadmap for acquiring the IBM Certified Database Administrator—DB2 Universal Database V8.1 for Linux, UNIX, and Windows certification can be seen in Figure 1–2.

Candidates who already hold the IBM Certified Solutions Expert—DB2 UDB V7.1 Database Administration for UNIX, Windows, and OS/2 certification may opt to take the **DB2 UDB V8.1 for Linux, UNIX, and Windows Database Administration Upgrade Exam** (Exam 706) to acquire the IBM Certified Database Administrator—DB2 Universal Database V8.1 for Linux, UNIX, and Windows certification. This exam, which is half the length and half the cost of the **DB2 UDB V8.1 for Linux, UNIX, and Windows Database Administration** exam (Exam 701), is designed to test a candidate's knowledge of the new features and functions that are provided in DB2 UDB Version 8.1. Essentially, the upgrade exam provides certified DB2 UDB Version 7.1 DBAs with an accelerated approach for acquiring an equivalent Version 8.1 certification. This accelerated approach is outlined in Figure 1–3.

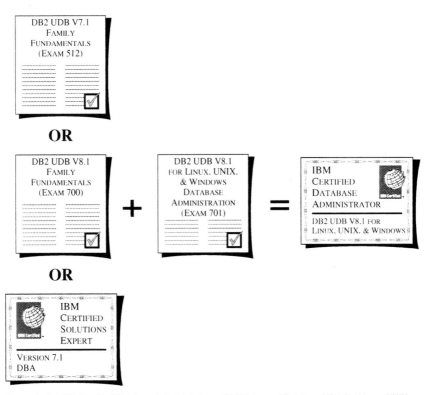

Figure 1-2   IBM Certified Database Administrator—DB2 Universal Database V8.1 for Linux, UNIX, and Windows certification roadmap.

Figure 1-3   The accelerated approach for acquiring IBM Certified Database Administrator—DB2 Universal Database V8.1 for Linux, UNIX, and Windows certification.

IBM Certified Database Administrator— DB2 Universal Database V8.1 for z/OS and OS/390

The *IBM Certified Database Administrator—DB2 Universal Database V8.1 for z/OS and OS/390* certification is intended for experienced DB2 UDB users who possess the knowledge and skills necessary to perform the day-to-day administration of DB2 UDB, Version 8.1 instances and databases residing on OS/390 platforms. In addition to being knowledgeable about the fundamental concepts of DB2 UDB, Version 8.1, and having significant hands-on experience as a DB2 UDB Database Administrator, individuals seeking this certification should:

➤ Know how to convert a logical database design to a physical database design.

➤ Know how to create, access, modify, and manage the various DB2 UDB objects available.

➤ Know how to interpret the contents of system catalogs and directories.

➤ Possess a strong knowledge about the activities associated with enabling stored procedures.

➤ Be familiar with the different types of constraints available and know how each is used.

➤ Possess an in-depth knowledge of the Structured Query Language (SQL), Data Definition Language (DDL), Data Manipulation Language (DML), and Data Control Language (DCL) statements that are available with DB2 UDB, Version 8.1.

➤ Know the difference between static and dynamic SQL.

➤ Know how to manage storage allocation with tools such as VSAM DELETE, VSAM DEFINE, and STOGROUP.

➤ Be familiar with DB2 Disaster Recovery.

➤ Possess a basic understanding of the different object statuses available (for example, RECP, GRECP, LPL, and RESTP).

➤ Be able to describe the effects of COMMIT frequency.

➤ Know how to capture and analyze Explain information.

➤ Know how to capture and analyze DB2 Trace data.

➤ Be able to determine the best characteristics for an index.

➤ Be able to describe the benefits of data sharing.

➤ Be able to describe the features that enable around-the-clock availability.

➤ Know how to use the REORG, BIND, REPAIR, UNLOAD, RUNSTATS, LOAD, and MODIFY utilities, including being able to restart a failed utility.

➤ Know how to use the DISPLAY, START, STOP, ALTER, RECOVER, and TERM UTILITY commands.

➤ Possess a basic understanding of the CHECK DATA/INDEX/LOB utility.

➤ Be able to demonstrate how DB2I is used.

➤ Be able to identify the functions of the Control Center.

➤ Possess a strong knowledge about the mechanisms DB2 UDB uses to protect data and database objects against unauthorized access and/or modification.

Candidates who have either taken and passed the **DB2 UDB V7.1 Family Fundamentals** exam (Exam 512) or acquired the IBM Certified Solutions Expert—DB2 UDB V7.1 Database Administration for OS/390 certification must take and pass the **DB2 UDB V8.1 for z/OS Database Administration** exam (Exam 702) to acquire the IBM Certified Database Administrator—DB2 Universal Database V8.1 for z/OS and OS/390 certification. All other candidates must take and pass both the **DB2 UDB V8.1 Family Fundamentals** exam (Exam 700) and the **DB2 UDB V8.1 for z/OS Database Administration** exam (Exam 702). The roadmap for acquiring the IBM Certified Database Administrator—DB2 Universal Database V8.1 for z/OS and OS/390 certification can be seen in Figure 1–4.

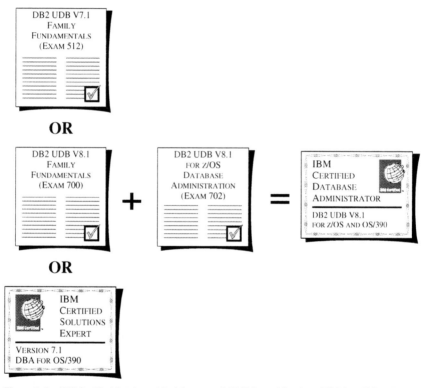

Figure 1–4   IBM Certified Database Administrator—DB2 Universal Database V8.1 for z/OS and OS/390 certification roadmap.

IBM Certified Application Developer— DB2 Universal Database V8.1 Family

The *IBM Certified Application Developer—DB2 Universal Database V8.1 Family* certification is intended for intermediate- to advanced-level application developers who possess the knowledge and skills necessary to create applications that interact with DB2 UDB for iSeries (AS/400), V5R2 and/or DB2 UDB, Version 8.1, databases residing on supported platforms including Linux, AIX, HP-UX, Sun Solaris, Windows, zSeries (z/OS, OS/390), and iSeries (AS/400). In addition to being knowledgeable about the fundamental concepts of DB2 UDB, Version 8.1, and having strong skills in embedded SQL programming, ODBC/CLI programming, JDBC programming, or SQLJ programming, individuals seeking this certification should:

➤ Be familiar with the naming conventions used to identify DB2 UDB objects.

➤ Know how to create, access, modify, and manage the various DB2 UDB objects available.

➤ Possess an in-depth knowledge of the Structured Query Language (SQL), Data Definition Language (DDL), Data Manipulation Language (DML), and Data Control Language (DCL) statements that are available with DB2 UDB, Version 8.1, or DB2 UDB for iSeries (AS/400), V5R2.

➤ Know the difference between static and dynamic SQL.

➤ Possess an in-depth knowledge of the SQL functions available.

➤ Know when to use ODBC/CLI, JDBC, SQLJ, OLE DB, and embedded SQL.

➤ Be able to establish a connection to a database within an ODBC/CLI, JDBC, or SQLJ application.

➤ Be able to query tables across multiple databases, including federated databases.

➤ Be able to identify the types of cursors available, as well as know when to use cursors in an application and what their scope will be.

➤ Know when to use Compound SQL, parameter markers, and distributed units of work.

➤ Know when to use user-defined functions (UDFs) and stored procedures.

➤ Be able to cast user-defined data types (UDTs) within an application.

➤ Know what authorities and privileges are needed in order to access data with an application.

➤ Be familiar with the steps involved in creating an embedded SQL application.

➤ Know when to declare host variables, as well as how to use host variables in a query.

➤ Possess the ability to analyze the contents of an SQL Communications Area (SQLCA) data structure.

➤ Be familiar with the steps involved in creating an ODBC/CLI application.

➤ Be familiar with the different ODBC/CLI handle types available.

➤ Know how to configure a DB2 ODBC driver.

➤ Possess the ability to obtain and analyze ODBC/CLI diagnostic information.

➤ Know the correct sequence for calling ODBC/CLI functions.

➤ Be familiar with the steps involved in creating a JDBC application.

➤ Be familiar with the steps involved in creating an SQLJ application.

➤ Know the difference between JDBC and SQLJ.

➤ Be familiar with the various JDBC objects available.

➤ Possess the ability to obtain and analyze JDBC trace, SQL exception, and JDBC error log information.

➤ Know how to manage transactions across multiple databases using JTA.

➤ Be familiar with the DB2 Development Center.

Candidates who have either taken and passed the **DB2 UDB V7.1 Family Fundamentals** exam (Exam 512) or acquired the IBM Certified Solutions Expert—DB2 UDB V7.1 Family Application Development certification must take and pass the **DB2 UDB V8.1 Family Application Development** exam

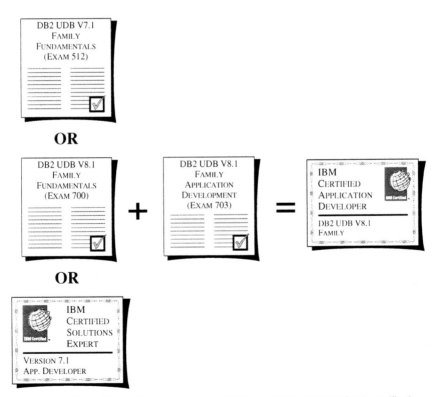

Figure 1–5   IBM Certified Application Developer—DB2 Universal Database V8.1 Family certification roadmap.

(Exam 703) to acquire the IBM Certified Application Developer—DB2 Universal Database V8.1 Family certification. All other candidates must take and pass both the **DB2 UDB V8.1 Family Fundamentals** exam (Exam 700) and the **DB2 UDB V8.1 Family Application Development** exam (Exam 703). The roadmap for acquiring the IBM Certified Application Developer—DB2 Universal Database V8.1 Family certification can be seen in Figure 1–5.

IBM Certified Advanced Database Administrator—DB2 Universal Database V8.1 for Linux, UNIX, and Windows

The *IBM Certified Advanced Database Administrator—DB2 Universal Database V8.1 for Linux, UNIX, and Windows* certification is intended for lead Database Administrators who possess extensive knowledge about DB2 UDB, Version 8.1, and who have extensive experience using DB2 UDB on one or more of the following supported platforms: Linux, AIX, HP-UX, Sun Solaris, and Windows. In addition to being knowledgeable about the more complex concepts of DB2 UDB, Version 8.1, and having significant experience as a DB2 UDB Database Administrator, individuals seeking this certification should:

➤ Know how to design, create, and manage both SMS and DMS tablespaces.

➤ Know how to design, create, and manage buffer pools.

➤ Be able to take full advantage of intraparallelism and interparallelism.

➤ Be able to design and configure federated database access.

➤ Know how to manage distributed units of work.

➤ Be able to develop a logging strategy.

➤ Be able to create constraints on and between table objects.

➤ Know how to perform database-level and tablespace-level backup, restore, and roll-forward recovery operations.

➤ Be able to use the advanced backup and recovery features available.

➤ Know how to implement a standby database using log shipping, replication, failover, and fault monitoring.

➤ Be able to identify and modify the DB2 Database Manager and database configuration file parameter values that have the most impact on performance.

➤ Possess a strong knowledge of query optimizer concepts.

➤ Be able to tune memory and I/O.

➤ Be able to correctly analyze, isolate, and correct database performance problems.

➤ Know how to manage a large number of users and connections, including connections to host systems.

➤ Know how to create, configure, and manage a partitioned database spanning multiple servers.

➤ Be able to create and manage multidimensional clustered tables.

➤ Know when the creation of an index will improve database performance.

➤ Be able to identify and resolve database connection problems.

➤ Possess a strong knowledge about the external authentication mechanisms DB2 UDB uses to protect data and database objects against unauthorized access and/or modification.

➤ Know how to implement data encryption.

To acquire the IBM Certified Advanced Database Administrator—DB2 Universal Database V8.1 for Linux, UNIX, and Windows certification, candidates must hold the IBM Certified Database Administrator—DB2 Universal Database V8.1 for Linux, UNIX, and Windows certification and they must take and pass the **DB2 UDB V8.1 for Linux, UNIX, and Windows Advanced Database Administration** exam (Exam 704). The roadmap for acquiring the IBM Certified Advanced Database Administrator—DB2 Universal Database V8.1 for Linux, UNIX, and Windows certification can be seen in Figure 1–6.

Figure 1–6   IBM Certified Advanced Database Administrator—DB2 Universal Database V8.1 for Linux, UNIX, and Windows certification roadmap.

IBM Certified Solution Designer— Business Intelligence V8.1

The *IBM Certified Solution Designer—Business Intelligence V8.1* certification is intended for individuals who are knowledgeable about IBM's Business Intelligence solutions, as well as the fundamental concepts of DB2 Universal Database, Version 8.1. In addition to having the knowledge and skills necessary to design, develop, and support Business Intelligence applications, anyone seeking this certification should:

➤ Be familiar with Business Intelligence terms, as well as be able to describe the benefits of Business Intelligence.

➤ Know how the characteristics and purpose of data marts differ from that of data warehouses.

➤ Know how the characteristics and purpose of operational data stores differ from that of data warehouses.

➤ Know how the characteristics and purpose of multidimensional databases differ from that of data warehouses.

➤ Know how network communications can impact Business Intelligence architecture.

➤ Be able to select the appropriate tools to perform transformation, extraction, data modeling, data cleansing, loading, and propagation when given Business Intelligence data and customer requirements.

➤ Be able to select the appropriate visualization and presentation techniques to use when given Business Intelligence data and customer requirements.

➤ Be able to select the appropriate analysis techniques to use when given Business Intelligence data.

➤ Be able to select the appropriate front-end features to use based on presentation, level of interactivity, Web-versus-FAT client, static versus dynamic, and user skill level when given customer requirements.

➤ Be able to define and distinguish metadata, as well as be able to describe metadata management processes and techniques.

➤ Know how to implement a metadata strategy when given Business Intelligence data and customer requirements.

➤ Know how to identify the business requirements of the customer as they relate to a Business Intelligence solution.

➤ Know how to define a customer's business goals and objectives, determine growth requirements, evaluate existing hardware and software, identify constraints, identify critical success factors, and determine availability and recovery requirements.

➤ Possess an in-depth knowledge of methods of extraction, methods for transformation, methods for cleansing, methods for workload balancing, methods for moving data, methods for scheduling, and methods for error detection and handling.

➤ Be able to differentiate between full differential capturing and snapshot capturing.

➤ Possess an in-depth knowledge of data warehouse management.

➤ Be able to design a solution for producing a searchable metadata repository for business users.

Candidates who have either taken and passed the **DB2 UDB V7.1 Family Fundamentals** exam (Exam 512) or acquired the IBM Certified Solutions Expert—DB2 UDB V7.1 Business Intelligence certification must take and pass the **Business Intelligence Solutions V8.1** exam (Exam 705) to acquire the IBM Certified Solution Designer—Business Intelligence V8.1 certification. All other candidates must take and pass both the **DB2 UDB V8.1 Family Fundamentals** exam (Exam 700) and the **Business Intelligence Solutions V8.1** exam (Exam 705). The roadmap for acquiring the IBM Certified Solution Designer—Business Intelligence V8.1 certification can be seen in Figure 1–7.

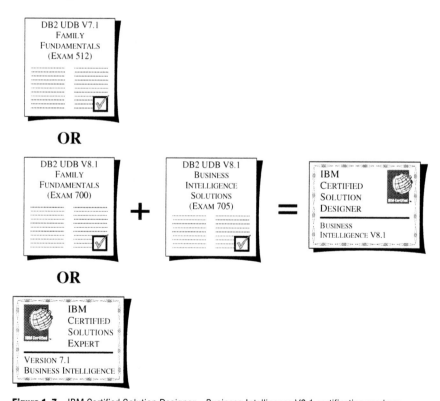

Figure 1–7   IBM Certified Solution Designer—Business Intelligence V8.1 certification roadmap.

The Certification Process

A close examination of the IBM certification roles available quickly reveals that, in order to obtain a particular DB2 UDB, Version 8.1, certification, you must take and pass one or more exams that have been designed specifically for that certification role. (Each exam is a software-based exam that is neither platform nor product specific.) Thus, once you have chosen the certification role you wish to pursue and familiarized yourself with the requirements for that particular role, the next step is to prepare for and take the appropriate certification exams.

Preparing for the Certification Exams

If you already have experience using DB2 UDB in the context of the certification role you have chosen, you may already possess the skills and knowledge needed to pass the exam(s) required for that role. However, if your experience with DB2 UDB is limited (and even if it is not), you can prepare for any of the certification exams available by taking advantage of the following resources:

➤ **Formal education.** IBM Learning Services offers courses that are designed to help you prepare for DB2 UDB certification. A listing of the courses that are recommended for each certification exam can be found using the Certification Navigator tool provided on IBM's "Professional Certification Program from IBM" Web site (*www.ibm.com/certify*). Recommended courses can also be found at IBM's "DB2 Data Management" Web site (*www.ibm.com/software/data/education.html*). For more information on course schedules, locations, and pricing, contact IBM Learning Services or visit their Web site.

IBM also offers two free Computer Based Training (CBT) programs that you can download and install on your personal computer. The first of these, *CT10—DB2 UDB Programmer Fastpath*, is geared toward the IBM Certified Application Developer—DB2 Universal Database V8.1 Family certification role. The second, *CT28—DB2 UDB Administration Fastpath*, was written with the IBM Certified Database Administrator—DB2 Universal Database V8.1 for Linux, UNIX, and Windows certification role in mind. Both are GUI-based and interactive.

➤ **Publications.** All the information you need to pass any of the available certification exams can be found in the documentation that is provided with DB2 UDB. A complete set of manuals comes with the product and is accessible through the Information Center once you have installed the DB2 UDB software. DB2 UDB documentation can also be downloaded from IBM's Web site in both HTML and PDF formats. (The IBM Web site that contains the DB2 UDB documentation can be found at *www.ibm.com/software/data/db2/library.*)

Self-study books (such as this one) that focus on one or more DB2 UDB certification exams/roles are also available. Most of these books can be found at your local bookstore or ordered from many online book retailers. (A listing of possible reference materials for each certification exam can be found using the Certification Navigator tool provided on IBM's "Professional Certification Program from IBM" Web site (*www.ibm.com/certify*). Ordering information is often included with the listing.

In addition to the DB2 UDB product documentation, IBM often produces manuals, known as "RedBooks," that cover advanced DB2 UDB topics (as well as other topics). These manuals are available as downloadable PDF files on IBM's RedBook Web site (*www.redbooks.ibm.com*). Or, if you prefer to have a bound hard copy, you can obtain one for a modest fee by following the appropriate links on the RedBook Web site. (There is no charge for the downloadable PDF files.)

IBM also offers a series of six interactive online tutorials designed to prepare you for the DB2 UDB V8.1 for Linux, UNIX, and Windows Database Administration exam (Exam 701). These tutorials can be found at *www7b.software.ibm.com/dmdd/library/tutorials/db2cert/701_prep.html.*

➤ **Exam objectives**. Objectives that provide an overview of the basic topics that are covered on a particular certification exam can be found using the Certification Navigator tool provided on IBM's "Professional Certification Program from IBM" Web site (*www.ibm.com/certify*). Exam objectives for the DB2 UDB V8.1 for Linux, UNIX, and Windows Database Administration exam (Exam 701) can also be found in Appendix A of this book; exam objectives for the DB2 UDB V8.1 for Linux, UNIX, and Windows Database Administration certification upgrade exam (Exam 706) can be found in Appendix B of this book.

➤ **Sample questions/exams**. Sample questions and sample exams allow you to become familiar with the format and wording used on the actual certification exams. They can help you decide whether you possess the knowledge needed to pass a particular exam. Sample questions, along with descriptive answers, are provided at the end of every chapter in this book.

Sample exams for each DB2 UDB certification role available can also be found using the Certification Exam tool provided on IBM's "Professional Certification Program from IBM" Web site (*http://certify.torolab.ibm.com*).

It is important to note that the certification exams are designed to be rigorous. Very specific answers are expected for most exam questions. Because of this, and because the range of material covered on a certification exam is usually broader than the knowledge base of many DB2 UDB professionals, you should take advantage of the exam preparation resources available if you want to guarantee your success in obtaining the certification(s) you desire.

Arranging to Take a Certification Exam

When you are confident that you are ready to take a specific DB2 UDB certification exam, your next step is to contact an IBM-authorized testing vendor. The DB2 UDB certification exams are administered by VUE, Prometric, Inc., and in rare cases by IBM (for example, IBM administers the DB2 UDB certifications free of charge at some of the larger database conferences, such as the International DB2 User's Group North American conference). However, before you contact either testing vendor, you should visit their Web site (*www.vue.com/ibm* and *www.2test.com*, respectively) and use the navigation tools provided there to locate a testing center that is convenient for you to get to. Once you have located a testing center, you should then contact the vendor and make arrangements to take the certification exam. (Contact information for the testing vendors can also be found on their respective Web sites; in some cases, you are able to schedule an exam online.)

You must make arrangements to take a certification exam at least 24 hours in advance and when you contact the testing vendor, you should be ready to provide the following information:

➤ Your name (as you want it to appear on your certification certificate)

➤ An identification number (this can be, but does not have to be, your Social Security/Social Insurance number). If an identification number is not provided, the testing vendor will supply one.

➤ A telephone number at which you can be reached

➤ A fax number

➤ The mailing address where you want all certification correspondence, including your certification welcome package, to be sent

➤ Your billing address, if it is different from your mailing address

➤ Your email address

➤ The number that identifies the exam you wish to take (for example, Exam 701)

➤ The method of payment (credit card or check) you wish to use, along with any relevant payment information (such as credit card number and expiration date)

➤ Your company's name (if applicable)

➤ The testing center where you would like to take the certification exam

➤ The date you would like to take the certification exam

Before you make arrangements to take a certification exam, you should have pencil/pen and paper handy so you can write down the test applicant identification number the testing center will assign you. You will need this information when you arrive at the testing center to take the certification exam. (If time permits, you will be sent a letter of confirmation containing the number of the certification exam you have been scheduled to take, along with corresponding date, time, and location information; if you register within 48 hours of the scheduled testing date, you will not receive a letter.)

If you have already taken one or more of the certification exams offered, you should make the testing vendor aware of this and ask them to assign you the same applicant identification number that was used before. This will allow the certification team at IBM to quickly recognize when you have met all the exam requirements for a particular certification role. (If you were assigned a unique applicant identification number each time you took an exam, you should send each applicant identification number used to the certification team at IBM (certify@us.ibm.com) and ask them to combine all of your exam results under one ID.)

With the exception of the DB2 UDB V8.1 for Linux, UNIX, and Windows Database Administration Upgrade Exam (Exam 706), each certification exam costs $120.00 (in the United States). Scheduling procedures vary according to how you choose to pay for the exam. If you decide to pay by credit card, you can make arrangements to take the exam immediately after providing the testing vendor with the appropriate information. However, if you elect to pay by check, you will be required to wait until the check has been received and payment has been confirmed before you will be allowed to make arrangements to take the exam. (Prometric, Inc., recommends that if you pay by check, you write your registration ID on the front and contact them seven business days after the check is mailed. At that time, they should have received and confirmed your payment, and you should be able to make arrangements to take the exam you have paid for.)

If, for some reason, you need to reschedule or cancel your testing appointment after it is made, you must do so at least 24 hours before your scheduled test time. Otherwise, you will still be charged the price of the exam.

Taking an IBM Certification Exam

On the day you are scheduled to take a certification exam, you should arrive at the testing center at least 15 minutes before the scheduled start time to sign in. As part of the sign-in process, you will be asked to provide the applicant identification number you were assigned when you made arrangements to take the exam, and two forms of identification. One form of identification must contain a recent photograph and the other must contain your signature. Examples of valid forms of identification include a driver's license (photograph) and a credit card (signature).

Once you are signed in, the exam administrator will instruct you to enter the testing area and select an available workstation. The exam administrator will then enter your name and identification number into the workstation you have chosen, provide you with a pencil and some paper, and instruct you to begin the exam when you are ready. At that point, the title screen of the IBM Certification Exam testing software should be displayed on the computer monitor in front of you. Figure 1–8 illustrates what this screen looks like.

As you can see in Figure 1–8, the title screen of the IBM Certification Exam testing software consists of the IBM Certification Logo along with the title "Professional Certification Program from IBM," the name of the exam that is about to be administered (for example, the title screen shown in Figure 1–8 indicates that the DB2 UDB V8.1 Family Fundamentals exam is about to be administered), and a welcome message comprised of your name and some basic information on how to get started. Before proceeding, you should:

➤ Verify that the exam you are about to take is indeed the exam you expected to take. If the name of the exam shown on the title screen is different from the name of the exam you had planned to take, bring this to the attention of the exam administrator immediately.

➤ Verify that your name is spelled correctly. The way your name appears in the welcome message shown on the title screen reflects how it has been stored in the IBM Certification database. This is how all correspondence to you will be addressed, and more importantly, this is how your name will appear on the certification credentials you will receive if you pass the exam you are about to take.

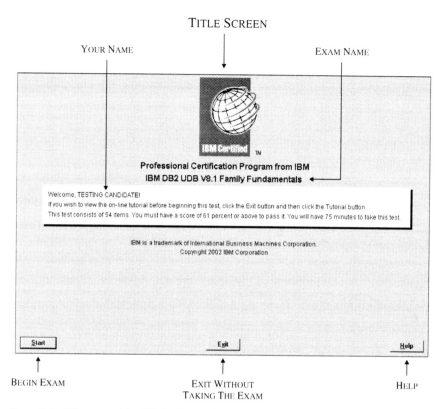

Figure 1–8   Title screen of the IBM Certification Exam testing software.

In addition to telling you which exam is about to be administered, the title screen of the IBM Certification Exam testing software lets you know how many questions you can expect to see on the exam you are about to take, what kind of score you must receive in order to pass, and the time frame in which the exam must be completed. With two exceptions, each exam contains between 50 and 70 questions and is allotted 75 minutes for completion. The DB2 UDB V8.1 for Linux, UNIX, and Windows Database Administration exam (Exam 701) is allotted 90 minutes, and the DB2 UDB V8.1 for Linux, UNIX, and Windows Database Administration Upgrade Exam (Exam 706) is allotted 40 minutes. Although each certification exam must be completed within a predefined time limit, you should never rush through an exam just because the "clock is running"; the time limits imposed are more than adequate for you to work through the exam at a relaxed, but steady pace.

When you are ready, begin by selecting the "Start" push button located in the lower left corner of the screen (refer to Figure 1–8). If instead you would like a quick refresher course on how to use the IBM Certification Exam testing software, select the "Help" push button located in the lower right corner of the screen. (If you panic and decide you're not ready to take the exam, you can select the "Exit" push button located between the "Start" and "Help" push buttons at the bottom of the screen to get out of the testing software altogether, but I recommend you talk with the exam administrator about your concerns before selecting this push button.)

If you plan to take a quick refresher course on how to use the IBM Certification Exam testing software, make sure you do so *before* you select the "Start" push button to begin the exam. Although help is available at any time, the clock does not start running until the "Start" push button is pressed. By viewing help information before the clock is started, you avoid using what could prove to be valuable testing time reading documentation instead of test questions.

Once the "Start" button on the title screen of the IBM Certification Exam testing software is selected, the clock will start running, and the first exam question will be presented in a question panel that looks something like the screen shown in Figure 1–9.

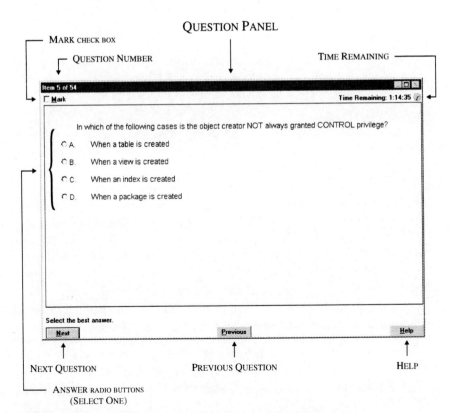

Figure 1–9   Typical question panel of the IBM Certification Exam testing software.

Aside from the question itself, one of the first things you may notice when you examine the question panel of the IBM Certification Exam testing software is the question number displayed in the top left corner of the screen. If you answer each question in the order they are presented, this portion of the screen can act as a progress indicator, because the current question number is displayed along with the total number of questions contained in the exam.

Immediately below the question number, you will find a special check box that is referred to as the "Mark" check box. If you would like to skip the current question for now and come back to it later, or if you're uncertain about the answer(s) you have chosen and would like to look at this question again after you have completed the rest of the exam, you should mark this check box (by placing the mouse pointer over it and pressing the left mouse button). When every question has been viewed once, you will be given the opportunity to review just the marked questions again. At that time, you can answer any unanswered questions remaining and/or reevaluate any answers you provided that you have some concerns about.

Another important feature that can be found on the question panel is the "Time Remaining" information that is displayed in the top right corner of the screen. As the title implies, this area of the question panel provides continuous feedback on the amount of time you have available to finish and review the exam. If you would like to see more detailed information, such as the actual wall-clock time at which you began the exam and the time frame in which you are expected to complete the exam, you can view that information by selecting the clock icon located just to the right of the time-remaining information. When this icon is selected (by placing the mouse pointer over it and pressing the left mouse button), a dialog similar to the one shown in Figure 1–10 is displayed.

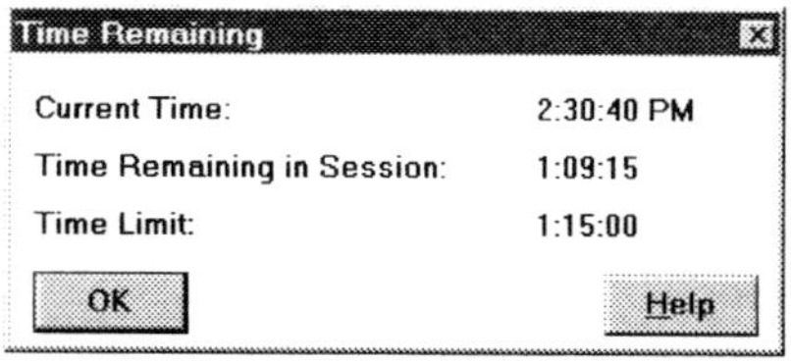

Time Remaining	
Current Time:	2:30:40 PM
Time Remaining in Session:	1:09:15
Time Limit:	1:15:00
OK	Help

Figure 1–10   Time Remaining dialog.

Obviously, the most important part of the question panel is the exam question itself, along with the corresponding list of possible answers provided. Take the time to read each question carefully. When you have located the correct answer in the list provided, you should mark it by selecting the answer radio-button positioned just to the left of the answer text (by placing the mouse pointer over the desired answer radio-button and pressing the left mouse button). Once you have selected an answer for the question being displayed (or marked it with the "Mark" check box), you can move to the next question by selecting the "Next" push button, which is located in the lower left corner of the screen (refer to Figure 1–9).

If, at any time, you would like to return to the previous question, you can do so by pressing the "Previous" push button, located at the bottom of the screen, just to the right of the "Next" push button. And, if you would like to access help on how to use the IBM Certification Exam testing software, you can do so by selecting the "Help" push button located in the lower right corner of the screen. It is important to note that, although the "Next" and "Previous" push buttons can be used to navigate through the questions provided with the exam, the navigation process itself is not cyclic in nature—that is, when you are on the first question you cannot go to the last question by selecting the "Previous" push button (in fact, the "Previous" push button will not be displayed if you are on the first question). Likewise, when you are on the last question, you cannot go to the first question simply by selecting the "Next" push button. However, there is a way to quickly navigate to a specific question from the item review panel, which we will look at shortly.

Although, in most cases, only one answer in the list provided is the correct answer to the question shown, there are times when multiple answers are valid. On those occasions, the answer radio-buttons will be replaced with answer check boxes and the question will be worded in such a way that you will know how many answers are expected. An example of such a question can be seen in Figure 1–11.

These types of questions are answered by selecting the answer check box positioned just to the left of the text *for every correct answer found*. (Again, this is done by placing the mouse pointer over each desired answer check box and pressing the left mouse button.)

Once in a while, an illustration or the output from some diagnostic tool will accompany a question. You will be required to view that illustration or output (referred to as an exhibit) before you can successfully answer the question presented. On those occasions, a message instructing you to display the exhibit for the question will precede the actual test question and a special push button called the "Exhibit" push button will be positioned at the bottom of the screen, between the "Previous" push button and the "Help" push button. An example of such a question can be seen Figure 1–12.

To view the exhibit associated with such a question, you simply select the "Exhibit" push button located at the bottom of the screen. This action will cause the corresponding exhibit panel to be displayed. (A sample exhibit panel can be seen in Figure 1–13.)

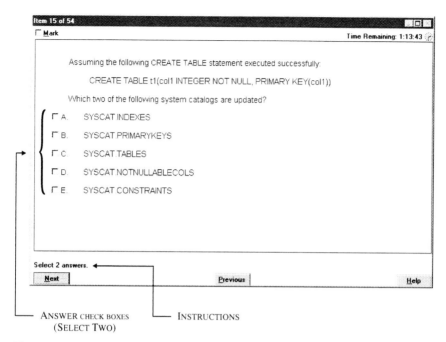

Figure 1–11 Question panel for questions expecting multiple answers.

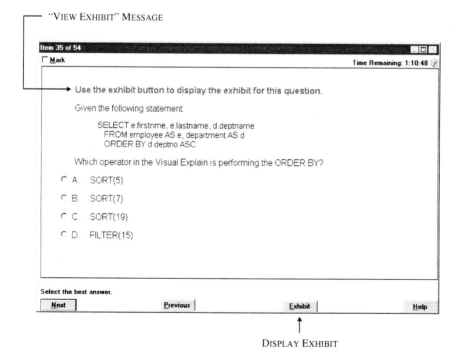

Figure 1–12 Question panel for questions that contain an exhibit.

EXHIBIT PANEL

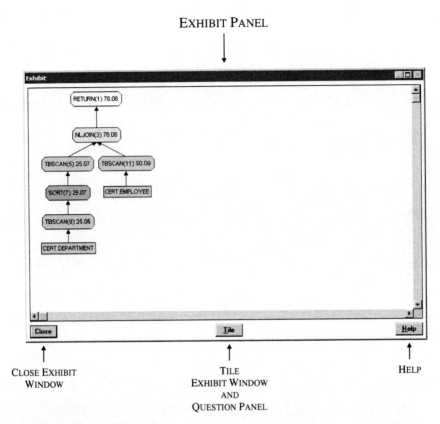

CLOSE EXHIBIT
WINDOW

TILE
EXHIBIT WINDOW
AND
QUESTION PANEL

HELP

Figure 1–13 Sample exhibit panel.

Exhibit panels are relatively simple. In fact, once an exhibit panel is displayed, there are only two things you can do with it: You can close it by selecting the "Close" push button located at the bottom of the screen, or you can tile it (i.e., make it share screen real estate) with its corresponding question panel by selecting the "Tile" push button, which is located beside the "Close" push button. Aside from having to view the exhibit provided, the process used to answer questions that have exhibits is no different from the process used to answer questions that do not.

When you have viewed every exam question available (by selecting the "Next" push button on every question panel shown), an item review panel that looks something like the panel shown in Figure 1–14 will be displayed.

As you can see in Figure 1–14, the item review panel contains a numerical listing of the questions that make up the certification exam you are taking, along with the answers you have provided for each. Questions that you marked (by selecting the "Mark" check box) are preceded by the letter "M"

ITEM (QUESTION) REVIEW PANEL

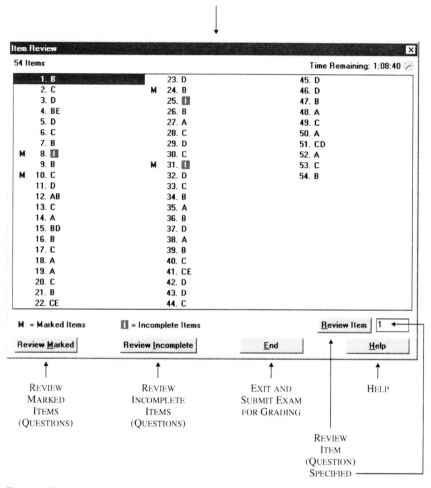

Figure 1–14   Item (question) review panel of the IBM Certification Exam testing software.

and questions that you skipped or did not provide the correct number of answers for are assigned the answer "I" to indicate they are incomplete. By selecting the "Review Marked" push button located in the lower left corner of the screen (refer to Figure 1–14), you can quickly go back through just the questions that have been marked. When reviewing marked items in this manner, each time the "Next" push button is selected on a question panel, you are taken to the next marked question in the list until eventually you are returned to the item review panel. Likewise, by selecting the "Review Incomplete" push button located just to the right of the "Review Marked" push button, you can go back though just the questions that have been identified as being incomplete. (Navigation works the same as when the "Review Marked" push button is pressed.) If instead you would like to review a specific question, you can do so by highlighting that question's number or typing that question's number in the entry field provided just to the right of the "Review Item" push button (which is located just above the "Help" push button in the lower right corner of the screen) and selecting the "Review Item" push button.

If you elect to use the "Review Item" push button to review a particular question, the only way you can return to the item review screen is by selecting the "Next" push button found on that question panel and every subsequent question panel presented until no more question panels exist.

One of the first things you should do when the item review panel is displayed is resolve any incomplete items found. (When the exam is graded, each incomplete item found is marked incorrect, and points are deducted from your final score.) Then, if time permits, you should go back and review the questions that you marked. It is important to note that when you finish reviewing a marked question, you should unmark it (by placing the mouse pointer over the "Mark" check box and pressing the left mouse button) before going on to the next marked question or returning to the item review panel. This will make it easier for you to keep track of which questions have been reviewed and which have not.

As soon as every incomplete item found has been resolved, the "Review Incomplete" push button is automatically removed from the item review panel. Likewise, when there are no more marked questions, the "Review Marked" push button is removed from the item review panel. Thus, when every incomplete and marked item found has been resolved, the item review panel will look similar to the one shown in Figure 1–15.

Keep in mind that, even when the "Review Incomplete" and "Review Marked" push buttons are no longer available, you can still go back and review a specific question by highlighting that question's number or typing that question's number in the entry field provided and selecting the "Review Item" push button (refer to Figure 1–15).

As soon as you feel comfortable with the answers you have provided, you can end the exam and submit it for grading by selecting the "End" push button, which should now be located in the lower left corner of the item review panel. When this push button is selected (by placing the mouse pointer over it and pressing the left mouse button), a dialog similar to the one shown in Figure 1–16 should be displayed.

If you select the "End" push button on the item review panel before every incomplete item found has been resolved, a dialog similar to the one shown in Figure 1–17 will be displayed instead.

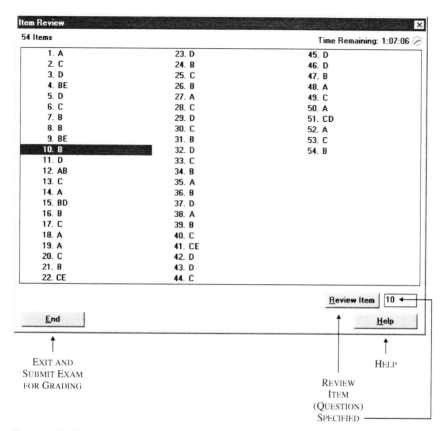

Figure 1–15   Item (question) review panel with all incomplete and marked items (questions) resolved.

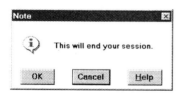

Figure 1–16   End exam session confirmation dialog.

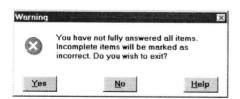

Figure 1–17   Ending exam with incomplete items warning dialog.

Both of these dialogs gives you the opportunity to confirm your decision to end the exam and submit it for grading or to reconsider and continue resolving and/or reviewing exam questions. If you wish to do the former, you should select either the "OK" or the "Yes" push button when either of these dialogs is presented; if you wish to do the latter, you should select the "Cancel" or "No" push button, in which case you will be returned to the item review panel. Keep in mind that if you select the "Yes" push button when the dialog shown in Figure 1–17 is displayed, all incomplete items found will be marked as wrong and this will have a negative impact on your final score.

As soon as you confirm that you do indeed wish to end the exam, the IBM Certification Exam testing software will evaluate your answers and produce a score report that indicates whether or not you passed the exam. This report will then be displayed on an exam results panel that looks something like the panel shown in Figure 1–18 and a corresponding hard copy (printout) will be generated.

EXAM RESULTS PANEL

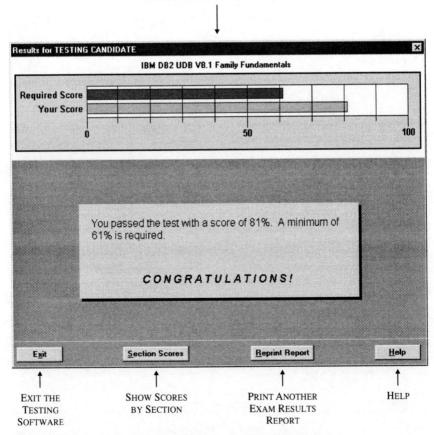

Figure 1–18 Exam results panel of the IBM Certification Exam testing software.

As you can see in Figure 1–18, the exam results panel shows the required score along with your actual score in a horizontal percent bar graph. Directly below this graph is a message that contains the percentage score you received, along with the percentage score needed to pass the exam. If you received a passing score, this message will end with the word "Congratulations!" However, if you received a score that is below the score needed to pass, the message you see will begin with the words "You did not pass the test" and your score will follow.

Each certification exam is broken into sections, and regardless of whether you pass or fail, you should take a few moments to review the score you received for each section. This information can help you evaluate your strengths and weaknesses. If you failed to pass the exam, it can help you identify the areas you should spend some time reviewing before you attempt to take the exam again. To view the section scores for the exam you have just completed, you simply select the "Section Scores" push button located at the bottom of the screen. This action will cause a section scores panel similar to the one shown in Figure 1–19 to be displayed.

SECTION SCORES PANEL

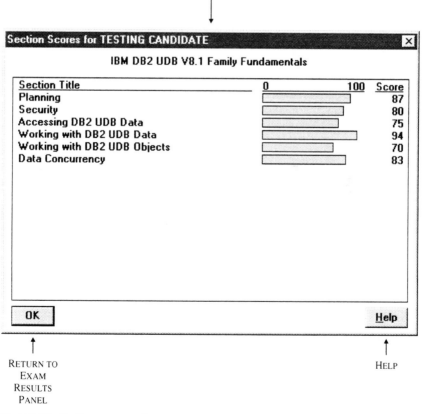

Figure 1–19 Section scores panel.

When you have finished reviewing your section scores, you may return to the exam results panel by selecting the "OK" push button located at the bottom left corner of the screen. From there, you can exit the IBM Certification Exam testing software by selecting the "Exit" push button, which is also located at the bottom left corner of the screen.

Shortly after you take a certification exam (usually within five working days), the testing vendor sends your results, along with your demographic data (i.e., name, address, phone number, etc.) to the IBM Certification Group for processing. If you passed the exam, you will receive credit toward the certification role the exam was designed for and if the exam you took completes the requirements that have been outlined for a particular certification role, you will receive an email (at the email address you provided during registration) that contains a copy of the IBM Certification Agreement and a welcome package that includes a certificate that is suitable for framing (in .PDF format), camera-ready artwork of the IBM certification logo, and guidelines for using the "IBM Certified" mark. (If this email cannot be delivered, the welcome package will be sent to you via regular mail.) You can also receive a printed certificate, along with a wallet-sized certificate, via regular mail by going to the Web site referenced in the email you receive and asking for it. You will be asked to provide your Fulfillment ID and Validation Number (also provided in the email) as verification that you have met the requirements for certification.

Upon receipt of the welcome package, you will become certified and you can begin using the IBM Professional Certification title and trademark. (You should receive the IBM Certification Agreement and welcome package within four to six weeks after IBM processes the exam results.) However, if you failed to pass the exam and you still wish to become DB2 UDB certified, you must make arrangements to take it again (including paying the testing fee again). There are no restrictions on the number of times you can take a particular certification exam; however, you cannot take the same certification exam more than two times within a 30-day period.

PART 2
DB2 UDB Linux, UNIX, and Windows Database Administration

2

Server Management

Nineteen percent (19%) of the DB2 UDB V8.1 for Linux, UNIX, and Windows Database Administration certification exam (Exam 701) and twenty percent (20%) of the DB2 UDB V8.1 for Linux, UNIX, and Windows Database Administration certification upgrade exam (Exam 706) is designed to test your knowledge about basic DB2 Universal Database server management. The questions that make up this portion of the exam are intended to evaluate the following:

➤ Your ability to create and manage DB2 instances.

➤ Your ability to create and manage the DB2 Administration Server (DAS).

➤ Your ability to identify the methods that can be used to restrict access to data stored in a DB2 UDB database.

➤ Your ability to identify each authorization level used by DB2 UDB.

➤ Your ability to identify each privilege used by DB2 UDB.

➤ Your ability to identify how specific authorizations and/or privileges are given to a user.

➤ Your ability to configure client/server connectivity.

➤ Your ability to configure clients and servers using DB2 Discovery.

➤ Your ability to gain exclusive control of a database.

➤ Your ability to schedule jobs.

➤ Your ability to interpret information found in the Administration Notification Log

This chapter is designed to introduce you to the various concepts you need to be familiar with in order to manage a DB2 UDB server. This chapter will also provide you with information about some of the tools that are available for server management.

Terms you will learn:

DB2 Database Manager

Instance

DB2 Administration Server (DAS)

ATTACH

DETACH

TCP/IP

DB2COMM

db2set

DB2 Discovery

Authentication

Authentication Type

Kerberos

Trusted Client

Untrusted Client

Authorities

Privileges

System Administrator authority

System Control authority

System Maintenance authority

Database Administrator authority

Load authority

Database Privileges

Object Privileges

GRANT

REVOKE

LIST APPLICATIONS

FORCE APPLICATION

QUIESCE

UNQUIESCE

Task Center

Journal

Error Codes

Reason Codes

First Failure Data Capture (FFDC)

db2diag.log

Administration notification log

Techniques you will master:

Understanding how to manage and configure DB2 instances, including the DB2 Administration Server (DAS).

Understanding how users are authenticated and how to control where authentication takes place.

Understanding how DB2 Universal Database controls data access through a wide variety of authorities and privileges.

Understanding the differences between authorities and privileges, and knowing how they compliment each other to protect data.

Recognizing the types of authorities available and knowing what each one allows a user to do.

Recognizing the types of privileges available and knowing what each one allows a user to do.

Understanding how authorities can be given to (granted) or taken away from (revoked) users and groups.

Understanding how privileges can be given to (granted) or taken away from (revoked) users and groups.

Understanding how to configure client/server connectivity, including how to configure clients and servers using DB2 Discovery.

Understanding how to gain exclusive control of a database.

Recognizing and interpreting information found in the Administration Notification Log.

Instances

When any edition of DB2 Universal Database is installed on a particular workstation, program files for a background process known as the *DB2 Database Manager* are physically copied to a specific location on that workstation and, in most cases, an *instance* of the DB2 Database Manager is created. Instances are responsible for managing system resources and databases that fall under their control and although only one instance is created initially, several instances can exist on a single server. Each instance behaves like a separate installation of DB2 UDB, even though all instances within a system share the same DB2 Database Manager program files (which were copied to the workstation during the installation process). And while multiple instances share the same binary code, each runs independently of the others and has its own environment (which can be modified by altering the contents of its associated configuration file).

The default instance for a particular system is defined by the DB2INSTANCE environment variable and in many cases this is the instance used for most operations. However, there are times when it is advantageous to create multiple instances on the same physical workstation. Reasons for creating multiple instances include:

➤ To separate your development environment from your production environment.

➤ To obtain optimum performance for special applications. (For example, you may choose to create an instance for one or more applications and then fine-tune each instance specifically for the application(s) it will service.)

➤ To prevent database administrators from accessing sensitive data. (For example, a company's payroll database could reside in its own instance, in which case owners of other databases in other instances on the same server will be unable to access payroll data.)

As you might imagine, DB2 UDB provides several commands that can be used to create and manage instances. These commands, which are referred to as *system commands* because they are executed from the system command prompt rather than from the DB2 Command Line Processor (CLP), are shown in Table 2–1.

Table 2–1 DB2 UDB Instance Management Commands	
Command	**Purpose**
db2icrt [*InstanceName*]	Creates a new instance.
db2idrop [*InstanceName*]	Deletes (drops) an existing instance.
db2ilist	Lists all instances that have been defined.
db2imigr [*InstanceName*]	Migrates an existing instance to a newer version of DB2 UDB.
db2iupdt [*InstanceName*]	Updates an existing instance to take advantage of new functionality that is provided when product fix packs are installed. (Also used to convert a 32-bit instance to a 64-bit instance.)
	(continues)

Table 2–1 DB2 UDB Instance Management Commands (Continued)	
Command	Purpose
db2start	Starts the DB2 Database Manager background processes for the current instance.
db2stop	Stops the DB2 Database Manager background processes for the current instance.

NOTE Although basic syntax is presented for the instance management commands shown in Table 2–1, the actual syntax supported may be more complex. To view the complete syntax for a specific DB2 UDB command or to obtain more information about a particular command, refer to the *IBM DB2 Universal Database, Version 8 Command Reference* product documentation.

Attaching to an Instance

Although the default instance for a particular system is defined by the DB2INSTANCE environment variable, you can *attach* to any instance available, including instances that reside on other workstations. And once attached, you can perform maintenance and utility tasks such as create a new database or monitor database activity, which can only be done at the instance level. Applications and users can attach to any instance by executing the ATTACH command. The basic syntax for this command is:

```
ATTACH <TO [InstanceName]>
<USER [UserID] <USING [Password]
    <NEW [NewPassword] CONFIRM [NewPassword]>>>
```

where:

InstanceName	Identifies the name assigned to the instance an attachment is to be made to.
UserID	Identifies the user (by authorization ID) that the instance attachment is to be made under.
Password	Identifies the password that corresponds to the authorization ID specified.
NewPassword	Identifies the password that is to replace the current password associated with the authorization ID specified.

So, if you wanted to attach to the default instance that is defined by the DB2INSTANCE environment variable using the authentication ID

DB2ADMIN and the password IBMDB2, you could do so by executing an `ATTACH` command that looks something like this:

```
ATTACH USER DB2ADMIN USING IBMDB2
```

On the other hand, if you wanted to attach to an instance named DB2_PROD using the same authentication ID and password, you could do so by executing an `ATTACH` command that looks something like this:

```
ATTACH TO DB2_PROD USER DB2ADMIN USING IBMDB2
```

Instance-level attachments can also be made using the Attach dialog, which can be activated by selecting the appropriate action from the *Instances* menu found in the Control Center. Figure 2–1 shows the Control Center menu items that must be selected to activate the Attach dialog; Figure 2–2 shows how the Attach dialog might look after its input fields have been populated.

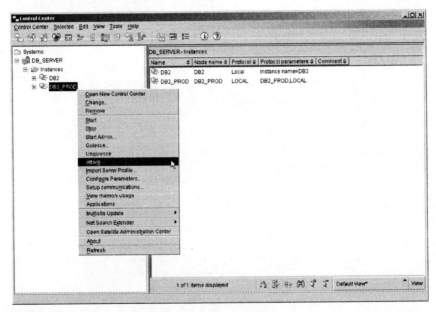

Figure 2–1   Invoking the Attach dialog from the Control Center.

Figure 2–2   The Attach dialog.

NOTE Unless you have explicitly established an attachment to a particular instance, all instance-level commands executed are done so against the current instance (which is identified by the DB2INSTANCE environment variable).

Detaching from an Instance

Once an attachment to an instance has been made and all necessary tasks have been performed against that instance, the instance attachment should be terminated if it is no longer needed; by terminating an instance attachment, you eliminate the potential to accidentally perform new operations against the wrong instance. The easiest way to terminate an attachment to an instance is by establishing an attachment to another. That's because an application or user can only be attached to one instance at a time—if an attachment is made to another instance, the current instance attachment is automatically terminated.

Applications and users can also detach from an instance by executing the DETACH command. The basic syntax for this command is:

```
DETACH
```

As you can see, the DETACH command requires no additional parameters.

The DB2 Administration Server (DAS)

All of the tools that come with DB2 UDB (such as the Control Center) require a separate server process that operates independently of, yet concurrently with, all other instances that have been defined for a particular workstation. For this reason, a special process, known as the DB2 Administration Server (DAS), is also created as part of the DB2 UDB installation process. Only one DAS process can exist on a single workstation. (The DB2 UDB global-level profile registry variable DB2ADMINSERVER contains the name of the DAS process that has been defined for a particular workstation.)

Once created, the DAS process runs continuously in the background whenever the system on which it was created is online; the DAS process is usually started automatically each time the workstation on which it resides is started (or rebooted). Furthermore, the DAS process must be running on every DB2 UDB server that you wish to administer remotely. That's because, among other things, the DAS process provides remote clients with the information needed to establish communications with other instances. (It is important to note that in order to administer a server from a remote client, a user must have System Administration [SYSADM] authority for the DAS process used. Furthermore, once a remote instance and database have been registered on a client workstation, the user must hold the authorities and privileges needed to perform administrative tasks.)

In addition to enabling remote administration of DB2 UDB servers, the DAS process assists the Control Center and the Configuration Assistant in:

➤ Providing job (task) management, including the ability to schedule and run user-defined shell scripts/batch files that contain both DB2 UDB and operating system commands.

➤ Scheduling jobs, viewing the results of completed jobs, and performing administrative tasks against jobs located either remotely or locally using the Task Center.

➤ Providing a means for discovering information about the configuration of other DAS instances, DB2 UDB instances, and databases using DB2 Discovery. (The Configuration Assistant and the Control Center use such information to simplify and automate the configuration of client connectivity to DB2 UDB servers.)

In most cases, you rarely have to interact directly with the DAS process, or for that matter, even concern yourself with its existence. However, in the event you do need to work with a DAS process on any server, several DAS-specific system commands are available. These commands can be seen in Table 2–2.

Table 2–2	DAS Instance Management Commands
Command	**Purpose**
dascrt	Creates the DAS process. (UNIX)
db2admin create	Creates the DAS process. (Windows)
dasdrop	Deletes (drops) the DAS process. (UNIX)
db2admin drop	Deletes (drops) the DAS process. (Windows)
daslist	Displays the name of the DAS process. (UNIX)
db2admin	Displays the name of the DAS process. (Windows)
dasmigr	Migrates an existing DAS instance to a newer version of DB2 UDB. (Prior to Version 8.1, the DAS process was a special instance.)
dasupdt	Updates an existing DAS process to take advantage of new functionality that is provided when product fix packs are installed. (UNIX)
	(continues)

Table 2–2 DAS Instance Management Commands (Continued)	
`db2admin start`	Starts the DAS process.
`db2admin stop`	Stops the DAS process.
`db2admin setid`	Specifies the login account that is to be used to administer the DAS process.
`db2admin setschedid`	Specifies the login account that is to be used by the scheduler to connect to the tools catalog database. (Only required if the scheduler is enabled and the tools catalog database is remote to the DAS process.)
`get admin cfg`	Displays the contents of the DB2 Database Manager configuration file associated with the DAS process.
`update admin cfg`	Allows you to alter the settings of one or more parameters in the DB2 Database Manager configuration file associated with the DAS process.
`reset admin cfg`	Changes the settings of all parameters in the DB2 Database Manager configuration file associated with the DAS process back to their original values.

NOTE
Again, basic syntax is presented for the DAS instance management commands shown in Table 2–2, but the actual syntax supported may be more complex. To view the complete syntax for a specific DB2 UDB command or to obtain more information about a particular command, refer to the *IBM DB2 Universal Database, Version 8 Command Reference* product documentation.

Distributed Connections and Communications

In a typical client/server environment, databases stored on a server are accessed by applications stored on remote client workstations using what is known as a distributed connection. In addition to providing clients with a way to access a centralized database located on a remote server, a distributed connection also allows a Database Administrator (DBA) to perform administrative operations on a remote database from any client workstation that has appropriate access to that database (with DB2 UDB, the client workstation must have the DB2 Administration Client software installed).

In order to communicate with a server workstation, each client must use some type of communications protocol that is recognized by the server. Likewise, each server must use some type of communications protocol to detect inbound requests from client workstations. In most cases, the communications protocol support needed is provided by the operating system being used on both workstations; however, in some cases, it may be provided by a separate add-on product. In either case, both clients and servers must be configured to use a communications protocol that is recognized by DB2 UDB. DB2 UDB recognizes the following communications protocols:

➤ Named pipe

➤ NetBIOS

➤ Transmission Control Protocol/Internet Protocol (TCP/IP) (which is used today in an overwhelming majority of cases)

➤ Advanced Peer-to-Peer Networking (APPN)

➤ Advanced Program-to-Program Communications (APPC)

➤ Advanced Program-to-Program Communications/Logical Unit (APPCLU)

Configuring Communications

When DB2 UDB is installed on a workstation, it is automatically configured to take advantage of any communications protocols that have been set up for that particular workstation (provided the protocols found are recognized by DB2 UDB). At that time, information about each supported communications protocol available is collected and stored in the configuration files for the DAS instance and the default instance as they are created on the workstation. However, this information is not updated automatically when a new protocol is activated or when an existing protocol is reconfigured. Instead, you must manually configure communications for each instance before such changes will be reflected.

The easiest way to make communications configuration changes is by using the Setup communications dialog, which can be activated by selecting the appropriate action from the *Instances* menu found in the Control Center. Figure 2–3 shows the Control Center menu items that must be selected in order to activate the Setup communications dialog; Figure 2–4 shows how the Setup communications dialog might be used to configure the TCP/IP protocol for a particular instance.

You can also configure communications for a particular instance by modifying the appropriate parameters of the DB2 Database Manager configuration file that is associated with that instance. (The DB2 Database Manager configuration file is covered in detail in Chapter 5, "Monitoring DB2 Activity.") The DB2 Database Manager configuration parameters that are used to configure communications are outlined in Table 2–3.

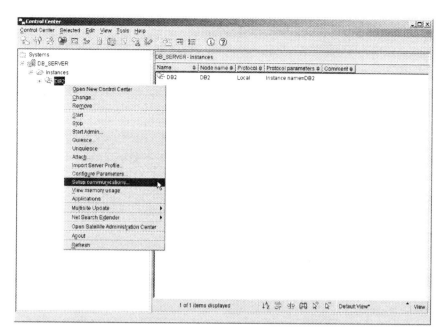

Figure 2–3   Invoking the Setup communications dialog from the Control Center.

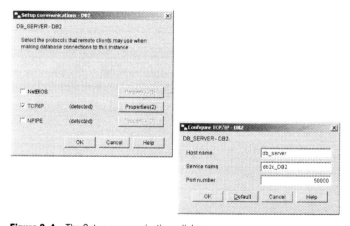

Figure 2–4   The Setup communications dialog.

Table 2–3 DB2 Database Manager Configuration Parameters Used to Configure Communications

Parameter	Description
dft_client_comm	Identifies the communication protocols client workstations can use to establish a connection to a remote server. Valid values include TCPIP, APPC, and NETBIOS. If multiple protocols are specified, they must be separated by a comma.
dir_obj_name	The unique object name that represents the DB2 Database Manager instance (or database). The concatenation of this value with the *dir_path_name* value yields a unique global name in the namespace.
dir_path_name	The unique name of the DB2 Database Manager instance (or database) in the global namespace. (The complete name is made up of the concatenation of this value and the value of the *dir_obj_name* parameter.)
dir_type	Indicates whether or not DCE directory services is used.
discover	Identifies the default DB2 Discovery action that is to be used by the instance.
discover_comm	Identifies the communications protocols that client workstations are to use when issuing search discovery requests, and that server workstations are to use to listen for search discovery requests. Valid values include TCPIP, APPC, and NETBIOS. If multiple protocols are specified, they must be separated by a comma.
fileserver	Identifies the name of the Novell NetWare file server where the internetwork address of the DB2 Database Manager is registered. If no value is specified for this parameter, the workstation is not configured to use the IPX/SPX communication protocol.
ipx_socket	Identifies the socket number that represents the connection end point in a DB2 server's Novell NetWare internetwork address (879E by default). If no value is specified for this parameter, the workstation is not configured to use the IPX/SPX communication protocol.
nname	Identifies the unique node or workstation name that is used to identify the workstation in a NetBIOS LAN environment. If no value is specified for this parameter, the workstation is not configured to use the NetBIOS communication protocol.
objectname	Identifies the unique name of the DB2 Database Manager instance in an IPX/SPX (Novell NetWare) environment. If no value is specified for this parameter, the workstation is not configured to use the IPX/SPX communication protocol.
route_obj_name	Identifies the name of the object that will be used to route information on behalf of all client applications that attempt to access a DRDA server.

(continues)

Table 2–3 DB2 Database Manager Configuration Parameters Used to Configure Communications (Continued)	
Parameter	**Description**
svcename	Identifies the name of the TCP/IP port that a server workstation will use to receive communications from remote client workstations. If no value is specified for this parameter, the workstation is not configured to use the TCP/IP communication protocol. (On Windows platforms, this may be a name that corresponds to an entry in the services file [c:\winnt\system32\drivers\etc\services].)
tpname	Identifies the name of the remote transaction program client workstations must use when issuing allocate requests to the server (in an APPC environment). If no value is specified for this parameter, the workstation is not configured to use the Advanced-Program-to-Program-Communications protocol.

The DB2COMM Registry Variable

Whenever you configure communications for an instance by updating the appropriate parameters of its DB2 Database Manager configuration file, you must also update the value of a special registry variable before the instance can actually begin using the designated protocol. This registry variable is known as the DB2COMM registry variable and its value determines which communications managers will be activated when the DB2 Database Manager for the instance is started. (If this variable is not set properly, one or more errors may be generated when the DB2 Database Manager attempts to start protocol support during instance initialization.)

The value of the DB2COMM registry variable, or any other DB2 registry variable for that matter, can be viewed or set/changed by executing the db2set command. The basic syntax for this command is:

```
db2set
<[Variable] = [Value]>
<-g>
<-i [InstanceName]>
<-all>
<-null>
<-r [InstanceName]>
<-l | -lr>
<-v>
<-h | -?>
```

where:

Variable	Identifies the registry variable whose value is to be displayed, set, or removed.
Value	Identifies the value that is to be assigned to the registry variable specified. If no value is provided, but a registry variable is specified, the registry variable specified is deleted.
InstanceName	Identifies the instance profile that the registry variable specified is associated with.

All other options shown with this command are described in Table 2–4.

Table 2–4 `db2set` Command Options	
Option	**Meaning**
-g	Indicates that a global profile variable is to be displayed, set, or removed.
-i	Indicates that an instance profile variable is to be displayed, set, or removed.
-all	Indicates that all occurrences of the registry variable, as defined in the following, are to be displayed: The environment, denoted by [-e] The node-level registry, denoted by [-n] The instance-level registry, denoted by [-i] The global-level registry, denoted by [-g]
-null	Indicates that the value of the variable at the specified registry level is to be set to NULL.
-r	Indicates that the profile registry for the given instance is to be reset.
-l	Indicates that all instance profiles will be listed.
-lr	Indicates that all registry variables supported will be listed.
-v	Executes in verbose mode.
-h | -?	Displays help information. When this option is specified, all other options are ignored, and only the help information is displayed.

So, if you wanted to see the current value of the DB2COMM registry variable, you could do so by executing a db2set command that looks something like this:

```
db2set -l DB2COMM
```

On the other hand, if you wanted to assign a value to the DB2COMM registry variable for an instance named PAYROLL, you could do so by executing a db2set command that looks something like this:

```
db2set -i PAYROLL DB2COMM=[Protocol, ...]
```

where:

> *Protocol*   Identifies one or more communications proto-
> cols that are to be started when the DB2 Data-
> base Manager for the instance is started. Any
> combination of the following values is valid:
> APPC, IPXSPX, NETBIOS, NPIPE, and
> TCPIP.

Thus, if you wanted to set the DB2COMM instance-level registry variable
such that the DB2 Database Manager would start the TCP/IP communication manager each time the instance is started, you could do so by executing a
db2set command that looks something like this:

```
db2set -i PAYROLL DB2COMM=TCPIP
```

It is important to note that because the communication managers for one or
more protocols are started when the instance is started, the DB2 Database
Manager for the instance must be stopped and restarted before any changes
made to the DB2COMM registry variable will take effect.

NOTE   Before a DB2 client can communicate with a DB2 server, the DB2 server must be configured to accept inbound requests for the communications protocol the client has
been configured to use. Therefore, in order for a specific communications protocol to
be used between a client and a server, the value assigned to the DB2COMM registry
variable on both the client and the server workstation must include the keyword for
that particular protocol.

DB2 Discovery

It's easy to see how manually configuring communications between client and
server workstations can become an involved process, especially in complex
network environments. And establishing communications between clients
and servers is only the beginning; before a client can send requests to a DB2
server for processing, both the server and the database stored on the server
must be cataloged on the client workstation as well.

This is where DB2 Discovery comes in. DB2 Discovery also allows you to
easily catalog a remote server and a database (and set up a distributed connection between a client and a server) without having to know any detailed com-
munication-specific information. Here's how DB2 Discovery works. When
invoked from a client workstation, DB2 Discovery broadcasts a discovery
request over the network, and each DB2 server on the network that has been

configured to support the discovery process responds by returning a list of instances found on the server, information about the communication protocol each instance supports, and a list of databases found within each instance. The Control Center and the Configuration Assistant can then use this information to catalog any instance or database returned by the discovery process.

When initiating a discovery request, DB2 Discovery can use one of two methods: *search* and *known*. When the search discovery method is used, the entire network is searched for valid DB2 servers/databases, and a list of all servers, instances, and databases found is returned to the client, along with the communications information needed to catalog and connect to each. In contrast, when the known discovery method is used, the network is searched for a specific server using a specific communications protocol. (Since the client knows the name of the server and the communications protocol used by that server, the server is said to be "known" by the client.) Again, when the specified server is located, a list of all instances and databases found on the server is returned to the client, along with the information needed to catalog and connect to each one.

A search discovery can take a very long time (many hours) to complete if the network the client and server are on contains hundreds of machines. Furthermore, some network devices, such as routers, may actually block a search discovery request. (Known discovery requests will still be processed.)

Configuring Instances and Databases for DB2 Discovery

Whether or not, and if so, how a client can launch a DB2 Discovery request and whether or not, and if so, how a particular server will respond is determined by the values of parameters found in the configuration file for the DAS process, the DB2 Database Manager configuration file for each instance (both on the client and on the server), and the database configuration file for each database within an instance. Specifically, these parameters control:

➤ Whether or not a client can launch a DB2 Discovery request.

➤ The communications protocol(s) that a client will use when broadcasting search discovery requests.

➤ Whether or not a server can be located by DB2 Discovery, and if so whether the server can only be located when the search discovery method is used or when the known discovery method is used.

➤ The communications protocol(s) that a server will use to listen for and respond to search discovery requests.

➤ Whether or not an instance can be located with a discovery request.

➤ Whether or not a database can be located with a discovery request.

The DAS process, DB2 Database Manager (instance), and database configuration parameters that are used to control the behavior of DB2 Discovery are described in Table 2–5.

Table 2–5 Configuration Parameters That Control the Behavior of DB2 Discovery		
Parameter	Values / Default	Description
Client Instance **(DB2 Database Manager Configuration File)**		
discover	DISABLE, KNOWN, or SEARCH Default: SEARCH	Identifies the DB2 Discovery action that is to be used by the client instance. If this parameter is set to SEARCH, the client instance can issue either search or known discovery requests; if this parameter is set to KNOWN, the client instance can only issue known discovery requests; and if this parameter is set to DISABLE, the client instance cannot issue discovery requests.
discover_comm	NETBIOS, TCPIP, or both (separated with a comma)	Identifies the communications protocols that the client instance will use to issue search discovery requests. (This parameter has no affect on known discovery requests.)
Server DAS Process **(DAS Configuration File)**		
discover	DISABLE, KNOWN, or SEARCH Default: SEARCH	Identifies the DB2 Discovery action that is to be used when the server is started. If this parameter is set to SEARCH, the server will respond to both search and known discovery requests; if this parameter is set to KNOWN, the server will only respond to known discovery requests; and if this parameter is set to DISABLE, the server will ignore all discovery requests.
discover_comm	NETBIOS, TCPIP, or both (separated with a comma)	Identifies the communications protocols that the DAS process will use to issue or listen for search discovery requests. (This parameter has no affect on known discovery requests.) *(continues)*

Table 2–5	Configuration Parameters That Control the Behavior of DB2 Discovery	
Parameter	Values / Default	Description
	Server Instance **(DB2 Database Manager Configuration File)**	
discover_inst	ENABLE or DISABLE Default: ENABLE	Identifies whether or not information about a particular instance found on a server will be included in the server's response to a discovery request.
		If this parameter is set to ENABLE, the server will include information about the instance in its response to both search and known discovery requests. On the other hand, if this parameter is set to DISABLE, the server will not include information about the instance in its response to discovery requests (nor will it include information about any databases that come under the instance's control in its response to discovery requests).
		This parameter provides a way to hide an instance and all of its databases from DB2 Discovery.
	Server Database **(Database Configuration File)**	
discover_db	ENABLE or DISABLE Default: ENABLE	Identifies whether or not information about a particular database found on a server will be included in the server's response to a discovery request.
		If this parameter is set to ENABLE, the server will include information about the database in its response to both search and known discovery requests. On the other hand, if this parameter is set to DISABLE, the server will not include information about the database in its response to discovery requests.
		This parameter provides a way to hide an individual database from DB2 Discovery.

As you can see, it is possible to enable or disable DB2 Discovery at the server level, instance level, and database level, as well as control how clients initiate discovery requests. It is also possible to configure a server so that DB2 Discovery will not see one or more of its instances and/or databases when discovery requests are made. Figure 2–5 shows how the configuration parameters that control the behavior of DB2 Discovery can be used to prevent DB2 Discovery from seeing certain instances and databases stored on a server.

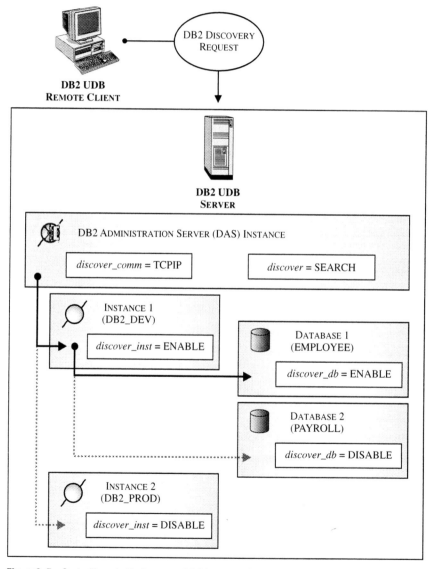

Figure 2–5 Controlling what instances and databases can be seen by DB2 Discovery. In this example, the server, Instance 1, and Database 1 will be returned by a discovery request; Instance 2 and Database 2 will not.

Controlling Database Access

Although disabling DB2 Discovery at the DAS level, instance level, and/or database level prevents a client from quickly locating a DB2 server, instance, or database on a network, it does not stop a savvy user from setting up connectivity by cataloging a server and a database on a client workstation using the CATALOG ... NODE and CATALOG DATABASE commands. Client workstations can still attach to remote instances and connect to remote databases even when DB2 Discovery has been disabled. Therefore, even though DB2 Discovery can be used to prevent most users from gaining access to servers and databases containing sensitive data, it is not the only security method used.

Every database management system must be able to protect data against unauthorized access and/or modification and DB2 UDB is no exception. DB2 UDB uses a combination of external security services and internal access control mechanisms to perform this vital task. In most cases, three different levels of security are employed: The first level controls access to the instance a database was created under, the second controls access to the database itself, and the third controls access to the data and data objects that reside within the database.

Authentication

The first security portal most users must pass through on their way to gaining access to a DB2 UDB instance or a database is a process known as *authentication*. The purpose of authentication is to verify that a user really is who they say they are. Typically, authentication is performed by an external security facility that is not part of DB2 UDB. This security facility may be part of the operating system (as is the case with AIX, Solaris, Linux, HP-UX, Windows 2000/NT, and many others), may be a separate add-on product (for example, Distributed Computing Environment [DCE] Security Services), or may not exist at all (which, by default, is the case with Windows 95, Windows 98, and Windows Millennium Edition). If a security facility does exist, it must be presented with two specific items before a user can be authenticated: a unique user ID and a corresponding password. The user ID identifies the user to the security facility, while the password, which is information that is known only by both the user and the security facility, is used to verify that the user is indeed who they claim to be.

Because passwords are a very important tool for authenticating users, you should always require passwords at the operating system level if you want the operating system to perform the authentication for your database. Keep in mind that on most UNIX operating systems, undefined passwords are treated as NULL, and any user that has not been assigned a password will be treated as if they have a NULL password—from the operating system's perspective, such a password will be evaluated as being valid and the user will be authenticated.

Where Does Authentication Take Place?

Because DB2 UDB can reside in environments comprised of multiple clients, gateways, and servers, each of which may be running on a different operating system, deciding where authentication is to take place can be a daunting task. So to simplify things, DB2 UDB uses a parameter in the DB2 Database Manager configuration file associated with every instance to determine how and where users are to be authenticated. The value assigned to this configuration parameter, often referred to as the *authentication type*, is set initially when an instance is created. (On the server side, the authentication type is specified during the instance creation process; on the client side, the authentication type is specified when a remote database is cataloged, which is usually performed using the Configuration Assistant.) Only one authentication type exists for each instance, and it controls access to that instance, as well as to all databases that fall under the instance's control.

In Version 8.1 of DB2 UDB, the following authentication types are available:

SERVER. Authentication occurs at the server workstation using the security facility provided by the server's operating system. (The user ID and password provided by the user wishing to attach to an instance or connect to a database are compared to the user ID and password combinations stored at the server to determine whether the user is permitted to access the instance/database.) By default, this is the authentication type used when an instance is first created.

SERVER_ENCRYPT. Authentication occurs at the server workstation using the security facility that is provided by the server's operating system. However, the password provided by the user wishing to attach to an instance or connect to a database stored on the server may be encrypted at the client workstation before it is sent to the server workstation for validation.

CLIENT. Authentication occurs at the client workstation or database partition where a client application is invoked using the security facility that is provided by the client's operating system, assuming one is available. If no security facility is available, authentication is handled in a slightly different manner. (The user ID and password provided by the user wishing to attach to an instance or connect to a database are compared to the user ID and password combinations stored at the client/node to determine whether the user is permitted to access the instance or the database.)

KERBEROS. Authentication occurs at the server workstation using a security facility that supports the Kerberos security protocol. The Kerberos security protocol is a protocol that performs authentication as a third-party service by using conventional cryptography to create a shared secret key. The key becomes the credentials used to verify the identity of users whenever local or network services are requested; this eliminates the need to pass a user ID and password across the network as ASCII text. (If both the client and the server support the Kerberos security protocol, the user ID and password provided by the user wishing to attach to an instance or connect to a database are encrypted at the client workstation and sent to the server for validation.) It should be noted that the KERBEROS authentication type is only supported on clients and servers that are using the Windows 2000, Windows XP, or Windows .NET operating system. In addition, both client and server workstations must either belong to the same Windows domain or belong to trusted domains.

KRB_SERVER_ENCRYPT. Authentication occurs at the server workstation using either the KERBEROS or the SERVER _ENCRYPT authentication method. If the client's authentication type is set to KERBEROS, authentication is performed at the server using the Kerberos security system. On the other hand, if the client's authentication type is set to anything other than KERBEROS or if the Kerberos authentication service is unavailable, the server acts as if the SERVER_ENCRYPT authentication type was specified, and the rules of this authentication method apply.

Just as the authentication type for an instance on a server is set when the instance is first created, an authentication type is usually specified at each client workstation that will communicate with a server. Furthermore, the combination of authentication types specified at both the client and the server determine which authentication method is actually used. Figure 2–6 shows the combination of client and server authentication types that should be used when users are to be authenticated at the client workstation. Figure 2–7 shows the combinations of client and server authentication types that should be used when users are to be authenticated at the server.

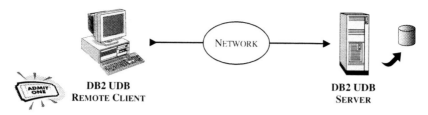

Client Authentication Type	Server Authentication Type	Authentication Type Used
CLIENT	CLIENT	CLIENT

Figure 2–6   Authentication type combinations to use for client authentication.

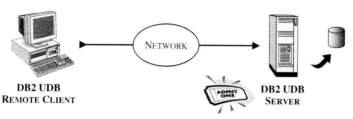

Client Authentication Type	Server Authentication Type	Authentication Type Used
SERVER	SERVER	SERVER
SERVER	SERVER_ENCRYPT	SERVER
SERVER_ENCRYPT	SERVER_ENCRYPT	SERVER_ENCRYPT
KERBEROS	KERBEROS	KERBEROS
KERBEROS	KRB_SERVER_ENCRYPT	KERBEROS
KRB_SERVER_ENCRYPT	KRB_SERVER_ENCRYPT	KRB_SERVER_ENCRYPT
SERVER	KRB_SERVER_ENCRYPT	SERVER_ENCRYPT
SERVER_ENCRYPT	KRB_SERVER_ENCRYPT	SERVER_ENCRYPT

Figure 2–7   Authentication type combinations to use for server authentication.

Trusted Clients versus Untrusted Clients

As you can see in Figure 2–6, if both the server and the client are configured to use the CLIENT authentication type, authentication occurs at the client workstation (if the database is a nonpartitioned database) or at the database partition from which the client application is invoked (if the database is a partitioned database), using the security facility that is provided by the client's operating system. But what happens if the client workstation is using an operating system that does not contain a tightly integrated security facility, and no separate add-on security facility has been made available? Does such a configuration compromise security? The answer is no. However, in such environments, the DB2 Database Manager for the instance at the server must be able to determine which clients will be responsible for validating users and which clients will be forced to let the server handle user authentication. To make this distinction, clients that use an operating system that contains an integrated security facility (for example, Windows NT, Windows 2000, all supported versions of UNIX, MVS, OS/390, VM, VSE, and AS/400) are classified as *trusted clients*, and clients that use an operating system that does not provide an integrated security facility (for example, Windows 95, Windows 98, and Windows Millennium Edition) are classified as *untrusted clients*.

The *trust_allclnts* parameter of a DB2 Database Manager configuration file helps the DB2 Database Manager for an instance on a server anticipate whether its clients are to be treated as trusted or untrusted. If this configuration parameter is set to YES (which is the default), the DB2 Database Manager assumes that any client that accesses the instance is a trusted client and that authentication will take place at the client. However, if this configuration parameter is set to NO, the DB2 Database Manager assumes that one or more untrusted clients will be used to access the server; therefore, all users must be authenticated at the server. (If this configuration parameter is set to DRDA-ONLY, only MVS, OS/390, VM, VSE, and OS/400 clients will be treated as trusted clients.) It is important to note that regardless of how the *trust_allclnts* parameter is set, whenever an untrusted client attempts to access an instance or a database, user authentication always takes place at the server.

In some situations, it may be desirable to authenticate users at the server, even when no untrusted clients will need access. In such situations, the *trust_clntauth* configuration parameter of a DB2 Database Manager configuration file can be used to control where trusted clients are to be validated. By accepting the default value for this parameter (which is CLIENT), authentication for trusted clients will take place at the client workstation. However, if the value for this parameter is changed to SERVER, authentication for all trusted clients will take place at the server.

Authorities and Privileges

Once a user has been authenticated and an attachment to an instance or a connection to a database has been established, the DB2 Database Manager evaluates any *authorities* and *privileges* that have been assigned to the user (these can be assigned directly to a user, or they can be obtained indirectly from group privileges that have been assigned to a group the user is a member of) to determine what operations the user is allowed to perform. Authorities convey a set of privileges and/or the right to perform high-level administrative and maintenance/utility operations against an instance or a database. Privileges, on the other hand, convey the rights to perform certain actions against specific database resources (such as tables and views). Together, authorities and privileges

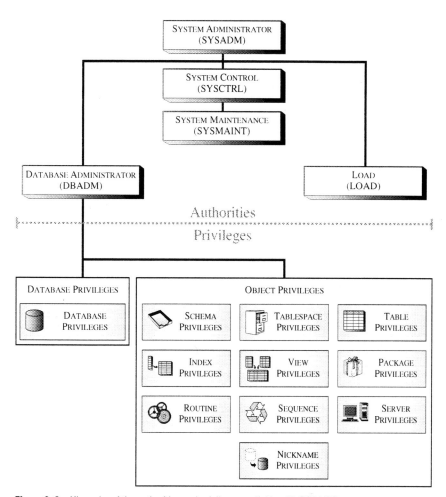

Figure 2–8 Hierarchy of the authorities and privileges available with DB2 UDB.

act to control access to the DB2 Database Manager for an instance, to one or more databases running under that instance's control, and to a particular database's objects. Users can only work with those objects for which they have been given the appropriate authorization—that is, the required authority or privilege. Figure 2–8 provides a hierarchical view of the authorities and privileges that are recognized by DB2 UDB.

Authorities

DB2 UDB uses five different levels of authority to control how users perform administrative and/or maintenance operations against an instance or a database. These five levels are:

➤ System Administrator (SYSADM) authority

➤ System Control (SYSCTRL) authority

➤ System Maintenance (SYSMAINT) authority

➤ Database Administrator (DBADM) authority

➤ Load (LOAD) authority

The first three of these levels apply to the DB2 Database Manager instance (and to all databases that are managed by that instance), while the remaining two apply only to specific databases within an instance. Furthermore, the three instance-level authorities can only be assigned to groups; the names of the groups that are assigned these authorities are stored in the DB2 Database Manager configuration file that is associated with the instance. Conversely, the two database-level authorities can be assigned to an individual user and/or to a group of users; groups and users that have been assigned database-level authorities are recorded in the system catalog tables of the database to which the authority applies.

System Administrator Authority

System Administrator (SYSADM) authority is the highest level of administrative authority available with DB2 UDB. Users that have been given this authority are allowed to run any available DB2 UDB utilities, execute any DB2 UDB command, perform any SQL operation, and control all objects within an instance, including databases, database partition groups, buffer pools, tablespaces, tables, views, indexes, schemas, aliases, data types, functions, procedures, triggers, packages, servers, and event monitors. In addition, users who have been given this authority are allowed to perform the following tasks:

➤ Migrate an existing database to make it compatible with a new version of DB2 UDB.

➤ Modify the parameter values of the DB2 Database Manager configuration file associated with the instance, including specifying which groups have System Control and/or System Maintenance authority. (The DB2 Database Manager configuration file is used to control the amount of system resources allocated to a single instance.)

➤ Quiesce (restrict access to) an instance, database, or tablespace.

➤ Give (grant) Database Administrator authority to groups and/or individual users.

➤ Take away (revoke) Database Administrator authority from groups and/or individual users.

SYSADM authority can only be assigned to a group, and this assignment is made by storing the appropriate group name in the *sysadm_group* parameter of the DB2 Database Manager configuration file associated with a particular instance. Individual membership in the group itself is controlled through the security facility used on the workstation where the instance has been defined.

System Control Authority

System Control (SYSCTRL) authority is the highest level of system/instance control authority available with DB2 UDB. Users that have been given this authority are allowed to perform maintenance and utility operations against both a DB2 Database Manager instance and any databases that fall under that instance's control. However, because SYSCTRL authority is designed to allow special users to maintain an instance containing sensitive data that they most likely do not have the right to access, users who are granted this authority do not implicitly receive authority to access the data stored in the databases on which they are allowed to perform maintenance and utility operations. On the other hand, because a connection to a database must exist before some utility operations can be performed, users who are granted SYSCTRL authority for a particular instance also receive the privileges needed to connect to each database under that instance's control.

Users with SYSCTRL authority (or higher) are allowed to perform the following tasks:

➤ Update a database, node, or distributed connection services (DCS) directory (by cataloging/uncataloging databases, nodes, or DCS databases).

➤ Modify the parameter values of one or more DB2 database configuration files. (A database configuration file is used to control the amount of system resources allocated to a single database during normal operation.)

➤ Force users off the system.

➤ Create or destroy (drop) a database.

➤ Create, alter, or drop a tablespace.

➤ Make a backup image of a database or a tablespace.

➤ Restore an existing database using a backup image.

➤ Restore a tablespace using a backup image.

➤ Create a new database from a database backup image.

➤ Perform a roll-forward recovery operation on a database.

➤ Start or stop a DB2 Database Manager instance.

➤ Run a trace on a database operation.

➤ Take database system monitor snapshots of a DB2 Database Manager instance or any database under the instance's control.

➤ Query the state of a tablespace.

➤ Update recovery log history files.

➤ Quiesce (restrict access to) an instance or a tablespace.

➤ Reorganize a table.

➤ Collect catalog statistics using the RUNSTATS utility.

Like SYSADM authority, SYSCTRL authority can only be assigned to a group. This assignment is made by storing the appropriate group name in the *sysctrl_group* parameter of the DB2 Database Manager configuration file that is associated with a particular instance. Again, individual membership in the group itself is controlled through the security facility that is used on the workstation where the instance has been defined.

System Maintenance Authority

System Maintenance (SYSMAINT) authority is the second highest level of system/instance control authority available with DB2 UDB. Users that have been given this authority are allowed to perform maintenance and utility operations against any database that falls under an instance's control—but not against the instance itself. Like SYSCTRL authority, SYSMAINT authority is designed to allow special users to maintain a database containing sensitive data that they most likely do not have access to. Therefore, users who are granted this authority do not implicitly receive authority to access the data stored in the databases on which they are allowed to perform maintenance and utility operations. However, because a connection to a database must exist before some utility operations can be performed, users who are granted SYSMAINT authority for a particular instance automatically receive the privileges needed to connect to each database under that instance's control.

Users with SYSMAINT authority (or higher) are allowed to perform the following tasks:

➤ Modify the parameter values of one or more DB2 database configuration files.

➤ Make a backup image of a database or a tablespace.

➤ Restore an existing database using a backup image.

➤ Restore a tablespace using a backup image.

➤ Perform a roll-forward recovery operation on a database.

➤ Start or stop a DB2 Database Manager instance.

➤ Run a trace on a database operation.

➤ Take database system monitor snapshots of a DB2 Database Manager instance or any database under the instance's control.

➤ Query the state of a tablespace.

➤ Update recovery log history files.

➤ Quiesce (restrict access to) a tablespace.

➤ Reorganize a table.

➤ Collect catalog statistics using the RUNSTATS utility.

Like SYSADM and SYSCTRL authority, SYSMAINT authority can only be assigned to a group. This assignment is made by storing the appropriate group name in the *sysmaint_group* parameter of the DB2 Database Manager configuration file that is associated with a particular instance. Again, individual membership in the group itself is controlled through the security facility that is used on the workstation where the instance has been defined.

Database Administrator Authority

Database Administrator (DBADM) authority is the second highest level of administrative authority (below SYSADM) available with DB2 UDB. Users that have been given this authority are allowed to run most DB2 UDB utilities, issue database-specific DB2 commands, perform most SQL operations, and access data stored in any table in a database. However, they can only perform these functions on the database for which DBADM authority is held.

Users with DBADM authority (or higher) are allowed to perform the following tasks:

➤ Query the state of a tablespace.

➤ Update recovery log history files.

➤ Quiesce (restrict access to) a database or a tablespace.

➤ Reorganize a table.

➤ Collect catalog statistics using the RUNSTATS utility.

On the other hand, only users with DBADM authority (or SYSADM authority) are allowed to:

➤ Read database log files.

➤ Create, activate, and drop event monitors.

➤ Give (grant) database privileges to groups and/or individual users.

➤ Take away (revoke) any privilege from any group and/or individual user, regardless of how it was granted.

Unlike SYSADM, SYSCTRL, and SYSMAINT authority, DBADM authority can be assigned to both individual users and groups. This assignment is made by executing the appropriate form of the GRANT SQL statement (which we will look at shortly). When a user is given DBADM authority for a particular database, they automatically receive CONNECT, QUIESCE_CONNECT, CREATETAB, BINDADD, CREATE_NOT_FENCED, CREATE_EXTERNAL_ROUTINE, LOAD, and IMPLICIT_SCHEMA database privileges for that database as well. (We will look at each of these privileges in greater detail a little later.)

> Any time a user with SYSADM or SYSCTRL authority creates a new database, they automatically receive DBADM authority on that database. Furthermore, if a user with SYSADM or SYSCTRL authority creates a database and is later removed from the SYSADM or SYSCTRL group (i.e., their SYSADM or SYSCTRL authority is revoked), they retain DBADM authority for that database until it is explicitly removed (revoked).

Load Authority

Load (LOAD) authority is a special database level of administrative authority that has a much smaller scope than the DBADM authority. Users that have been given this authority, along with INSERT and in some cases DELETE privileges, on a particular table are allowed to bulk-load data into that table, using either the AutoLoader utility (db2atld command) or the LOAD command/API. LOAD authority is designed to allow special users to perform bulk-load operations against a database that they most likely cannot do anything else with. This authority level provides a way for Database Administrators to allow more users to perform special database operations without having to sacrifice control.

In addition to being able to load data into a database table, users with LOAD authority (or higher) are allowed to perform the following tasks:

➤ Query the state of a tablespace using the LIST TABLESPACES command.

➤ Quiesce (restrict access to) a tablespace.

➤ Collect catalog statistics using the RUNSTATS utility.

Like DBADM authority, LOAD authority can be assigned to both individual users and groups. This assignment is made by executing the appropriate form of the GRANT SQL statement.

Privileges

As mentioned earlier, privileges are used to convey the rights to perform certain actions on specific database resources to both individual users and groups. With DB2 UDB, two distinct types of privileges exist: *database privileges* and *object privileges.*

Database Privileges

Database privileges apply to a database as a whole, and for most users, they act as identification that gets verified at the second security checkpoint that must be cleared before access to data is provided. Figure 2–9 shows the different types of database privileges available.

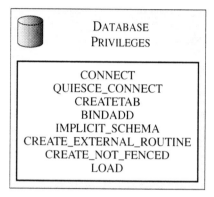

Figure 2–9   Database privileges available with DB2 UDB.

As you can see in Figure 2–9, eight different database privileges exist. They are:

CONNECT. Allows a user to establish a connection to the database.

QUIESCE_CONNECT. Allows a user to establish a connection to the database while it is quiesced (while access to it is restricted).

CREATETAB. Allows a user to create new tables in the database.

BINDADD. Allows a user to create packages in the database (by precompiling embedded SQL application source code files against the database and/or by binding application bind files to the database).

CREATE_EXTERNAL_ROUTINE. Allows a user to create a procedure that can be invoked by applications and other database users and store it in the database.

CREATE_NOT_FENCED. Allows a user to create unfenced user-defined functions (UDFs) and store them in the database. (Unfenced UDFs are considered "safe" enough to be run in the DB2 Database Manager operating environment's process or address space. Unless a function is registered as being unfenced, the DB2 Database Manager insulates its internal resources in such a way that they cannot be utilized by that function.)

IMPLICIT_SCHEMA. Allows a user to implicitly create a new schema in the database by creating an object and assigning that object a schema name that is different from any of the schema names already existing in the database.

LOAD. Allows a user to bulk-load data into one or more existing tables in the database.

At a minimum, a user must have a CONNECT privilege on a database before they can work with any object in that database.

Object Privileges

Unlike database privileges, which apply to a database as a whole, object privileges only apply to specific objects within a database. These objects include schemas, tablespaces, tables, indexes, views, packages, routines, sequences, servers, and nicknames. Because the nature of each available database object varies, the individual privileges that exist for each object can vary as well. The following sections describe the different sets of object privileges that are available with DB2 UDB.

Schema privileges. Schema privileges control what users can and cannot do with a particular schema. (A schema is an object that is used to logically classify and group other objects in the database; most objects are named using a naming convention that consists of a schema name, followed by a period, followed by the object name.) Figure 2–10 shows the different types of schema privileges available.

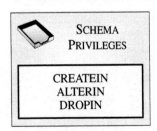

Figure 2–10   Schema privileges available with DB2 UDB.

As you can see in Figure 2–10, three different schema privileges exist. They are:

CREATEIN. Allows a user to create objects within the schema.

ALTERIN. Allows a user to change the comment associated with any object in the schema or to alter any object that resides within the schema.

DROPIN. Allows a user to remove (drop) any object within the schema.

Objects that can be manipulated within a schema include: tables, views, indexes, packages, user-defined data types, user-defined functions, triggers, stored procedures, and aliases. The owner of a schema (usually the individual who created the schema) automatically receives these privileges, along with the right to grant any combination of these privileges to other users and groups.

Tablespace privileges. Tablespace privileges control what users can and cannot do with a particular tablespace. (Tablespaces are used to control where data in a database physically resides.) Figure 2–11 shows the different types of tablespace privileges available.

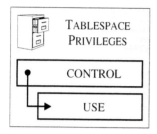

Figure 2–11   Tablespace privileges available with DB2 UDB.

As you can see in Figure 2–11, two different tablespace privileges exist. They are:

CONTROL. Provides a user with every tablespace privilege available, allows the user to remove (drop) the tablespace from the database, and gives the user the ability to grant to or revoke from other users and groups the USE tablespace privilege. (Only users who hold SYSADM or DBADM authority are allowed to grant and revoke CONTROL privileges for an object.)

USE. Allows a user to create tables within the tablespace. (This privilege is used to control which tablespaces a particular user is allowed to create tables in.)

The owner of a tablespace (usually the individual who created the tablespace) automatically receives CONTROL privilege and USE privilege for that tablespace. By default, whenever a new database is created, the USE privilege for tablespace USERSPACE1 is given to the group PUBLIC; however, this privilege can be revoked.

The USE privilege cannot be used to provide a user with the ability to create tables in the SYSCATSPACE tablespace or in any system temporary tablespace that might exist.

Table privileges. Table privileges control what users can and cannot do with a particular table in a database. (A table is a logical structure that is used to present data as a collection of unordered rows with a fixed number of columns.) Figure 2–12 shows the different types of table privileges available.

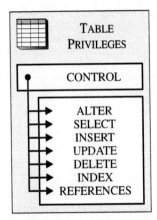

Figure 2–12   Table privileges available with DB2 UDB.

As you can see in Figure 2–12, eight different table privileges exist. They are:

CONTROL. Provides a user with every table privilege available, allows the user to remove (drop) the table from the database, and gives the user the ability to grant to or revoke from other users and groups any available table privileges (except the CONTROL privilege).

ALTER. Allows a user to execute the ALTER TABLE SQL statement against the table. In other words, allows a user to add columns to the table, add or change comments associated with the table and/or any of its columns, create a primary key for the table, create a unique constraint for the table, create or drop a check constraint for the table, and create triggers for the table (provided the user holds the appropriate privileges for every object referenced by the trigger).

SELECT. Allows a user to execute a SELECT SQL statement against the table. In other words, allows a user to retrieve data from a table, create a view that references the table, and run the EXPORT utility against the table.

INSERT. Allows a user to execute the INSERT SQL statement against the table. In other words, allows a user to add data to the table and run the IMPORT utility against the table.

UPDATE. Allows a user to execute the UPDATE SQL statement against the table. In other words, allows a user to modify data in the table. (This privilege can be granted for the entire table or limited to one or more columns within the table.)

DELETE. Allows a user to execute the DELETE SQL statement against the table. In other words, allows a user to remove rows of data from the table.

INDEX. Allows a user to create an index for the table.

REFERENCES. Allows a user to create and drop foreign key constraints that reference the table in a parent relationship. (This privilege can be granted for the entire table or limited to one or more columns within the table, in which case only those columns can participate as a parent key in a referential constraint.)

The owner of a table (usually the individual who created the table) automatically receives CONTROL privilege, along with all other available table privileges, for that table. If the CONTROL privilege is later revoked from the table owner, all other privileges that were automatically granted to the owner for that particular table are not automatically revoked. Instead, they must be explicitly revoked in one or more separate operations.

Index privileges. The index privilege controls what users can and cannot do with a particular index. (An index is an ordered set of pointers that refer to one or more key columns in a base table; indexes are used to improve query performance.) Figure 2–13 shows the only index privilege available.

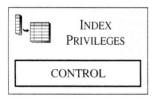

Figure 2–13   Index privilege available with DB2 UDB.

As you can see in Figure 2–13, only one index privilege exists. That privilege is the CONTROL privilege, which allows a user to remove (drop) the index from the database. Unlike the CONTROL privilege for other objects, the CONTROL privilege for an index does not provide a user with the ability to grant to or revoke from other users and groups any available index privilege.

That's because only users who hold SYSADM or DBADM authority are allowed to grant and revoke CONTROL privileges for an object.

The owner of an index (usually the individual who created the index) automatically receives CONTROL privilege for that index.

View privileges. View privileges control what users can and cannot do with a particular view. (A view is a virtual table, residing in memory, that provides an alternative way of working with data that resides in one or more base tables.) Figure 2–14 shows the different types of view privileges available.

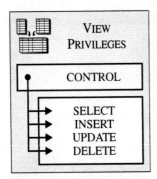

Figure 2–14 View privileges available with DB2 UDB.

As you can see in Figure 2–14, five different view privileges exist. They are:

CONTROL. Provides a user with every view privilege available, allows the user to remove (drop) the view from the database, and gives the user the ability to grant to or revoke from other users and groups any available view privileges (except the CONTROL privilege).

SELECT. Allows a user to retrieve data from the view, create a second view that references the view, and run the EXPORT utility against the view.

INSERT. Allows a user to add data to the view.

UPDATE. Allows a user to modify data in the view. (This privilege can be granted for the entire view or limited to one or more columns within the view.).

DELETE. Allows a user to remove rows of data from the view.

In order to create a view, a user must hold appropriate privileges on each base table the view references. Once a view is created, the owner of that view (usually the individual who created the view) automatically receives all available view privileges—with the exception of the CONTROL privilege—for that view. A view owner will only receive CONTROL privilege for the view if they also hold CONTROL privilege for every base table the view references.

Package privileges. Package privileges control what users can and cannot do with a particular package. (A package is an object that contains the information needed by the DB2 Database Manager to process SQL statements in the most efficient way possible on behalf of an embedded SQL application.) Figure 2–15 shows the different types of package privileges available.

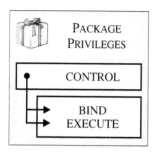

Figure 2–15   Package privileges available with DB2 UDB.

As you can see in Figure 2–15, three different package privileges exist. They are:

CONTROL. Provides a user with every package privilege available, allows the user to remove (drop) the package from the database, and gives the user the ability to grant to or revoke from other users and groups any available package privileges (except the CONTROL privilege).

BIND. Allows a user to rebind or add new package versions to a package that has already been bound to a database. (In addition to the BIND package privilege, a user must hold the privileges needed to execute the SQL statements that make up the package before the package can be successfully rebound.)

EXECUTE. Allows a user to execute the package. (A user that has EXECUTE privilege for a particular package can execute that package, even if they do not have the privileges that are needed to execute the SQL statements stored in the package. That is because any privileges needed to execute the SQL statements are implicitly granted to the package user. It is important to note that for privileges to be implicitly granted, the creator of the package must hold privileges as an individual user or as a member of the group PUBLIC—not as a member of another named group.)

The owner of a package (usually the individual who created the package) automatically receives CONTROL privilege, along with all other available package privileges, for that package. If the CONTROL privilege is later revoked from the package owner, all other privileges that were automatically granted to the owner for that particular package are not automatically revoked. Instead, they must be explicitly revoked in one or more separate operations.

 Users who have EXECUTE privilege for a package that contains nicknames do not need additional authorities or privileges for the nicknames in the package; however, they must be able to pass any authentication checks performed at the data source(s) in which objects referenced by the nicknames are stored, and they must hold the appropriate authorizations and privileges needed to access all referenced objects.

Routine privileges. Routine privileges control what users can and cannot do with a particular routine. (A routine can be a user-defined function, a stored procedure, or a method that can be invoked by several different users.) Figure 2–16 shows the different types of routine privileges available.

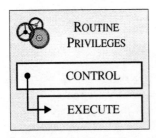

Figure 2–16   Routine privileges available with DB2 UDB.

As you can see in Figure 2–16, two different routine privileges exist. They are:

CONTROL. Provides a user with every routine privilege available, allows the user to remove (drop) the routine from the database, and gives the user the ability to grant to or revoke from other users and groups any available routine privileges (except the CONTROL privilege).

EXECUTE. Allows a user to invoke the routine, create a function that is sourced from the routine (provided the routine is a function), and reference the routine in a DDL statement or when creating a constraint.

The owner of a routine (usually the individual who created the routine) automatically receives CONTROL and EXECUTE privileges for that routine. If the CONTROL privilege is later revoked from the owner, the EXECUTE privilege will be retained and must be explicitly revoked in a separate operation.

Sequence privileges. Sequence privileges control what users can and cannot do with a particular sequence. (A sequence is an object that can be used to generate values automatically—sequences are ideal for generating unique key values. Applications can use sequences to avoid the possible concurrency and performance problems that can occur when unique counters residing outside the database are used for data generation.) Figure 2–17 shows the different types of sequence privileges available.

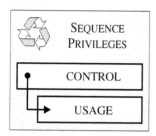

Figure 2–17   Sequence privileges available with DB2 UDB.

As you can see in Figure 2–17, two different sequence privileges exist. They are:

CONTROL. Provides a user with every sequence privilege available, allows the user to remove (drop) the sequence from the database, and gives the user the ability to grant to or revoke from other users and groups any available sequence privileges (except the CONTROL privilege).

USAGE. Allows a user to use the PREVVAL and NEXTVAL expressions that are associated with the sequence. (The PREVVAL expression returns the most recently generated value for the specified sequence; the NEXTVAL expression returns the next value for the specified sequence.)

The owner of a sequence (usually the individual who created the sequence) automatically receives CONTROL and USAGE privilege for that sequence. If the CONTROL privilege is later revoked from the owner, the USAGE privilege will be retained and must be explicitly revoked in a separate operation.

Server privileges. The server privilege controls what users can and cannot do with a particular federated database server. (A DB2 federated system is a distributed computing system that consists of a DB2 server, known as a *federated server,* and one or more data sources to which the federated server sends queries. Each data source consists of an instance of some supported relational database management system—such as Oracle—plus the database or databases that the instance supports.) Figure 2–18 shows the only type of server privilege available.

Figure 2–18   Server privilege available with DB2 UDB.

As you can see in Figure 2–18, only one server privilege exists. That privilege is the PASSTHRU privilege, which allows a user to issue Data Definition Language (DDL) and Data Manipulation Language (DML) SQL statements (as pass-through operations) directly to a data source via a federated server.

Nickname privileges. Nickname privileges control what users can and cannot do with a particular nickname. (When a client application submits a distributed request to a federated database server, the server forwards the request to the appropriate data source for processing. However, such a request does not identify the data source itself; instead, it references tables and views within the data source by using nicknames that map to specific table and view names at the data source. Nicknames are not alternate names for tables and views in the same way that aliases are; instead, they are pointers by which a federated server references external objects.) Figure 2–19 shows the different types of nickname privileges available.

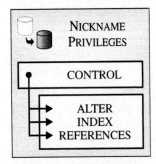

Figure 2–19   Nickname privileges available with DB2 UDB.

As you can see in Figure 2–19, four different nickname privileges exist. They are:

> **CONTROL.** Provides a user with every nickname privilege available, allows the user to remove (drop) the nickname from the database, and gives the user the ability to grant to or revoke from other users and groups any available nickname privileges (except the CONTROL privilege).

ALTER. Allows a user to change column names in the nickname, add or change the DB2 data type that a particular nickname column's data type maps to, and specify column options for a particular nickname column.

INDEX. Allows a user to create an index specification for the nickname.

REFERENCES. Allows a user to create and drop foreign key constraints that reference a nickname in a parent relationship. (This privilege can be granted for the entire nickname or limited to one or more columns within the nickname.)

The owner of a nickname (usually the individual who created the nickname) automatically receives CONTROL privilege, along with all other available nickname privileges, for that nickname. If the CONTROL privilege is later revoked from the nickname owner, all other privileges that were automatically granted to the owner for that particular nickname are not automatically revoked. Instead, they must be explicitly revoked in one or more separate operations.

Requirements for Granting and Revoking Authorities and Privileges

Not only do authorization levels and privileges control what a user can and cannot do, they also control what authorities and privileges a user can grant to and revoke from other users and groups. A list of the authorities and privileges a user who has been given a specific authority level or privilege is allowed to grant and revoke is shown in Table 2–6.

Table 2–6 Requirements for Granting/Revoking Authorities and Privileges		
If a user holds ...	**They can grant ...**	**They can revoke ...**
System Administrator (SYSADM) authority	System Control (SYSCTRL) authority	System Control (SYSCTRL) authority
	System Maintenance (SYSMAINT) authority	System Maintenance (SYSMAINT) authority
	Database Administrator (DBADM) authority	Database Administrator (DBADM) authority
	Load (LOAD) authority	Load (LOAD) authority
	Any database privilege, including CONTROL privilege	Any database privilege, including CONTROL privilege
	Any object privilege, including CONTROL privilege	Any object privilege, including CONTROL privilege
		(continues)

Table 2–6 Requirements for Granting/Revoking Authorities and Privileges (Continued)		
If a user holds ...	**They can grant ...**	**They can revoke ...**
System Control (SYSCTRL) authority	The USE tablespace privilege	The USE tablespace privilege
System Maintenance (SYSMAINT) authority	No authorities or privileges	No authorities or privileges
Database Administrator (DBADM) authority	Any database privilege, including CONTROL privilege Any object privilege, including CONTROL privilege	Any database privilege, including CONTROL privilege Any object privilege, including CONTROL privilege
Load (LOAD) authority	No authorities or privileges	No authorities or privileges
CONTROL privilege on an object (but no other authority)	All privileges available (with the exception of the CONTROL privilege) for the object the user holds CONTROL privilege on	All privileges available (with the exception of the CONTROL privilege) for the object the user holds CONTROL privilege on
A privilege on an object that was assigned with the WITH GRANT OPTION option specified	The same object privilege that was assigned with the WITH GRANT OPTION option specified.	No authorities or privileges

Granting Authorities and Privileges

There are three different ways that users (and groups) can obtain database-level authorities and database/object privileges. They are:

Implicitly. When a user creates a database, they implicitly receive DBADM authority for that database, along with several database privileges. Likewise, when a user creates a database object, they implicitly receive all privileges available for that object along with the ability to grant any combination of those privileges (with the exception of the CONTROL privilege), to other users and groups. Privileges can also be implicitly given whenever a higher-level privilege is explicitly granted to a user (for example, if a user is explicitly given CONTROL privilege for a tablespace, they will implicitly receive the USE privilege for that tablespace as well). Keep in mind that such implicitly assigned privileges are not automatically revoked when the higher-level privilege that caused them to be granted is revoked.

Indirectly. Indirectly assigned privileges are usually associated with packages; when a user executes a package that requires privileges to execute that the user does not have (for example, a package that deletes a row of data from a table requires the DELETE privilege on that table), the user is indirectly given those privileges for the express purposes of executing the package. Indirectly granted privileges are temporary and do not exist outside the scope in which they are granted.

Explicitly. Database-level authorities, database privileges, and object privileges can be explicitly given to or taken from an individual user or a group of users by any user that has the authority to do so. To explicitly grant privileges on most database objects, a user must have SYSADM authority, DBADM authority, or CONTROL privilege on that object. Alternately, a user can explicitly grant any privilege they were assigned with the WITH GRANT OPTION specified. To grant CONTROL privilege for any object, a user must have SYSADM or DBADM authority; to grant DBADM authority, a user must have SYSADM authority.

Granting and Revoking Authorities and Privileges from the Control Center

One way to explicitly grant and revoke database-level authorities, as well as several available privileges, is by using the various authorities and privileges management dialogs that are provided with the Control Center. These dialogs are activated by highlighting the appropriate database or object name shown in the Control Center panes and selecting either *Authorities* or *Privileges* from the corresponding database or object menu. Figure 2–20 shows the menu items that must be selected in the Control Center in order to activate the Table Privileges dialog for a particular table. Figure 2–21 shows how the Table Privileges dialog might look immediately after a table is first created. (A single check mark under a privilege means that the individual or group shown has been granted that privilege; a double check mark means the individual or group has also been granted ability to grant that privilege to other users and groups.)

To assign privileges to an individual user from the Table Privileges dialog (or a similar authorities/privileges dialog), you simply identify a particular user by highlighting their entry in the recognized users list—if the desired user is not in the list, they can be added by selecting the "Add User" push button—and assign the appropriate privileges (or authorities) using the "Privileges" (or "Authorities") drop-down list or the "Grant All" or "Revoke All" push buttons. To assign privileges to a group of users, select the "Group" tab to

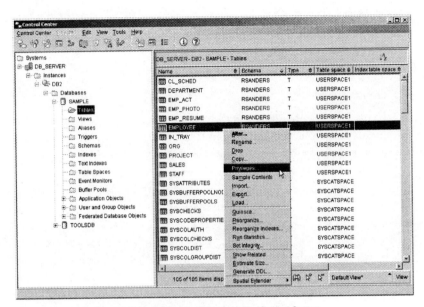

Figure 2–20   Invoking the Table Privileges dialog from the Control Center.

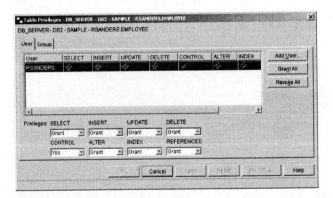

Figure 2–21   The Table Privileges dialog.

display a list of recognized groups and repeat the process (using the "Add Group" push button instead of the "Add User" push button to add a desired group to the list if they are not already there).

Granting Authorities and Privileges with the GRANT SQL Statement

Not all privileges can be explicitly given to users/groups with the privileges management dialogs available. However, in situations where no privileges dialog exists (and in situations where you elect not to use the Control Center), database-level authorities and database/object privileges can be explicitly given to users and/or groups by executing the appropriate form of the GRANT SQL statement. The syntax for the GRANT SQL statement varies according to the authority or privilege being granted—the following sections show the syntax used to grant each database-level authority and database/object privilege available.

Database-Level Authorities and Privileges

```
GRANT [DBADM | Privilege, ...] ON DATABASE TO [Recipient,
...]
```

where:

Privilege	Identifies one or more database privileges that are to be given to one or more users and/or groups.
Recipient	Identifies the name of the user(s) and/or group(s) that are to receive DBADM authority or the database privileges specified.

Schema Privileges

```
GRANT [Privilege, ...] ON SCHEMA [SchemaName] TO
[Recipient, ...] <WITH GRANT OPTION>
```

where:

Privilege	Identifies one or more schema privileges that are to be given to one or more users and/or groups.
SchemaName	Identifies by name the specific schema that all schema privileges specified are to be associated with.
Recipient	Identifies the name of the user(s) and/or group(s) that are to receive the schema privileges specified.

Tablespace Privilege

```
GRANT USE OF TABLESPACE [TablespaceName] TO [Recipient,
...] <WITH GRANT OPTION>
```

where:

TablespaceName	Identifies by name the specific tablespace that the USE privilege is to be associated with.
Recipient	Identifies the name of the user(s) and/or group(s) that are to receive the USE privilege.

Table Privileges

```
GRANT [ALL <PRIVILEGES> | Privilege <( ColumnName, ... )>
, ...] ON TABLE [TableName] TO [Recipient, ...] <WITH
GRANT OPTION>
```

where:

Privilege	Identifies one or more table privileges that are to be given to one or more users and/or groups.
ColumnName	Identifies by name one or more specific columns that UPDATE or REFERENCES privileges are to be associated with. This option is not used if *Privilege* is not equal to UPDATE or REFERENCES.
TableName	Identifies by name the specific table that all table privileges specified are to be associated with.
Recipient	Identifies the name of the user(s) and/or group(s) that are to receive the table privileges specified.

Index Privilege

```
GRANT CONTROL ON INDEX [IndexName] TO [Recipient, ...]
```

where:

IndexName	Identifies by name the specific index that the CONTROL privilege is to be associated with.
Recipient	Identifies the name of the user(s) and/or group(s) that are to receive the CONTROL privilege.

View Privileges

```
GRANT [ALL <PRIVILEGES> | Privilege <( ColumnName, ... )>
, ...] ON [ViewName] TO [Recipient, ...] <WITH GRANT OPTION>
```

where:

Privilege	Identifies one or more view privileges that are to be given to one or more users and/or groups.

ColumnName	Identifies by name one or more specific columns that UPDATE privilege is to be associated with. This option is not used if *Privilege* is not equal to UPDATE.
ViewName	Identifies by name the specific view that all view privileges specified are to be associated with.
Recipient	Identifies the name of the user(s) and/or group(s) that are to receive the view privileges specified.

Package Privileges

```
GRANT [Privilege, ...] ON PACKAGE <SchemaName.> [Pack-
ageID] TO [Recipient, ...] <WITH GRANT OPTION>
```

where:

Privilege	Identifies one or more package privileges that are to be given to one or more users and/or groups.
SchemaName	Identifies by name the schema in which the specified package is found.
PackageName	Identifies by name the specific package that all package privileges specified are to be associated with.
Recipient	Identifies the name of the user(s) and/or group(s) that are to receive the package privileges specified.

Routine Privilege

```
GRANT EXECUTE ON [RoutineName | FUNCTION <SchemaName.> * |
METHOD * FOR [TypeName] | METHOD * FOR <SchemaName.> * |
PROCEDURE <SchemaName.> *] TO [Recipient, ...] <WITH GRANT
OPTION>
```

where:

RoutineName	Identifies by name the routine that the EXE-CUTE privilege is to be associated with.
TypeName	Identifies by name the type in which the specified method is found.
SchemaName	Identifies by name the schema in which all functions, methods, or procedures—including those

that may be created in the future—are to have the EXECUTE privilege granted on.

Recipient   Identifies the name of the user(s) and/or group(s) that are to receive the EXECUTE privilege.

Sequence Privilege

```
GRANT USAGE ON SEQUENCE [SequenceName] TO PUBLIC
```

where:

SequenceName   Identifies by name the specific sequence that the USAGE privilege is to be associated with.

Server Privilege

```
GRANT PASSTHRU ON SERVER [ServerName] TO [Recipient, ...]
```

where:

ServerName   Identifies by name the specific server that the PASSTHRU privilege is to be associated with.

Recipient   Identifies the name of the user(s) and/or group(s) that are to receive the PASSTHRU privilege.

Nickname Privileges

```
GRANT [ALL <PRIVILEGES> | Privilege <( ColumnName, ... )>
, ...] ON [Nickname] TO [Recipient, ...] <WITH GRANT OPTION>
```

where:

Privilege   Identifies one or more nickname privileges that are to be given to one or more users and/or groups.

ColumnName   Identifies by name one or more specific columns that the REFERENCES privilege is to be associated with. This option is not used if *Privilege* is not equal to REFERENCES.

Nickname   Identifies by name the specific nickname that all privileges specified are to be associated with.

Recipient   Identifies the name of the user(s) and/or group(s) that are to receive the nickname privileges specified.

If the ALL PRIVILEGES option is specified, all privileges available for the object, with the exception of the CONTROL privilege, will be granted to the user and/or group specified. If the WITH GRANT OPTION clause is specified with the GRANT statement, the user and/or group receiving the privileges specified is given the ability to grant the privilege received (except for the CONTROL privilege) to other users. In all cases, the value specified for the *Recipient* parameter can be any combination of the following:

USER [*UserName*]   Identifies a specific user that the privileges specified are to be given to.

GROUP [*GroupName*]   Identifies a specific group that the privileges specified are to be given to.

PUBLIC   Indicates that the specified privilege(s) are to be given to the special group PUBLIC. (All users are a member of the group PUBLIC.)

GRANT SQL Statement Examples

Now that we've seen the basic syntax for the various forms of the GRANT SQL statement, let's take a look at some examples.

Example 1. A server has both a user and a group named TESTER. Give the group TESTER the ability to bind applications to the database SAMPLE:

```
CONNECT TO SAMPLE
GRANT BINDADD ON DATABASE TO GROUP tester
```

Example 2. Give all table privileges available (except CONTROL privilege) for the table PAYROLL.EMPLOYEE to the group PUBLIC:

```
GRANT ALL PRIVILEGES ON TABLE payroll.employee TO PUBLIC
```

Example 3. Give user USER1 and user USER2 the privileges needed to perform just DML operations on the table DEPARTMENT using the view DEPTVIEW:

```
GRANT SELECT, INSERT, UPDATE, DELETE ON deptview TO USER
user1, USER user2
```

Example 4. Give user JOHN_DOE the privilege needed to query the table INVENTORY, along with the ability to grant this privilege to other users whenever appropriate:

```
GRANT SELECT ON TABLE inventory TO john_doe WITH GRANT
OPTION
```

Example 5. Give user USER1 the ability to run an embedded SQL application that requires package GET_INVENTORY:

```
GRANT EXECUTE ON PACKAGE get_inventory TO USER user1
```

Example 6. Give user USER1 the ability to use a user-defined function named PAYROLL.CALC_SALARY that has an input parameter of type CHAR(5) in a query:

```
GRANT EXECUTE ON FUNCTION payroll.calc_salary(CHAR(5)) TO
USER user1
```

Example 7. Give user USER1 the ability to define a referential constraint between the tables EMPLOYEE and DEPARTMENT, using column EMPID in table EMPLOYEE as the parent key:

```
GRANT REFERENCES(empid) ON TABLE employee TO USER user1
```

Example 8. Give the group PUBLIC the ability to modify information stored in the ADDRESS and HOME_PHONE columns of the table EMP_INFO:

```
GRANT UPDATE(address, home_phone) ON TABLE emp_info TO
PUBLIC
```

Revoking Authorities and Privileges with the REVOKE SQL Statement

Just as there is an SQL statement that can be used to grant database-level authorities and database/object privileges, there is an SQL statement that can be used to revoke database-level authorities and database/object privileges. This statement is the REVOKE SQL statement, and like the GRANT statement, the syntax for the REVOKE statement varies according to the authority or privilege being revoked. The following sections show the syntax used to revoke each database-level authority and database/object privilege available.

Database-Level Authorities and Privileges

```
REVOKE [DBADM | Privilege, ...] ON DATABASE FROM [For-
feiter, ...] <BY ALL>
```

where:

Privilege	Identifies one or more database privileges that are to be taken from one or more users and/or groups.

Forfeiter	Identifies the name of the user(s) and/or group(s) that are to lose DBADM authority or the database privileges specified.

Schema Privileges

```
REVOKE [Privilege, ...] ON SCHEMA [SchemaName] FROM [For-
feiter, ...] <BY ALL>
```

where:

Privilege	Identifies one or more schema privileges that are to be taken from one or more users and/or groups.
SchemaName	Identifies by name the specific schema that all schema privileges specified are to be associated with.
Forfeiter	Identifies the name of the user(s) and/or group(s) that are to lose the schema privileges specified.

Tablespace Privilege

```
REVOKE USE OF TABLESPACE [TablespaceName] FROM [Forfeiter,
...] <BY ALL>
```

where:

TablespaceName	Identifies by name the specific tablespace that the USE privilege is to be associated with.
Forfeiter	Identifies the name of the user(s) and/or group(s) that are to lose the USE privilege.

Table Privileges

```
REVOKE [ALL <PRIVILEGES> | Privilege, ...] ON TABLE
[TableName] FROM [Forfeiter, ...] <BY ALL>
```

where:

Privilege	Identifies one or more table privileges that are to be taken from one or more users and/or groups.
TableName	Identifies by name the specific table that all table privileges specified are to be associated with.
Forfeiter	Identifies the name of the user(s) and/or group(s) that are to lose the table privileges specified.

Index Privilege

```
REVOKE CONTROL ON INDEX [IndexName] FROM [Forfeiter, ...]
<BY ALL>
```

where:

IndexName	Identifies by name the specific index that the CONTROL privilege is to be associated with.
Forfeiter	Identifies the name of the user(s) and/or group(s) that are to lose the CONTROL privilege.

View Privileges

```
REVOKE [ALL <PRIVILEGES> | Privilege, ...] ON [ViewName]
FROM [Forfeiter, ...] <BY ALL>
```

where:

Privilege	Identifies one or more view privileges that are to be taken from one or more users and/or groups.
ViewName	Identifies by name the specific view that all view privileges specified are to be associated with.
Forfeiter	Identifies the name of the user(s) and/or group(s) that are to lose the view privileges specified.

Package Privileges

```
REVOKE [Privilege, ...] ON PACKAGE <SchemaName.> [Pack-
ageID] FROM [Forfeiter, ...] <BY ALL>
```

where:

Privilege	Identifies one or more package privileges that are to be taken from one or more users and/or groups.
SchemaName	Identifies by name the schema in which the specified package is found.
PackageName	Identifies by name the specific package that all package privileges specified are to be associated with.
Forfeiter	Identifies the name of the user(s) and/or group(s) that are to lose the package privileges specified.

Routine Privilege

```
REVOKE EXECUTE ON [RoutineName | FUNCTION <SchemaName.> *
| METHOD * FOR [TypeName] | METHOD * FOR <SchemaName.> * |
PROCEDURE <SchemaName.> *] FROM [Forfeiter, ...] <BY ALL>
RESTRICT
```

where:

RoutineName	Identifies by name the routine that the EXECUTE privilege is to be associated with.
TypeName	Identifies by name the type in which the specified method is found.
SchemaName	Identifies by name the schema in which all functions, methods, or procedures—including those that may be created in the future—are to have the EXECUTE privilege revoked on.
Forfeiter	Identifies the name of the user(s) and/or group(s) that are to lose the package privileges specified.

Sequence Privilege

```
REVOKE USAGE ON SEQUENCE [SequenceName] FROM PUBLIC
```

where:

SequenceName	Identifies by name the specific sequence that the USAGE privilege is to be associated with.

Server Privilege

```
REVOKE PASSTHRU ON SERVER [ServerName] FROM [Forfeiter,
...] <BY ALL>
```

where:

ServerName	Identifies by name the specific server that the PASSTHRU privilege is to be associated with.
Forfeiter	Identifies the name of the user(s) and/or group(s) that are to lose the PASSTHRU privilege.

Nickname Privileges

```
REVOKE [ALL <PRIVILEGES> | Privilege, ...] ON [Nickname]
FROM [Forfeiter, ...] <BY ALL>
```

where:

Privilege	Identifies one or more nickname privileges that are to be given to one or more users and/or groups.
Nickname	Identifies by name the specific nickname that all privileges specified are to be associated with.
Forfeiter	Identifies the name of the user(s) and/or group(s) that are to lose the nickname privileges specified.

The BY ALL syntax is optional and is provided as a courtesy for administrators who are familiar with the syntax of the DB2 for OS/390 REVOKE SQL statement. Whether it is included or not, the results will always be the same—the privilege(s) specified will be revoked from all users and/or groups specified, regardless of who granted it originally.

In all cases, the value specified for the *Forfeiter* parameter can be any combination of the following:

USER [*UserName*]	Identifies a specific user that the privileges specified are to be taken from.
GROUP [*GroupName*]	Identifies a specific group that the privileges specified are to be taken from.
PUBLIC	Indicates that the specified privilege(s) are to be taken from the special group PUBLIC. (All users are a member of the group PUBLIC.)

REVOKE SQL Statement Examples

Now that we've seen the basic syntax for the various forms of the REVOKE SQL statement, let's take a look at some examples.

Example 1. A server has both a user and a group named Q045. Remove the ability to connect to the database named SAMPLE from the group Q045:

```
CONNECT TO SAMPLE
REVOKE CONNECT ON DATABASE FROM GROUP q045
```

Example 2. Revoke all table privileges available (except CONTROL privilege) for the table DEPARTMENT from the user USER1 and the group PUBLIC:

```
REVOKE ALL PRIVILEGES ON TABLE department FROM user1, PUBLIC
```

Example 3. Take away user USER1's ability to use a user-defined function named CALC_BONUS:

```
REVOKE EXECUTE ON FUNCTION calc_bonus FROM USER user1
```

Example 4. Take away user USER1's ability to modify information stored in the ADDRESS and HOME_PHONE columns of the table EMP_INFO, regardless of who granted it:

```
REVOKE UPDATE(address, home_phone) ON TABLE emp_info FROM
user1 BY ALL
```

Authorities and Privileges Needed to Perform Common Tasks

So far, we have identified the authorities and privileges that are available, and we have examined how these authorities and privileges are granted and revoked. But to use authorities and privileges effectively, you must be able to determine which authorities and privileges are appropriate for an individual user and which are not. Often, a blanket set of authorities and privileges is assigned to an individual, based on their job title and/or their job responsibilities. Then, as the individual begins to work with the database, the set of authorities and privileges they have is modified as necessary. Some of the more common job titles used, along with the tasks that usually accompany them and the authorities /privileges needed to perform those tasks, can be seen in Table 2–7.

Table 2–7 Common Job Titles, Tasks, and Authorities/Privileges Needed		
Job Title	**Tasks**	**Authorities/Privileges Needed**
Department Administrator	Oversees the departmental system; designs and creates databases.	System Control (SYSCTRL) authority or System Administrator (SYSADM) authority (if the department has its own instance)
Security Administrator	Grants authorities and privileges to other users and revokes them, if necessary.	System Administrator (SYSADM) authority or Database Administrator (DBADM) authority
Database Administrator	Designs, develops, operates, safeguards, and maintains one or more databases.	Database Administrator (DBADM) authority over one or more databases and System Maintenance (SYSMAINT) authority, or in some cases System Control (SYSCTRL) authority, over the same databases
		(continues)

Table 2–7 Common Job Titles, Tasks, and Authorities/Privileges Needed (Continued)		
Job Title	**Tasks**	**Authorities/Privileges Needed**
System Operator	Monitors the database and performs routine backup operations. Also performs recovery operations if needed.	System Maintenance (SYSMAINT) authority
Application Developer/ Programmer	Develops and tests database/DB2 Database Manager application programs; may also create test tables and populate them with data.	CONNECT and CREATETAB privilege for one or more databases, BINDADD and BIND privilege on one or more existing packages, one or more schema privileges for one or more schemas, and one or more table privileges for one or more tables.
User Analyst	Defines the data requirements for an application program by examining the database structure using the system catalog views.	CONNECT privilege for one or more databases and SELECT privilege on the system catalog views
End User	Executes one or more application programs.	CONNECT privilege for one or more databases and EXECUTE privilege on the package associated with each application used. If an application program contains dynamic SQL statements, SELECT, INSERT, UPDATE, and DELETE privileges for one or more tables may be needed as well.
Information Center Consultant	Defines the data requirements for a query user; provides the data needed by creating tables and views and by granting access to one or more database objects.	Database Administrator (DBADM) authority for one or more databases.

Table 2-7 Common Job Titles, Tasks, and Authorities/Privileges Needed (Continued)		
Query User	Issues SQL statements (usually from the Command Line Processor) to retrieve, add, update, or delete data. (May also save results of queries in tables.)	CONNECT privilege on one or more databases, SELECT, INSERT, UPDATE, and DELETE privilege on each table used, and CREATEIN privilege on the schema in which tables and views are to be created.

Adapted from Table 6 on Pages 261–262 of the *IBM DB2 Administration Guide—Implementation* manual.

Taking Control of a Server

Because any number of users can be granted the privileges needed to work with a particular database, it can be difficult, if not impossible, to coordinate the work efforts of everyone using a specific database at any given point in time. This can create a problem because there are times when a Database Administrator will need all users to stop using a particular instance or database so special maintenance operations can be performed. If your organization is small, it may be possible to contact each database user and ask them to disconnect long enough to perform any maintenance operations needed. But what if your organization consists of several hundred users? Or what if an employee went home early and inadvertently left an instance attachment or database connection open? In these situations, you must first find out which users and applications are attached to the instance or connected to the database you need exclusive access to.

Finding Out Who is Using an Instance or a Database

If you have System Administrator (SYSADMN) or System Control (SYSC-TRL) authority for a server, you can find out who is using an instance or a database on that server by executing the LIST APPLICATIONS command. The basic syntax for this command is:

```
LIST APPLICATIONS
<FOR [DATABASE | DB] [DatabaseName]>
<SHOW DETAIL>
```

where:

> *DatabaseName*   Identifies the name assigned to the database that application information is to be obtained for.

Thus, if you wanted to find out what applications are currently connected to a database named SAMPLE (along with the authorization IDs associated with the users running those applications), you could do so by executing a LIST APPLICATIONS command that looks something like this:

```
LIST APPLICATIONS FOR DATABASE SAMPLE
```

When this command is executed, you might see output that looks something like this:

```
Auth Id   Application Appl.  Application Id            DB     # of
          Name        Handle                           Name   Agents
--------  ----------- ------ ------------------------ ------ ------
RSANDERS  db2bp.exe   3      *LOCAL.DB2.00CB46014904  SAMPLE 1
```

You can also find out what applications are attached to an instance (or connected to a database within that instance) by selecting the *Applications* action from the *Instances* menu found in the Control Center. Figure 2–22 shows the Control Center menu items that must be selected in order to activate the Applications dialog. Figure 2–23 shows how this dialog might look if an application is connected to a database within the instance specified.

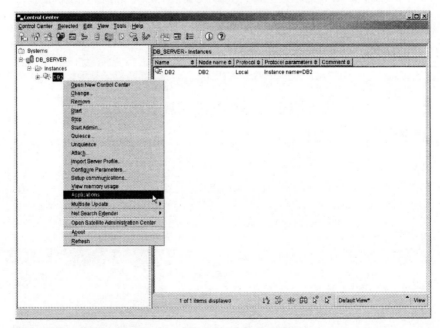

Figure 2–22   Invoking the Applications dialog from the Control Center.

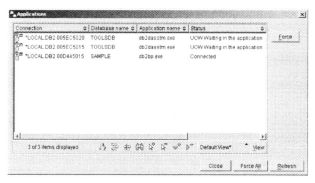

Figure 2–23 The Applications dialog.

The FORCE APPLICATION Command

Once you know what applications are using a particular instance or database, you can terminate instance attachments and database connections, provided you have SYSADMN or SYSCTRL authority for a server, by executing the FORCE APPLICATION command. The basic syntax for this command is:

    FORCE APPLICATION ALL

or

    FORCE APPLICATION ([ApplicationHandle] ,...)

where:

> *ApplicationHandle* Identifies the handle associated with one or more applications whose instance attachments and/or database connections are to be terminated.

Therefore, if you needed all users to stop using a particular instance or database so you could install a DB2 FixPak, but were unable to contact each user to ask them to terminate their attachments or connections gracefully, you could force them off a server by executing some form of the FORCE APPLICATION command. For example, suppose you wanted to force all users/applications that are using a database named SAMPLE to terminate their database connections. You could do so by executing a FORCE APPLICATION command that looks something like this:

    FORCE APPLICATION ALL

On the other hand, if you only wanted to force a specific application (whose handle is 3) to terminate its connection to a database named SAMPLE, you could do so by executing a FORCE APPLICATION command that looks something like this:

```
FORCE APPLICATION (3)
```

It is important to note that when an application's instance attachment or database connection is terminated by the FORCE APPLICATION command, any SQL operations that have been performed by the application but not yet committed are rolled back.

In order to preserve database integrity, only applications that are idle or that are performing interruptible database operations can be terminated when the FORCE APPLICATION command is processed. (For example, applications in the process of creating or backing up a database would not be terminated). In addition, the DB2 Database Manager for the instance cannot be stopped (by the db2stop command) during a force operation (neither can it be stopped while there are still active connections to the database); the DB2 Database Manager must remain active so that subsequent DB2 Database Manager operations can be handled without having to be restarted. Finally, because the FORCE APPLICATION command is run asynchronously, other applications/users can attach to the instance or connect to a database within the instance after this command has been executed. Multiple FORCE APPLICATION commands may be required to completely terminate all instance attachments and database connections.

If you are using the Applications dialog to see which users and/or applications are currently attached to an instance or connected to a database, you can terminate instance attachments and database connections by highlighting one or more entries in the list shown on the Applications dialog and selecting the "Force" push button located in the upper right corner of the screen (refer to Figure 2–23). You can also terminate all instance attachments and database connections from the Applications dialog by selecting the "Force All" push button located between the "Close" and "Refresh" push buttons at the bottom of the screen (again, refer to Figure 2–23).

The QUIESCE and UNQUIESCE Commands

An alternative approach to using the FORCE APPLICATIONS command to force all users off an instance or a database is to temporarily place an instance or database in what is known as *quiesced* (restricted access) mode long enough to perform any maintenance activities necessary. Instances and databases can be placed in quiesced mode by executing the QUIESCE command. The basic syntax for this command is:

```
QUIESCE INSTANCE [InstanceName]
<FOR USER [UserName] | FOR GROUP [GroupName]>
IMMEDIATE
<FORCE CONNECTIONS>
```

or

```
QUIESCE [DATABASE | DB]
IMMEDIATE
<FORCE CONNECTIONS>
```

where:

InstanceName	Identifies the name assigned to the instance that is to be placed in quiesced mode. (If an instance is placed in quiesce mode, all databases under the instances control will be placed in quiesce mode as well.)
UserName	Identifies the name of a specific user who is to be allowed access to the instance specified while it is in quiesced mode.
GroupName	Identifies the name of a specific group of users who is to be allowed access to the instance specified while it is in quiesced mode.

Thus, if you wanted to place an instance named DEV_INST into quiesced mode immediately, but allow a user named DB2ADMIN to continue using a database under its control, you could do so by executing a QUIESCE command that looks something like this:

```
QUIESCE INSTANCE DEV_INST FOR USER DB2ADMIN IMMEDIATE
FORCE CONNECTIONS
```

On the other hand, if you wanted to place a database named SAMPLE in quiesced mode immediately, you could do so by establishing a connection to the database and executing a QUIESCE command that looks something like this:

```
QUIESCE DATABASE IMMEDIATE
```

It is important to note that when an instance or database is placed in quiesced mode, any transactions running against the database that have not yet been committed (with the exception of transactions that belong to a user or group that have been given access to the quiesced instance and its databases) will be rolled back.

One of the advantages of using the QUIESCE command instead of the FORCE APPLICATION command is that the QUIESCE command provides exclusive access to an instance or database without having to force applications/users off the instance or database and then trying to prevent other attachments or connections from occurring. Remember, because the FORCE APPLICATION command is run asynchronously, other applications/users can attach to an instance or connect to a database within the instance after it has been executed; when an instance or database is in quiesced mode, attachments and connections cannot be made from outside of the database engine. Only users with SYSADM, SYSMAINT, or SYSCTRL authority can attach to a quiesced instance; only users with SYSADM or DBADM authority can connect to a quiesced database.

Once the appropriate administrative operations have been completed, instances and databases can be removed from quiesce mode and returned to normal by executing the UNQUIESCE command. The basic syntax for this command is:

```
UNQUIESCE INSTANCE [InstanceName]
```

or

```
UNQUIESCE DB
```

where:

      InstanceName   Identifies the name assigned to the instance that is to be removed from quiesced mode.

Therefore, if you wanted to take an instance named DEV_INST out of quiesced mode, you could do so by executing an UNQUIESCE command that looks like this:

```
UNQUIESCE INSTANCE DEV_INST
```

Likewise, if you wanted to take a database named SAMPLE out of quiesced mode, you could do so by establishing a connection to the database and executing an UNQUIESCE command that looks like this:

```
UNQUIESCE DB
```

You can also quiesce and unquiesce instances and databases by selecting the *Quiesce* or *Unquiesce* action from either the *Instances* menu or the *Databases* menu found in the Control Center. Figure 2–24 shows the Control Center menu items that must be selected in order to activate the Quiesce instance dialog. Figure 2–25 shows how this dialog might look once its input fields have been populated.

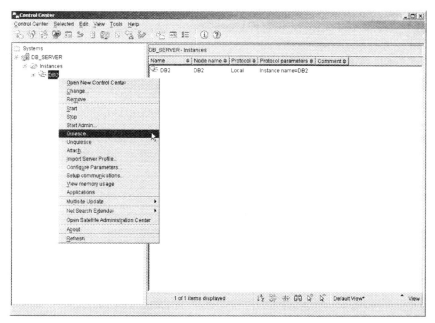

Figure 2–24   Invoking the Quiesce dialog from the Control Center.

Figure 2–25   The Quiesce dialog.

Using the Task Center

As you might imagine, terminating instance attachments and database connections with the FORCE APPLICATION or QUIESCE commands can have a significant impact on all users and applications affected. A better alternative is to schedule maintenance operations so that they are performed at a time when there is little or no database activity. That's where the Task Center comes in. The Task Center is an easy-to-use graphical user interface (GUI) tool that allows users to organize task flow, schedule frequently occurring tasks, and distribute notifications regarding the status of tasks that have been completed. Figure 2–26 shows what the Task Center looks like on a Windows 2000 server.

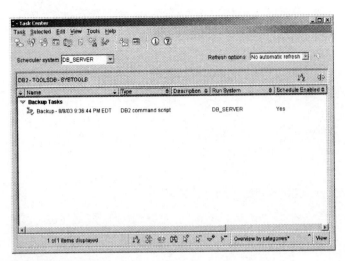

Figure 2-26 The Task Center.

So just what is a task? A task is simply a script that has been bundled together with success conditions/actions, schedules, and notifications. The script used to perform a task can be created within the Task Center, within another tool and saved to the Task Center, imported from an existing UNIX shell script/ Windows batch file, or it can be generated from a Control Center dialog or wizard (for example, the Backup Wizard will create a database backup operation that can be scheduled). Furthermore, the script used to perform a task can contain any combination of DB2 UDB commands, SQL statements, and operating system commands. Although a task is not just a script, a script is often an integral part of a task; once a script has been created, the process of converting it into a task involves:

➤ Scheduling when the script will run.

➤ Specifying success and failure conditions.

➤ Specifying actions that should be performed when the script executes successfully and when it fails.

➤ Specifying e-mail addresses (including pager addresses) that should be notified when the script has completed or if the script failed. (The task center can either notify contacts or place information in the Journal.)

With the Task Center, it is also possible to create a *grouping task*, which is a special task that combines several scripts into a single logical unit of work. When the grouping task meets the success or failure conditions that you define, any follow-on tasks are run. For example, you could combine three backup scripts into a grouping task and then specify a table reorganization operation as a follow-on task that is to be executed if all of the backup scripts execute successfully. Regardless of whether a task completes successfully or fails, any number of actions can be performed, including:

➤ Running another task

➤ Scheduling another task

➤ Disabling another scheduled task

➤ Deleting itself

So just who can create and schedule tasks? Anyone who has the authorities and privileges needed to execute the task. In fact, the Task Center provides a way for users who create a task to grant read, write, and execute (run) privileges to other users for the task being created. This can be useful when a number of different users are creating and maintaining tasks.

A Word about the Journal

The Journal is an interactive GUI application that tracks historical information about tasks, database actions and operations, Control Center actions, messages, and alerts. To present this information in an organized manner, the Journal uses several different views. They are:

➤ Task History

➤ Database History

➤ Messages

➤ Notification Log

The *Task History* view shows the results of tasks that have already been executed. This view contains one entry for each individual task (regardless of how many times the task was executed) and allows users to:

➤ View details of any task that has been executed.

➤ View the results of any task that has been executed.

➤ Edit any task that has been executed.

➤ View execution statistics associated with any task that has been executed.

➤ Remove any task execution record from the Journal.

The *Database History* view shows information stored in a database's recovery history file. The recovery history file is automatically updated whenever any of the following operations are performed:

➤ Database or tablespace backup

➤ Database or tablespace restore

➤ Roll-forward recovery

➤ Load

➤ Table reorganization

The *Messages* view shows a running history of messages that were issued from the Control Center and any other GUI tool, and the *Notification Log* view shows information from the administration notification log.

Figure 2–27 shows what the Task History view of the Journal looks like on a Windows 2000 server.

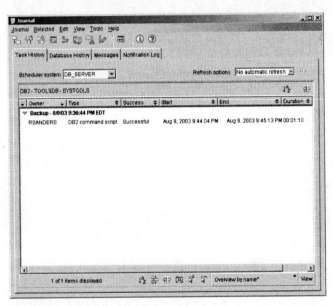

Figure 2–27   The Task History view of the Journal.

As you might imagine, the Task History view of the Journal is commonly used to view the status of completed tasks.

Problem Determination

Because the potential for errors to occur can never be completely eliminated from a database environment, DB2 UDB comes equipped with a variety of tools that can be used to help pinpoint the cause in the event an error does occur. And in many cases, these tools can provide recommendations that, when followed, may resolve the situation that caused the error to be generated in the first place.

When an error occurs within a database system, the DB2 Database Manager notifies the user by generating a specific error code and presenting this code in a variety of ways. If the Command Line Processor (CLP) is being used when an error occurs, the error code generated, along with a corresponding message, will be displayed at the CLP prompt. On the other hand, if any of the administration tools that come with DB2 UDB are being used when an error occurs, the error code generated, along with a corresponding message, will be displayed in a pop-up dialog and recorded in the Journal, along with the date and time the error occurred.

Obtaining Information about an Error Code

When an error code is returned by the DB2 Database Manager, there are a variety of ways in which you can find out what that error code means:

➤ By looking up the error code generated in the *IBM DB2 Universal Database Message Reference Volume 1* or the *IBM DB2 Universal Database Message Reference Volume 2* product documentation.

➤ By executing the GET ERROR MESSAGE API (this API must be executed from within an application program).

➤ By instructing the DB2 Database Manager to provide information associated with the error code generated. You can tell the DB2 Database Manager to provide information associated with an error code by executing a command that consists of a question mark followed by the error code from the Command Line Processor (CLP). For example, if you wanted to view information associated with the error code CCA3002N, you could do so by executing the command ? CCA3002N from the CLP. The results returned would look something like this:

```
CCA3002N An I/O error occurred.

Explanation:

An error was encountered while attempting to open, read,
change the file position, or close a file.

User Response:

If a file name was specified, verify that the file name is
valid and that the user has permission to access the file.
Also check for any disk and operating system errors.
```

Reason Codes

In some cases, an error message will contain a reference to what is known as a *reason code*. Reason codes are used when a single error code can be generated by several different events and they are designed to provide additional information associated with the error code returned. For example, the error message associated with the error code SQL0866N looks something like this:

```
Connection redirection failed. Reason code: " [Reason-
Code]"
```

where:

> *ReasonCode*   Identifies the reason code associated with the error message. Usually, this is a numerical value. (For error code SQL0866N, *ReasonCode* can be the number 1 or 2.)

In most cases, you can find out what a particular reason code means by looking up the error code generated in the *IBM DB2 Universal Database Message Reference Volume 1* or the *IBM DB2 Universal Database Message Reference Volume 2* product documentation, or by instructing the DB2 Database Manager to provide information associated with the error code the reason code is associated with.

First Failure Data Capture (FFDC)

One of the most important diagnostic tools available with DB2 UDB is a facility that is known as First Failure Data Capture (FFDC). FFDC runs quietly in the background until a significant event occurs and at that time, diagnostic information about the event is automatically captured by the DB2 Database Manager and recorded in special ASCII-format files. This information contains crucial details that may help in the diagnosis and resolution of problems. And because this information is collected at the actual time an event takes place, the need to reproduce errors in order to obtain diagnostic information is greatly reduced or in some cases eliminated. The information captured by FFDC is externalized in several different ways, including:

> **DB2 diagnostic log file entries..** Whenever any significant event occurs, an entry containing diagnostic information about that event is automatically recorded in a file named "db2diag.log", which acts as the primary diagnostic log file for DB2 UDB.

> **Administration notification log entries.** When significant events occur, supplemental information for any SQL return code generated

is written to the Windows Event Log (on Windows NT, Windows 2000, and Windows XP systems) or to a file named *Instance-Name*.nfy"—where *InstanceName* is the name of the instance that generated the information (on all other supported operating systems). This information is noncryptic and can be viewed with the Windows Event Viewer (on Windows systems) or with any text editor (on all other systems).

Dump files. In some cases, when a DB2 UDB-specific process or thread fails, extra information is logged in external binary dump files (that are assigned a name based on the ID of the failing process/thread). These files are more-or-less unreadable and are intended to be forwarded to DB2 Customer Support for interpretation.

Trap files. If the DB2 Database Manager cannot continue processing because a trap, segmentation violation, or exception has occurred, it generates a trap file that contains the sequence of function calls made for the last steps executed before the trap, segmentation violation, or exception event occurred.

Core files (UNIX only). If DB2 terminates abnormally on a UNIX platform, the operating system will generate a core file, which is a binary file that contains information that is similar to the information recorded in a DB2 trap file. (Core files may also contain the entire memory image of the terminated DB2 process.)

Where FFDC Information is Stored

By default, all FFDC information collected on a UNIX platform is stored in the directory $HOME/sqllib/db2dump, where $HOME is the home directory of the instance owner. On Windows platforms, if the location of the instance directory has not been stored in the DB2INSTPROF environment variable, FFDC information collected is stored in the directory *DB2Path\DB2Instance*, where *DB2Path* is the path stored in the DB2PATH environment variable and *DB2Instance* is the value stored in the DB2INSTDEF environment variable (which is "DB2" by default). On the other hand, if the location of the instance directory has been stored in the DB2INSTPROF environment variable, FFDC information is stored in the directory *Drive:\DB2InstProfile\DB2Instance*, where *Drive* is the drive referenced in the DB2PATH environment variable, *DB2InstProfile* is the name of the instance profile directory, and *DB2Instance* is the value stored in the DB2INSTDEF environment variable.

However, where FFDC information is actually recorded is controlled by the value of the *diagpath* parameter of a DB2 Database Manager instance's configuration file. Thus, if you wish to change the location where all FFDC information is stored, you may do so by changing the value of this parameter (which contains a null string when an instance is first created).

Regardless of where FFDC information is stored, it is up to the System Administrator to ensure that the location used is cleaned periodically; DB2 UDB does not automatically remove dump files, trap files, and core files that are generated by the FFDC tool.

Controlling How Much FFDC Information is Collected

The type (which controls the amount) of administrative and diagnostic information recorded is also controlled by parameters (*notifylevel* and *diaglevel*) in a DB2 Database Manager instance's configuration file. Based on their current value, these parameters tell FFDC what type of administrative and diagnostic information to collect:

0. Do not collect administrative information and diagnostic data (not recommended).

1. Collect administrative information and diagnostic data for severe (fatal or unrecoverable) errors only.

2. Collect administrative information and diagnostic data for all types of errors (both severe and nonsevere) but not for warnings.

3. Collect administrative information and diagnostic data for all errors and warnings.

4. Collect administrative information and diagnostic data for all errors and warnings, including informational messages and other internal diagnostic information.

When an instance is first created, the *notifylevel* and *diaglevel* parameters in a DB2 Database Manager instance's configuration file are set to 3 by default and administrative information/diagnostic data for errors and warnings is collected by FFDC whenever such events occur. However, these parameters should be set to 4 (except in parallel database environments where this setting can cause too much data to be produced) when DB2 UDB is set up initially, each time configuration parameter values are changed, or whenever a large number of errors seem to be occurring. It is important to keep in mind that if the the *notifylevel* and *diaglevel* configuration parameters are set to 4, DB2 UDB will run slower when the DB2 Database Manager for the instance is first started, when an initial connection to a database within the instance is established, and each time an error condition occurs.

The DB2 Diagnostic Log File

Earlier, we saw that whenever any significant event occurs, an entry containing diagnostic information about that event is automatically recorded in a file named "db2diag.log", which acts as the primary diagnostic log file for DB2 UDB. The db2diag.log file is an ASCII format file that is comprised of diagnostic records that have been generated by the FFDC tool. Each record (or entry) in this file contains either information about a particular administrative event that has occurred or specific error information. Entries for administrative events are valuable because they indicate whether events such as backup and restore operations were started and if so, whether or not they finished successfully. Entries for error information, on the other hand, are only useful when trying to diagnose an external symptom, or if the source of a particular error has been isolated and you are looking for more information (for example, if an application receives an unexpected SQL code or if a database crashes). If a database is behaving normally, error information entries are not important and can usually be ignored.

Once created, the db2diag.log file grows continuously. As a result, the most recent entries are always found near the end of the file. If storage space for this file becomes an issue, the existing file can be deleted (or moved to a secure location such as an archive directory)—a new db2diag.log file will be created automatically the next time one is needed.

The Administration Notification Log

In earlier versions of DB2 UDB, the DB2 diagnostics log (db2diag.log file) acted as a single diagnostic facility that could be used by both system/database administrators and DB2 Customer Service. Unfortunately, because diagnostic information needed by system/database administrators is very different from that needed by DB2 Customer Service personnel, and because the information needed by DB2 Customer Service personnel is often cryptic (i.e., memory structure dumps, internal return codes, and benign diagnostic entries) and is only useful to people with a working knowledge of the DB2 source code, forcing this one file to serve two purposes often caused system and database administrators to become unnecessarily concerned about file entries they did not understand. To remedy this situation, IBM introduced the user-friendly administration notification log in Version 8.1. This log is designed to drastically change the diagnostic landscape of DB2 UDB; now the administration notification log serves as the primary diagnostic facility for system and database administrators while the DB2 diagnostics log exists for the sole purpose of providing special, customized information to DB2 Customer Service personnel.

One of the noticeable differences about administration notification log entries as opposed to DB2 diagnostic log entries is the lack of confusing hex dumps. Meaningful, helpful messages that were reviewed and written with the help of real, professional DB2 DBAs (DB2 customers) are provided in their place. Most of these messages provide supplemental information for each associated SQL return code value returned to an application or the CLP. Other messages provide notification of unexpected errors or asynchronous events such as a crash, a signal from the operating system, or a suboptimal configuration. The format of administration notification log entries and DB2 diagnostic log entries are essentially identical. However, all messages written to the administration notification log are written using the end-user language specified during the installation process (messages written to the DB2 diagnostics log are always written in English, regardless of the end-user language used).

Another significant difference is that on Windows platforms, administration notification log entries are written to the Windows Event Log, rather than a predefined file. However, when a predefined file is used (which is the case on all non-Windows platforms), this file behaves like the DB2 diagnostics log: once created, it grows continuously; the most recent entries are always found near the end of the file, and if the file is deleted a new one will be created automatically the next time it is needed.

It is important to note that entries written to the Windows Event Log can be viewed using the Windows Event Viewer. Figure 2–28 shows how a DB2 administration notification log entry might appear in the Windows Event Viewer on a Windows 2000 server.

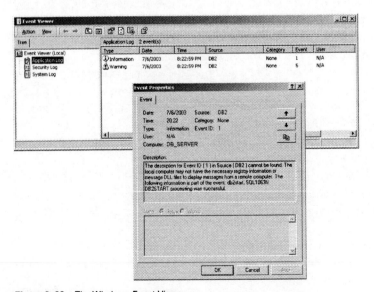

Figure 2–28   The Windows Event Viewer.

Interpreting DB2 Diagnostic Log and Administration Notification Log Entry Headers

Every entry in the administration notification log file and the DB2 diagnostic log file begins with a specific set of values that are intended to help identify the particular event the entry corresponds to. Because this block of information is recorded for all entries and because it is always recorded in a specific format, it is referred to as the *entry header*. Figure 2–29 illustrates how a typical administration notification log entry header looks.

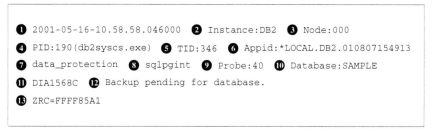

Figure 2–29   Individual components of an administration notification log/DB2 diagnostic log entry header.

All entry headers consist of the following components (refer to the numbered bullets in Figure 2–29):

1. A timestamp that identifies when the entry was made.

2. The name of the instance that generated the entry.

3. The number that corresponds to the node that generated the entry. If a nonpartitioned database is being used, the node number will always be 000.

4. The unique identifier that has been assigned (by the operating system) to the process that generated the entry. This value is more applicable in a UNIX environment where DB2 UDB operates using multiple processes. In a Windows environment, DB2 UDB operates with multiple threads rather than multiple processes; therefore, the process ID provided is usually that of the main DB2 UDB executable. In the entry shown in Figure 2–29, the process that has been assigned the process ID 190 is responsible for the entry. The name of this process is *db2syscs.exe* and it is interacting with the database named SAMPLE. (If the application is operating in a Distributed Unit of Work [DUOW] environment, the Process ID shown will be the DUOW correlation token.)

5. The unique transaction identifier of the transaction that generated the entry. In the entry shown in Figure 2–29, the transaction that was assigned the transaction ID 346 is responsible for the entry.

6. The unique identifier that has been assigned to the application for which the process that generated the event is working. In the entry shown in Figure 2–29, the process that is responsible for the entry was working on behalf of an application that has been assigned the ID "*LOCAL.DB2.010807154913". To find out more about a particular application ID, execute the LIST APPLICATIONS command on a DB2 UDB server or execute the LIST DCS APPLICATIONS command on a DB2 UDB Connect gateway to obtain a list of all application IDs available. Then, using this list, you can obtain information about the client experiencing the error (such as its node name and its TCP/IP address) or you can execute the GET SNAPSHOT FOR APPLICATION command (providing snapshot monitoring has been turned on) to obtain specific information about the application in question.

7. The DB2 UDB component that produced the entry. If the entry was generated by a user application that executed the db2AdminMsgWrite() API, this component of the entry header will read "User Application." (Applications can write messages to the administration notification log file and the DB2 diagnostic log file by invoking the db2AdminMsgWrite() API.)

8. The name of the function that produced the entry. This function operates within the DB2 UDB subcomponent that produced the entry. (If the entry was generated by a user application that executed the db2AdminMsgWrite() API, this component of the entry header will read "User Function.")

To find out more about the type of activity performed by the function that produced the entry, look at the fourth letter of its name. The following shows some of the letters used in the fourth position of DB2 UDB function names, along with the type of activity each function performs:

b Buffer pool management and manipulation

c Communications between clients and servers

d Data management

e Database engine processes

o Operating system calls (such as opening and closing files)

p Data protection (such as locking and logging)

r Relational database services

s Sorting operations

x Indexing operations

In the entry shown in Figure 2–29, the fourth letter of the function named **sqlpgint** (p) indicates that a problem was encountered by a function that was attempting to perform some type of data protection operation.

9. The ID of the internal error that was reported. (This number provides a way for DB2 UDB developers to quickly locate the section in the DB2 UDB source code that generated the entry.)

10. The database on which the error occurred.

11. When available, a diagnostic error code (often beginning with the letters "DIA") that attempts to explain the reason for the entry.

12. When available, a diagnostic error message (which corresponds to the diagnostic error code generated) that attempts to explain the reason for the entry.

13. When available, the hexadecimal representation of an internal return code (DB2 diagnostics log only).

If you are familiar with SQL, you are probably aware that a special structure known as the SQL Communications Area (SQLCA) structure is updated each time an SQL statement or an administrative API function is executed. When severe errors occur, the contents of the SQLCA data structure being used at that time may be written to the DB2 diagnostics log file. Figure 2–30 shows how such an SQLCA structure "dump" to the DB2 diagnostics log file will look. (Notice that an SQLCA structure dump follows a normal entry header.)

```
2001-05-16-10.58.58.046000    Instance:DB2    Node:000
PID:1157(db2agent (instance))    Appid:none
relation_data_serv  sqlrerlg    Probe:17    Database:SAMPLE
DIA9999E An internal error occurred. Report the following error
code: "FFFF813C".
❶ Data Title:SQLCA pid(14358)
❷ sqlcaid :SQLCA    sqlcabc:136  ❸ sqlcode:-980    sqlerrml:0
❹ sqlerrmc:
  sqlerrp :sqlrita
❺ sqlerrd : (1)0xFFFFE101    (2)0x00000000    (3)0x00000000
           (4)0x00000000    (5)0x00000000    (6)0x00000000
  sqlwarn : (1)        (2)        (3)        (4)        (5)        (6)
           (7)        (8)        (9)        (10)       (11)
  sqlstate:
```

Figure 2–30   Individual components of an SQLCA structure dump to the DB2 diagnostics log file.

All SQLCA entries consist of the following components (refer to the numbered bullets in Figure 2–30):

1. A title that marks the beginning of the SQLCA structure dump.

2. An eye catcher that identifies the beginning of the SQLCA data structure data.

3. The SQL return code value. A value of 0 means "Successful execution," a positive value means "Successful execution with warnings," and a negative value means "Error."

4. One or more reason codes, separated by the value 0xFF, which are associated with the SQL return code value shown.

5. A hexadecimal representation of up to six minor errors, which occurred in the sequence shown, that caused the final SQL return code value to be generated.

For the most part, the information found in the administration notification log file and the DB2 diagnostic log file is easy to read once you understand the format used. However, certain pieces of data such as hexadecimal dumps and internal DB2 codes can be somewhat difficult to interpret. In fact, in order to obtain a description for any internal error code that has been recorded as a hexadecimal value, you must connect to IBM's DB2 Support Web site (the URL for that site is http://www-3.ibm.com/cgi-bin/db2www/ data/db2/udb/winos2unix/support/index.d2w/report) and search for the appropriate TechNote using the keywords "Internal Return Codes".

Practice Questions

Question 1

Which of the following commands must be executed before an instance named DB2 will accept incoming connections using TCP/IP?

○ A. `db2set -i DB2COMM=TCPIP`

○ B. `db2set -i SVCENAME=TCPIP`

○ C. `UPDATE DBM CFG USING DB2COMM TCPIP`

○ D. `UPDATE DBM CFG USING SVCENAME TCPIP`

Question 2

An AIX workstation running DB2 UDB ESE needs to connect to a DB2 UDB ESE Linux server and have users authenticated there. Which of the following authentication levels satisfies this need while providing authentication for other clients needing access to the AIX server?

○ A. CLIENT

○ B. SERVER

○ C. KERBEROS

○ D. CLIENT_SERVER

Question 3

In a client-server environment, which two of the following can be used to verify passwords?

❑ A. System Catalog

❑ B. Client Applications

❑ C. Client Operating System

❑ D. DB2 Database Manager

❑ E. Application Server

Question 4

Given an application with the following embedded SQL statement:

UPDATE department SET dept_name = 'PLANNING' WHERE dept_no = 'B01'

Which of the following privileges must a user hold in order to run the application?

○ A. ALTER privilege on DEPARTMENT
○ B. UPDATE privilege on DEPARTMENT
○ C. REFERENCES privilege on DEPARTMENT
○ D. EXECUTE privilege on the package

Question 5

An index named EMPID_X exists for a table called EMPLOYEE. Which of the following will allow USER1 to drop the index?

○ A. GRANT DELETE ON TABLE employee TO user1
○ B. GRANT DELETE ON INDEX empid_x TO user1
○ C. GRANT INDEX ON TABLE employee TO user1
○ D. GRANT CONTROL ON INDEX empid_x TO user1

Question 6

Which of the following identifies the group that has SYSMAINT authority?

○ A. The system catalog
○ B. The database manager configuration file
○ C. The system database directory
○ D. The system registry

Question 7

Given the following output from the `LIST APPLICATIONS` command:

```
Auth Id  Application  Appl.  Application Id           DB      # of
         Name         Handle                          Name    Agents
-------- -----------  ------ ---------------------- ------  ------
R.SANDERS db2bp.exe    3      *LOCAL.DB2.00CB46014904 SAMPLE  1
DB2ADMIN db2dasstm.exe 5      *LOCAL.DB2.0065C7013401 TOOLSDB 1
```

Which two of the following commands will terminate all client application connections?

❏ A. `FORCE APPLICATION (3, 5)`
❏ B. `FORCE APPLICATION ALL`
❏ C. `KILL APPLICATION (3, 5)`
❏ D. `DROP ALL APPLICATIONS`
❏ E. `DROP APPLICATION (3, 5)`

Question 8

Which of the following must be set to allow clients to discover all instances, but no databases on a server?

○ A. DISCOVER parameter set to ENABLE
   DISCOVER_DB parameter set to DISABLE
○ B. DISCOVER_INST parameter set to ENABLE
   DISCOVER parameter set to DISABLE
○ C. DISCOVER_INST parameter to ENABLE
   DISCOVER_DB parameter set to DISABLE
○ D. DISCOVER_INST parameter to KNOWN
   DISCOVER_DB parameter set to DISABLE

Question 9

The information in the administration notification log is intended to be used by:

○ A. DB2 customer service and support
○ B. Hardware service and support staff
○ C. System and database administrators
○ D. Application development and testing staff

Question 10

What is the minimum level of authority required to administer a remote server using Control Center functions that utilize the DAS process?

- ○ A. SYSADM
- ○ B. DASADM
- ○ C. SYSMAINT
- ○ D. SYSCTRL

Question 11

Which of the following actions can NOT be specified to take place when a task fails to execute successfully?

- ○ A. Start a new task
- ○ B. Cancel a scheduled task
- ○ C. Delete itself
- ○ D. Re-run itself

Question 12

If an entry in the administrative notification log has "User Application" listed as the component ID, which of the following is most likely to have caused the entry to be produced?

- ○ A. An application ended gracefully
- ○ B. An application called the db2AdminMsgWrite() API
- ○ C. An application was unable to start
- ○ D. A user did not have the authorization needed to run a particular application

Question 13

A FixPack needs to be applied to a DB2 UDB ESE Linux server. Which of the following will allow a system administrator to obtain a list of all instances on the server that will need to be updated once the FixPack has been applied?

○ A. dascrt, db2icrt

○ B. dascvt, db2icvt

○ C. daslist, db2ilist

○ D. dasupdt, db2iupdt

Question 14

Which of the following authority levels are allowed to terminate database connections with the FORCE APPLICATION command?

○ A. SYSADMN

○ B. SYSMAINT

○ C. DBADM

○ D. DBCTRL

Question 15

Which of the following commands allows a database administrator to prevent users that do not have SYSADM or DBADM authority from connecting to a database named DBASE1 long enough to perform maintenance on the database?

○ A. FORCE APPLICATION ALL

○ B. DEACTIVATE DATABASE dbase1

○ C. QUIESCE INSTANCE dbase1 ALLOW (SYSADMN, DBADM)

○ D. QUIESCE DATABASE dbase1 IMMEDIATE

Question 16

Which of the following is required before using the `FORCE APPLICATION` command to force users off a remote database?

○ A. Connect to the remote instance
○ B. Attach to the remote instance
○ C. Connect to the remote database
○ D. Attach to the remote database

Question 17

The status of jobs scheduled by the Task Center can be monitored using all but which of the following?

○ A. Email
○ B. Journal
○ C. Pager
○ D. Snapshot monitor

Question 18

Which of the following is NOT true about the administration notification log?

○ A. If the administration notification log is deleted, a new one will be created
○ B. The administration notification log is designed to be easier for system and database administrators to interpret than the db2diag.log file
○ C. On Windows platforms, administration notification log entries are written to the Windows Event Log and can be seen with the Windows Event Viewer.
○ D. If the file system where the administration notification log resides becomes full, a new log will be created in the location specified by the NEWLOGPATH database configuration parameter.

Answers

Question 1

The correct answer is **A**. The DB2COMM registry variable's value determines which communications managers will be activated when the DB2 Database Manager for the instance is started. (In this case, we want the TCP/IP communications manager to be started on the server.) The value of the DB2COMM registry variable, or any other DB2 registry variable for that matter, can be viewed or set/changed by executing the db2set command.

Question 2

The correct answer is **B**. Because the AIX workstation needs to provide authentication for other client workstations, it should use the SERVER authentication level. The Linux server should use the SERVER authentication level as well. (User IDs and passwords for both the AIX workstation and the Linux workstations will be managed by the respective operating systems.)

Question 3

The correct answers are **C** and **E**. Authentication is performed by an external security facility that is not part of DB2 UDB, so answers A and D are automatically eliminated. The security facility used to authenticate users is often part of the operating system and the combination of authentication types specified at both the client and the server determine which authentication method is actually used.

Question 4

The correct answer is **D**. A user that has EXECUTE privilege for a particular package can execute that package, even if they do not have the privileges that are needed to execute the SQL statements stored in the package. That is because any privileges needed to execute the SQL statements within a package are implicitly granted to the package user.

Question 5

The correct answer is **D**. The first GRANT statement (answer A) provides USER1 with the ability to delete rows from the EMPLOYEE table; the second GRANT statement (answer B) is not valid because DELETE is not an index privilege (DELETE is a table or view privilege); and the third GRANT statement (answer C) provides USER1 with the ability to create indexes for the EMPLOYEE table. The only thing that a person who has CONTROL privilege for an index can do with that index is delete (drop) it.

Question 6

The correct answer is **B**. SYSMAINT authority group assignment is made by storing the appropriate group name in the *sysmaint_group* parameter of the DB2 Database Manager configuration file that is associated with a particular instance. (Like SYSMAINT authority, SYSADM and SYSCTRL authority can only be assigned to a group and this assignment is made by storing the appropriate group name in the *sysadmn_group* and *sysctrl_group* parameters of the DB2 Database Manager configuration file that is associated with a particular instance.)

Question 7

The correct answers are **A** and **B**. The FORCE APPLICATION command is used to terminate client application connections. In this example, the connections for applications 3 and 5 are to be terminated so either the command FORCE APPLICATION (3, 5) or the command FORCE APPLICATION ALL can be used to accomplish this task.

Question 8

The correct answer is **C**. The DISCOVER_INST parameter controls whether or not instances can be seen by DB2 Discovery (if set to ENABLE, instances can be seen; if set to DISABLE, instances cannot be seen). The DISCOVER_DB parameter controls whether or not databases can be seen by DB2 Discovery (if set to ENABLE, databases can be seen; if set to DISABLE, databases cannot be seen). Both parameters must be set for *each* instance and *each* database found on a server.

Question 9

The correct answer is **C**. The administration notification log serves as the primary diagnostic facility for system and database administrators while the DB2 diagnostics log exists for the sole purpose of providing special, customized information to DB2 Customer Service personnel.

Question 10

The correct answer is **A**. In order to administer a server from a remote client using the Control Center, a user must have System Administration (SYSADM) authority for the DAS process used.

Question 11

The correct answer is **D**. Regardless of whether a task completes successfully, or fails, any number of actions can be performed, including:

➤ Running another task

➤ Scheduling another task

➤ Disabling another scheduled task

➤ Deleting itself

Question 12

The correct answer is **B**. If an entry in the administration notification log indicates that the DB2 UDB component that produced the entry was a user application that executed the db2AdminMsgWrite() API, a portion of the entry header will read "User Application." (Applications can write messages to the administration notification log file and the DB2 diagnostic log file by invoking the db2AdminMsgWrite() API.)

Question 13

The correct answer is **C**. The commands dascrt and db2icrt will create the DAS process and DB2 instances, respectively; the commands dasupdt and db2iupdt will update the DAS process and DB2 instances, respectively (and should be executed once the FixPack has been installed); and the commands dascvt and db2icvt are not valid. On the other hand, the command `daslist` will show the name of the DAS process on the server and the command `db2ilist` will list the names of all DB2 instances that have been defined for the server.

Question 14

The correct answer is **A**. You can terminate instance attachments and database connections by executing the FORCE APPLICATION command, provided you have SYSADMN or SYSCTRL authority for a server.

Question 15

The correct answer is **D**. Instances and databases can be placed in quiesced (restricted access) mode by executing the QUIESCE command. The appropriate syntax for quiescing a database is:

```
QUIESCE [DATABASE | DB] [DatabaseName]
IMMEDIATE
<FORCE CONNECTIONS>
```

Only users with SYSADM or DBADM authority can connect to a quiesced database.

Question 16

The correct answer is **C**. You must connect to a remote database before you can issue the FORCE APPLICATION command.

Question 17

The correct answer is **D**. The task center can either store information about the status of a completed task in the Journal or it can notify contacts via e-mail or pager (using the e-mail address or pager address provided when the task was created).

Question 18

The correct answer is **D**. The NEWLOGPATH database configuration parameter is used to specify a new location to store database transaction log files.

3

Data Placement

Seventeen percent (17%) of the DB2 UDB V8.1 for Linux, UNIX, and Windows Database Administration certification exam (Exam 701) and thirteen percent (13%) of the DB2 UDB V8.1 for Linux, UNIX, and Windows Database Administration certification upgrade exam (Exam 706) is designed to test your ability to create a DB2 UDB database, as well as to test your knowledge of the methods used to create and modify the various DB2 UDB storage objects available. The questions that make up this portion of the exam are intended to evaluate the following:

➤ Your ability to create a DB2 UDB database.

➤ Your ability to construct and alter DB2 UDB storage objects.

➤ Your ability to discuss the differences between System Managed Space (SMS) tablespaces and Database Managed Space (DMS) tablespaces.

➤ Your knowledge of tablespace states.

➤ Your ability to describe how schemas are used.

This chapter is designed to introduce you to instances and databases, to walk you through the database creation process, and to provide you with an overview of the various storage objects that can be constructed once a database exists. This chapter is also designed to show you how to construct storage objects, as well as modify storage objects as the storage requirements of a database change.

Terms you will learn:

> Instance

> DB2 Database Manager

Database

Registry Variables

Instance Configuration File

Database Configuration File

System Objects

Recovery Objects

Storage Objects

Buffer Pools

Containers

Tablespaces

System Managed Space (SMS) Tablespaces

Database Managed Space (DMS) Tablespaces

Database Objects

CREATE DATABASE

Recovery History File

Transaction Log Files

Create Database Wizard

CREATE BUFFERPOOL

ALTER BUFFERPOOL

CREATE TABLESPACE

ALTER TABLESPACE

Rows

Columns

Record

Field

Value

Base Table

Result Table

Materialized Query Table

Declared Temporary Table

Typed Table

CREATE TABLE

ALTER TABLE

Declared Temporary Tables

Schemas

LIST TABLESPACES

LIST TABLESPACE CONTAINERS

Tablespace States

Techniques you will master:

Understanding how to construct a new database.

Understanding what happens when a DB2 UDB database is created.

Recognizing the types of storage objects that are available and understanding when each is to be used.

Recognizing the major differences between System Managed Space (SMS) tablespaces and Database Managed Space (DMS) tablespaces.

Understanding how to obtain detailed information about one or more tablespaces.

Recognizing the various states a tablespace can be in.

Instances and Databases

Earlier, we saw that when any edition of DB2 Universal Database is installed on a particular workstation, program files for a background process known as the DB2 Database Manager are physically copied to a specific location on that workstation and, in most cases, an instance of the DB2 Database Manager is created. Instances are responsible for managing system resources and databases that fall under their control. Although only one instance is created initially, several instances can exist. Each instance behaves like a separate installation of DB2 UDB, even though all instances within a system share the same DB2 Database Manager program files (which were copied to the workstation during the installation process). And although multiple instances share the same binary code, each runs independently of the others and has its own environment (which can be modified by altering its associated configuration parameters).

 In the event one or more fix packs are applied to one instance but not another, the instances will no longer share the same binary files. Instead, each instance will have their own copy.

Every instance controls access to one or more databases. Databases are responsible for managing the storage, modification, and retrieval of data. Like instances, databases work independently of each other. Each database has its own environment (also controlled by a set of configuration parameters), as well as its own set of grantable authorities and privileges to govern how users interact with the data and database objects it controls. From a user's perspective, a database is a collection of tables (preferably related in some way) that are used to store data. However, from a database administrator's viewpoint, a DB2 UDB database is much more; a database is an entity that is comprised of many physical and logical components. Some of these components help determine how data is organized, while others determine how and where data is physically stored. So how do you create a database and allocate storage space for it? In order to answer that question, you must have a basic understanding of the different types of objects that are used by DB2 UDB.

DB2 UDB Objects

DB2 UDB uses both a logical and a physical storage model that is comprised of several different, yet related objects. Four types of objects exist. They are:

➤ System objects
➤ Recovery objects
➤ Storage objects
➤ Database (or data) objects

System Objects

System objects consist of registry variables, instance configuration files, and individual database configuration files. Registry variables can be set at the system level and at the instance level; all system level settings affect every instance that resides on a particular server. Instance configuration files (also known as DB2 Database Manager configuration files) are created and assigned to individual instances during the instance creation process. Values in an instance's configuration file control how resources are allocated for that particular instance, and changes to them affect every database that falls under that instance's control. (Values for many of the parameters in an instance configuration file can be modified to improve overall performance or increase concurrency.) Database configuration files are created and associated with individual databases during the database creation process. Values in a database's configuration file control how resources are allocated for that particular database, and changes to them can improve performance or increase capacity, depending on the type of activity the database encounters.

Recovery Objects

Recovery objects consist of transaction log files (often referred to a log files or logs) and recovery history files. By default, one recovery history file and three transaction log files are automatically created when a database is created. Recovery log files are used, together with database backup images and transaction log files, to coordinate database recovery operations. The recovery history file contains information about every backup operation executed, while transaction log files contain records of each database operation performed. In the event a database has to be recovered from an application, user, or system error, events stored in the transaction log files can be replayed to return the database to a consistent and stable state, or to return a database to the state it was in up to the point in time that the error occurred, provided roll-forward recovery has been enabled. You cannot modify transaction log files or recovery history files directly; however, you will find that their contents are important should you need to repair a database that has been damaged or destroyed.

Storage Objects

Storage objects control where data is physically stored and how data is moved between storage and memory during normal operation. Three types of storage objects are used. They are:

> Buffer pools

> Containers

> Tablespaces

Buffer Pools

A buffer pool is a section of memory that has been reserved for the sole purpose of caching data pages as they are read from physical storage. Whenever data is needed to resolve a query, the page that the data is stored on (data is stored in sections called *pages*) is located in physical storage and transferred to a buffer pool, where it is then read and/or modified. If the page is modified, it is copied back to physical storage; however, all pages read stay in memory until the space they occupy is needed or until all connections to the database are terminated. Furthermore, whenever a page of data is retrieved, the DB2 Database Manager uses a set of heuristic algorithms to try to determine which pages will be needed next and those pages are retrieved as well (this is referred to as *prefetching*). Retaining all pages loaded and prefetching are done to improve overall performance; data can be accessed much faster when it is stored in memory than when it is stored on disk.

Buffer Pool Page Cleaners. As pages accumulate in a buffer pool, the pool will eventually become full. If a buffer pool becomes full of unmodified pages, this usually does not present a problem unless a large number of random select operations are being performed and the buffer pool being used is very large. On the other hand, if a buffer is filled with modified pages, performance can decrease significantly because the DB2 Database Manager must decide which pages should be written to disk, write them, and then discard them to make room for any new pages needed.

To prevent a buffer pool from filling up with "dirty" pages (pages that have been modified but not yet written to disk), DB2 UDB utilizes special agents known as page cleaners to write dirty pages to disk at a predetermined interval. (The interval at which dirty pages are written to disk is determined by the value of the *chngpgs_thresh* database configuration parameter; by default, this parameter is set such that page cleaning occurs whenever 60% of a buffer pool consists of dirty pages). By automatically writing pages to disk at regular intervals, page cleaners ensure that some amount of buffer pool space always remains available for future read operations.

Containers

A container is some form of physical storage that the DB2 Database Manager has unique access to. A container can be a directory that may or may not already exist within a file system, a fixed-size, preallocated file that may or may not already exist, or a physical (raw) device that is recognized by the operating system. (On Linux and UNIX operating systems, a physical device can be any logical volume that uses a character special interface; on Windows operating systems, a physical device is any unformatted partition or any physical disk.) A single tablespace can span many containers, but each container can only belong to one tablespace.

Tablespaces

Tablespaces are used to control where data is physically stored and to provide a layer of indirection between a table and one or more containers in which the table's data actually resides. A single tablespace can span many containers, but each container can only belong to one tablespace. When a tablespace spans multiple containers, data is written in a round-robin fashion (in groups of pages called *extents*) to each container assigned to that tablespace; this helps balance data across all containers that belong to a given tablespace.

Two types of tablespaces can exist: system managed space (SMS) tablespaces and database managed space (DMS) tablespaces. With SMS tablespaces, only directory containers can be used for storage, and the operating system's file manager is responsible for controlling how that space is used. With DMS tablespaces, only file and/or device containers can be used for storage, and the DB2 Database Manager is responsible for controlling how the space is used. These and other differences between SMS and DMS tablespaces are outlined in Table 3–1.

Table 3–1 Differences between SMS and DMS Tablespaces	
SMS Tablespaces	**DMS Tablespaces**
Storage space is allocated and managed by the operating system's file manager.	Storage space is allocated, if so specified, and managed by the DB2 Database Manager.
Only directory containers can be used for storage.	File or device containers can be used as storage; directory containers cannot be used.
No additional containers can be added to a tablespace (using the ALTER TABLESPACE SQL statement) once it has been created.	Additional containers can be added to a tablespace after it has been created. When new containers are added, existing data can automatically be rebalanced across the new set of containers to retain optimal I/O efficiency.
Storage space is allocated as it is needed. (The amount of space available for use is limited only by the size of the file system being used.)	Storage space is preallocated. (If more space is needed later, additional containers will have to be added or existing containers will need to be extended.)
A container's size cannot be changed once a tablespace has been created.	A container's size can be increased or decreased after a tablespace has been created.
A single table must reside in a single tablespace.	A single table can be split across multiple tablespaces. (Table data can reside in one tablespace, index data can reside in a separate tablespace, and large data can reside in another tablespace.)
Tablespaces are easier to create and manage.	Table access is slightly faster so overall performance is better.

If you look closely at how DB2 UDB manages data, you will discover that, depending on how a table has been defined, each corresponding record can be stored as three distinct values: as a regular data value, which is how values produced by an application, user, or trigger are stored; as an index value, which is how all related index data values are stored; and as one or more long data values, which is how each long data and large object (LOB) value is stored. Consequently, three types of tablespaces can exist: *regular*, *large*, and *temporary*. Regular data and index data can reside in regular tablespaces, while long field data and large object data can reside in large tablespaces—but only if DMS tablespaces are used. (The use of large tablespaces is optional since long data can reside in regular tablespaces as well.) A regular tablespace can be up to 16,777,215 pages in size, therefore, the maximum amount of data that can be stored in any one tablespace is determined by the page size used for that tablespace: 64 G (gigabytes) if 4 K (kilobyte) pages are used, 128 G if 8 K pages are used, 256 G if 32 K pages are used, and 512 G if 32 K pages are used. Large tablespaces, on the other hand, can contain up to 2 T (terabytes) of data.

Temporary tablespaces are used for a much different purpose. Temporary tablespaces are classified as either *system* or *user*. System temporary tablespaces are used to store internal temporary data generated when some types of operations are performed (for example, sorting data, reorganizing tables, creating indexes, and joining tables), while user temporary tablespaces are used to store declared global temporary tables, which in turn are used to store application-specific data for a brief period of time. Temporary tablespaces can contain up to 2 T of data.

Database (or Data) Objects

Database objects—otherwise known as data objects—are used to logically store and manipulate data, as well as to control how all user data (and some system data) is organized. Data objects include tables, indexes, views, aliases, schemas, triggers, user-defined data types, user-defined functions, stored procedures, and sequences.

Creating a DB2 UDB Database with the CREATE DATABASE Command

Now that you have a basic understanding of the types of DB2 UDB objects available, let's look at how a database is created. There are two ways to create a DB2 UDB database: by using the Create Database Wizard or by using the CREATE DATABASE command. Because the Create Database Wizard is essentially a graphical user interface (GUI) for the CREATE DATABASE command, we will look at the command method first.

In its simplest form, the syntax for the CREATE DATABASE command is:

```
CREATE [DATABASE | DB] [DatabaseName]
```

where:

> *DatabaseName*   Identifies the unique name to be assigned to the
> database to be created.

The only value you must provide when executing this command is the name
to assign the database once it is created. This name:

➤ Can only consist of the characters a–z, A–Z, 0–9, @, #, $, and _.

➤ Cannot begin with a number.

➤ Cannot begin with the letter sequences "SYS", "DBM", or "IBM".

➤ Cannot be the same as the name already assigned to another database
within the same instance.

Of course, a more complex form of the CREATE DATABASE command, which
provides you with much more control over database parameters, is available,
and we will look at it shortly. But for now, let's look at what happens when
this form of the CREATE DATABASE command is executed.

What Happens When a DB2 UDB Database is Created

Regardless of how the process is initiated, whenever a new database is created, the following tasks are performed, in the order shown:

1. All physical directories needed are created in the appropriate location.

Information about each database created is stored in a special hierarchical
directory tree. Where this directory tree is actually created is determined by
information provided with the CREATE DATABASE command. If no location
information is provided, this directory tree is created in the location specified
by the *dftdbpath* DB2 Database Manager configuration parameter associated
with the instance the database is being created under. The root directory of
this hierarchical tree is assigned the name of the instance the database is associated with. This directory will contain a subdirectory that has been assigned
a name corresponding to the partition's node. If the database is a partitioned
database, this directory will be named NODE*xxxx*, where *xxxx* is the unique
node number that has been assigned to the partition; if the database is a non-
partitioned database, this directory will be named NODE0000. The node-

name directory, in turn, will contain one subdirectory for each database that has been created under the node. The name assigned to each subdirectory corresponds to the database token that has been assigned to the database (the subdirectory for the first database created will be named SQL00001, the subdirectory for the second database will be named SQL00002, and so on). Figure 3–1 illustrates how this directory hierarchy typically looks in a non-partitioned database environment.

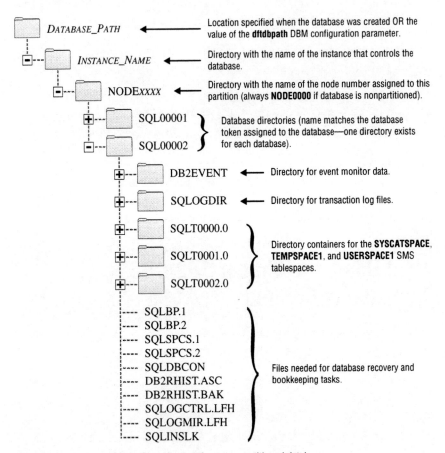

Figure 3–1 Typical directory hierarchy tree for a non-partitioned database.

 Never attempt to modify this directory structure or any of the files stored in it. Such actions could destroy one or more databases or make them unusable.

2. Files that are needed for database recovery and other bookkeeping tasks are created.

After the appropriate database-name directory has been created, the following files are created in that directory:

SQLBP.1 This file contains buffer pool information.

SQLBP.2 This file is a backup copy of SQLBP.1.

SQLSPCS.1 This file contains tablespace information.

SQLSPCS.2 This file is a backup copy of SQLSPCS.1.

SQLDBCON. This file contains database configuration information.

DB2RHIST.ASC This file contains historical information about backup operations, restore operations, table load operations, table reorganization operations, tablespace alterations, and similar database changes (i.e., the recovery history file).

DB2RHIST.BAK This file is a backup copy of DB2RHIST.ASC.

SQLOGCTL.LFH This file contains information about active transaction log files. Recovery operations use information stored in this file to determine how far back in the logs to begin the recovery process.

SQLOGMIR.LFH This file is a mirrored copy of SQLOGCTL.LFH.

SQLINSLK This file contains information used to ensure that a database is only assigned to one instance of the DB2 Database Manager.

A subdirectory named SQLOGDIR is also created, and three files (named S0000000.LOG, S0000001.LOG, and S0000002.LOG) are created in this subdirectory. These three files are used to store transaction log records as SQL operations are performed against the database.

3. The database is cataloged in the system and local database directory (a system and/or local database directory is created first if they don't exist).

DB2 Universal Database uses a set of special files to keep track of where databases are stored and to provide access to those databases. Because the information stored in these files is used like the information stored in an office building directory is used, they are referred to as directory files. Whenever a database is created, these directories are updated with the database's name and alias. If specified, a comment and code set values are also stored in these directories.

4. One buffer pool is created

During the database creation process, a buffer pool is created and assigned the name IBMDEFAULTBP. On Linux and UNIX platforms, this buffer pool is 1,000 4K (kilobyte) pages in size; on Windows platforms, this buffer pool is 250 4K pages in size. The actual memory used by this buffer pool (and for that matter, by any other buffer pools that may exist) is allocated when the first connection to the database is established and freed when all connections to the database have been terminated.

5. One system temporary tablespace and two regular tablespaces are created.

Once the buffer pool IBMDEFAULTBP has been created, three tablespaces associated with this buffer pool are created. These three tablespaces are:

➤ A regular tablespace named SYSCATSPACE1, which is used to store the system catalog tables and views associated with the database.

➤ A regular tablespace named USERSPACE1, which is used to store all user-defined objects (such as tables, indexes, and so on) along with user data, index data, and long value data.

➤ A system temporary tablespace named TEMPSPACE1, which is used as a temporary storage area for operations such as sorting data, reorganizing tables, and creating indexes.

Unless otherwise specified, all three of these tablespaces will be SMS tablespaces with an extent size of 32 4K pages; characteristics for each of these tablespaces can be provided as input to the Create Database Wizard or the CREATE DATABASE command.

6. The system catalog tables and views are created and populated.

Once the tablespace SYSCATSPACE has been created, a special set of tables, known as the *system catalog tables*, are constructed and populated within that tablespace. The DB2 Database Manager uses these system catalog tables to keep track of information like database object definitions, database object dependencies, database object privileges, column data types, and table constraints. A set of system catalog views is created along with the system catalog tables, and these views are typically used when accessing data stored in the system catalog tables. The system catalog tables and views cannot be modified with SQL statements (however, their contents can be viewed). Instead, they are modified by the DB2 Database Manager whenever:

➤ A database object (such as a table or index) is created, altered, or dropped

➤ Authorizations and/or privileges are granted or revoked.

➤ Statistical information is collected for a table.

➤ Packages are bound to the database.

In most cases, the complete characteristics of a database object are stored in one or more system catalog tables when the object is created. However, in some cases, such as when triggers and constraints are defined, the actual SQL used to create the object is stored instead.

7. Four schemas are created.

During the database creation process, the following schemas are created: SYSIBM, SYSCAT, SYSSTAT, and SYSFUN. A special user named SYSIBM is made the owner of each.

8. The database configuration file for the database is initialized.

Some of the parameters in the database configuration file (such as code set, territory, and collating sequence) will be set using values that were specified as input for the Create Database Wizard or CREATE DATABASE command. Others will be assigned system default values.

9. A set of utility programs are bound to the database.

Before some of the DB2 UDB utilities available can work with a database, the packages needed to run those utilities must be created. Such packages are created by binding a set of defined DB2 Database Manager bind files to the database (the set of bind files used are stored in the utilities bind list file *db2ubind.lst*).

10. Authorities and privileges are granted to the appropriate users.

To connect to and work with a particular database, a user must have the authorities and privileges needed to use that database. Therefore, whenever a new database is created, the following authorities and privileges are granted:

➤ DBADM authority, along with CONNECT, QUIESCE_CONNECT, CREATETAB, BINDADD, CREATE_NOT_FENCED, CREATE _EXTERNAL_ROUTINE, IMPLICIT_SCHEMA, and LOAD privileges, are granted to the user who created the database.

➤ USE privilege on the tablespace USERSPACE1 is granted to the group PUBLIC.

➤ CONNECT, CREATETAB, BINDADD, and IMPLICIT_SCHEMA privileges are granted to the group PUBLIC.

➤ SELECT privilege on each system catalog table is granted to the group PUBLIC.

➤ EXECUTE privilege on all procedures found in the SYSIBM schema is granted to the group PUBLIC.

➤ EXECUTE WITH GRANT privilege on all functions found in the SYSFUN schema is granted to the group PUBLIC.

➤ BIND and EXECUTE privileges for each successfully bound utility are granted to the group PUBLIC.

The CREATE DATABASE Command

So how do you create a database that uses a DMS tablespace to hold the system catalog tables? Or a database whose tablespaces are to have an extent size of 64? You can create these and other databases by using any combination of the options available with the CREATE DATABASE command. The complete syntax for this command is:

```
CREATE [DATABASE | DB] [DatabaseName] <AT DBPARTITIONNUM>
```

or

```
CREATE [DATABASE | DB] [DatabaseName]
<ON [Path]>
<ALIAS [Alias]>
<USING CODESET [CodeSet] TERRITORY [Territory]>
<COLLATE USING [CollateType]>
<NUMSEGS [NumSegments]>
<DFT_EXTENT_SZ [DefaultExtentSize]>
<CATALOG TABLESPACE [TS_Definition]>
<USER TABLESPACE [TS_Definition]>
<TEMPORARY TABLESPACE [TS_Definition]>
<WITH "[Description]">
<AUTOCONFIGURE <USING [Keyword] [Value] ,... >
    <APPLY [DB ONLY | DB AND DBM | NONE>>
```

where:

DatabaseName	Identifies the unique name to be assigned to the database to be created.
Path	Identifies the location (drive and/or directory) where the directory hierarchy and files associated with the database to be created are to be physically stored.
Alias	Identifies the alias to be assigned to the database to be created.
CodeSet	Identifies the code set to be used for storing data in the database to be created. (In a DB2 UDB database, each single-byte character is represented internally as a unique number between 0 and 255. This number is referred to as the *code point* of the character; assignments of code points to every character in a particular character set are called the *code page*; and the International Organiza-

tion for Standardization term for a code page is *code set.*)

Territory	Identifies the territory to be used for storing data in the database to be created.
CollateType	Identifies the collating sequence (i.e., the sequence in which characters are ordered for the purpose of sorting, merging, and making comparisons) to be used by the database to be created. Valid values include COMPATABILITY (DB2 v2 collating sequence), IDENTITY (byte for byte comparisons), NLSCHAR (code set/territory comparisons), and SYSTEM (territory comparisons).
NumSegments	Identifies the number of directories that will be created and used to store files for each of the default SMS tablespaces used by the database to be created (SYSCATSPACE, USERSPACE1, and TEMPSPACE1 only).
DefaultExtentSize	Identifies the default extent size to be used whenever a tablespace is created and no extent size is specified during the creation process.
Description	A comment used to describe the database entry that will be made in the database directory for the database to be created. The description must be enclosed by double quotation marks.
Keyword	One or more keywords recognized by the AUTO-CONFIGURE command. Valid values include mem_percent, workload_type, num_stmts, tpm, admin_priority, is_populated, num_local_apps, num_remote_apps, isolation, and bp_resizable. Refer to the *DB2 UDB Command Reference* for more information on how the AUTOCONFIGURE option is used.
Value	Identifies the value that is to be associated with the *Keyword* specified.
TS_Definition	Specifies the definition that is to be used to create the tablespace that will be used to hold the system catalog tables (SYSCATSPACE), user-defined objects (USERSPACE1), and/or tempo-

rary objects (TEMPSPACE1). The syntax used to define a system managed (SMS) tablespace is:

```
MANAGED BY SYSTEM
USING ( '[Container]' ,... )
<EXTENTSIZE [ExtentSize]>
<PREFETCHSIZE [PrefetchSize]>
<OVERHEAD [Overhead]>
<TRANSFERRATE [TransferRate]>
```

The syntax used to define a database managed (DMS) tablespace is:

```
MANAGED BY DATABASE
USING ( [FILE | DEVICE] '[Container]' NumberOfPages ,... )
<EXTENTSIZE [ExtentSize]>
<PREFETCHSIZE [PrefetchSize]>
<OVERHEAD [Overhead]>
<TRANSFERRATE [TransferRate]>
```

where:

Container Identifies one or more containers to be used to store data that will be assigned to the tablespace specified. For SMS tablespaces, each container specified must identify a valid directory; for DMS FILE containers, each container specified must identify a valid file; and for DMS DEVICE containers, each container specified must identify an existing device.

NumberOfPages Specifies the number of 4K pages to be used by the tablespace container.

ExtentSize Specifies the number of 4K pages of data that will be written in a round-robin fashion to each tablespace container.

PrefetchSize Specifies the number of 4K pages of data that will be read from the specified tablespace when data prefetching is performed.

Overhead Identifies the I/O controller overhead and disk-seek latency time (in number of milliseconds) associated with the containers that belong to the specified tablespace.

TransferRate Identifies the time, in number of milliseconds, that it takes to read one 4K page of data from a tablespace container and store it in memory.

Now that we have seen the complete syntax for the CREATE DATABASE command, let's go back to our original question. The way you would create a database that uses a DMS tablespace to hold the system catalog tables would be to execute a CREATE DATABASE command that looks something like this:

```
CREATE DATABASE SAMPLEDB ON E:
USING CODESET 1252
TERRITORY US
COLLATE USING SYSTEM
CATALOG TABLESPACE MANAGED BY DATABASE
   (FILE 'E:\SYSCATSPACE.DAT', 5000)
```

When executed, this statement would create a database that

➤ Is physically located on drive E:.

➤ Has been assigned the name SAMPLEDB.

➤ Recognizes the United States/Canada code set. (The code page, along with the territory, is used to convert alphanumeric data to binary data that is stored in the database.)

➤ Uses a collating sequence that is based on the territory used (which in this case is United States/Canada).

➤ Will store the system catalog in a DMS tablespace that uses the file SYSCATSPACE.DAT as its container. (This file is stored on drive E: and is capable of holding up to 5,000 pages that are 4K in size.)

➤ Is created using default values for all other parameters not specified (i.e., USERSPACE1 and TEMPSPACE1 will be SMS tablespaces, extent sizes will be 32, etc.).

Creating a DB2 UDB Database with the Create Database Wizard

If you have ever installed software on a computer using a graphical installation program, more than likely the interface you used is what is known as a *wizard*. A wizard is a GUI tool consisting of a sequenced set of dialogs that have been designed to guide a user through the steps needed to perform a complex operation. More often than not, the dialogs (often referred to as *pages*) that make up a wizard are processed in the order that they appear; thus, they orchestrate a step one, step two, step three. . . input scenario. The Create Database Wizard is no exception, and the pages it contains are designed to capture information about the characteristics of the database to be created.

The Control Center, which is the most important and versatile GUI tool DB2 UDB has to offer, is comprised of several elements, including:

➤ An objects pane (located on the left-hand side of the Control Center), which contains a hierarchical representation of every object type that can be managed from the Control Center.

➤ A contents pane (located on the right-hand side of the Control Center), which contains a listing of existing objects that correspond to the object type selected in the objects pane. (For example, if the Tables object type were selected in the objects pane, a list of all tables available would be listed in the contents pane.)

By highlighting the *Databases* object shown in the objects pane of the Control Center and right-clicking the mouse button, you will bring up a menu that contains a list of options available for database objects. The Create Database Wizard is invoked by selecting *Create*, followed by *Database Using Wizard...* from this menu. Figure 3–2 shows the Control Center menu items that must be selected in order to activate the Create Database Wizard; Figure 3–3 shows what the first page of the Create Database Wizard looks like when it is activated.

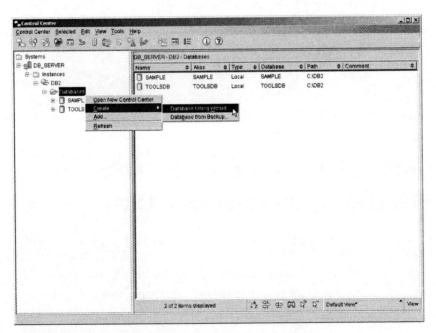

Figure 3–2 Invoking the Create Database Wizard from the Control Center.

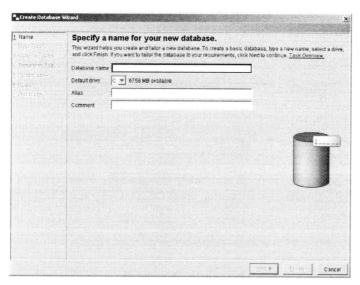

Figure 3–3   The first page of the Create Database Wizard.

Once the Create Database Wizard is displayed, you simply follow the directions shown on each panel presented to define the characteristics of the database that is to be created. (These same characteristics can be specified through the various options available with the CREATE DATABASE command.) When you have provided enough information for the DB2 Database Manager to create the database, the "Finish" push button displayed in the lower right corner of the wizard (see Figure 3–3) will be enabled. When this button is selected, the specified database will be created.

The Configuration Advisor

If you have had the opportunity to create a database using an earlier version of DB2 UDB, one of the biggest differences you will see when creating databases with DB2 UDB, Version 8.1, is that a tool known as the Configuration Advisor is automatically launched immediately after a database is created, provided the Create Database Wizard database is used to create a new database. The Configuration Advisor is designed to capture specific information about your database environment and recommend/make changes to configuration parameters based on the information provided. (This functionality is also provided when the AUTOCONFIGURE option of the CREATE DATABASE command is specified along with various keyword/value pairs.) Figure 3–4 shows what the first page of the Configuration Advisor looks like when it is activated.

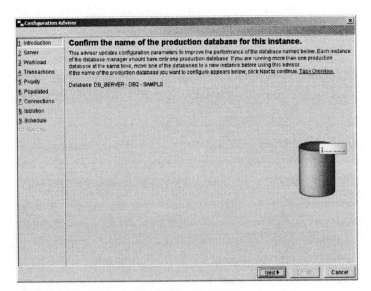

Figure 3–4   The first page of the Configuration Advisor.

Once the Configuration Advisor wizard is activated, you simply follow the directions shown on each panel presented to identify your server environment and to describe what a typical transaction workload for your database will look like. When you have provided the information requested, the Configuration Advisor will recommend changes that should improve overall performance if made to instance and/or database to configuration parameters. At that time, the "Finish" push button displayed in the lower right corner of the wizard (see Figure 3–4) will be enabled and when this button is selected, all configuration parameter changes recommended will be applied.

Creating Additional Storage Objects

Earlier, we saw that when a DB2 UDB database is created, one buffer pool named IBMDEFAULTBP is created and three tablespaces are created and associated with this buffer pool as part of the database initialization process. The three tablespaces that are created are:

➤ A regular tablespace named SYSCATSPACE1, which is used to store the system catalog tables and views associated with the database.

➤ A regular tablespace named USERSPACE1, which is used to store all user-defined objects (such as tables, indexes, and so on) along with user data.

➤ A system temporary tablespace named TEMPSPACE1, which is used as a temporary storage area for operations such as sorting data, reorganizing tables, and creating indexes.

These basic storage objects are usually sufficient for small databases. However, large databases are typically made up of many different buffer pool and tablespace objects. Therefore, as a database administrator, it is important to know how new storage objects are created as well as how existing storage objects are modified.

Creating Buffer Pools

Earlier, we saw that a buffer pool is an area of main memory that has been allocated to the DB2 Database Manager for the purpose of caching table and index data pages as they are read from disk. By default, one buffer pool (named IBMDEFAULTBP) is created for a particular database when that database is first created. On Linux and UNIX platforms, this buffer pool is 1,000 4K (kilobyte) pages in size; on Windows platforms, this buffer pool is 250 4K pages in size. Additional buffer pools can be created by executing the CREATE BUFFERPOOL SQL statement. The basic syntax for this statement is:

```
CREATE BUFFERPOOL [BufferPoolName]
<IMMEDIATE | DEFERRED>
SIZE [Size]
<PAGESIZE [PageSize] <K>>
<NOT EXTENDED STORAGE | EXTENDED STORAGE>
```

where:

BufferPoolName	Identifies the name to be assigned to the buffer pool to be created.
Size	Identifies the number of pages (of *PageSize* size) to be allocated for the buffer pool to be created.
PageSize	Specifies the size that each page used by the buffer pool being created is to be. (Valid values include 4096, 8192, 16384, or 32768 bytes—if the suffix K [for kilobytes] is provided, this parameter must be set to 4, 8, 16, or 32.) Unless otherwise specified, pages used by buffer pools are 4K in size. (It is important to note that the page size used by a buffer pool determines what tablespaces can be used with it; a buffer pool can only be used by a tablespace that has the same page size.)

If the DEFERRED clause is specified with the CREATE BUFFERPOOL statement, the buffer pool will not be created until all connections to the database the buffer pool is to be created for have been terminated. If the IMMEDIATE clause is specified, the buffer pool will be created immediately unless the amount of memory required is not available, in which case a warning message will be generated and the buffer pool creation process will behave as if the DEFERRED clause were specified. If neither clause is specified, the buffer pool will not be created until all connections to the database the buffer pool is to be created for have been terminated.

Although basic syntax is presented for most of the SQL statements covered in this chapter, the actual syntax supported may be much more complex. To view the complete syntax for a specific SQL statement or to obtain more information about a particular statement, refer to the *IBM DB2 Universal Database, Version 8 SQL Reference Volume 2* product documentation.

So, if you wanted to create a buffer pool that has the name TEMP_BP, consists of 100 pages that are 8 kilobytes in size, and is to be created immediately if enough free memory is available, you could do so by executing a CREATE BUFFERPOOL SQL statement that looks something like this:

```
CREATE BUFFERPOOL TEMP_BP
IMMEDIATE
SIZE 100
PAGESIZE 8 K
```

Buffer pools can also be created using the Create Buffer Pool dialog, which can be activated by selecting the appropriate action from the *Buffer Pools* menu found in the Control Center. Figure 3–5 shows the Control Center menu items that must be selected to activate the Create Buffer Pool dialog; Figure 3–6 shows how the Create Buffer Pool dialog might look after its input fields have been populated.

So why would you want to create additional buffer pools? If you want to create tablespaces that have a page size of 8K, 16K, or 32K, you must first create a buffer pool that uses the same page size. (When you create a tablespace, it must be associated with a buffer pool that has a matching page size). You may also choose to create additional buffer pools to improve database performance (for example, you may want to create a separate buffer pool for system temporary tablespaces to improve the performance of sort operations).

Modifying Existing Buffer Pools

Because the way a buffer pool is configured is an important factor in how well some database operations perform, you may end up modifying a single buffer

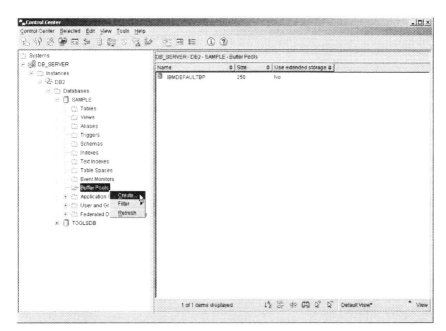

Figure 3–5   Invoking the Create Buffer Pool dialog from the Control Center.

Figure 3–6   The Create Buffer Pool dialog.

pool several times when tuning a database for optimum performance. Once a buffer pool has been created, you cannot alter its page size; however, you can control how many pages get allocated for it by executing the ALTER BUFFER-POOL SQL statement. The basic syntax for this statement is:

```
ALTER BUFFERPOOL [BufferPoolName]
<IMMEDIATE | DEFERRED>
SIZE [Size]
```

where:

> *BufferPoolName*   Identifies the name assigned to the buffer pool to be altered.

Size	Identifies the number of pages that are to be allocated for the buffer pool specified.

If the DEFERRED clause is specified with the ALTER BUFFERPOOL statement, the buffer pool's size will not be changed until all connections to the database the buffer pool is associated with have been terminated. If the IMMEDIATE clause is specified, the number of pages needed for the buffer pool will be allocated immediately unless the amount of memory required is not available, in which case a warning message will be generated and the buffer pool resize process will behave as if the DEFERRED clause were specified. If neither clause is specified, the buffer pool will not be resized until all connections to the database the buffer pool is associated with have been terminated.

Thus, if you wanted to resize an existing buffer pool that has the name TEMP_BP so that it consists of 500 pages, and if you wanted the buffer pool to be resized after all connections to the database the buffer pool is associated with have been terminated, you could do so by executing an ALTER BUFFER-POOL SQL statement that looks something like this:

```
ALTER BUFFERPOOL TEMP_BP
SIZE 500
```

Buffer pools can also be altered using the Alter Buffer Pool dialog, which can be activated by selecting the appropriate action from the *Buffer Pools* menu found in the Control Center. Figure 3–7 shows the Control Center menu items that must be selected in order to activate the Alter Buffer Pool dialog; Figure 3–8 shows how the Alter Buffer Pool dialog might look after its input fields have been populated.

Creating Tablespaces

As mentioned earlier, tablespaces are used to control where data is physically stored and to provide a layer of indirection between database objects and the directories, files, or raw devices (referred to as containers) in which the data physically resides. Depending on how it is defined, a tablespace can be either a system managed space (SMS) tablespace or a database managed space (DMS) tablespace. With SMS tablespaces, each container used must be a directory that resides within the file space of the operating system, and the operating system's file manager is responsible for managing data storage. With DMS tablespaces, each container used must be either a fixed-size preallocated file or a raw device, and the DB2 Database Manager is responsible for managing data storage. By default, three tablespaces (named SYSCATSPACE, USERSPACE1, and TEMPSPACE1) are created for a database as part of the database creation pro-

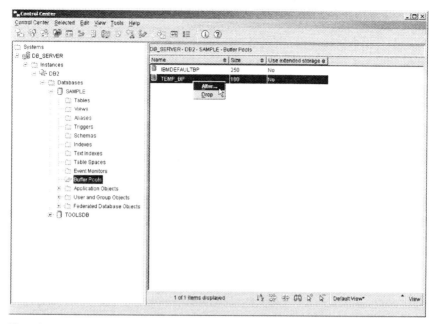

Figure 3–7   Invoking the Alter Buffer Pool dialog from the Control Center.

Figure 3–8   The Alter Buffer Pool dialog.

cess. Additional tablespaces can be created by executing the CREATE TABLESPACE SQL statement. The basic syntax for this statement is:

```
CREATE
<REGULAR | LARGE | SYSTEM TEMPORARY | USER TEMPORARY>
TABLESPACE [TablespaceName]
<PAGESIZE [PageSize] <K>>
MANAGED BY SYSTEM USING
    ( '[Container]' ,... )
<EXTENTSIZE [ExtentPages | ExtentSize <K | M | G>]>
<PREFETCHSIZE [PrefetchPages | PrefetchSize <K | M | G>]>
<BUFFERPOOL [BufferPoolName]>
```

or

```
CREATE
<REGULAR | LARGE | SYSTEM TEMPORARY | USER TEMPORARY>
TABLESPACE [TablespaceName]
<PAGESIZE [PageSize] <K>>
MANAGED BY DATABASE USING
    ( [FILE | DEVICE] '[Container]' [ContainerSize] ,... )
<EXTENTSIZE [ExtentPages | ExtentSize <K | M | G>]>
<PREFETCHSIZE [PrefetchPages | PrefetchSize <K | M | G>]>
<BUFFERPOOL [BufferPoolName]>
```

where:

TablespaceName	Identifies the name to be assigned to the tablespace to be created.
PageSize	Specifies the size that each page used by the tablespace being created is to be. Valid values include 4096, 8192, 16384, or 32768 bytes. If the suffix K (for kilobytes) is provided, this parameter must be set to 4, 8, 16, or 32. Unless otherwise specified, pages used by tablespaces are 4K in size.
Container	Identifies one or more containers that are to be used to store the data associated with the tablespace to be created. (If multiple containers are used, data is written to each in a round-robin fashion, one extent at a time.)
ContainerSize	Identifies the number of pages (of *PageSize* size) to be stored in the tablespace container specified.
ExtentPages	Identifies the number of pages of data to be written to a single tablespace container before another container will be used.
ExtentSize	Identifies the amount of data to be written to a single tablespace container before another container will be used. The value specified for this parameter is treated as the total number of bytes, unless the letter K (for kilobytes), M (for megabytes), or G (for gigabytes) is also specified. (If an *ExtentSize* value is specified, it is converted to an *ExtentPages* value using the *PageSize* value provided.)
PrefetchPages	Identifies the number of pages of data to be read from the tablespace when data prefetching is per-

formed (prefetching allows data needed by a query to be read before it is referenced so that the query spends less time waiting for I/O).

PrefetchSize Identifies the amount of data to be read from the tablespace when data prefetching is performed. The value specified for this parameter is treated as the total number of bytes, unless the letter K (for kilobytes), M (for megabytes), or G (for gigabytes) is also specified. (If a *PrefetchSize* value is specified, it is converted to a *PrefetchPages* value using the *PageSize* value provided.)

BufferPoolName Identifies the name of the buffer pool to be used by the tablespace to be created. (The page size of the buffer pool specified must match the page size of the tablespace to be created, or the CREATE TABLESPACE statement will fail.)

If the MANAGED BY SYSTEM version of this statement is executed, the resulting tablespace will be an SMS tablespace. On the other hand, if the MANAGED BY DATABASE version is executed, the resulting tablespace will be a DMS tablespace. Furthermore, if an SMS tablespace is to be created, only existing directories can be used as that tablespace's storage container(s), and if a DMS tablespace is to be created, only fixed-size, preallocated files or physical raw devices can be used as that tablespace's storage container(s).

The size of each container assigned to a single DMS tablespace can differ; however, optimal performance is achieved when all containers used are the same size.

Thus, if you wanted to create a DMS tablespace that has the name PAYROLL_TS, consists of pages that are 8 kilobytes in size, uses the file DMS_TBS, which is 1000 megabytes in size and resides in the directory C:\TABLESPACES as its storage container, and uses the buffer pool PAYROLL_BP, you could do so by executing a CREATE TABLESPACE SQL statement that looks something like this:

```
CREATE REGULAR TABLESPACE PAYROLL_TS
PAGESIZE 8K
MANAGED BY DATABASE USING
   (FILE 'C:\TABLESPACES\DMS_TBSP.TSF', 1000 M)
BUFFERPOOL PAYROLL_BP
```

Tablespaces can also be created using the Create Table Space Wizard, which can be activated by selecting the appropriate action from the *Table Spaces* menu found in the Control Center. Figure 3–9 shows the Control Center menu items that must be selected to activate the Create Table Space Wizard; Figure 3–10 shows how the first page of the Create Table Space Wizard might look after its input fields have been populated.

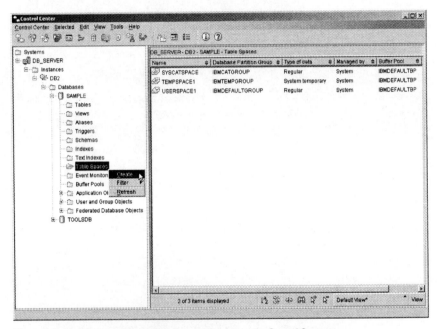

Figure 3–9   Invoking the Create Table Space Wizard from the Control Center.

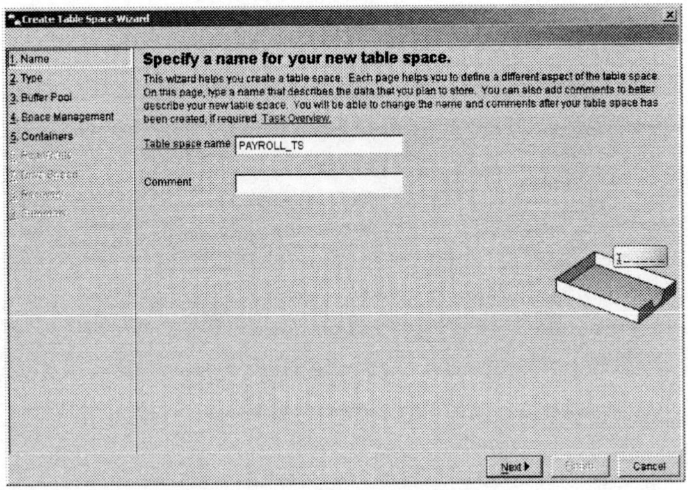

Figure 3–10   The first page of the Create Table Space Wizard.

Unlike buffer pools, which may or may not be usable immediately after they have been created, tablespaces can be used as soon as they have been successfully created.

Modifying Existing Tablespaces

Because SMS tablespaces rely on the operating system for physical storage space management, they rarely need to be modified after they have been successfully created. (In fact, the only thing that can be changed for an existing SMS tablespace is the prefetch size used and the buffer pool the tablespace is associated with.) DMS tablespaces, on the other hand, have to be monitored closely to ensure that the fixed-size, preallocated file(s) or physical raw device(s) that they use for storage always have enough free space available to meet the database's needs. When the amount of free storage space available to a DMS tablespace becomes dangerously low (typically less than 10 percent), more free space can be added either by increasing the size of one or more of its containers or by making one or more new containers available to it. Existing tablespace containers can be resized, new containers can be made available to an existing tablespace, and an existing tablespace's properties can be altered by executing the ALTER TABLESPACE SQL statement. The basic syntax for this statement is:

```
ALTER TABLESPACE [TablespaceName]
ADD ( [FILE | DEVICE] '[Container]' [ContainerSize] ,... )
```

or

```
ALTER TABLESPACE [TablespaceName]
DROP ( [FILE | DEVICE] '[Container]' ,... )
```

or

```
ALTER TABLESPACE [TablespaceName]
[EXTEND | REDUCE | RESIZE]
   ( [FILE | DEVICE] '[Container]' ,... )
```

or

```
ALTER TABLESPACE [TablespaceName]
[EXTEND | REDUCE | RESIZE]
   ( ALL <CONTAINERS> [NumPages | Size <K | M | G>]> )
```

or

```
ALTER TABLESPACE [TablespaceName]
<PREFETCHSIZE [PrefetchPages | PrefetchSize <K | M | G>]>
<BUFFERPOOL [BufferPoolName]>
<DROPPED TABLE RECOVERY [ON | OFF]>
```

where:

TablespaceName	Identifies the name assigned to the tablespace to be altered.
Container	Identifies one or more containers that are to be used to store the data associated with the tablespace to be altered.
ContainerSize	Identifies the number of pages to be stored in the tablespace container specified.
NumPages	Specifies the number of pages that are to be added to, removed from, or allocated for every container used by the tablespace specified.
Size	Identifies the amount of storage space that is to be added to, removed from, or allocated for every container used by the tablespace specified. The value specified for this parameter is treated as the total number of bytes, unless the letter K (for kilobytes), M (for megabytes), or G (for gigabytes) is also specified. (If a *Size* value is specified, it is converted to a *NumPages* value using the page size of the tablespace specified.)
PrefetchPages	Identifies the number of pages of data to be read from the tablespace when data prefetching is performed.
PrefetchSize	Identifies the amount of data to be read from the tablespace when data prefetching is performed. The value specified for this parameter is treated as the total number of bytes, unless the letter K (for kilobytes), M (for megabytes), or G (for gigabytes) is also specified. (If a *PrefetchSize* value is specified, it is converted to a *PrefetchPages* value using the page size of the tablespace being altered.)
BufferPoolName	Identifies the name of the buffer pool to be used by the tablespace to be altered. (The page size of the buffer pool specified must match the page size used by the tablespace to be altered.)

Thus, if you wanted a fixed-size, preallocated file named NEWFILE.TSF, which is 1000 megabytes in size and resides in the directory C:\TABLESPACES, to be used as a new storage container for an existing

DMS tablespace named PAYROLL_TS, you could make the PAYROLL_TS tablespace use this file as a new storage container by executing an ALTER TABLESPACE SQL statement that looks like this:

```
ALTER TABLESPACE PAYROLL_TS
ADD (FILE 'C:\TABLESPACES\NEWFILE.TSF', 1000 M)
```

On the other hand, if you wanted to expand the size of all containers associated with an existing DMS tablespace named PAYROLL_TS by 200 megabytes, you could do so by executing an ALTER TABLESPACE SQL statement that looks like this:

```
ALTER TABLESPACE PAYROLL_TS
EXTEND (ALL CONTAINERS 200 M)
```

Tablespaces can also be altered using the Alter Table Space dialog, which can be activated by selecting the appropriate action from the *Table Spaces* menu found in the Control Center. Figure 3–11 shows the Control Center menu items that must be selected in order to activate the Alter Table Space dialog; Figure 3–12 shows how the first page of the Alter Table Space dialog might look after its input fields have been populated.

It is important to note that when new containers are added to an existing tablespace or, to a much lesser extent, when existing containers are extended, a process known as rebalancing may occur. Rebalancing involves moving tablespace data from one location to another, and is done in an attempt to

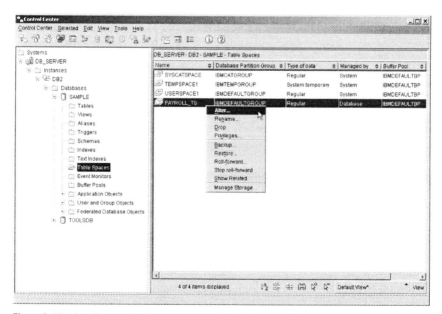

Figure 3–11 Invoking the Alter Table Space dialog from the Control Center.

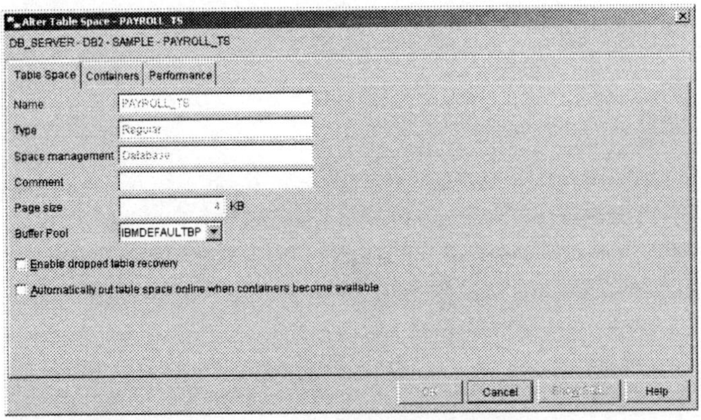

Figure 3–12 The first page of the Alter Table Space dialog.

keep data evenly distributed across all tablespace containers used. Access to the tablespace is not restricted during rebalancing and objects can be created, populated, queried, and dropped as usual. However, the rebalancing operation can have a significant negative impact on performance. If you need to add multiple containers to an existing tablespace, you should add them all at the same time using a single ALTER TABLESPACE statement to prevent the DB2 Database Manager from having to rebalance the data more than once.

Tables

A table is a logical database object that acts as the main repository in a database. Tables present data as a collection of unordered rows with a fixed number of columns. Each column contains values of the same data type or one of its subtypes, and each row contains a set of values for every column available. Usually, the columns in a table are logically related, and additional relationships can be defined between two or more tables. The storage representation of a row is called a *record*, the storage representation of a column is called a *field*, and each intersection of a row and column is called a *value*. Figure 3–13 shows the structure of a simple database table.

With DB2 UDB, five types of tables are available:

> **Base tables.** User-defined tables designed to hold persistent user data.
>
> **Result tables.** DB2 Database Manager-defined tables populated with rows retrieved from one or more base tables in response to a query.
>
> **Materialized query tables.** User-defined tables whose definition is based on the result of a query, and whose data is in the form of precomputed results that are taken from one or more tables upon which

DEPARTMENT TABLE

DEPTID	DEPTNAME	COSTCENTER
A000	ADMINISTRATION	10250
B001	PLANNING	10820
C001	ACCOUNTING	20450
D001	HUMAN RESOURCES	30200
E001	R & D	50120
E002	MANUFACTURING	50220
E003	OPERATIONS	50230
F001	MARKETING	42100
F002	SALES	42200
F003	CUSTOMER SUPPORT	42300
G010	LEGAL	60680

RECORD (ROW)

FIELD (COLUMN)   VALUE

Figure 3–13   A simple database table.

the materialized query table definition is based. (Prior to Version 8.1, DB2 UDB supported summary tables, also known as automatic summary tables [ASTs]. Summary tables are now considered to be a special type of MQT whose fullselect contains a GROUP BY clause that summarizes data from the tables referenced in the fullselect.)

Declared temporary tables. User-defined tables used to hold non-persistent data temporarily, on behalf of a single application. Declared temporary tables are explicitly created by an application when they are needed and implicitly destroyed when the application that created them terminates its last database connection.

Typed tables. User-defined tables whose column definitions are based on the attributes of a user-defined structured data type.

Data associated with base tables, materialized query tables, and typed tables is physically stored in tablespaces—the actual tablespace used is specified during the table creation process.

Declared Temporary Tables

Of the five different types of tables available, base tables are the most common type of table used, followed by declared temporary tables. Unlike base tables, whose descriptions and constraints are stored in the system catalog tables of the database to which they belong, declared temporary tables are not persistent and can only be used by the application that creates them—and only for the life of the application. When the application that creates a declared temporary table terminates, the rows of the table are deleted, and the description of the table is dropped. Whereas base tables are created with the CREATE TABLE SQL statement, declared temporary tables are created with the DECLARE GLOBAL TEMPORARY TABLE statement.

 Before an application can create and use a declared temporary table, a user temporary tablespace must be defined for the database the application will be working with.

A Word about Schemas

Schemas are objects that are used to logically classify and group other objects in the database. And because schemas are objects themselves, they have privileges associated with them that allow the schema owner to control which users can create, alter, and drop objects within them.

Most objects in a database are named using a two-part naming convention. The first (leftmost) part of the name is called the *schema name* or *qualifier* and the second (rightmost) part is called the *object name*. Syntactically, these two parts are concatenated and delimited with a period (for example, HR.EMPLOYEE). Each time an object that can be qualified by a schema name is created, it is assigned to the schema that is provided with its name. (If no schema name is provided, the object is assigned to the default schema, which is usually the user ID of the individual that created the object.) Some schema names, such as the names assigned to the four schemas that are implicitly created when a database is created (SYSIBM, SYSCAT, SYSSTAT, and SYSFUN) are reserved and cannot be used. Schemas are usually created implicitly when other objects are created. (When a new database is created, all users are granted IMPLICIT_SCHEMA privileges. This allows any user to create objects in any schema that is not already in existence.) However, schemas can be created explicitly as well.

So how does this apply to storage objects such as buffer pools and tablespaces? Unlike database objects, which will always be assigned a schema name either implicitly or explicitly, storage objects *cannot* be assigned to a schema. Thus, if you attempt to provide a schema with a buffer pool name or tablespace name when attempting to create either of these objects, the creation process will fail.

Obtaining Information About Existing Tablespaces

As with other objects, whenever a tablespace object is created, information about that tablespace is recorded in the system catalog. As a result, you can obtain specific information about any tablespace in a database by querying the appropriate system catalog tables or system catalog views. You can also obtain information about all tablespaces that have been created for a particular database by executing the LIST TABLESPACES command. The syntax for this command is:

```
LIST TABLESPACES
<SHOW DETAIL>
```

If this command is executed without the SHOW DETAIL option specified, the following information will be displayed for every tablespace that has been created for a database:

➤ The internal ID that was assigned to the tablespace when it was created.

➤ The name that has been assigned to the tablespace.

➤ Indication that the tablespace is an SMS tablespace or a DMS tablespace.

➤ The type of data the tablespace is designed to hold (i.e., regular data, long/large object data, system temporary, or user temporary data).

➤ The current state of the tablespace. (Table 3–2 contains a list of the tablespace states available).

Table 3–2 Tablespace States and Their Corresponding Hexadecimal Values	
Tablespace State	**Hexadecimal Value**
Normal	0x0
Quiesced:SHARE	0x1
Quiesced:UPDATE	0x2
Quiesced:EXCLUSIVE	0x4
Load pending	0x8
Delete pending	0x10
Backup pending	0x20
Roll-forward recovery in progress	0x40
Roll-forward recovery pending	0x80
	(continues)

Table 3–2 Tablespace States and Their Corresponding Hexadecimal Values (Continued)	
Restore pending	0x100
Recovery pending (no longer used)	0x100
Disable pending	0x200
Reorg in progress	0x400
Backup in progress	0x800
Storage must be defined	0x1000
Restore in progress	0x2000
Offline and not accessible	0x4000
Drop pending	0x8000
Storage may be defined	0x2000000
StorDef is in "Final" state	0x4000000
StorDef was changed prior to roll forward recovery	0x8000000
DMS rebalancer is active	0x10000000
Tablespace deletion in progress	0x20000000
Tablespace creation in progress	0x40000000
A single tablespace can be in more than one state at a given point in time. If this is the case, multiple tablespace state hexadecimal values will be ANDed together to keep track of the multiple states. The Get Tablespace State command (db2tbst) can be used to obtain the tablespace state associated with any given hexadecimal value.	

On the other hand, if the LIST TABLESPACES command is executed with the SHOW DETAIL option specified, the information produced when the LIST TABLESPACES command is executed with no option specified will be returned along with the following additional information:

➤ The total number of pages the tablespace is designed to hold. For DMS tablespaces, this is the sum of all pages available from all containers associated with the tablespace. For SMS tablespaces, this is the total amount of file space currently being used.

➤ The number of pages in the tablespace that user data can be stored in. For DMS tablespaces, this number is calculated by subtracting the number of pages required for overhead from the total number of pages available. For SMS tablespaces, this number is equal to the total number of pages the tablespace is designed to hold.

➤ The number of pages in the tablespace that already contain data. (For SMS tablespaces, this value is equal to the total number of pages the tablespace is designed to hold.)

➤ The number of pages in the tablespace that are currently empty. (This information is only applicable for DMS tablespaces.)

➤ The number of pages that mark the current "high water mark" or "end" of the tablespace's address space (i.e., the page number of the first free page following the last allocated extent of the tablespace). (This information is only applicable to DMS tablespaces.)

➤ The size, in bytes, that one page of data in the tablespace will occupy.

➤ The number of pages that are contained in one extent of the tablespace.

➤ The number of pages of data that will be read from the tablespace in advance of those pages currently being referenced by a query, in anticipation that they will be needed to resolve the query (prefetched).

➤ The number of containers used by the tablespace.

➤ The earliest point in time that may be specified if a point-in-time roll-forward recovery operation is to be performed on the tablespace.

➤ The ID of the tablespace that caused the tablespace being queried to be placed in the "Load Pending" or "Delete Pending" state. (This information is only displayed if the tablespace being queried has been placed in the "Load Pending" or "Delete Pending" state.)

➤ The ID of the object that caused the tablespace being queried to be placed in the "Load Pending" or "Delete Pending" state. (This information is only displayed if the tablespace being queried has been placed in the "Load Pending" or "Delete Pending" state.)

➤ The number of users and/or applications that have placed the tablespace in a "Quiesced" (restricted access) state. (This information is only displayed if the tablespace being queried has been placed in the "Quiesced:SHARE", "Quiesced:UPDATE", or "Quiesced:EXCLUSIVE" state.)

➤ The ID of the tablespaces and objects that caused the tablespace being queried to be placed in a "Quiesced" state. (This information is only displayed if the number of users and/or applications that have placed the tablespace in a "Quiesced" state is greater than zero.)

So, if you wanted to obtain basic information about all tablespaces that have been created for a database named SAMPLE, you could do so by executing a `LIST TABLESPACES` command that looks like this:

```
LIST TABLESPACES
```

And when this `LIST TABLESPACES` command is executed, you might see output that looks something like this:

```
                 Tablespaces for Current Database

Tablespace ID                        = 0
Name                                 = SYSCATSPACE
Type                                 = System managed space
Contents                             = Any data
State                                = 0x0000
   Detailed explanation:
      Normal

Tablespace ID                        = 1
Name                                 = TEMPSPACE1
Type                                 = System managed space
Contents                             = System Temporary data
State                                = 0x0000
   Detailed explanation:
      Normal

Tablespace ID                        = 2
Name                                 = USERSPACE1
Type                                 = System managed space
Contents                             = Any data
State                                = 0x0000
   Detailed explanation:
      Normal

Tablespace ID                        = 3
Name                                 = PAYROLL_TS
Type                                 = Database managed space
Contents                             = Any data
State                                = 0x0000
   Detailed explanation:
      Normal
```

Obtaining Information about the Containers Used by a Tablespace

Just as you can obtain information about the tablespaces that have been created for a particular database, you can obtain information about the containers that are used to physically hold tablespace data. You obtain information about the containers that are associated with a particular tablespace by executing the LIST TABLESPACE CONTAINERS command. The syntax for this command is:

```
LIST TABLESPACE CONTAINERS FOR [TablespaceID]
<SHOW DETAIL>
```

where:

>   *TablespaceID*   Identifies the internal identification number that
>   has been assigned to the tablespace that con-
>   tainer information is to be obtained for. (This
>   identification number can be obtained by execut-
>   ing the LIST TABLESPACES command.)

If this command is executed without the SHOW DETAIL option specified, the
following information will be displayed for every tablespace that has been
created for a database:

➤ The internal ID that was assigned to the container when it was associated
  with the tablespace specified.

➤ The name that was used to reference the container when it was assigned to
  the tablespace specified.

➤ Indication that the container is a directory (path) container, a file container, or a device container.

On the other hand, if the LIST TABLESPACE CONTAINERS command is executed with the SHOW DETAIL option specified, the information produced
when the LIST TABLESPACE CONTAINERS command is executed with no
option specified will be returned along with the following additional information:

➤ The total number of pages the tablespace container is designed to hold.
  (For SMS tablespaces, this is the total amount of storage space that is currently being used by the container.)

➤ The number of pages in the tablespace container that user data can be
  stored in. For DMS tablespaces, this number is calculated by subtracting
  the number of pages needed for overhead from the total number of pages
  available. For SMS tablespaces, this value is equal to the total number of
  pages the tablespace container is designed to hold.

➤ An indication of whether the container is accessible.

So, if you wanted to obtain detailed information about the containers that are
associated with the tablespace (in a database named SAMPLE) whose internal ID is 0, you could do so by executing a LIST TABLESPACE CONTAINERS
command that looks like this:

```
LIST TABLESPACE CONTAINERS FOR 0 SHOW DETAIL
```

And when this LIST TABLESPACE CONTAINERS command is executed, you
might see output that looks something like this:

```
                Tablespace Containers for Tablespace 0

Container ID       = 0
Name               = C:\DB2\NODE0000\SQL00002\SQLT0000.0
Type               = Path
Total pages        = 4424
Useable pages      = 4424
Accessible         = Yes
```

It is important to note that if, for some reason, a particular tablespace container becomes inaccessible (Accessible = No), the tablespace associated with that container will automatically be placed in the "Offline" state. When the issue that made the container inaccessible is resolved, the associated tablespace can be returned to the "Normal" state by executing the ALTER TABLESPACE SQL statement with the SWITCH ONLINE option specified. For more information about the SWITCH ONLINE option of the ALTER TABLESPACE statement, or to obtain more information about the ALTER TABLESPACE statement, refer to the *IBM DB2 Universal Database, Version 8 SQL Reference Volume 2* product documentation.

Practice Questions

Question 1

Which of the following can NOT have their default location changed when the CREATE DATABASE command is issued?

- ○ A. SYSCATSPACE
- ○ B. USERSPACE1
- ○ C. TEMPSPACE1
- ○ D. IBMDEFAULTBP

Question 2

Given the following command:

```
CREATE DATABASE test_db
ON /home/db2data/db_dir
USER TABLESPACE MANAGED BY DATABASE
     USING (FILE '/home/db2data/user' 16777215)
```

How many SMS tablespaces are created?

- ○ A. 1
- ○ B. 2
- ○ C. 3
- ○ D. 4

Question 3

Which of the following characteristics of a Database Managed Space (DMS) tablespace cannot be modified with the ALTER TABLESPACE statement?

- ○ A. Buffer pool
- ○ B. Container size
- ○ C. Extent size
- ○ D. Prefetch size

Question 4

Assuming roll-forward recovery has been enabled for a database, what state will a tablespace be in immediately after it has been restored, but before a roll-forward recovery operation completes?

○ A. Normal
○ B. Restore in progress
○ C. Roll-forward recovery pending
○ D. Roll-forward recovery in progress

Question 5

Which of the following is NOT true about SMS tablespaces?

○ A. Space for the objects in the tablespace is not allocated until required.
○ B. A table can be split across multiple tablespaces.
○ C. Only directory containers can be used for storage.
○ D. A container's size cannot be changed with the ALTER TABLESPACE statement once the tablespace has been created.

Question 6

Given the following statement:

```
CREATE TABLESPACE tbsp1
    MANAGED BY DATABASE USING (FILE 'tbsp1a' 200M,
                               FILE 'tbsp1b' 300M,
                               FILE 'tbspc1c' 400M)
```

Which of the following commands would be used to add 100 megabytes of storage space to each container associated with tablespace TBSP1?

○ A. ALTER TABLESPACE tbsp1 EXPAND (ALL CONTAINERS 100M)
○ B. ALTER TABLESPACE tbsp1 RESIZE (ALL CONTAINERS 100M)
○ C. ALTER TABLESPACE tbsp1 EXTEND (ALL CONTAINERS 100M)
○ D. ALTER TABLESPACE tbsp1 ENLARGE (ALL CONTAINERS 100M)

Question 7

Given the following set of commands/statements:

```
CREATE DATABASE test_db ON C:\
CATALOG TABLESPACE MANAGED BY SYSTEM
    USING ('C:\tspaces\system')
TEMPORARY TABLESPACE MANAGED BY SYSTEM
    USING ('C:\tspaces\temp')
CREATE BUFFERPOOL TEMP_BP IMMEDIATE SIZE 100
```

How many buffer pools are associated with the database TEST_DB?

- ○ A. 0
- ○ B. 1
- ○ C. 2
- ○ D. 3

Question 8

Which of the following commands is used to determine the number of containers associated with a tablespace?

- ○ A. GET TABLESPACES
- ○ B. LIST TABLESPACES
- ○ C. LIST TABLESPACE CONTAINERS SHOW DETAIL
- ○ D. LIST TABLESPACES SHOW DETAIL

Question 9

Which of the following must occur in order to separate long data from regular data and index data?

- ○ A. Use SMS tablespaces
- ○ B. Use DMS tablespaces
- ○ C. Use a combination of SMS and DMS tablespaces
- ○ D. Use two different tablespace containers; one for index and regular data, one for long data

Question 10

Which of the following is NOT granted to PUBLIC when a database is created?

○ A. CONNECT
○ B. CREATETAB
○ C. LOAD
○ D. IMPLICIT_SCHEMA

Question 11

Which of the following is NOT true about DMS tablespaces?

○ A. Storage space is pre-allocated.
○ B. A table can be split across multiple tablespaces.
○ C. Only directory containers can be used for storage.
○ D. A container's size can be changed with the ALTER TABLESPACE statement once the tablespace has been created.

Question 12

Which of the following SQL statements will create a buffer pool named MY_BP and make it available for use right away (provided the amount of memory required is available)?

○ A. CREATE BUFFERPOOL my_bp SIZE 20000
○ B. CREATE BUFFERPOOL my_bp DEFERRED SIZE 20000
○ C. CREATE BUFFERPOOL my_bp INSTANTLY SIZE 20000
○ D. CREATE BUFFERPOOL my_bp IMMEDIATE SIZE 20000

Question 13

Given the following statements:

```
CREATE REGULAR TABLESPACE reg_data
MANAGED BY DATABASE USING (FILE 'C:\tsp\datafile1' 5000)

CREATE REGULAR TABLESPACE ind_data
MANAGED BY DATABASE USING (FILE 'C:\tsp\datafile2' 2000)

CREATE TABLE tab1 (col1  INTEGER NOT NULL PRIMARY KEY, col2
CHAR(100))
IN reg_data INDEX IN ind_data
```

In which of the following locations will data for table TAB1 be stored?

○ A. COL1 and COL2 data values will be stored in the file C:\tsp\datafile1;
       Index data values for COL1 will be stored in the file C:\tsp\datafile2

○ B. COL1 and COL2 data values will be stored in the file C:\tsp\datafile2;
       Index data values for COL1 will be stored in the file C:\tsp\datafile1

○ C. COL1 and COL2 data values will be stored in the file C:\tsp\datafile1;
       Index data values for COL1 will be stored in the file C:\tsp\datafile1

○ D. COL1 and COL2 data values will be stored in the file C:\tsp\datafile2;
       Index data values for COL1 will be stored in the file C:\tsp\datafile2

Question 14

What is the purpose of the Configuration Advisor?

○ A. Configure communications
○ B. Recommend/make changes to configuration parameters
○ C. Recommend tablespace/container configurations
○ D. Recommend buffer pool/tablespace configurations

Answers

Question 1

The correct answer is **D**. When a database is created, one buffer pool named IBMDEFAULTBP is created. The following three tablespaces are also created and associated with the buffer pool named IBMDEFAULTBP as part of the database initialization process:

➤ A *catalog* tablespace named SYSCATSPACE1, which is used to store the system catalog tables and views associated with the database.

➤ A *user* tablespace named USERSPACE1, which is used to store all user-defined objects (such as tables, indexes, and so on) along with user data.

➤ A *temporary* tablespace named TEMPSPACE1, which is used to store temporary tables that might be created in order to resolve a query.

By default, these tablespaces are SMS tablespaces that use the subdirectory under the directory in which the database is created as their storage containers. However, different tablespace types (DMS vs. SMS) and different storage containers can be specified for each.

Question 2

The correct answer is **B**. Again, by default, when a database is created, three SMS tablespaces are created and assigned the names SYSCATSPACE, USERSPACE1, and TEMPSPACE1. This particular CREATE DATABASE command overrides this default behavior and makes the USERSPACE1 tablespace a DMS tablespace; therefore, this database will have two SMS tablespaces and one DMS tablespace.

Question 3

The correct answer is **C**. The ALTER TABLESPACE statement can be used to change the size of one or more DMS tablespace containers, change the buffer pool a particular tablespace is associated with, or change the prefetch size of a particular tablespace. Extent sizes, on the other hand, can only be specified when a tablespace is created; the only way in which you can change the extent size of a tablespace is by dropping (deleting) the tablespace and recreating it with the new extent size. (Note: With SMS tablespaces, you cannot make any changes related to containers.)

Question 4

The correct answer is **D**. Once a tablespace has been restored from a backup image, it will be placed in "Roll-forward recovery pending" state until a roll-forward recovery operation is started. Once the roll-forward operation is started, it is placed in "Roll-forward recovery in progress" state until the roll-forward recovery completes. At that time, it will be returned to "Normal" state (provided the restoration and roll-forward recovery operations executed successfully).

Question 5

The correct answer is **B**. A single table cannot be split across multiple tablespaces unless DMS tablespaces are used; when DMS tablespaces are used, regular data can reside in one tablespace, index data can reside in a second tablespace, and long data can reside in a third tablespace.

Question 6

The correct answer is **C**. When the ALTER TABLESPACE ... EXTEND (ALL CONTAINERS ...) statement is executed, the size of all containers associated with the DMS tablespace specified is expanded by the number of bytes specified. (The ALTER TABLESPACE ... REDUCE (ALL CONTAINERS ...) statement has the opposite effect—the size of all containers associated with the tablespace specified are reduced by the specified number of bytes; the ALTER TABLESPACE ... RESIZE (ALL CONTAINERS ...) statement sets all containers associated with the tablespace specified to the size specified.)

Question 7

The correct answer is **C**. When a new database is created, one buffer pool (named IBMDEFAULTBP) is created as part of the database creation process. And in this example, the CREATE BUFFERPOOL statement creates a second buffer pool named TEMP_BP.

Question 8

The correct answer is **D**. You can obtain information about all tablespaces that have been created for a particular database by executing the LIST TABLESPACES command. You can find out how many containers are associated with a particular tablespace by executing the LIST TABLESPACES command with the SHOW DETAIL option specified.

Question 9

The correct answer is **B**. When DMS tablespaces are used, regular data can reside in one tablespace, index data can reside in a second tablespace, and long data can reside in a third tablespace. When SMS tablespaces are used, regular data, index data, and long data must reside in the same tablespace. The number of containers used has no impact on whether or not data for a single table can be split across multiple tablespaces.

Question 10

The correct answer is **C**. When a new database is created, the following authorities and privileges are granted:

➤ DBADM authority, along with CONNECT, QUIESCE_CONNECT, CREATETAB, BINDADD, CREATE_NOT_FENCED, CREATE _EXTERNAL_ROUTINE, IMPLICIT_SCHEMA, and LOAD privileges, are granted to the user who created the database.

➤ USE privilege on the tablespace USERSPACE1 is granted to the group PUBLIC.

➤ CONNECT, CREATETAB, BINDADD, and IMPLICIT_SCHEMA privileges are granted to the group PUBLIC.

➤ SELECT privilege on each system catalog table is granted to the group PUBLIC.

➤ EXECUTE privilege on all procedures found in the SYSIBM schema is granted to the group PUBLIC.

➤ EXECUTE WITH GRANT privilege on all functions found in the SYS-FUN schema is granted to the group PUBLIC.

➤ BIND and EXECUTE privileges for each successfully bound utility are granted to the group PUBLIC.

Question 11

The correct answer is **C**. Only system files or raw devices can be used as containers for DMS tablespaces.

Question 12

The correct answer is **D**. If the IMMEDIATE clause is specified with the CRE-ATE BUFFERPOOL statement, the buffer pool will be created immediately unless the amount of memory required is not available, in which case a warning message will be generated and the buffer pool creation process will behave as if the DEFERRED clause were specified.

Question 13

The correct answer is **A**. The CREATE TABLE statement specifies that data for all columns is to reside in the DMS tablespace named REG_DATA (whose storage container is the file C:\tsp\datafile1) and index data for the index that gets created to support the COL1 primary key is to reside in the DMS tablespace IND_DATA (whose storage container is the file C:\tsp\datafile2).

Question 14

The correct answer is **B**. The Configuration Advisor is designed to capture specific information about your database environment and recommend/make changes to configuration parameters based on the information provided.

4

Database Access

Seventeen percent (17%) of the DB2 UDB V8.1 for Linux, UNIX, and Windows Database Administration certification exam (Exam 701) and thirteen percent (13%) of the DB2 UDB V8.1 for Linux, UNIX, and Windows Database Administration certification upgrade exam (Exam 706) is designed to test your ability to create tables, indexes, and views as well as to test your knowledge of when and how the different constraints that are available with DB2 Universal Database should be used in a table definition. The questions that make up this portion of the exam are intended to evaluate the following:

➤ Your knowledge of the basic objects that are used to manage data in a database (tables, indexes, and views).

➤ Your knowledge of the various constraints available and your ability to identify when and how NOT NULL constraints, default constraints, check constraints, unique constraints, referential integrity constraints, and informational constraints should be used.

➤ Your ability to create base tables that contain one or more constraints.

➤ Your ability to identify how operations performed on the parent table of a referential integrity constraint are reflected in the child table of the constraint.

➤ Your ability to create indexes, including clustering indexes.

➤ Your ability to create views.

➤ Your ability to automate routine maintenance operations using the Task Center.

This chapter is designed to introduce you to the various constraints that are available with DB2 Universal Database, and to show you how to construct

DB2 UDB base tables, indexes, and views. This chapter is also designed to remind you how the Task Center can be used to automate routine maintenance operations.

Terms you will learn:

Table

Record

Field

Value

Base tables

Result tables

Materialized Query tables

Declared Temporary tables

Typed tables

Constraints

NOT NULL Constraint

Default Constraint

Check Constraint

Unique Constraint

Referential Integrity Constraint

Referential Constraint

Foreign Key Constraint

Unique Key

Primary Key

Foreign Key

Parent Key

Parent Table

Parent Row

Dependent Table

Child Table

Dependent Row

Child Row

Descendant Table

Descendant Row

Referential Cycle

Self-Referencing Table

Self-Referencing Row

ON UPDATE NO ACTION

ON UPDATE RESTRICT

ON DELETE CASCADE

ON DELETE SET NULL

ON DELETE NO ACTION

ON DELETE RESTRICT

Informational Constraint

SET INTEGRITY

"Check Pending"

Exception Table

Create Table Wizard

CREATE TABLE

Identity Columns

Index

CREATE INDEX

Clustering Indexes

Multidimensional Clustering (MDC) Table Indexes

Type-1 Indexes

Type-2 Indexes

"Next-Key Locking"

View

CREATE VIEW

WITH CHECK OPTION

Task Center

Techniques you will master:

Understanding how NOT NULL constraints, default constraints, check constraints, unique constraints, referential constraints, and informational constraints are defined.

Understanding what NOT NULL constraints, default constraints, check constraints, unique constraints, referential constraints, and informational constraints are used for.

Recognizing how operations performed on the parent table of a referential integrity constraint are reflected in the child table of the constraint.

Understanding how a base table is created.

Understanding how an index is created, as well as what indexes are used for.

Understanding how clustering indexes can be used to improve query performance.

Recognizing the difference between Type-1 and Type-2 indexes.

Understanding how a view is created, as well as what views are used for.

Recognizing how the Task Center is used to automate routine operations.

Tables

If you have had the opportunity to work with a relational database in the past, you are probably already aware that a table is a logical database object that acts as the main repository in a database. Tables present data as a collection of unordered rows with a fixed number of columns. Each column contains values of the same data type or one of its subtypes, and each row contains a set of values for every column available. Usually, the columns in a table are logically related, and additional relationships can be defined between two or more tables. The storage representation of a row is called a *record*, the storage representation of a column is called a *field*, and each intersection of a row and column is called a *value*. Figure 4–1 shows the structure of a simple database table.

DEPARTMENT TABLE

DEPTID	DEPTNAME	COSTCENTER
A000	ADMINISTRATION	10250
B001	PLANNING	10820
C001	ACCOUNTING	20450
D001	HUMAN RESOURCES	30200
E001	R & D	50120
E002	MANUFACTURING	50220
E003	OPERATIONS	50230
F001	MARKETING	42100
F002	SALES	42200
F003	CUSTOMER SUPPORT	42300
G010	LEGAL	60680

RECORD (ROW)

FIELD (COLUMN)

VALUE

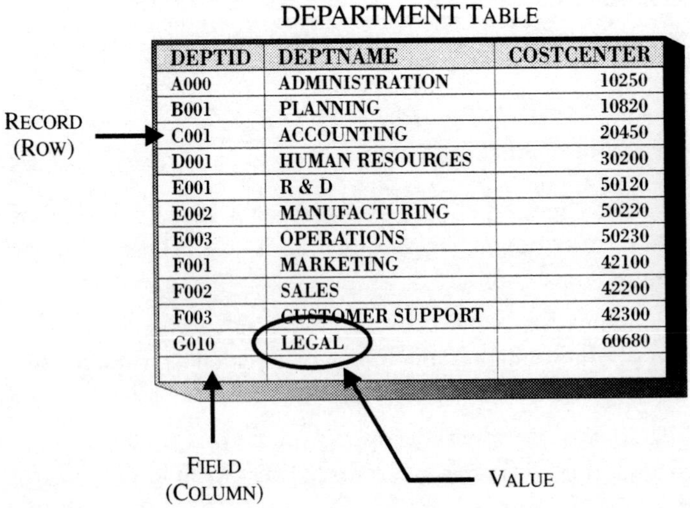

Figure 4–1 A simple database table.

With DB2 UDB, five types of tables are available:

Base tables. User-defined tables designed to hold persistent user data.

Result tables. DB2 Database Manager-defined tables populated with rows retrieved from one or more base tables in response to a query.

Materialized query tables. User-defined tables whose definition is based on the result of a query, and whose data is in the form of pre-computed results that are taken from one or more tables upon which the materialized query table definition is based. (Prior to Version 8.1, DB2 UDB supported summary tables, also known as automatic summary tables [ASTs]. Summary tables are now considered to be a special type of MQT whose fullselect contains a GROUP BY clause that summarizes data from the tables referenced in the fullselect.)

Declared temporary tables. User-defined tables used to hold non-persistent data temporarily, on behalf of a single application. Declared temporary tables are explicitly created by an application when they are needed and implicitly destroyed when the application that created them terminates its last database connection.

Typed tables. User-defined tables whose column definitions are based on the attributes of a user-defined structured data type.

Because tables are the basic data objects used to store information, many are often created for a single database.

Constraints

Within most businesses, data often must adhere to a certain set of rules and restrictions. For example, companies typically have a specific format and numbering sequence they use when generating purchase orders. With DB2 UDB *constraints* can be used to enforce data integrity and ensure that data that is added to a database adheres to one or more business rules. Essentially, constraints are rules that govern how data values can be added to a table, as well as how those values can be modified once they have been added. The following types of constraints are available:

➤ NOT NULL constraints

➤ Default constraints

➤ Check constraints

➤ Unique constraints

➤ Referential integrity constraints

➤ Informational Constraints

Constraints are usually defined during table creation; however, constraints can also be added to existing tables using the ALTER TABLE SQL statement.

NOT NULL Constraints

With DB2 UDB, null values (not to be confused with empty strings) are used to represent missing or unknown data and/or states. And by default, every column in a table will accept a null value. This allows you to add records to a table when not all of the values that pertain to the record are known. However, there may be times when this behavior is unacceptable (for example, a tax identification number might be required for every employee that works for a company). When such a situation arises, the NOT NULL constraint can be used to ensure that a particular column in a base table is never assigned a null value; once the NOT NULL constraint has been defined for a column, any operation that attempts to place a null value in that column will fail. Figure 4–2 illustrates how the NOT NULL constraint is used.

Because NOT NULL constraints are associated with a specific column in a base table, they are usually defined during the table creation process.

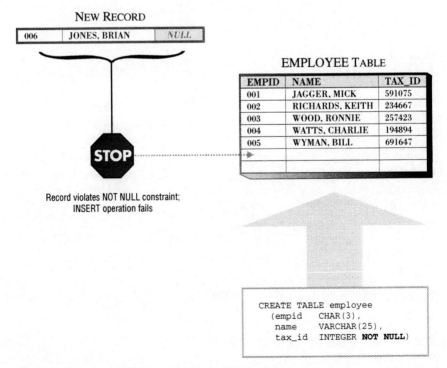

Figure 4–2 How the NOT NULL constraint prevents null values.

Default Constraints

Just as there are times when it is objectionable to accept a null value, there may be times when it is desirable to have the system provide a specific value for you (for example, you might want to automatically assign the current date to a particular column whenever a new record is added to a table). In these situations, the default constraint can be used to ensure that a particular column in a base table is assigned a predefined value (unless that value is overridden) each time a record is added to the table. The predefined value provided could be null (if the NOT NULL constraint has not been defined for the column), a user-supplied value compatible with the column's data type, or a value furnished by the DB2 Database Manager. Table 4–1 shows the default values that can be provided by the DB2 Database Manager for the various DB2 UDB data types available.

Figure 4–3 illustrates how the default constraint is used.

Table 4–1 DB2 Database Manager-Supplied Default Values		
Column Data Type	Definition	Default Value Provided
Small integer	SMALLINT	0
Integer	INTEGER or INT	0
Decimal	DECIMAL, DEC, NUMERIC, or NUM	0
Single-precision floating point	REAL or FLOAT	0
Double-precision floating point	DOUBLE, DOUBLE PRECISION, or FLOAT	0
Fixed-length character string	CHARACTER or CHAR	A string of blank characters
Varying-length character string	CHARACTER VARYING, CHAR VARYING, or VARCHAR	A zero-length string
Long varying-length character string	LONG VARCHAR	A zero-length string
Fixed-length double-byte character string	GRAPHIC	A string of blank characters
Varying-length double-byte character string	VARGRAPHIC	A zero-length string
Long varying-length double-byte character string	LONG VARGRAPHIC	A zero-length string *(continues)*

Table 4–1 DB2 Database Manager-Supplied Default Values (Continued)		
Column Data Type	**Definition**	**Default Value Provided**
Date	DATE	The system date at the time the record is added to the table. (When a date column is added to an existing table, existing rows are assigned the date January 01, 0001.)
Time	TIME	The system time at the time the record is added to the table. (When a time column is added to an existing table, existing rows are assigned the time 00:00:00.)
Timestamp	TIMESTAMP	The system date and time (including microseconds) at the time the record is added to the table. (When a timestamp column is added to an existing table, existing rows are assigned a timestamp that corresponds to January 01, 0001 - 00:00:00.000000)
Binary large object	BLOB	A zero-length string
Character large object	CLOB	A zero-length string
Double-byte character large object	DBCLOB	A zero-length string
Any distinct user-defined data type		The default value provided for the built-in data type the distinct user-defined data type is based on (typecast to the distinct user-defined data type).

Adapted from Table 2 on page 51 of the *DB2 SQL Reference—Volume 2* manual

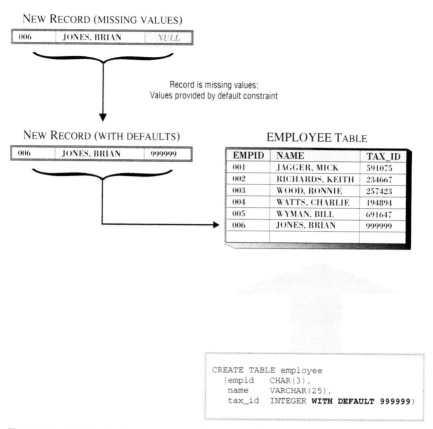

NEW RECORD (MISSING VALUES)

| 006 | JONES, BRIAN | *NULL* |

Record is missing values:
Values provided by default constraint

NEW RECORD (WITH DEFAULTS)

| 006 | JONES, BRIAN | 999999 |

EMPLOYEE TABLE

EMPID	NAME	TAX_ID
001	JAGGER, MICK	591075
002	RICHARDS, KEITH	234667
003	WOOD, RONNIE	257423
004	WATTS, CHARLIE	194894
005	WYMAN, BILL	691647
006	JONES, BRIAN	999999

```
CREATE TABLE employee
(empid   CHAR(3),
 name    VARCHAR(25),
 tax_id  INTEGER WITH DEFAULT 999999)
```

Figure 4–3   How the default constraint is used to provide data values.

Like NOT NULL constraints, default constraints are associated with a specific column in a base table and are usually defined during the table creation process.

Check Constraints

Sometimes it is desirable to control what values will be accepted for a particular item and what values will not (for example, a company might decide that all nonexempt employees must be paid, at a minimum, the federal minimum wage). When this is the case, the logic needed to determine whether a value is acceptable can be incorporated directly into the data entry program being used to collect the data. A better way to achieve the same objective is by defining a check constraint for the column in the base table that is to receive the data value. A check constraint (also known as a *table check constraint*) can be used to ensure that a particular column in a base table is never assigned an unacceptable value. Once a check constraint has been defined for a column, any operation that attempts to place a value in that column that does not meet specific criteria will fail.

Check constraints are comprised of one or more predicates (which are connected by the keywords AND or OR) that collectively are known as the *check condition*. This check condition is then compared with the data value provided and the result of this comparison is returned as the value "TRUE", "FALSE", or "Unknown". If the check constraint returns the value "TRUE", the value is acceptable, and is added to the database. If, on the other hand, the check constraint returns the value "FALSE" or "Unknown", the operation attempting to place the value in the database fails, and all changes made by that operation are backed out of the database. However, it is important to note that when the results of a particular operation are rolled back because of a check constraint violation, the transaction that invoked that operation is not terminated, and other operations within that transaction are unaffected. Figure 4–4 illustrates how a simple check constraint is used.

Like NOT NULL constraints and default constraints, check constraints are associated with a specific column in a base table and are usually defined during the table creation process.

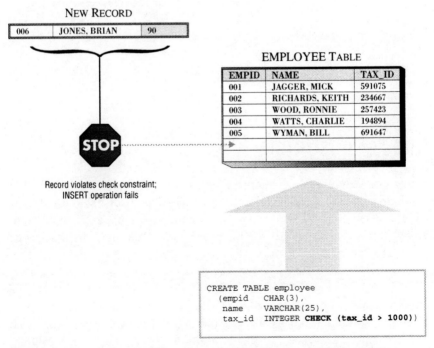

Figure 4–4   How a check constraint is used to control what values are accepted by a column.

Unique Constraints

By default, records that are added to a base table can have the same values assigned to any of the columns available any number of times. As long as the records stored in the table do not contain information that should not be duplicated, this kind of behavior is acceptable. However, there are times when certain pieces of information that make up a record should be unique (for example, if an employee identification number is assigned to each individual that works for a particular company, each number used should be unique—two employees should never be assigned the same employee identification number). In these situations, the unique constraint can be used to ensure that the value(s) assigned to one or more columns when a record is added to a base table are always unique; once a unique constraint has been defined for one or more columns, any operation that attempts to place duplicate values in those columns will fail. Figure 4–5 illustrates how the unique constraint is used.

Unlike NOT NULL constraints, default constraints, and check constraints, which are only associated with single columns in a base table, unique constraints can be associated with an individual column or with a group of columns. However, like the other constraints, unique constraints are usually defined during the table creation process.

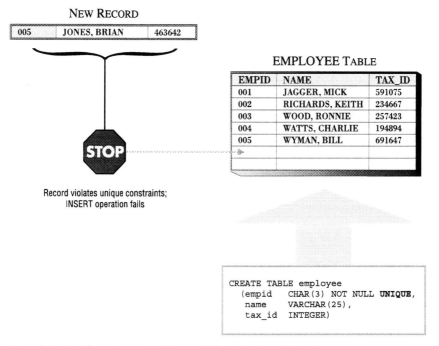

Figure 4–5   How the unique constraint prevents the duplication of data values.

Regardless of when a unique constraint is defined, when it is created the DB2 Database Manager looks to see if an index for the columns the unique constraint refers to already exists. If so, that index is marked as being unique and system-required. If not, an appropriate index is created and marked as being unique and system-required. This index is then used to enforce uniqueness whenever new records are added to the column(s) the unique constraint was defined for.

 Although a unique, system-required index is used to enforce a unique constraint, there is a distinction between defining a unique constraint and creating a unique index. Although both enforce uniqueness, a unique index allows nullable columns and generally cannot be used in a referential constraint. (The value "NULL" means a field's value is undefined *and* distinct from any other value, *including* other NULL values.)

A *primary key*, which we will look at next, is a special form of unique constraint. Only one primary key is allowed per table, and every column that is used to define a primary key must be assigned the NOT NULL constraint. In addition to ensuring that every record added to a table has some unique characteristic, primary keys allow tables to participate in referential constraints.

A table can have any number of unique constraints; however, a table cannot have more than one unique constraint defined on the same set of columns. And because unique constraints are enforced by indexes, all the limitations that apply to indexes (for example, a maximum of 16 columns with a combined length of 255 bytes is allowed; none of the columns used can have a large object or long character string data type, etc.) apply to unique constraints.

Referential Integrity Constraints

If you've had the opportunity to design a database in the past, you are probably aware that data normalization is a technique used to ensure that there is only one way to get to a fact stored in a database. Data normalization is possible because two or more individual base tables can have some type of relationship with one another, and information stored in related base tables can be combined, if necessary, using a join operation. Data normalization is also where referential integrity constraints come into play; referential integrity constraints (also known as referential constraints and foreign key constraints) are used to define required relationships between two base tables.

To understand how referential constraints work, it helps to look at an example. Suppose you own a small auto parts store and you use a database to keep track of the inventory you have on hand. Many of the parts you stock will only work with a particular "make" and "model" of an automobile; therefore, your database has one table named MAKE to hold make information and another table named MODEL to hold model information. Since these two tables are related (every model must belong to a make), a referential constraint can be used to ensure that every record that is stored in the MODEL table has a corresponding record in the MAKE table; the relationship between these two tables is established by comparing values that are to be added to the "MAKE" column of the MODEL table (known as the *foreign key* of the *child table*) with the values that currently exist for the set of columns

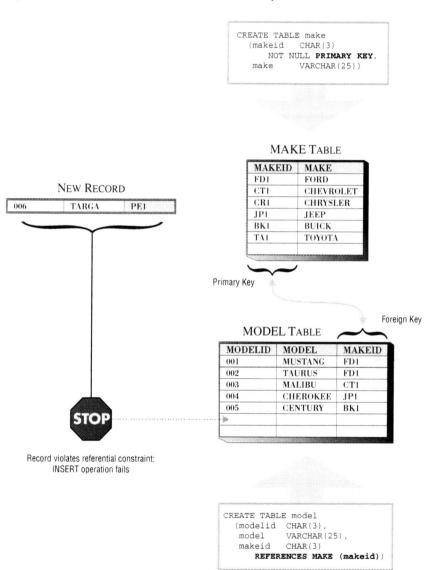

Figure 4–6 How a referential constraint is used to define a relationship between two tables.

that make up the primary key of the MAKE table (known as the *parent key* of the *parent table*). To create the referential constraint just described, you would define a primary key, using one or more columns in the MAKE table, and you would define a foreign key for one or more corresponding columns in the MODEL table that reference the MAKE table's primary key. Assuming a column named MAKEID is used to create the primary key for the MAKE table and a column also named MAKEID is used to create the foreign key for the MODEL table, the referential constraint created would look something like the one shown in Figure 4–6.

In this example, a single column is used to define the parent key and the foreign key of the referential constraint. However, as with unique constraints, multiple columns can be used to define the parent key and the foreign key of a referential constraint.

> The name of the column(s) used to create the foreign key of a referential constraint name do not have to be the same as the column(s) used to create the primary key of the constraint (as was the case in the previous example). However, the data types used for the column(s) that make up the primary key and the foreign key of a referential constraint must be identical.

As you can see, referential constraints are more complex than NOT NULL constraints, default constraints, check constraints, and unique constraints. In fact, they can be so complex that a set of special terms are used to identify the individual components that can make up a single referential constraint. You may already be familiar with some of them; the complete list of terms used can be seen in Table 4–2.

Table 4–2 DB2 UDB Referential Integrity Constraint Terminology	
Term	**Meaning**
Unique key	A column or set of columns in which every row of values is different from the values of all other rows.
Primary key	A special unique key that does not accept null values.
Foreign key	A column or set of columns in a child table whose values must match those of a parent key in a parent table.
Parent key	A primary key or unique key in a parent table that is referenced by a foreign key in a referential constraint.
Parent table	A table that contains a parent key of a referential constraint. (A table can be both a parent table and a dependent table of any number of referential constraints.)
Parent row	A row in a parent table that has at least one matching row in a dependent table.

(continues)

Table 4–2	DB2 UDB Referential Integrity Constraint Terminology (Continued)
Term	**Meaning**
Dependent or child table	A table that contains at least one foreign key that references a parent key in a referential constraint. (A table can be both a dependent table and a parent table of any number of referential constraints.)
Dependent or child row	A row in a dependent table that has at least one matching row in a parent table.
Descendent table	A dependent table or a descendent of a dependent table.
Descendent row	A dependent row or a descendent of a dependent row.
Referential cycle	A set of referential constraints defined in such a way that each table in the set is a descendent of itself.
Self-referencing table	A table that is both a parent table and a dependent table in the same referential constraint. (The constraint is known as a self-referencing constraint.)
Self-referencing row	A row that is a parent of itself.

The primary reason referential constraints are created is to guarantee that data integrity is maintained whenever one table object references another. As long as a referential constraint is in effect, the DB2 Database Manager guarantees that, for every row in a child table that has a value in any column that is part of a foreign key, there is a corresponding row in the parent table. So what happens when an SQL operation attempts to manipulate data in a way that would violate a referential constraint? To answer this question, let's look at what could compromise data integrity if the checks and balances provided by a referential constraint were not in place:

➤ An insert operation could add a row of data to a child table that does not have a matching value in the corresponding parent table. (For example, using our MAKE / MODEL scenario, a record could be added to the MODEL table that does not have a corresponding value in the MAKE table.)

➤ An update operation could change an existing value in a child table such that it no longer has a matching value in the corresponding parent table. (For example, a record could be changed in the MODEL table so that it no longer has a corresponding value in the MAKE table.)

➤ An update operation could change an existing value in a parent table, leaving rows in a child table with values that no longer match those in the parent table. (For example, a record could be changed in the MAKE table, leaving records in the MODEL table that no longer have a corresponding MAKE value.)

➤ A delete operation could remove a value from a parent table, leaving rows in a child table with values that no longer match those in the parent table. (For example, a record could be removed from the MAKE table, leaving records in the MODEL table that no longer have a corresponding MAKE value.)

The DB2 Database Manager can either prohibit ("restrict") these types of operations from being performed on tables that are part of a referential constraint or it can attempt to carry out these actions in a way that will safeguard data integrity. In either case, DB2 UDB uses a set of rules to control the operation's behavior. Each referential constraint has its own set of rules (which consist of an Insert Rule, an Update Rule, and a Delete Rule), and the way a particular rule will function can be specified as part of the referential constraint creation process.

The Insert Rule for Referential Constraints

The Insert Rule guarantees that a value can never be inserted into the foreign key of a child table unless a matching value can be found in the corresponding parent key of the associated parent table. Any attempt to insert records into a child table that violates this rule will result in an error, and the insert operation will fail. In contrast, no checking is performed when records are added to the parent key of the parent table.

The Insert Rule for a referential constraint is implicitly created when the referential constraint itself is created. Figure 4–7 illustrates how a row that conforms to the Insert Rule for a referential constraint is successfully added to a child table; Figure 4–8 illustrates how a row that violates the Insert Rule causes an insert operation to fail.

It is important to note that because the Insert Rule exists, records must be inserted in the parent key of the parent table before corresponding records can be inserted into the child table. (Going back to our MAKE/MODEL example, this means that a record for a new MAKE must be added to the MAKE table *before* a record that references the new MAKE can be added to the MODEL table.)

The Update Rule for Referential Constraints

The Update Rule controls how update operations performed against either table (child or parent) participating in a referential constraint are to be processed. The following two types of behaviors are possible, depending on how the Update Rule is defined:

> **ON UPDATE NO ACTION.** This definition ensures that whenever an update operation is performed on either table in a referential

constraint, the value for the foreign key of each row in the child table will have a matching value in the parent key of the corresponding parent table; however, the value may not be the same as it was before the update operation occurred.

ON UPDATE RESTRICT. This definition ensures that whenever an update operation is performed on the parent table of a referential constraint, the value for the foreign key of each row in the child table will have the same matching value in the parent key of the parent table it had before the update operation was performed.

```
CREATE TABLE color
   (c_id    INTEGER
         NOT NULL PRIMARY KEY,
    c_desc  CHAR(20))
```

```
CREATE TABLE object
   (o_id   CHAR(2),
    o_desc CHAR(20),
    c_id   INTEGER
         REFERENCES COLOR (c_id))
```

COLOR TABLE

C_ID	C_DESC
1	RED/ROJO
2	BLUE/AZUL
3	YELLOW/AMARILLO
4	BLACK/NEGRO
5	WHITE/BLANCO

OBJECT TABLE

O_ID	O_DESC	C_ID
01	STOP SIGN	1
02	SKY	2
03	SCHOOL BUS	3
04	COAL	4

Primary Key

Foreign Key

INSERT OPERATION (CHILD TABLE)

```
INSERT INTO object VALUES('05', 'SNOW', 5)
```

INSERT operation successful

COLOR TABLE

C_ID	C_DESC
1	RED/ROJO
2	BLUE/AZUL
3	YELLOW/AMARILLO
4	BLACK/NEGRO
5	WHITE/BLANCO

OBJECT TABLE

O_ID	O_DESC	C_ID
01	STOP SIGN	1
02	SKY	2
03	SCHOOL BUS	3
04	COAL	4
05	SNOW	5

Figure 4–7 An insert operation that conforms to the Insert Rule of a referential constraint.

```
CREATE TABLE color
   (c_id    INTEGER
       NOT NULL PRIMARY KEY,
   c_desc   CHAR(20))
```

```
CREATE TABLE object
   (o_id    CHAR(2),
   o_desc CHAR(20),
   c_id    INTEGER
       REFERENCES COLOR (c_id))
```

COLOR TABLE

C_ID	C_DESC
1	RED/ROJO
2	BLUE/AZUL
3	YELLOW/AMARILLO
4	BLACK/NEGRO
5	WHITE/BLANCO

OBJECT TABLE

O_ID	O_DESC	C_ID
01	STOP SIGN	1
02	SKY	2
03	SCHOOL BUS	3
04	COAL	4

Primary Key

Foreign Key

INSERT OPERATION (CHILD TABLE)

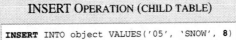

```
INSERT INTO object VALUES('05', 'SNOW', 8)
```

STOP

The value **8** does not exist in the primary key;
INSERT operation fails

COLOR TABLE

C_ID	C_DESC
1	RED/ROJO
2	BLUE/AZUL
3	YELLOW/AMARILLO
4	BLACK/NEGRO
5	WHITE/BLANCO

OBJECT TABLE

O_ID	O_DESC	C_ID
01	STOP SIGN	1
02	SKY	2
03	SCHOOL BUS	3
04	COAL	4

Figure 4–8 An insert operation that violates the Insert Rule of a referential constraint.

Figure 4–9 illustrates how the Update Rule is enforced when the ON UPDATE NO ACTION definition is used; Figure 4–10 illustrates how the Update Rule is enforced when the ON UPDATE RESTRICT definition is used.

Like the Insert Rule, the Update Rule for a referential constraint is implicitly created when the referential constraint itself is created. If no Update Rule defi-

```
CREATE TABLE color
    (c_id    INTEGER
        NOT NULL PRIMARY KEY,
    c_desc  CHAR(20))
```

```
CREATE TABLE object
    (o_id    CHAR(2),
    o_desc  CHAR(20),
    c_id    INTEGER
        REFERENCES COLOR (c_id)
        ON UPDATE NO ACTION)
```

COLOR TABLE

C_ID	C_DESC
1	RED/ROJO
2	BLUE/AZUL
3	YELLOW/AMARILLO
4	BLACK/NEGRO
5	WHITE/BLANCO

OBJECT TABLE

O_ID	O_DESC	C_ID
01	STOP SIGN	1
02	SKY	2
03	SCHOOL BUS	3
04	COAL	4

Primary Key   Foreign Key

UPDATE OPERATION (PARENT TABLE)

UPDATE color SET c_id = c_id - 1

UPDATE operation successful

COLOR TABLE

C_ID	C_DESC
0	RED/ROJO
1	BLUE/AZUL
2	YELLOW/AMARILLO
3	BLACK/NEGRO
4	WHITE/BLANCO

OBJECT TABLE

O_ID	O_DESC	C_ID
01	STOP SIGN	1
02	SKY	2
03	SCHOOL BUS	3
04	COAL	4

Figure 4–9   How the ON UPDATE NO ACTION Update Rule of a referential constraint is enforced.

nition is provided when the referential constraint is defined, the ON UPDATE NO ACTION definition is used as the default. Regardless of which form of the Update Rule is used, if the condition of the rule is not met, the update operation will fail, an error message will be displayed, and any changes made to the data in either table participating in the referential constraint will be backed out.

The Delete Rule for Referential Constraints

The Delete Rule controls how delete operations performed against the parent table of a referential constraint are to be processed. The following

```
CREATE TABLE color
   (c_id    INTEGER
       NOT NULL PRIMARY KEY,
    c_desc  CHAR(20))
```

```
CREATE TABLE object
   (o_id    CHAR(2),
    o_desc  CHAR(20),
    c_id    INTEGER
       REFERENCES COLOR (c_id)
       ON UPDATE RESTRICT)
```

COLOR TABLE

C_ID	C_DESC
1	RED/ROJO
2	BLUE/AZUL
3	YELLOW/AMARILLO
4	BLACK/NEGRO
5	WHITE/BLANCO

OBJECT TABLE

O_ID	O_DESC	C_ID
01	STOP SIGN	1
02	SKY	2
03	SCHOOL BUS	3
04	COAL	4

Primary Key   Foreign Key

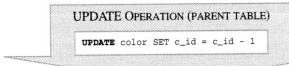

UPDATE OPERATION (PARENT TABLE)

```
UPDATE color SET c_id = c_id - 1
```

Operation violates ON UPDATE RESTRICT rule;
UPDATE operation fails

COLOR TABLE

C_ID	C_DESC
1	RED/ROJO
2	BLUE/AZUL
3	YELLOW/AMARILLO
4	BLACK/NEGRO
5	WHITE/BLANCO

OBJECT TABLE

O_ID	O_DESC	C_ID
01	STOP SIGN	1
02	SKY	2
03	SCHOOL BUS	3
04	COAL	4

Figure 4–10   How the ON UPDATE RESTRICT Update Rule of a referential constraint is enforced.

four types of behaviors are possible, depending on how the Delete Rule is defined:

ON DELETE CASCADE. This definition ensures that when a parent row is deleted from the parent table of a referential constraint, all dependent rows in the child table that have matching primary key values in their foreign key are deleted as well.

ON DELETE SET NULL. This definition ensures that when a parent row is deleted from the parent table of a referential constraint, all dependent rows in the child table that have matching primary key values in their foreign key are located and their foreign key values are changed to null. Other values for the dependent row are not affected.

ON DELETE NO ACTION. This definition ensures that whenever a delete operation is performed on the parent table of a referential constraint, the value for the foreign key of each row in the child table will have a matching value in the parent key of the parent table (after all other referential constraints have been applied).

ON DELETE RESTRICT. This definition ensures that whenever a delete operation is performed on the parent table of a referential constraint, the value for the foreign key of each row in the child table will have a matching value in the parent key of the parent table (before any other referential constraints are applied).

Figure 4–11 illustrates how the Delete Rule is enforced when the ON DELETE CASCADE definition is used; Figure 4–12 illustrates how the Delete Rule is enforced when the ON DELETE SET NULL definition is used; Figure 4–13 illustrates how the Delete Rule is enforced when the ON DELETE NO ACTION definition is used; and Figure 4–14 illustrates how the Delete Rule is enforced when the ON DELETE RESTRICT definition is used.

Like the Insert Rule and the Update Rule, the Delete Rule for a referential constraint is implicitly created when the referential constraint itself is created. If no Delete Rule definition is provided when the referential constraint is defined, the ON DELETE NO ACTION definition is used as the default. No matter which form of the Delete Rule is used, if the condition of the rule is not met, an error message will be displayed, and the delete operation will fail.

If the ON DELETE CASCADE Delete Rule is used and the deletion of a parent row in a parent table causes one or more dependent rows to be deleted from the corresponding child table, the delete operation is said to have been *propagated* to the child table. In such a situation, the child table is said to be *delete-connected* to the parent table. Because a delete-connected child table can also be the parent table in another referential constraint, a delete operation that is propagated to one child table can, in turn, be propagated to another child table, and so on. Thus, the deletion of one parent row from a single parent table can result in the deletion of several hundred rows from any num-

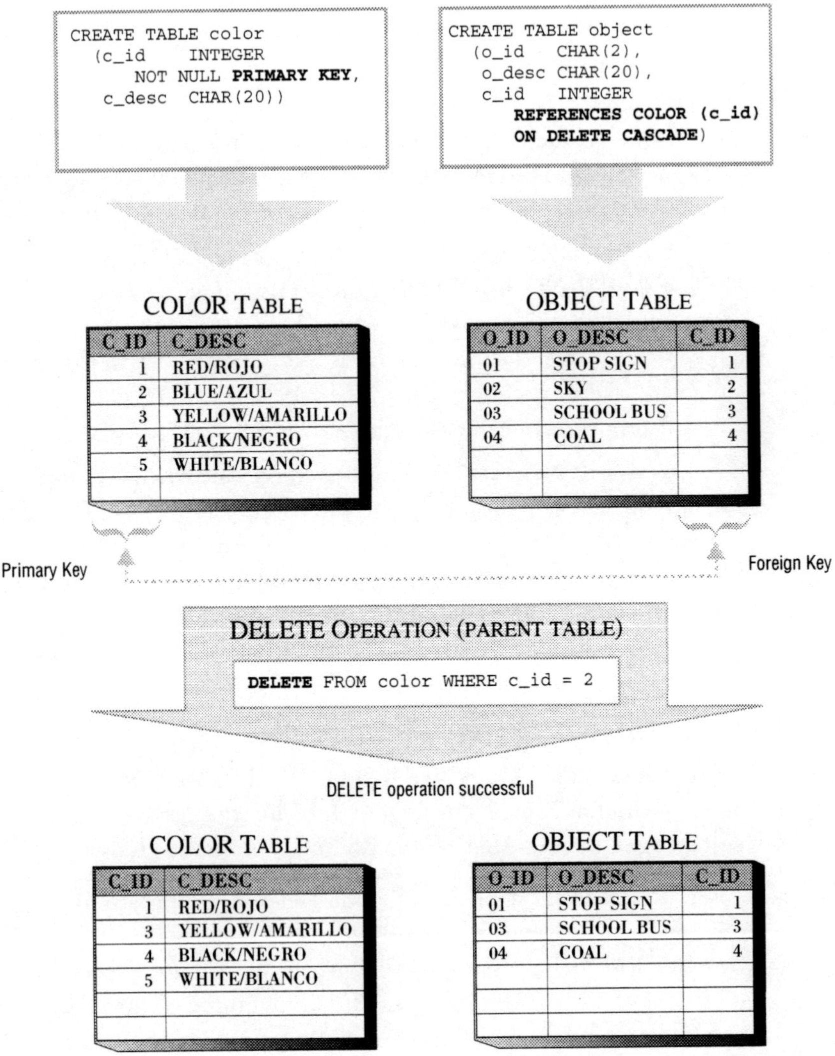

```
CREATE TABLE color
   (c_id    INTEGER
      NOT NULL PRIMARY KEY,
    c_desc  CHAR(20))
```

```
CREATE TABLE object
   (o_id    CHAR(2),
    o_desc  CHAR(20),
    c_id    INTEGER
      REFERENCES COLOR (c_id)
      ON DELETE CASCADE)
```

COLOR Table

C_ID	C_DESC
1	RED/ROJO
2	BLUE/AZUL
3	YELLOW/AMARILLO
4	BLACK/NEGRO
5	WHITE/BLANCO

OBJECT Table

O_ID	O_DESC	C_ID
01	STOP SIGN	1
02	SKY	2
03	SCHOOL BUS	3
04	COAL	4

Primary Key   Foreign Key

DELETE Operation (parent table)

```
DELETE FROM color WHERE c_id = 2
```

DELETE operation successful

COLOR Table

C_ID	C_DESC
1	RED/ROJO
3	YELLOW/AMARILLO
4	BLACK/NEGRO
5	WHITE/BLANCO

OBJECT Table

O_ID	O_DESC	C_ID
01	STOP SIGN	1
03	SCHOOL BUS	3
04	COAL	4

Figure 4–11   How the ON DELETE CASCADE Delete Rule of a referential constraint is enforced.

```
CREATE TABLE color
   (c_id    INTEGER
     NOT NULL PRIMARY KEY,
     c_desc  CHAR(20))
```

```
CREATE TABLE object
   (o_id    CHAR(2),
    o_desc CHAR(20),
    c_id    INTEGER
       REFERENCES COLOR (c_id)
       ON DELETE SET NULL)
```

COLOR TABLE

C_ID	C_DESC
1	RED/ROJO
2	BLUE/AZUL
3	YELLOW/AMARILLO
4	BLACK/NEGRO
5	WHITE/BLANCO

OBJECT TABLE

O_ID	O_DESC	C_ID
01	STOP SIGN	1
02	SKY	2
03	SCHOOL BUS	3
04	COAL	4

Primary Key

Foreign Key

DELETE OPERATION (PARENT TABLE)

```
DELETE FROM color WHERE c_id = 2
```

DELETE operation successful

COLOR TABLE

C_ID	C_DESC
1	RED/ROJO
3	YELLOW/AMARILLO
4	BLACK/NEGRO
5	WHITE/BLANCO

OBJECT TABLE

O_ID	O_DESC	C_ID
01	STOP SIGN	1
02	SKY	-
03	SCHOOL BUS	3
04	COAL	4

Figure 4–12   How the ON DELETE SET NULL Delete Rule of a referential constraint is enforced.

```
CREATE TABLE color
   (c_id     INTEGER
       NOT NULL PRIMARY KEY,
    c_desc   CHAR(20))
```

```
CREATE TABLE object
   (o_id    CHAR(2),
    o_desc  CHAR(20),
    c_id    INTEGER
       REFERENCES COLOR (c_id)
       ON DELETE NO ACTION)
```

COLOR Table

C_ID	C_DESC
1	RED/ROJO
2	BLUE/AZUL
3	YELLOW/AMARILLO
4	BLACK/NEGRO
5	WHITE/BLANCO

OBJECT Table

O_ID	O_DESC	C_ID
01	STOP SIGN	1
02	SKY	2
03	SCHOOL BUS	3
04	COAL	4

Primary Key

Foreign Key

DELETE Operation (parent table)

```
DELETE FROM color WHERE c_id = 2
```

Operation violates ON DELETE NO ACTION rule;
DELETE operation fails

COLOR Table

C_ID	C_DESC
1	RED/ROJO
2	BLUE/AZUL
3	YELLOW/AMARILLO
4	BLACK/NEGRO
5	WHITE/BLANCO

OBJECT Table

O_ID	O_DESC	C_ID
01	STOP SIGN	1
02	SKY	2
03	SCHOOL BUS	3
04	COAL	4

Figure 4–13   How the ON DELETE NO ACTION Delete Rule of a referential constraint is enforced.

```
CREATE TABLE color
    (c_id    INTEGER
        NOT NULL PRIMARY KEY,
    c_desc  CHAR(20))
```

```
CREATE TABLE object
    (O_id    CHAR(2),
    o_desc  CHAR(20),
    c_id    INTEGER
        REFERENCES COLOR (c_id)
        ON DELETE RESTRICT)
```

COLOR TABLE

C_ID	C_DESC
1	RED/ROJO
2	BLUE/AZUL
3	YELLOW/AMARILLO
4	BLACK/NEGRO
5	WHITE/BLANCO

OBJECT TABLE

O_ID	O_DESC	C_ID
01	STOP SIGN	1
02	SKY	2
03	SCHOOL BUS	3
04	COAL	4

Primary Key   Foreign Key

DELETE OPERATION (PARENT TABLE)

```
DELETE FROM color WHERE c_id = 2
```

Operation violates ON DELETE RESTRICT rule;
DELETE operation fails

COLOR TABLE

C_ID	C_DESC
1	RED/ROJO
2	BLUE/AZUL
3	YELLOW/AMARILLO
4	BLACK/NEGRO
5	WHITE/BLANCO

OBJECT TABLE

O_ID	O_DESC	C_ID
01	STOP SIGN	1
02	SKY	2
03	SCHOOL BUS	3
04	COAL	4

Figure 4–14   How the ON DELETE RESTRICT Delete Rule of a referential constraint is enforced.

ber of tables, depending on how tables are delete-connected. Therefore, the ON DELETE CASCADE Delete Rule should be used with extreme caution when a hierarchy of referential constraints permeates a database.

 Only users with System Administrator (SYSADM) authority, System Control (SYSC-TRL) authority, CONTROL privilege on the parent table, or REFERENCES privilege on the parent table are allowed to create referential constraints between two tables.

Informational Constraints

The DB2 Database Manager automatically enforces all of the constraints that we have looked at so far whenever new data values are added to a table or existing data values are modified. As you might imagine, if a large number of constraints have been defined, a large amount of system overhead can be required to enforce those constraints—particularly when large amounts of data are loaded into a table.

If an application is coded in such a way that it validates data before inserting it into a DB2 UDB database, it may be more efficient to create one or more *informational constraints*, instead of creating any of the "normal" constraints available. Unlike other constraints, informational constraints are not enforced during insert and update processing. However, the DB2 SQL optimizer will use information provided by an informational constraint when considering the best access plan to use to resolve a query. As a result, an informational constraint may result in better query performance even though the constraint itself will not be used to validate data. Figure 4–15 illustrates how a simple informational constraint is used.

Because informational constraints are not enforced, you must ensure that all data added to or modified in a table that has one or more informational constraints defined conforms to each constraint's definition. Therefore, the best case for using informational constraints is when it can be guaranteed that the only applications that are allowed to perform insert and update operations against the table containing the informational constraint are applications that have been designed to check data values for validity.

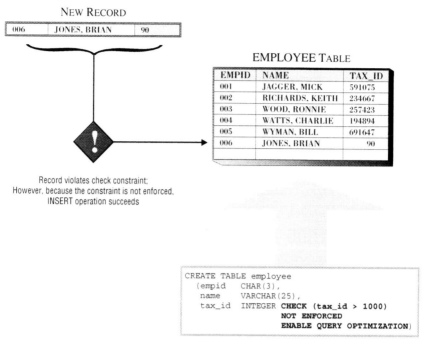

Figure 4–15 begins below.

```
CREATE TABLE employee
  (empid   CHAR(3),
   name    VARCHAR(25),
   tax_id  INTEGER CHECK (tax_id > 1000)
                   NOT ENFORCED
                   ENABLE QUERY OPTIMIZATION)
```

Figure 4–15   How an informational constraint is used.

Temporarily Suspending Constraint Checking with the SET INTEGRITY SQL Statement

Although constraints provide a means of ensuring that some level of integrity is maintained as data is manipulated within a base table, their enforcement can prevent some types of operations from executing successfully. For example, suppose you want to bulk-load 10,000 rows of data into a base table using the LOAD utility. If the data that is to be loaded contains values that will violate a constraint defined for the table the data is to be loaded into, the load operation will fail. Or suppose you wish to add a new constraint to an existing table that already contains several hundred rows of data. If one or more rows in the table contain data values that violate the constraint you wish to add, any attempt to add the constraint will fail. In situations like these, it can be advantageous to suspend constraint checking just long enough to perform the desired operation. However, when constraint checking is suspended, at some point it must be resumed, and at that time, rows in the table that cause a constraint to be violated must be located and dealt with.

Constraint checking for a table can be suspended temporarily by executing the SET INTEGRITY SQL statement. When used to suspend constraint checking, the syntax for the simplest form of this statement is:

```
SET INTEGRITY FOR [TableName ,...] OFF <AccessMode>
```

where:

TableName	Identifies the name of one or more base tables that constraint checking is to be temporarily suspended for.
AccessMode	Specifies whether or not the table(s) specified can be accessed in read-only mode while constraint checking is suspended. (Valid values include NO ACCESS and READ ACCESS—if no access mode is specified, NO ACCESS is used as the default.)

So, if you wanted to temporarily suspend constraint checking for a table named EMPLOYEES and deny read-only access to that table while constraint checking is turned off, you could do so by executing a SET INTEGRITY statement that looks something like this:

```
SET INTEGRITY FOR EMPLOYEES OFF
```

When constraint checking is suspended for a particular table, that table is placed in "Check Pending" state to indicate that it contains data that has not been checked (and that may not be free of constraint violations). While a table is in "Check Pending" state, it cannot be used in insert, update, or delete operations, nor can it be used by any DB2 UDB utility that needs to perform these types of operations. In addition, indexes cannot be created for a table while it is in "Check Pending" state, and data stored in the table can only be retrieved if the access mode specified when the SET INTEGRITY statement was used to place the table in "Check Pending" state allows read-only access.

Just as one form of the SET INTEGRITY statement is used to temporarily suspend constraint checking, another form is used to resume it. In this case, the syntax for the simplest form of the SET INTEGRITY statement is:

```
SET INTEGRITY FOR [TableName] IMMEDIATE CHECKED FOR
EXCEPTION [IN [TableName] USE [ExceptionTable] ,...]
```

or

```
SET INTEGRITY FOR [[TableName] [ConstraintType] ,...]
IMMEDIATE UNCHECKED
```

where:

TableName	Identifies the name of one or more base tables that suspended constraint checking is to be resumed for as well as one or more base tables where all rows that are in violation of a referential constraint or a check constraint are to be copied from.
ExceptionTable	Identifies the name of a base table where all rows that are in violation of a referential constraint or a check constraint are to be copied to.
ConstaintType	Identifies the type of constraint checking that is to be resumed. (Valid values include: FOREIGN KEY, CHECK, DATALINK RECONCILE PENDING, MATERIALIZED QUERY, GENERATED COLUMN, STAGING, and ALL. If no value is specified, constraint checking for ALL constraints defined for the table specified is resumed.)

NOTE Although basic syntax is presented for most of the SQL statements covered in this chapter, the actual syntax supported may be much more complex. To view the complete syntax for a specific SQL statement or to obtain more information about a particular statement, refer to the *IBM DB2 Universal Database, Version 8 SQL Reference Volume 2* product documentation.

Thus, if you wanted to resume constraint checking for the EMPLOYEES table that constraint checking was suspended for in the previous example, you could do so by executing a SET INTEGRITY statement that looks something like this:

```
SET INTEGRITY FOR EMPLOYEES
IMMEDIATE CHECKED
```

When this particular form of the SET INTEGRITY statement is executed, the table named EMPLOYEES is taken out of the "Check Pending" state, and each row of data stored in the table is checked for constraint violations. If an offensive row is found, constraint checking is stopped, and the EMPLOYEES table is returned to the "Check Pending" state. However, if this form of the SET INTEGRITY statement is executed:

```
SET INTEGRITY FOR EMPLOYEES
IMMEDIATE CHECKED
FOR EXCEPTION IN EMPLOYEES USE BAD_ROWS
```

each row found that violates one or more of the constraints that have been defined for the EMPLOYEES table will be copied to a table named BAD_ROWS, where it can be corrected and copied back to the EMPLOY-EES table if so desired. And finally, if this form of the SET INTEGRITY statement is executed:

```
SET INTEGRITY FOR EMPLOYEES ALL
IMMEDIATE UNCHECKED
```

the table named EMPLOYEES is taken out of the "Check Pending" state, and no constraint checking is performed. However, this is a very hazardous thing to do and should only be done if you have some independent means of ensuring that the EMPLOYEES table does not contain data that violates one or more constraints defined for the EMPLOYEES table.

You can determine whether or not constraint checking has been performed for a table (and if so, how) by examining the CONST_CHECKED column of the SYSCAT.TABLES system catalog table. This column contains encoded constraint checking information for each table that has been defined for the database. (Remember, information about each database object created is recorded in the database's system catalog.)

Creating Tables

Like many of the other database objects available, tables can be created using a GUI tool that is accessible from the Control Center. In this case, the tool is the Create Table Wizard, and it can be activated by selecting the appropriate action from the *Tables* menu found in the Control Center. Figure 4–16 shows the Control Center menu items that must be selected to activate the Create Table Wizard; Figure 4–17 shows how the first page of the Create Table Wizard might look after its input fields have been populated.

Tables can also be created using the CREATE TABLE SQL statement. However, the CREATE TABLE statement is probably the most complex SQL statement available (in fact, over 60 pages of the DB2 UDB SQL Reference manual are devoted to this statement alone). Because this statement is so complex, its syntax can be quite intimidating. Fortunately, you do not have to know all the nuances of the CREATE TABLE statement to pass the DB2 UDB V8.1 for Linux, UNIX, and Windows Database Administration certification exam (Exam 701) or the DB2 UDB V8.1 for Linux, UNIX, and Windows Database Administration certification upgrade exam (Exam 706). Still, you do need to know the basics, and the remainder of this section is devoted to

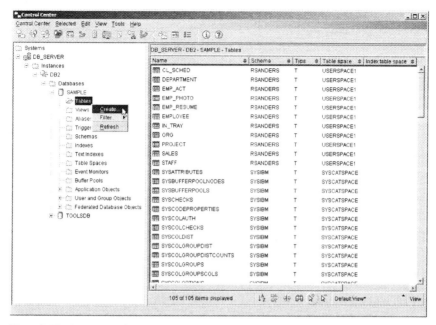

Figure 4–16   Invoking the Create Table Wizard from the Control Center.

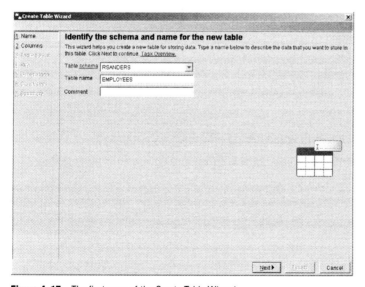

Figure 4–17   The first page of the Create Table Wizard.

the CREATE TABLE statement and to the syntax you need to be familiar with. With that said, let's begin by taking a look at the simplest form of the CREATE TABLE SQL statement.

In its simplest form, the syntax for the CREATE TABLE SQL statement is:

```
CREATE TABLE [TableName] ( [Element] ,...)
<IN [TablespaceName]>
<INDEX IN [TablespaceName]>
<LONG IN [TablespaceName]>
```

where:

TableName	Identifies the name to be assigned to the table to be created. (A table name must be unique within the schema the table is to be defined in.)
Element	Identifies one or more columns, unique/primary key constraints, referential constraints, and/or check constraints to be included in the table definition. The syntax used for defining each of these elements varies according to the element being defined.
TablespaceName	Identifies the tablespace that the table and its regular data, indexes, and/or long data/large object data is to be stored in. (Regular data, indexes, and long/large object data can only be stored in separate tablespaces if DMS tablespaces are used.)

The basic syntax used to define a column is:

```
[ColumnName] [DataType]
<NOT NULL>
<WITH DEFAULT <[DefaultValue] | CURRENT DATE |
CURRENT TIME | CURRENT TIMESTAMP>>
<UniqueConstraint>
<CheckConstraint>
<ReferentialConstraint>
```

where:

ColumnName	Identifies the unique name to be assigned to the column to be created.
DataType	Identifies the data type (built-in or user-defined) to be assigned to the column to be created; the data type specified determines the kind of data values that can be stored in the column. (Table 4–1 contains a list of the data type definitions that are valid.)

DefaultValue	Identifies the value to be provided for the column in the event no value is supplied for the column when an insert or update operation is performed against the table.
UniqueConstraint	Identifies a unique or primary key constraint to be associated with the column.
CheckConstraint	Identifies a check constraint to be associated with the column.
ReferentialConstraint	Identifies a referential constraint to be associated with the column.

The syntax used to create a unique or primary key constraint as part of a column definition is:

```
<CONSTRAINT [ConstraintName]> [UNIQUE | PRIMARY KEY]
```

where:

ConstraintName	Identifies the unique name to be assigned to the constraint to be created.

The syntax used to create a check constraint as part of a column definition is:

```
<CONSTRAINT [ConstraintName]> CHECK ( [CheckCondition] )
<ENFORCED | NOT ENFORCED>
<ENABLE QUERY OPTIMIZATION | DISABLE QUERY OPTIMIZATION>
```

where:

ConstraintName	Identifies the unique name to be assigned to the constraint to be created.
CheckCondition	Identifies a condition or test that must evaluate to TRUE before the value provided for the column will actually be stored in the table.

And finally, the syntax used to create a referential constraint as part of a column definition is:

```
<CONSTRAINT [ConstraintName]>
REFERENCES [PKTableName] < ( [PKColumnName] ,...) >
<ON UPDATE [NO ACTION | RESTRICT]>
<ON DELETE [CASCADE | SET NULL | NO ACTION | RESTRICT]>
<ENFORCED | NOT ENFORCED>
<ENABLE QUERY OPTIMIZATION | DISABLE QUERY OPTIMIZATION>
```

where:

ConstraintName	Identifies the unique name to be assigned to the constraint to be created.
PKTableName	Identifies the name of the parent table that is to participate in the referential constraint.
PKColumnName	Identifies the column(s) that make up the parent key of the parent table that is to participate in the referential constraint.

If the NOT ENFORCED clause is specified as part of a constraint's definition, an informational constraint will be created and the constraint will not be enforced during insert and update processing. Furthermore, if the ENABLE QUERY OPTIMIZATION clause is specified, the DB2 SQL optimizer will consider the information provided by the constraint when generating an access plan in response to a query. (When the ENABLE QUERY OPTIMIZATION is used, the constraint will be imposed when SELECT statements are issued against the table and records stored in the table that do not conform to the constraint are not returned.)

So, if you wanted to create a table that had three columns in it, two of which use an integer data type and another that uses a fixed-length character string data type, you could do so by executing a CREATE TABLE SQL statement that looks something like this:

```
CREATE TABLE EMPLOYEES
    (EMPID   INTEGER,
     NAME    CHAR(50)
     DEPT    INTEGER)
```

If you wanted to create the same table such that the EMPID column had both the NOT NULL constraint and a unique constraint associated with it, you could do so by executing a CREATE TABLE statement that looks something like this:

```
CREATE TABLE EMPLOYEES
    (EMPID   INTEGER NOT NULL PRIMARY KEY,
     NAME    CHAR(50)
     DEPT    INTEGER)
```

If you wanted to create the same table such that the DEPT column participates in a referential constraint with the DEPARTMENT table, you could do so by executing a CREATE TABLE statement that looks something like this:

```
CREATE TABLE EMPLOYEES
    (EMPID   INTEGER,
     NAME    CHAR(50)
     DEPT    INTEGER REFERENCES DEPARTMENT (DEPTID))
```

And if you wanted to create the same table such that the EMPID column has an informational constraint, you could do so by executing a CREATE TABLE statement that looks something like this:

```
CREATE TABLE EMPLOYEES
    (EMPID  INTEGER NOT NULL
        CONSTRAINT INF_CS CHECK (EMPID BETWEEN 1 AND 100)
        NOT ENFORCED
        ENABLE QUERY OPTIMIZATION,
    NAME   CHAR(50)
    DEPT   INTEGER)
```

As you can see, a unique constraint, a check constraint, a referential constraint, and/or an informational constraint that involves a single column can be defined as part of that particular column's definition. But what if you needed to define a constraint that encompasses multiple columns in the table? You do this by defining a constraint as another element, rather than as an extension to a single column's definition. The basic syntax used to define a unique constraint as an individual element is:

```
<CONSTRAINT [ConstraintName]> [UNIQUE | PRIMARY KEY]
( [ColumnName] ,...)
```

where:

ConstraintName	Identifies the unique name to be assigned to the constraint to be created.
ColumnName	Identifies one or more columns that are to be part of the unique or primary key constraint to be created.

The syntax used to create a check constraint as an individual element is the same as the syntax used to create a check constraint as part of a column definition:

```
<CONSTRAINT [ConstraintName]> CHECK ( [CheckCondition] )
<ENFORCED | NOT ENFORCED>
<ENABLE QUERY OPTIMIZATION | DISABLE QUERY OPTIMIZATION>
```

where:

ConstraintName	Identifies the unique name to be assigned to the constraint to be created.
CheckCondition	Identifies a condition or test that must evaluate to TRUE before the value provided for the column will actually be stored in the table.

And finally, the syntax used to create a referential constraint as an individual element is:

```
<CONSTRAINT [ConstraintName]>
FOREIGN KEY ( [ColumnName] ,...)
REFERENCES [PKTableName] < ( [PKColumnName] ,...) >
<ON UPDATE [NO ACTION | RESTRICT]>
<ON DELETE [CASCADE | SET NULL | NO ACTION | RESTRICT]>
<ENFORCED | NOT ENFORCED>
<ENABLE QUERY OPTIMIZATION | DISABLE QUERY OPTIMIZATION>
```

where:

ConstraintName	Identifies the unique name to be assigned to the constraint to be created.
ColumnName	Identifies one or more columns that are to be part of the referential constraint to be created.
PKTableName	Identifies the name of the parent table that is to participate in the referential constraint.
PKColumnName	Identifies the column(s) that make up the parent key of the parent table that is to participate in the referential constraint.

Thus, a table that was created by executing a CREATE TABLE statement that looks something like this:

```
CREATE TABLE EMPLOYEES
    (EMPID  INTEGER NOT NULL PRIMARY KEY,
    NAME   CHAR(50)
    DEPT   INTEGER REFERENCES DEPARTMENT (DEPTID))
```

could also be created by executing a CREATE TABLE statement that looks something like this:

```
CREATE TABLE EMPLOYEES
    (EMPID  INTEGER NOT NULL,
    NAME   CHAR(50)
    DEPT   INTEGER,
    PRIMARY KEY (EMPID),
    FOREIGN KEY (DEPT) REFERENCES DEPARTMENT (DEPTID))
```

Identity Columns

Many times, base tables are designed such that a single column will be used to store a unique identifier that represents an individual record (or row).

More often than not, this identifier is a number that is sequentially incremented each time a new record is added to the table. Numbers for such columns can be automatically generated using a *before* trigger, or the DB2 Database Manager can generate a sequence of numbers (or other values) for such a column and assign a value to that column, using the sequence generated, as new records are added.

Before the DB2 Database Manager can generate a sequence of values for a column, that column must be defined as an *identity column*. Identity columns are created by specifying the GENERATED ... AS IDENTITY clause along with one or more of the identity column attributes available as part of the column definition. The syntax used to create an identity column is:

```
[ColumnName] [DataType]
GENERATED <ALWAYS | BY DEFAULT> AS IDENTITY
<(
    <START WITH [1 | StartingValue]>
    <INCREMENT BY [1 | IncrementValue]>
    <NO MINVALUE | MINVALUE [MinValue]>
    <NO MAXVALUE | MAXVALUE [MaxValue]>
    <NO CYCLE | CYCLE>
    <NO CACHE | CACHE 20 | CACHE [CacheSize]>
    <NO ORDER | ORDER>
)>
```

or

```
[ColumnName] [DataType]
GENERATED <ALWAYS | BY DEFAULT> AS (Expression)
```

where:

ColumnName	Identifies the unique name to be assigned to the identity column to be created.
DataType	Identifies the data type (built-in or user-defined) to be assigned to the identity column to be created. (Table 4–1 contains a list of the data type definitions that are valid.)
StartingValue	Identifies the first value that is to be assigned to the identity column created.
IncrementValue	Identifies the interval that is to be used to calculate the next consecutive value that is to be assigned to the identity column created.
MinValue	Identifies the smallest value that can be assigned to the identity column created.

MaxValue	Identifies the largest value that can be assigned to the identity column created.
CacheSize	Identifies the number of values of the identity sequence that are to be preallocated and kept in memory.
Expression	Identifies an expression or user-defined external function that is to be used to generate values for the identity column created.

If the CYCLE clause is specified as part of the identity column's definition, values will continue to be generated for the column after any minimum or maximum value specified has been reached. (After an ascending identity column reaches the maximum value allowed, a minimum value will be generated and the cycle will begin again. Likewise, after a descending identity column reaches the minimum value allowed, a maximum value will be generated and the cycle will repeat itself.) On the other hand, if the NO CYCLE clause is specified or if neither clause is specified, values will not be generated for the column after any minimum or maximum value specified has been reached and any attempt to insert new data into the table will fail.

So, if you wanted to create a table that had a simple identity column in it, you could do so by executing a CREATE TABLE SQL statement that looks something like this:

```
CREATE TABLE EMPLOYEES
    (EMPID   INTEGER GENERATED ALWAYS AS IDENTITY,
     NAME    CHAR(50)
     DEPT    INTEGER)
```

It is important to note that a table can only have one identity column and the data type used by an identity column must be a numeric data type with a scale of 0 (SMALLINT, INTEGER, BIGINT, or DECIMAL) or a user-defined data type that is based on such a data type. All identity columns are implicitly assigned a NOT NULL constraint; identity columns cannot have a default constraint.

Creating Tables That Are Similar to Existing Tables

At times, it may be desirable to create a new table that has the same definition as an existing table. To perform such an operation, you could execute a CREATE TABLE statement that looks identical to the CREATE TABLE statement used to define the original table. Or better still, you could use a special form of the CREATE TABLE statement. The syntax for this form of the CREATE TABLE is:

```
CREATE TABLE [TableName] LIKE [SourceTable]
<[INCLUDING | EXCLUDING] COLUMN DEFAULTS>
<[INCLUDING | EXCLUDING] IDENTITY COLUMN ATTRIBUTES>
```

where:

TableName	Identifies the unique name to be assigned to the table to be created.
SourceTable	Identifies the name of an existing table whose structure is to be used to define the table to be created.

When this form of the CREATE TABLE is executed, the table that is ultimately created will have the same number of columns as the source table specified, and these columns will have the same names, data types, and nullability characteristics as those of the source table. In addition, unless the EXCLUDING COLUMN DEFAULTS option is specified, any default constraints defined for columns in the source table will be copied to the new table as well. However, no other attributes of the source table will be duplicated. Thus, the table that is created will not contain unique constraints, referential constraints, triggers, or indexes that have been defined for the source table used.

A Word about Declared Temporary Tables

Before we look at some more complex examples of the CREATE TABLE statement, another type of table that is commonly used should be mentioned. This type of table is known as a declared temporary table. Unlike base tables, whose descriptions and constraints are stored in the system catalog tables of the database to which they belong, declared temporary tables are not persistent and can only be used by the application that creates them—and only for the life of the application. When the application that creates a declared temporary table terminates, the rows of the table are deleted, and the description of the table is dropped. Whereas base tables are created with the CREATE TABLE SQL statement, declared temporary tables are created with the DECLARE GLOBAL TEMPORARY TABLE statement.

CREATE TABLE SQL Statement Examples

Now that we've seen the basic syntax for the CREATE TABLE statement and have examined some simple examples of the CREATE TABLE statement's use, let's take a look at a few more complex CREATE TABLE statement examples and identify the characteristics of the resulting tables that would be created if each statement shown were executed.

Example 1

If the following CREATE TABLE statement is executed:

```
CREATE TABLE PROJECT
      (PROJNO    CHAR(6) NOT NULL,
      PROJNAME   VARCHAR(24) NOT NULL,
      DEPTNO     SMALLINT,
      BUDGET     DECIMAL(6,2),
      STARTDATE  DATE,
      ENDDATE    DATE)
```

A table named PROJECT will be created as follows:

➤ The first column will be assigned the name PROJNO and will be used to store fixed-length character string data that is six characters in length (for example, 'PROJ01', 'PROJ02', etc.).

➤ The second column will be assigned the name PROJNAME and it will be used to store variable-length character string data that can be up to 24 characters in length (for example, 'DB2 Benchmarks Tool', 'Auto-Configuration Tool', etc.).

➤ The third column will be assigned the name DEPTNO and will be used to store numeric values in the range of –32,768 to +32,767.

➤ The fourth column will be assigned the name BUDGET and will be used to store numerical values that contain both whole and fractional parts. Up to six numbers can be specified—four for the whole number part and two for the fractional part (for example, 1500.00, 2000.50, etc.).

➤ The fifth column will be assigned the name STARTDATE and will be used to store date values.

➤ The sixth column will be assigned the name ENDDATE and will also be used to store date values.

➤ Whenever data is added to the PROJECT table, values must be provided for the PROJNO column and the PROJNAME column. (Null values are not allowed because the NOT NULL constraint was defined for both of these columns.)

➤ The PROJECT table will be created in the tablespace USERSPACE1 (which was not specified but is the default).

Example 2

If the following CREATE TABLE statement is executed:

```
CREATE TABLE SALES
     (PO_NUMBER  INTEGER NOT NULL CONSTRAINT UC1 UNIQUE,
      DATE       DATE NOT NULL WITH DEFAULT),
      OFFICE     CHAR(128) NOT NULL WITH DEFAULT 'HQ',
      AMT        DECIMAL(10,2) NOT NULL CHECK (AMT > 99.99)
     IN MY_SPACE
```

A table named SALES will be created as follows:

➤ The first column will be assigned the name PO_NUMBER (for Purchase Order Number) and will be used to store numeric values in the range of –32,768 to +32,767.

➤ The second column will be assigned the name DATE and will be used to store date values.

➤ The third column will be assigned the name OFFICE and will be used to store fixed-length character string data that can be up to 128 characters in length (for example, 'Baltimore/Washington', 'Dallas/Ft. Worth', etc.).

➤ The fourth column will be assigned the name AMT (for Amount) and will be used to store numerical values that contain both whole and fractional parts. Up to 10 numbers can be specified—eight for the whole number part and two for the fractional part (for example, 15000000.00, 20000000.50, etc.).

➤ Whenever data is added to the SALES table, values must be provided for the PO_NUMBER and the AMT columns. (Null values are not allowed in any column because the NOT NULL constraint was defined for each column; however, default values are provided for two columns.)

➤ Every value provided for the PO_NUMBER column must be unique. (Because a unique constraint named UC1 was created for the PO_NUMBER column.)

➤ An index will automatically be created for the PO_NUMBER column. As data is added to the table, the values provided for the PO_NUMBER column will be added to the index, and the index will be sorted in ascending order (which is the default behavior).

➤ If no value is provided for the DATE column, the system date at the time a row is inserted into the SALES table will be written to the column by default (because a default constraint was created for the DATE column).

➤ If no value is provided for the OFFICE column, the value HQ will be written to the column by default (because a default constraint was created for the OFFICE column).

➤ Every value provided for the AMT column must be greater than or equal to 100.00 (because a check constraint was created for the AMT column).

➤ The SALES table will be created in the tablespace MY_SPACE.

Example 3

If the following CREATE TABLE statements are executed:

```
CREATE TABLE EMPLOYEE
    (EMPID       INT NOT NULL PRIMARY KEY,
     EMP_FNAME   CHAR(30),
     EMP_LNAME   CHAR(30))

CREATE TABLE PAYROLL
    (EMPID        INTEGER,
     WEEKNUMBER   CHAR(3),
     PAYCHECK     DECIMAL(6,2),
    CONSTRAINT FKCONST FOREIGN KEY (EMPID)
       REFERENCES EMPLOYEE(EMPID) ON DELETE CASCADE,
    CONSTRAINT CHK1 CHECK (PAYCHECK > 0 AND WEEKNUMBER
       BETWEEN 1 AND 52))
```

A table named EMPLOYEE will be created as follows:

➤ The first column will be assigned the name EMPID (for Employee ID) and will be used to store numeric values in the range of –32,768 to +32,767.

➤ The second column will be assigned the name EMP_FNAME (for Employee First Name) and will be used to store fixed-length character string data that can be up to 30 characters in length (for example, 'Mark', 'Bob', etc.).

➤ The third column will be assigned the name EMP_LNAME (for Employee Last Name) and will be used to store fixed-length character string data that can be up to 30 characters in length (for example, 'Hay-akawa', 'Jancer', etc.).

➤ Whenever data is added to the EMPLOYEE table, values must be provided for the EMPID column. (Null values are not allowed because the NOT NULL constraint was defined for this column.)

➤ Every value provided for the EMPID column must be unique (because a unique constraint was created for the EMPID column).

➤ An index will automatically be created for the EMPID column. As data is added to the table, the values provided for the EMPID column will be added to the index, and the index will be sorted in ascending order.

➤ The EMPLOYEE table will be created in the tablespace USERSPACE1.

A table named PAYROLL will also be created as follows:

➤ The first column will be assigned the name EMPID and will be used to store numeric values in the range of –32,768 to +32,767.

➤ The second column will be assigned the name WEEKNUMBER and will be used to store fixed-length character string data that can be up to three characters in length (for example, '1', '35', etc.).

➤ The third column will be assigned the name PAYCHECK and will be used to store numerical values that contain both whole and fractional parts. Up to six numbers can be specified—four for the whole number part and two for the fractional part (for example, 1500.00, 2000.50, etc.).

➤ An index will automatically be created for the EMPID column. As data is added to the table, the values provided for the EMPID column will be added to the index, and the index will be sorted in ascending order.

➤ Every value entered in the EMPID column must have a matching value in the EMPID column of the EMPLOYEE table created earlier (because a referential constraint in which the EMPID column of the EMPLOYEE table is the parent key and the EMPID column of the PAYROLL table is the foreign key has been created—this referential constraint is assigned the name FKCONST).

➤ Whenever a row is deleted from the EMPLOYEE table created earlier, all rows in the PAYROLL table that have a value in the EMPID column matching the primary key of the row being deleted will also be deleted.

➤ Every value provided for the PAYCHECK column must be greater than 0 and every value provided for the WEEKNUMBER column must be greater than or equal to 1 and less than or equal to 52 (because a check constraint named CHK1 was created for the PAYCHECK and WEEKNUMBER columns).

➤ The EMPLOYEE table will be created in the tablespace USERSPACE1.

Indexes

An index is an object that contains an ordered set of pointers that refer to rows in a base table. Each index is based upon one or more columns in the base table

DEPARTMENT TABLE

DEPTID INDEX

KEY	ROW
A000	5
B001	2
C001	8
D001	11
E001	3
E002	6
E003	4
F001	1
F002	9
F003	7
G010	10

	DEPTID	DEPTNAME	COSTCENTER
Row 1 →	F001	ADMINISTRATION	10250
Row 2 →	B001	PLANNING	10820
Row 3 →	E001	ACCOUNTING	20450
Row 4 →	E003	HUMAN RESOURCES	30200
Row 5 →	A000	R & D	50120
Row 6 →	E002	MANUFACTURING	50220
Row 7 →	F003	OPERATIONS	50230
Row 8 →	C001	MARKETING	42100
Row 9 →	F002	SALES	42200
Row 10 →	G010	CUSTOMER SUPPORT	42300
Row 11 →	D001	LEGAL	60680

Figure 4–18   A simple index.

they refer to, yet they are stored as separate entities. Figure 4–18 shows the structure of a simple index, along with its relationship to a base table.

Indexes are important because they:

➤ Provide a fast, efficient method for locating specific rows of data in very large tables. (In some cases, all the information needed to resolve a query may be found in the index itself, in which case the actual table data does not have to be accessed.)

➤ Provide a logical ordering of the rows of a table. (Data is stored in a table in no particular order; when indexes are used, the values of one or more columns can be sorted in ascending or descending order. This is very beneficial when processing queries that contain ORDER BY and GROUP BY clauses.)

➤ Improve overall query performance. (If no index exists on a table, a table scan must be performed for each table referenced in a query. The larger the table, the longer a table scan takes because a table scan requires each table row to be accessed sequentially. Index files, on the other hand are generally smaller and require less time to read than tables, particularly as tables get larger. In addition, depending upon the predicates used in the query, only a portion of a particular index may need to be scanned.)

➤ Can enforce the uniqueness of records stored in a table.

➤ Can require a table to use *clustering* storage, which causes the rows of a table to be physically arranged according to the ordering of their index column values. (Although all indexes provide a logical ordering of data, only a clustering index provides a physical ordering of data.)

Indexes can also provide greater concurrency in multi-user environments. Because records can be located faster, acquired locks do not have to be held as long. However, there is a price for these benefits: Additional storage space is needed whenever indexes are used, and performance can actually decrease when new data is added to a base table and existing data is modified. In both cases, the operations performed must be applied to both the base table and to any corresponding indexes.

While some indexes are created implicitly to provide support for a table's definition (for example to provide support for a primary key), indexes are typically created explicitly, using the tools provided with DB2 UDB. Indexes can be explicitly created by executing the CREATE INDEX SQL statement. The basic syntax for this statement is:

```
CREATE <UNIQUE> INDEX [IndexName]
ON [TableName] ( [PriColumnName] <ASC | DESC> ,... )
<INCLUDE ( [SecColumnName] ,... )>
<CLUSTER>
<PCTFREE 10 | PCTFREE [PercentFree]>
<DISALLOW REVERSE SCANS | ALLOW REVERSE SCANS>
```

where:

IndexName	Identifies the name to be assigned to the index to be created.
TableName	Identifies the name assigned to the base table that the index to be created is to be associated with.
PriColumnName	Identifies one or more primary columns that are to be part of the index's key. (The combined values of each primary column specified will be used to enforce data uniqueness in the associated base table.)
SecColumnName	Identifies one or more secondary columns whose values are to be stored with the values of the primary columns specified, but are not to be used to enforce data uniqueness.
PercentFree	Identifies a percentage of each index page to leave as free space when building the index.

If the UNIQUE clause is specified when the CREATE INDEX statement is executed, rows in the table associated with the index to be created must not have two or more occurrences of the same values in the set of columns that make up the index key. If the base table the index is to be created for contains data, this uniqueness is checked when the DB2 Database Manager attempts to create the index specified; once the index has been created, this uniqueness is enforced each time an insert or update operation is performed against the table. In both cases, if the uniqueness of the index key is compromised, the index creation, insert, or update operation will fail, and an error will be generated. It is important to keep in mind that when the UNIQUE clause is used, it is possible to have an index key that contains one (and only one) NULL value.

So, if you wanted to create a unique index for a base table named EMPLOY-EES that has the following characteristics:

Column Name	Data Type
EMPNO	INTEGER
FNAME	CHAR(20)
LNAME	CHAR(30)
TITLE	CHAR(10)
DEPARTMENT	CHAR(20)
SALARY	DECIMAL(6,2)

such that the index key consists of the column named EMPNO, you could do so by executing a CREATE INDEX statement that looks something like this:

```
CREATE INDEX EMPNO_INDX
ON EMPLOYEES (EMPNO)
```

Indexes can also be created using the Create Index dialog, which can be activated by selecting the appropriate action from the *Indexes* menu found in the Control Center. Figure 4–19 shows the Control Center menu items that must be selected to activate the Create Indexes dialog; Figure 4–20 shows how the Create Indexes dialog might look after its input fields have been populated.

If an index is created for an empty table, that index will not have any entries stored in it until the table the index is associated with is populated. On the other hand, if an index is created for a table that already contains data, index entries will be generated for the existing data and added to the index as soon as it is created. Any number of indexes can be created for a table, using a wide variety of combinations of columns. However, each index comes at a price in both storage requirements and performance: Since each index replicates its key values, and this replication requires additional storage space, and each modification to a table results in a similar modification to all indexes defined on the table, performance can decrease when insert, update, and delete operations are performed. In fact, if a large number of indexes are created for a table that is modified frequently, overall performance will decrease rather

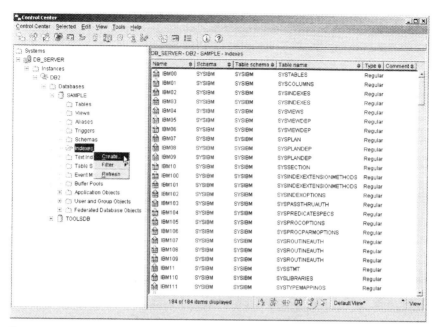

Figure 4–19   Invoking the Create Index dialog from the Control Center.

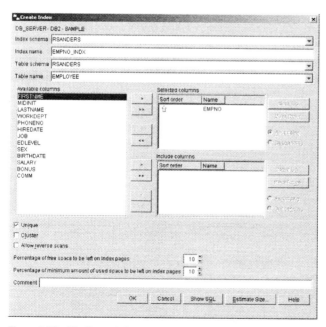

Figure 4–20   The Create Index dialog.

than increase. Tables that are used for data mining, business intelligence, business warehousing, and other applications that execute many (and often complex) queries while rarely modifying data are prime targets for multiple indexes. On the other hand, tables that are used in OLTP (On-Line Transaction Processing) environments or other environments where data throughput is high should use indexes sparingly.

Clustering Indexes

A clustering index is a special index that, when used, informs the DB2 Database Manager to always try to store records on a page that contains other records that have similar index key values. (If no space is available on that page, the DB2 Database Manager will attempt to store the record in a page that is nearby.) A clustering index usually increases performance by decreasing the amount of I/O required to access data: this results in fewer page fetches, since like data values are stored on the same physical page. (Only one index in a table can be a clustering index.)

When a logical set of rows are physically stored close together, a read operation on the set of rows will require less I/O, because adjacent rows are more likely to be found within the same extent (remember, data pages are written in batches called extents) instead of being widely distributed across multiple extents. And because similar key values are placed on the same data page whenever possible, often only a portion of a table will need to be read in response to a query. A clustering index is most useful for columns that have range predicates because it allows better sequential access of data in the base table.

A clustering index is created by specifying the CLUSTER option with the CREATE INDEX SQL statement. Thus, if you wanted to create a clustering index for a base table named EMPLOYEES that has the following characteristics:

Column Name	Data Type
EMPNO	INTEGER
FNAME	CHAR(20)
LNAME	CHAR(30)
TITLE	CHAR(10)
DEPARTMENT	CHAR(20)
SALARY	DECIMAL(6,2)

such that the index key consists of the column named EMPNO, you could do so by executing a CREATE INDEX statement that looks something like this:

```
CREATE INDEX EMPNO_CINDX
ON EMPLOYEES (EMPNO)
CLUSTER
```

When creating a clustering index, the PCTFREE option of the CREATE INDEX SQL statement can be used to control how much space is reserved for future insert and update operations. Specify a higher PCTFREE value (the default is 10 percent) at index creation time to reduce the likelihood of index page splits to occur when records are inserted into the index.

 Over time, update operations can cause rows to change page locations, thereby reducing the degree of clustering that exists between an index and its data pages. Reorganizing a table (with the REORG utility) using the appropriate index will return the index specified to its original level of clustering. (The REORG utility is covered in detail in Chapter 6—DB2 Utilities.)

Multidimensional Clustering (MDC) Table Indexes

Multidimensional clustering (MDC) provides a way to automatically cluster data along multiple dimensions. Such clustering results in significant improvement in query performance, as well as significant reduction in the overhead of data maintenance operations, such as table/index reorganization, and index maintenance operations during insert, update, and delete operations. Multidimensional clustering is primarily intended for data warehousing, online transaction processing (OLTP), and large database environments.

Earlier, we saw that when a clustering index is used, the DB2 Database Manager maintains the physical order of data on pages in the key order of the index, as records are inserted and updated in the table. With good clustering, only a portion of the table needs to be accessed in response to a query and, when the pages are stored sequentially, more efficient prefetching can be performed. With MDC, these benefits are extended to multiple keys (or dimensions); MDC allows a table to be physically clustered on more than one key (or dimension) simultaneously. Not only will queries access only those pages that contain records with the correct dimension values, these qualifying pages will be grouped by extents. Furthermore, although a table with a clustering index can become unclustered over time as space fills up in the table, an MDC table is able to maintain its clustering over all dimensions automatically and continuously, thus eliminating the need to reorganize a table in order to restore the original level of clustering used.

When you create a table, you can specify one or more keys as dimensions that are to be used to cluster data; each dimension can consist of one or more columns, just like regular index keys. A *dimension block index* will then be created automatically for each dimension specified, and the DB2 Optimizer will use this index to quickly and efficiently access data across each dimension. A *composite block index* that contains all dimension key columns will also be created, and this index will be used to maintain the clustering of data during insert and update operations. (A composite block index will only be created if a single dimension block index does not already contain all the dimension key columns specified for the table.) The composite block index can also be used by the DB2 Optimizer to efficiently access data. Every unique combination of dimension values form a logical *cell*, which is physically comprised of blocks of pages, where a block is a set of consecutive pages on disk. The set of blocks that contain pages with data having a certain key value of one of the dimension block indexes is called a *slice*. Every page of the table is part of exactly one block, and all blocks of the table consist of the same number of pages—the *blocking factor*. The blocking factor is equal to extent size, so that block boundaries line up with extent boundaries.

Type-1 and Type-2 Indexes

In DB2 UDB Version 8.1, the structure used to store index records was modified to help eliminate a phenomena known as "Next-key Locking". Next-key locking occurs during index insert and delete operations and during index scans; when a row is inserted into, updated, or deleted from a table, an Exclusive (X) lock is acquired for that row. When a corresponding key is inserted into or deleted from the table's index, the table row that corresponds to the key that follows the deleted or inserted key in the index is locked as well (with a Next-key Exclusive lock [NX]). (For update operations that affect the value of the key, the original key value is first deleted and the new value is inserted, so two Next-key Exclusive [NX] locks are acquired.) Thus, Next-key locking for Type-1 (older style) indexes during key value insertions and deletions could sometimes result in a deadlock cycle. With Type-2 indexes, such deadlocks do not occur because deleted keys are marked as being deleted and are not physically removed from the index. (Keys that have been marked as being deleted are overwritten by subsequent insert and update operations.)

By default, all new indexes created under DB2 UDB Version 8.1 will use the Type-2 index structure, while existing indexes will continue to use the Type-1 index structure until they are manually converted. To convert a Type-1 index to a Type-2 index, you can either reorganize it with the REORG ... CONVERT command, or you can drop and recreate it.

NOTE If you migrate a DB2 UDB V7.x table to DB2 UDB V8.1, all existing indexes for that table will remain as Type-1 indexes and any new indexes you create for that table will be Type-1 indexes as well. Likewise, if you drop and recreate a single index, the new index will be a Type-1 index. This behavior can only be changed by converting every index associated with the table to a Type-2 index.

Views

Views are used to provide a different way of looking at the data stored in one or more base tables. Essentially, a view is a named specification of a result table that is populated whenever the view is referenced in an SQL statement. Like base tables, views can be thought of as having columns and rows. And in most cases, data can be retrieved from a view the same way it can be retrieved from a table. However, whether or not a view can be used in insert, update, and delete operations depends on how it was defined. Views can be defined as being insertable, updatable, deletable, and read-only. (In general, a view is insertable, updateable, or deleteable if each row in the view can be uniquely mapped onto a single row of a base table.)

Although views look similar to base tables, they do not contain real data. Instead, views refer to data stored in other base tables. Only the view definition itself is actually stored in the database. (In fact, when changes are made to the data presented in a view, the changes are actually made to the data stored in the base table(s) the view references.) Figure 4–21 shows the structure of a simple view, along with its relationship to a base table.

Because views allow different users to see different presentations of the same data, they are often used to control data access. For example, suppose you had a table that contained information about all employees that worked for a particular company. Managers could be given access to this table using a view that only allows them to see information about the employees that work in their department. Members of the payroll department, on the other hand, could be given access to the table using a view that only allows them to see the information needed to generate employee paychecks. Both sets of users are given access to the same table; however, because each user works with a different view, it appears that they are working with their own tables. By creating views and coupling them with the view privileges available, a database administrator can have greater control over how individual users access specific pieces of data.

NOTE Because there is no way to grant SELECT privileges on specific columns within a table, the only way to prevent users from accessing every column in a table is by creating a result, materialized query, or declared temporary table that holds only the data a particular user needs, or by creating a view that only contains the table columns a user is allowed to access. Of these two methods, the view is easier to implement and manage.

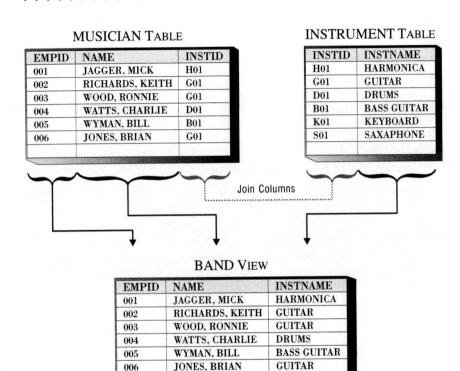

MUSICIAN TABLE

EMPID	NAME	INSTID
001	JAGGER, MICK	H01
002	RICHARDS, KEITH	G01
003	WOOD, RONNIE	G01
004	WATTS, CHARLIE	D01
005	WYMAN, BILL	B01
006	JONES, BRIAN	G01

INSTRUMENT TABLE

INSTID	INSTNAME
H01	HARMONICA
G01	GUITAR
D01	DRUMS
B01	BASS GUITAR
K01	KEYBOARD
S01	SAXAPHONE

Join Columns

BAND VIEW

EMPID	NAME	INSTNAME
001	JAGGER, MICK	HARMONICA
002	RICHARDS, KEITH	GUITAR
003	WOOD, RONNIE	GUITAR
004	WATTS, CHARLIE	DRUMS
005	WYMAN, BILL	BASS GUITAR
006	JONES, BRIAN	GUITAR

Figure 4-21 A simple view that references a base table.

Views can be created by executing the CREATE VIEW SQL statement. The basic syntax for this statement is:

```
CREATE VIEW [ViewName]
<( [ColumnName] ,... )>
AS [SELECTStatement]
<WITH CHECK OPTION>
```

where:

ViewName   Identifies the name to be assigned to the view to be created.

ColumnName   Identifies the names of one or more columns that are to be included in the view to be created. If a list of column names is specified, the number of column names provided must match the number of columns that will be returned by the SELECT statement used to create the view. (If a list of column names is not provided, the columns of the view will inherit the names that are assigned to the columns returned by the SELECT statement used to create the view.)

SELECTStatement   Identifies a SELECT SQL statement that, when executed, will produce data that can be seen using the view to be created.

Thus, if you wanted to create a view that references all data stored in a table named DEPARTMENT and assign it the name DEPT_VIEW, you could do so by executing a CREATE VIEW SQL statement that looks something like this:

```
CREATE VIEW DEPT_VIEW
AS SELECT * FROM DEPARTMENT
```

On the other hand, if you wanted to create a view that references specific data values stored in the table named DEPARTMENT and assign it the name ADV_DEPT_VIEW, you could do so by executing a CREATE VIEW SQL statement that looks something like this:

```
CREATE VIEW ADV_DEPT_VIEW
AS SELECT (DEPT_NO, DEPT_NAME, DEPT_SIZE) FROM DEPARTMENT
WHERE DEPT_SIZE > 25
```

The view created by this statement would only contain department number, department name, and department size information for each department that has more than 25 people in it.

Views can also be created using the Create View dialog, which can be activated by selecting the appropriate action from the *Views* menu found in the Control Center. Figure 4–22 shows the Control Center menu items that must be selected to activate the Create View dialog; Figure 4–23 shows how the Create View dialog might look after its input fields have been populated.

If the WITH CHECK OPTION clause of the CREATE VIEW SQL statement is specified (or if a Check option is selected on the Create View dialog), insert and update operations performed against the view that is created are validated to ensure that all rows being inserted into or updated in the base table the view refers to conform to the view's definition (otherwise, the insert/update operation will fail). So what exactly does this mean? Suppose a view was created using the following CREATE VIEW statement:

```
CREATE VIEW PRIORITY_ORDERS
AS SELECT * FROM ORDERS WHERE RESPONSE_TIME < 4
WITH CHECK OPTION
```

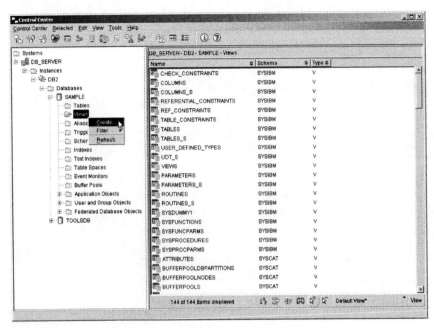

Figure 4–22 Invoking the Create View dialog from the Control Center.

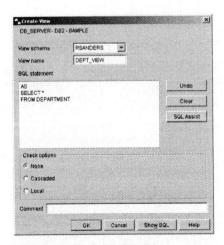

Figure 4–23 The Create View dialog.

Now, suppose a user tries to insert a record into this view that has a RESPONSE_TIME value of 6. The insert operation will fail because the record violates the view's definition. Had the view not been created with the WITH CHECK OPTION clause, the insert operation would have been successful, even though the new record would not be visible to the view that was used to add it. Figure 4–24 illustrates how the WITH CHECK OPTION works.

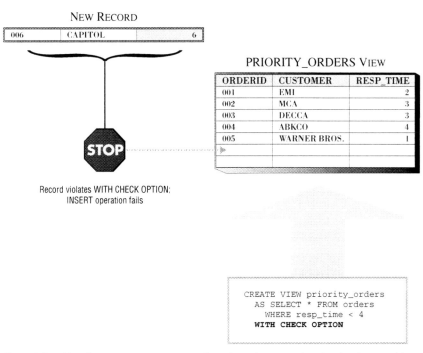

Figure 4–24 How the WITH CHECK OPTION clause is used to ensure insert and update operations conform to a view's definition.

 NOTE | Views created with the WITH CHECK OPTION clause specified are referred to as *symmetric views*, because every record that can be inserted into them can also be retrieved from them.

The Task Center (Revisited)

Managing a DB2 UDB server involves more than just the initial implementation of a database and its associated objects (i.e., tables, indexes, views, etc.). It also requires the performance of regular maintenance tasks. Such tasks can be administered manually on a regular basis, or they can be automated using a special tool known as the Task Center.

Earlier, we saw that the Task Center is an easy-to-use graphical user interface (GUI) tool that can be used to run tasks immediately, or that allows users to organize task flow, schedule frequently occurring tasks, and distribute notifications regarding the status of completed tasks. The Task Center contains all the functionality found in the Script Center, which was available in earlier versions of DB2 UDB, plus several additional new features. Figure 4–25 shows what the Task Center looks like on a Windows 2000 server.

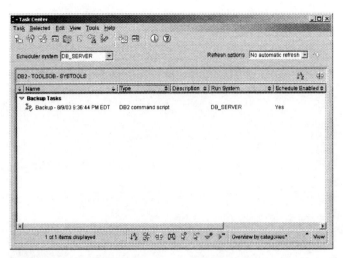

Figure 4–25 The Task Center.

In order to use the Task Center, the tools catalog database must exist on the DB2 UDB workstation. This database contains information about the administrative tasks that you configure with tools such as the Task Center and the Control Center. The tools catalog can be created automatically as part of the DB2 UDB installation process or it can be created manually, either from the Control Center or by executing the CREATE TOOLS CATALOG command from the DB2 Command Line Processor (CLP).

You may recall that a task is simply a script that has been bundled together with success conditions/actions, schedules, and notifications. The script used to perform a task can be created within the Task Center, within another tool and saved to the Task Center, imported from an existing UNIX shell script/Windows batch file, or they can be generated from a Control Center dialog or wizard (for example, the Backup Wizard will create a database backup operation that can be scheduled). Furthermore, the script used to perform a task can contain any combination of DB2 UDB commands, SQL statements, and operating system commands. Although a task is not just a script, a script is often an integral part of a task and once a script has been created, the process of converting it into a task involves:

➤ Scheduling when the script will run.

➤ Specifying success and failure conditions.

➤ Specifying actions that should be performed when the script executes successfully and when it fails.

➤ Specifying e-mail addresses (including pager addresses) that should be notified when the script has completed or if the script failed). (The task center can either notify contacts or place information in the Journal.)

By default, all output from the Task Center is recorded in the Journal.

It is also possible to create a *grouping task*, which is a special task that combines several individual scripts to create a single logical unit of work. When a grouping task meets the success or failure conditions that have been defined for it, the appropriate actions are performed. For example, you could combine three backup scripts into a grouping task and then specify a table reorganization operation as a follow-on task that is to be executed if all of the backup scripts execute successfully. Regardless of whether a task completes successfully or fails, any number of actions can be performed, including:

➤ Running another task

➤ Scheduling another task

➤ Disabling another scheduled task

➤ Deleting itself

So just who can create and schedule tasks? Anyone who has the authorities and privileges needed to execute the task. In fact the Task Center provides a way for users who create a task to grant read, write, and execute (run) privileges to other users for the task being created. This can be useful when a number of different users are creating and maintaining tasks.

Practice Questions

Question 1

Given the following table:

```
TABLEA
empid   name
1       USER1
2       USER2
```

Which of the following ensures that a TABLEA is created with column EMPID as the parent key for a foreign key relationship?

○ A. Create table TABLEA, then create a unique index on the EMPID column.

○ B. Create table TABLEA and indicate that the EMPID column is the partitioning key.

○ C. Create table TABLEA and indicate that the EMPID column is a primary key.

○ D. Create table TABLEA, then alter the table to define a unique constraint on the EMPID column.

Question 2

Which of the following statements is NOT a benefit of using a clustering index?

○ A. Rows with equal key values are stored close to each other on disk.

○ B. Read operations require less I/O.

○ C. Often, only a portion of a table has to be read in response to a query.

○ D. Disk space is saved when rows are added to a table.

Question 3

Given the following tables:

```
TABLEA                  TABLEB
empid    name           empid   weekno   payamt
1        USER1          1       1        1000.00
2        USER2          1       2        1000.00
                        2       1        2000.00
```

and the fact that TABLEB was defined as follows:

```
CREATE TABLE tableb  (  empid   SMALLINT,
                        weekno  SMALLINT,
                        payamt  DECIMAL(6,2),
     CONSTRAINT const1 FOREIGN KEY (empid) REFERENCES tablea(empid)
     ON DELETE NO ACTION)
```

If the following command is issued:

```
DELETE FROM tablea WHERE empid=2
```

How many rows will be deleted from TABLEA and TABLEB?

- ○ A. 0,0
- ○ B. 0,1
- ○ C. 1,0
- ○ D. 1,1

Question 4

Given the following table definition:

```
CREATE TABLE tablea  (  empidSMALLINT,
                        age   SMALLINT CHECK (age >= 18))
```

and the statement:

```
INSERT INTO tablea VALUES (1, 17), (2, 21), (3, 18)
```

How many records will be inserted into table TABLEA?

- ○ A. 0
- ○ B. 1
- ○ C. 2
- ○ D. 3

Question 5

Given the following CREATE TABLE statement:

```
CREATE TABLE newtable LIKE table1
```

Which two of the following would NOT occur as a result of the statement execution?

❏ A. NEWTABLE would have the same column names and column data types as TABLE1

❏ B. NEWTABLE would have the same column defaults as TABLE1

❏ C. NEWTABLE would have the same indexes as TABLE1

❏ D. NEWTABLE would have the same nullability characteristics as TABLE1

❏ E. NEWTABLE would have the same referential constraints as TABLE1

Question 6

Which two of the following privileges will allow a user to create a table named TABLE2 that contains a foreign key that references a table named TABLE1?

❏ A. SYSCTRL

❏ B. SYSMAINT

❏ C. DBADM

❏ D. REFERENCES on TABLE1

❏ E. REFERENCES on TABLE2

Question 7

Which of the following is a NOT a valid reason for defining a view on a table?

○ A. Restrict users' access to a subset of table data

○ B. Ensure that rows entered remain within the scope of a definition

○ C. Produce an action as a result of a change to a table

○ D. Provide users with an alternate view of table data

Question 8

Which of the following deletion rules on CREATE TABLE will allow parent table rows to be deleted if a dependent row exists?

○ A. ON DELETE RESTRICT
○ B. ON DELETE NO ACTION
○ C. ON DELETE SET NO VALUE
○ D. ON DELETE CASCADE

Question 9

Which of the following is NOT a purpose for creating a primary key on a table?

○ A. To ensure duplicate values are not entered
○ B. To support referential integrity between tables
○ C. To support creation of a table check constraint
○ D. To aid in ordering data

Question 10

Given the following table definition:

```
CREATE TABLE tablea  (   col1 SMALLINT CHECK (id >= 10) NOT ENFORCED,
                         col2 CHAR(5))
```

and the statement:

```
INSERT INTO tablea VALUES (5, 'abc'), (10, 'def'), (15, 'ghi')
```

How many records will be inserted into table TABLEA?

○ A. 0
○ B. 1
○ C. 2
○ D. 3

Question 11

Given the following statements:

```
CREATE TABLE table1 (col1 INTEGER, col2 CHAR(3))
CREATE VIEW view1 AS
SELECT col1, col2 FROM table1
WHERE col1 < 100
WITH CHECK OPTION
```

Which of the following INSERT statements will execute successfully?

- ○ A. INSERT INTO view1 VALUES (50, abc)
- ○ B. INSERT INTO view1 VALUES(100, abc)
- ○ C. INSERT INTO view1 VALUES(50, 'abc')
- ○ D. INSERT INTO view1 VALUES(100, 'abc')

Question 12

Given the following table:

```
TABLEB
empname       payamt
------------  ----------
Smith         1000.00
Jones         1000.00
Jancer        2000.00
```

and the following statements:

```
REVOKE SELECT ON tableb FROM PUBLIC
CREATE VIEW view2 AS SELECT empname FROM tableb
GRANT SELECT ON view2 TO PUBLIC
```

Which of the following can members of the group PUBLIC see?

- ○ A. Employee names and payment information assigned to records in TABLEB.
- ○ B. Employee names assigned to records in TABLEB.
- ○ C. Payment information assigned to records in TABLEB.
- ○ D. Members of the group PUBLIC are not allowed to see any information stored in TABLEB.

Question 13

What is the primary purpose of an IDENTITY column?

- ○ A. Generate a unique value for each row in a table
- ○ B. Generate a row ID for each row in a table
- ○ C. Identify the owner/creator of a table
- ○ D. Identify the current users of a table

Question 14

Which of the following CREATE INDEX statement options is used to tell DB2 to attempt to physically order the table data?

○ A. UNIQUE

○ B. CLUSTER

○ C. PCTFREE

○ D. ALLOW REVERSE SCANS

Question 15

Given the following table definitions:

```
        EMPLOYEES
---------------------------------------------
EMPID           INTEGER
NAME            CHAR(20)
DEPT            INTEGER
SALARY          DECIMAL(10,2)
COMMISSION      DECIMAL(8,2)


        DEPARTMENT
---------------------------------------------
DEPTID          INTEGER NOT NULL PRIMARY KEY
DEPTNAME        CHAR(20)
```

and the following information:

Employee IDs are unique
A query is run each month to obtain commission information for each department (departments are listed by name)

Which of the following will improve query performance?

○ A. A unique index on EMPID, COMMISSION

○ B. A unique clustered index on DEPTNAME

○ C. An index on DEPT

○ D. A unique clustered index on SALARY, COMMISSION

Question 16

Given the following table definitions:

```
CREATE TABLE tablea  (  empid    SMALLINT NOT NULL PRIMARY KEY,
                        name     CHAR(25))

CREATE TABLE tableb  (  empid    SMALLINT WITH DEFAULT,
                        weekno   SMALLINT,
                        payamt   DECIMAL(6,2),
     FOREIGN KEY (empid) REFERENCES tablea (empid)
     ON DELETE CASCADE)
```

If the following command is issued:

```
DELETE FROM tablea WHERE empid=2
```

What happens to the rows in TABLEB where EMPID = 2?

- ○ A. They are deleted
- ○ B. They are copied to an exception table
- ○ C. The EMPID value for each affected row is set to null
- ○ D. The EMPID value for each affected row is set to the system default value

Question 17

A DBA wants to create three related tasks in the Task Center. Which of the following tools can NOT be used to create these tasks?

- ○ A. The Task Center
- ○ B. Control Center Wizards
- ○ C. A text editor
- ○ D. The Journal

Question 18

What is the purpose of a grouping task?

- ○ A. To combine several tasks into a single unit of work
- ○ B. To control the order in which tasks are executed
- ○ C. To control who can modify a set of tasks
- ○ D. To control who can schedule a set of tasks to run

Answers

Question 1

The correct answer is **C**. When a primary key is created for a table, that key can be used in any number of referential constraints; if no primary key exists, the table cannot participate as a parent table in a referential constraint.

Question 2

The correct answer is **D**. Clustering indexes have no impact on the amount of disk space used to store data values. Instead, they attempt to store data with like key values in close proximity so that read operations require less I/O.

Question 3

The correct answer is **A**. The ON DELETE NO ACTION definition ensures that whenever a delete operation is performed on the parent table in a referential constraint, the value for the foreign key of each row in the child table will have a matching value in the parent key of the parent table (after all other referential constraints have been applied). Therefore, no row will be deleted from TABLEA because a row exists in TABLEB that references the row the DELETE statement is trying to remove. And because the ON DELETE CASCADE definition was not used, no row will be deleted from TABLEB.

Question 4

The correct answer is **A**. Because the value 17 in the values set (1, 17) violates the check constraint defined for the AGE column of table TABLEA (values must be greater than or equal to 18), the insert operation will fail and no rows will be added to the table.

Question 5

The correct answers are **C** and **E**. When the CREATE TABLE ... LIKE ... statement is executed, each column of the table that is created will have exactly the same name, data type, and nullability characteristic of the columns of the source table that was used to create the new table. Furthermore, if the EXCLUDING COLUMN DEFAULTS option is not specified, all column defaults will be copied as well. However, the new table will not contain any unique constraints, foreign key constraints, triggers, or indexes that exist in the original.

Question 6

The correct answers are **A** and **D**. Only users with System Administrator (SYSADM) authority, System Control (SYSCTRL) authority, CONTROL privilege on the parent table (which in this case is TABLE1), or REFERENCES privilege on the parent table are allowed to create referential constraints between two tables.

Question 7

The correct answer is **C**. A *trigger* is used to produce an action as a result of a change to a table. Views provide users with alternate ways to see table data. And because a view can reference the data stored in any number of columns found in the base table it refers to, views can be used, together with view privileges, to control what data a user can and cannot see. Furthermore, if a view is created with the WITH CHECK OPTION specified, it can be used to ensure that all rows added to a table through it conform to its definition.

Question 8

The correct answer is **D**. The ON DELETE RESTRICT delete rule and the ON DELETE NO ACTION delete rule prevents the deletion of parent rows in a parent table if dependent rows that reference the primary row being deleted exist in the corresponding child table and the ON DELETE SET NO VALUE delete rule is an invalid rule. On the other hand, the ON DELETE CASCADE delete rule will allow rows in the parent table to be deleted; if dependent rows that reference the primary row being deleted exist in the corresponding child table, they will be deleted as well.

Question 9

The correct answer is **C**. A check constraint can be created on a table at any time, regardless of whether or not a primary key exists. The main purpose for creating a primary key is to support referential integrity between tables, however, the existence of a primary key aids in the ordering of data and prevents duplicate key values from being entered.

Question 10

The correct answer is **D**. Because the constraint defined for column COL1 is an informational constraint, all three records will be added, even though the first record violates the check constraint ID <= 10.

Question 11

The correct answer is **C**. Because VIEW1 was created using a SELECT statement that only references rows that have a value less than 100 in COL1, and because VIEW1 was created with the WITH CHECK OPTION specified, each value inserted into COL1 (using VIEW1) must be less than 100. In addition, because COL2 was defined using a character data type, all values inserted into COL2 must be enclosed in single quotes. The INSERT statements shown in answers B and D will fail because the value to be assigned to COL1 exceeds 100; the INSERT statement shown in answer A will fail because the value abc is not enclosed in single quotation marks.

Question 12

The correct answer is **B**. View VIEW2 provides a way to see just employee names stored in the table TABLEB. Because members of the group PUBLIC have been given access to the view VIEW2 and have been revoked access to the table TABLEB, they are only allowed to see employee names assigned to records stored in TABLEB.

Question 13

The correct answer is **A**. When an IDENTITY column is used, the DB2 Database Manager will generate a sequence of numbers (or other values) for the column and assign a value to that column, using the sequence generated, as new records are added to the table.

Question 14

The correct answer is **B**. A clustering index is a special index that, when used, informs the DB2 Database Manager to always try to store records on a page that contains other records that have similar index key values. A clustering index is created by executing the CREATE INDEX SQL statement with the CLUSTER option specified.

Question 15

The correct answer is **C**. Because the two tables are joined in the query (SELECT DEPTNAME, COMMISSION FROM EMPLOYEES E, DEPARTMENT D WHERE D.DEPTID = E.DEPT), creating an index on the DEPT column of the EMPLOYEES table will improve overall query performance.

Question 16

The correct answer is **A**. When an IDENTITY column is used, the DB2 Database Manager will generate a sequence of numbers (or other values) for the column and assign a value to that column, using the sequence generated, as new records are added to the table.

Question 17

The correct answer is **D**. The Journal displays historical information about tasks, database actions and operations, Control Center actions, messages, and alerts. However, it is not used to create a task. On the other hand, the script used to perform a task can be created within the Task Center, within another tool and saved to the Task Center, imported from an existing UNIX shell script/Windows batch file, or they can be generated from a Control Center dialog or wizard (for example, the Backup Wizard will create a database backup operation that can be scheduled).

Question 18

The correct answer is **A**. A grouping task is a special task that combines several individual tasks (scripts) into a single logical unit of work. When the grouping task meets the success or failure conditions defined, any follow-on tasks are run. (For example, you could combine three backup scripts into a grouping task and then specify a table reorganization operation as a follow-on task that is to be executed if all of the backup scripts execute successfully.)

5

Monitoring DB2 Activity

Sixteen percent (16%) of the DB2 UDB V8.1 for Linux, UNIX, and Windows Database Administration certification exam (Exam 701) and thirteen percent (13%) of the DB2 UDB V8.1 for Linux, UNIX, and Windows Database Administration certification upgrade exam (Exam 706) is designed to test your ability to configure systems, instances, and databases and to evaluate your ability to use each of the database monitoring tools that are available with DB2 Universal Database. The questions that make up this portion of the exam are intended to evaluate the following:

➤ Your ability to view and modify DB2 system environment/registry variables.

➤ Your ability to view and modify DB2 Database Manager configuration information.

➤ Your ability to view and modify database configuration information.

➤ Your knowledge of the various monitoring tools available with DB2 UDB.

➤ Your ability to use the snapshot monitor, including capturing and analyzing snapshot data.

➤ Your ability to create and use event monitors, including capturing and analyzing event monitor data.

➤ Your ability to use the Health Center.

➤ Your ability to use the Explain Facility to capture and analyze both comprehensive Explain information and Explain snapshot data.

➤ Your ability to identify the basic functionality of the DB2 Governor and the DB2 Query Patroller.

This chapter is designed to introduce you to the environment/registry and configuration parameters that are used to control how resources are used by the DB2 Database Manager instance and databases under the instance's control. This chapter is also designed to introduce you to the set of monitoring tools that are available with DB2 Universal Database and to show you how each are used to monitor how well (or how poorly) your database system is operating.

Terms you will learn:

Environment/registry variables

The DB2 Global Level Profile Registry

The DB2 Instance Level Profile Registry

The DB2 Instance Node Level Profile Registry

DB2 Registry management tool

db2set

DB2 Database Manager Configuration

GET DATABASE MANAGER CONFIGURATION

UPDATE DATABASE MANAGER CONFIGURATION

Database Configuration

GET DATABASE CONFIGURATION

UPDATE DATABASE CONFIGURATION

AUTOMATIC

IMMEDIATE

DEFERRED

Database System Monitor

Snapshot Monitor

Event Monitors

Monitor Elements

Snapshot Monitor Switches

GET MONITOR SWITCHES

UPDATE MONITOR SWITCHES

GET SNAPSHOT

RESET MONITOR

CREATE EVENT MONITOR

SET EVENT MONITOR

FLUSH EVENT MONITOR

Event Analyzer

db2evmon

Health Monitor

Health Center

Health Indicators

Health Beacons

Package

Explain Facility

Explain Tables

Comprehensive Explain Data

Explain Snapshot Data

EXPLAIN

CURRENT EXPLAIN MODE

CURRENT EXPLAIN SNAPSHOT

SET CURRENT EXPLAIN MODE

SET CURRENT EXPLAIN SNAPSHOT

EXPLAIN Bind Option

EXPLSNAP Bind Option

db2expln

dynexpln

db2exfmt

Visual Explain

Operator

Operand

DB2 Governor

DB2 Query Patroller

Techniques you will master:

Understanding how DB2 system environment/registry variables are set and cleared.

Understanding what DB2 Database Manager configuration parameters are available, what each is used for, and how their current values can be obtained and/or altered.

Understanding what database configuration parameters are available, what each is used for, and how their current values can be obtained and/or altered.

Recognizing the different monitoring tools that are available with DB2 UDB.

Understanding how snapshot information is collected.

Understanding how event monitors are created and event monitor data is collected.

Understanding how the Health Monitor and the Health Center are used.

Recognizing the difference between comprehensive Explain data and Explain snapshot data.

Understanding how comprehensive Explain data can be collected.

Understanding how Explain snapshot data can be collected.

Understanding how Visual Explain is used to view Explain snapshot data.

Understanding the basic functionality of the DB2 Governor and the DB2 Query Patroller.

Configuring the DB2 System Environment

During normal operation, the behavior of the DB2 Database Manager is controlled, in part, by a collection of values that define the DB2 UDB operating environment. Some of these values are operating system environment variables and others are special DB2-specific system-level values known as *environment* or *registry* variables. Environment/registry variables provide a way to centrally control the database environment. Three different registry profiles are available and each controls the database environment at a different level. The registry profiles available are:

The **DB2 Global Level Profile Registry.** All machine-wide environment variable settings are kept in this registry; one global level profile registry exists on each DB2 UDB workstation. If an environment variable is to be set for all instances, this profile registry is used.

The **DB2 Instance Level Profile Registry.** The environment variable settings for a particular instance are kept in this registry; this is where the majority of the DB2 environment variables are set. (Values defined in this profile registry override any corresponding settings in the global level profile registry.)

The **DB2 Instance Node Level Profile Registry.** This profile registry level contains variable settings that are specific to a partition (node) in a multipartitioned database environment. (Values defined in this profile registry override any corresponding settings in the global level and instance level profile registry.)

DB2 looks for environment/registry variable values in the DB2 Global Level Profile
Registry first, then in the DB2 Instance Level Profile Registry, and finally, in the DB2
Instance Node Level Profile Registry. (Additional values may be set in individual ses-
sions, in which case DB2 will see these values last.)

A wide variety of environment/registry variables are available and they vary
depending on the operating system being used. A complete listing can be
found in Appendix A of the *IBM DB2 Universal Database, Version 8 Administration Guide—Performance* product documentation.

So how do you determine which environment/registry variables have been
set, and what they have been set to? With DB2 UDB, Version 8.1, there are
two ways to view and change registry variables: by using a tool known as the
DB2 Registry management tool and by executing the db2set system command. The DB2 Registry management tool is activated by selecting the
appropriate action from the *Configure* menu found in the Configuration
Assistant. Figure 5–1 shows the Configuration Assistant menu items that
must be selected in order to activate the DB2 Registry management tool;
Figure 5–2 shows how the main dialog of the DB2 Registry management tool
might look after it has been activated.

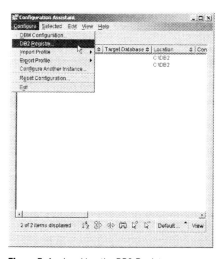

Figure 5–1   Invoking the DB2 Registry management tool from the Configuration Assistant.

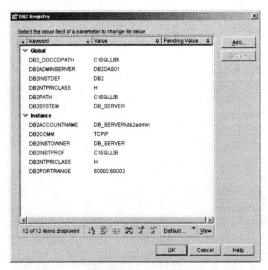

Figure 5–2   The DB2 Registry management tool dialog.

As mentioned earlier, values assigned to environment/registry variables can also be viewed, set, or changed by executing the db2set command. The complete syntax for this command is:

```
db2set
<[Variable] = [Value]>
<-g>
<-i [InstanceName] <NodeNumber>>
<-all>
<-null>
<-r [InstanceName] <NodeNumber>>
<-n [DASNode] <-u [UserID] <-p [Password]>>>
<-l | -lr>
<-v>
<-ul | -ur>
<-h | -?>
```

where:

Variable	Identifies the registry variable whose value is to be displayed, set, or removed.
Value	Identifies the value that is to be assigned to the registry variable specified. If no value is provided, but a registry variable is specified, the registry variable specified is deleted.
InstanceName	Identifies the instance profile that the registry variable specified is associated with.

NodeNumber	Identifies a specific node that is listed in the file **db2nodes.cfg**.
DASNode	Identifies the name of the node where the DB2 Administration Server instance resides.
UserID	Identifies the authentication ID that will be used to attach to the DB2 Administration Server instance.
Password	Identifies the password (for the authentication ID) that will be used to attach to the DB2 Administration Server instance.

All other options shown with this command are described in Table 5–1.

Table 5–1 `db2set` **Command Options**	
Option	**Meaning**
`-g`	Indicates that a global profile variable is to be displayed, set, or removed.
`-i`	Indicates that an instance profile variable is to be displayed, set, or removed.
`-all`	Indicates that all occurrences of the registry variable, as defined in the following, are to be displayed: • The environment, denoted by [`-e`] • The node-level registry, denoted by [`-n`] • The instance-level registry, denoted by [`-i`] • The global-level registry, denoted by [`-g`]
`-null`	Indicates that the value of the variable at the specified registry level is to be set to NULL.
`-r`	Indicates that the profile registry for the given instance is to be reset.
`-n`	Indicates that a remote DB2 Administration Server instance node name is specified.
`-u`	Indicates that an authentication ID that will be used to attach to the DB2 Administration Server process is specified.
`-p`	Indicates that a password for the authentication ID specified is provided.
`-l`	Indicates that all instance profiles will be listed.
`-lr`	Indicates that all registry variables supported will be listed.
`-v`	Execute in verbose mode.
`-ul`	Accesses the user profile variables. (This parameter is only supported on Windows operating systems.)
`-ur`	Refreshes the user profile variables. (This parameter is only supported on Windows operating systems.)
`-h` | `-?`	Displays help information. When this option is specified, all other options are ignored, and only the help information is displayed.

You may recall that in Chapter 2—Server Management, we saw that the DB2COMM environment/registry variable is used to determine which communications managers will be activated when the DB2 Database Manager for a particular instance is started. If you wanted to see the current value of the DB2COMM registry variable for all instances, you could do so by executing a db2set command that looks something like this:

```
db2set -l DB2COMM
```

On the other hand, if you wanted to assign a value to the DB2COMM environment/registry variable for an instance named TEST, you could do so by executing a db2set command that looks something like this:

```
db2set -i TEST DB2COMM=[Protocol, ...]
```

where:

Protocol   Identifies one or more communications protocols that are to be started when the DB2 Database Manager for the instance is started. Any combination of the following values is valid: APPC, IPX-SPX, NETBIOS, NPIPE, and TCPIP.

For example, if you wanted to set the DB2COMM instance level environment/registry variable such that the DB2 Database Manager would start the TCP/IP communication manager each time an instance is started, you could do so by executing a db2set command that looks like this:

```
db2set -i TEST DB2COMM=TCPIP
```

You can also remove the value of any environment/registry variable by providing just the variable name and the equal sign as input to the db2set command. Thus, if you wanted to disable the DB2COMM instance level registry variable for an instance named TEST, you could do so by executing a db2set command that looks like this:

```
db2set -i TEST DB2COMM=
```

It is important to note that if the db2set command is executed without options, a list containing every environment/registry variable that has been set, along with its value, will be returned.

Although environment/registry variables can be set at any time, the DB2 Database Manager for the instance all modified environment/registry variables are associated with must be stopped and restarted before any changes made will take effect.

Configuring Instances and Databases

Along with the comprehensive set of environment/registry variables available, DB2 UDB uses an extensive array of configuration parameters to control how system resources are allocated and utilized on behalf of a database. Unfortunately, the default values provided for many of these configuration parameters were produced with very simple systems in mind. (The goal was for DB2 UDB to run out of the box, on virtually any platform, not for DB2 UDB to run optimally on the platform it is installed on.) Thus, even though the default values provided for these configuration parameters are sufficient to meet most database needs, overall system and application performance can usually be greatly improved simply by changing the values of one or more configuration parameters. In fact, the values assigned to DB2 UDB configuration parameters should always be modified if your database environment contains one or more of the following:

➤ Large databases

➤ Databases that normally service large numbers of concurrent connections

➤ One or more special applications that have high performance requirements

➤ A special hardware configuration

➤ Unique query and/or transaction loads

➤ Unique query and/or transaction types

In a few moments, we'll look at ways to measure transaction loads and performance to determine how configuration parameter values should be altered, but for now let's take a closer look at the configuration parameters available.

The DB2 Database Manager Instance Configuration

Whenever an instance is created, a corresponding DB2 Database Manager configuration file is also created and initialized as part of the instance creation process. Each DB2 Database Manager configuration file is comprised of 91 different parameter values (some of which are only provided for backward compatibility) and most control the amount of system resources that will be allocated to a single DB2 Database Manager instance. The parameters that make up a DB2 Database Manager configuration file are shown in Table 5–2.

Table 5–2   DB2 Database Manager Instance Configuration Parameters

Parameter	Value Range / Default	Description
agent_stack_sz	8–1000 4k pages Default: 16	Specifies the amount of memory (in pages) that is to be allocated by the operating system for each DB2 agent used.
agentpri	–1, 41–125 4k pages or 0–6 4k pages, depending on the operating system being used. Default: –1	Specifies the execution priority that is to be assigned to DB2 Database Manager processes and threads on a particular workstation.
aslheapsz	1–524,288 4k pages Default: 15	Specifies the amount of memory (in pages) that is to be shared between a local client application and a DB2 Database Manager agent.
audit_buf_sz	0–65,000 4k pages Default: 0	Specifies the amount of memory (in pages) that is to be used to store audit records that are generated by the audit facility. If this parameter is set to 0, no audit buffer is used.
authentication	CLIENT, SERVER, SERVER_ENCRYPT, KERBEROS, KRB_SERVER_ENCRYPT Default: SERVER	Specifies how and where authentication of a user takes place. If this parameter is set to CLIENT, all authentication takes place at the client workstation. If this parameter is set to SERVER, the user ID and password are sent from the client workstation to the server workstation so that authentication can take place at the server.
backbufsz	16–524,288 4k pages Default: 1024	Specifies the size (in 4KB pages) of the buffer that is used for backing up a database (if a buffer size is not specified when the BACKUP utility is invoked).
catalog_noauth	YES, NO Default: YES	Specifies whether or not users without System Administrator (SYSADM) authority are allowed to catalog and uncatalog nodes, databases, or DCS and ODBC directories. *(continues)*

Table 5–2 DB2 Database Manager Instance Configuration Parameters (Continued)		
Parameter	**Value Range / Default**	**Description**
comm_bandwidth	0.1–100,000 megabytes per second Default: −1	Specifies the calculated value for the communications bandwidth (in megabytes per second) that is to be used by the DB2 Optimizer to estimate the cost of performing certain SQL operations between the database partition servers of a partitioned database system.
conn_elapse	−1, 0–100 seconds Default: 10	Specifies the number of seconds that a TCP/IP connection between two nodes is to be established within. (If a connection is not established within the time specified by this parameter, other attempts are made up to the number of times specified by the *max_connretries* parameter. If all attempts made fail, an error is returned.)
cpuspeed	−1, 1–10e−1 Default: −1	Specifies the speed of the CPU being used by the workstation DB2 UDB has been installed on.
datalinks	YES, NO Default: YES	Specifies whether or not Data Links support is enabled.
dft_account_str	Any valid character string Default: NULL	Specifies the default accounting string that is to be used when connecting to DRDA servers.
dft_client_adpt	0–15 Default: 0	Specified the default client adapter number for the NETBIOS protocol whose server is extracted from DCE Directory Services.
dft_client_comm	NULL, TCPIP, APPC, NETBIOS Default: NULL	Specifies the communication protocols that client applications on the instance can use to establish connections to remote servers. (Multiple values can be specified by separating each one with a comma.)
dft_mon_bufpool	ON, OFF Default: OFF	Specifies the value of the snapshot monitor's buffer pool switch.

(continues)

Table 5–2	DB2 Database Manager Instance Configuration Parameters (Continued)	
Parameter	**Value Range / Default**	**Description**
dft_mon_lock	ON, OFF Default: OFF	Specifies the value of the snapshot monitor's lock switch.
dft_mon_sort	ON, OFF Default: OFF	Specifies the value of the snapshot monitor's sort switch.
dft_mon_stmt	ON, OFF Default: OFF	Specifies the value of the snapshot monitor's statement switch.
dft_mon_table	ON, OFF Default: OFF	Specifies the value of the snapshot monitor's table switch.
dft_mon_timestamp	ON, OFF Default: OFF	Specifies the value of the snapshot monitor's timestamp switch.
dft_mon_uow	ON, OFF Default: OFF	Specifies the value of the snapshot monitor's unit of work (UOW) switch.
dftdbpath	Any valid character string Default: C: (Windows) or instance user's home directory (UNIX).	Specifies the default drive (Windows) or directory path (UNIX) that is to be used to store new databases. (If no path is specified when a database is created, the database is created in the location identified by this parameter.)
diaglevel	0–4 Default: 3	Specifies the diagnostic error capture level that is used to determine the severity of diagnostic errors that get recorded in the database administration notification log file and the DB2 diagnostics log file (**db2diag.log**).
diagpath	Any valid character string Default: NULL	Specifies the fully qualified path where DB2 diagnostic information is to be stored.
dir_cache	YES, NO Default: YES	Specifies whether or not directory cache support is enabled. (If this parameter is set to YES, node, database, and DCS directory files are cached in memory. This reduces connect overhead by eliminating directory file I/O, and minimizing the directory searches required to retrieve directory information.)
		(continues)

Table 5–2 DB2 Database Manager Instance Configuration Parameters (Continued)		
Parameter	Value Range / Default	Description
dir_obj_name	Any valid character string Default: NULL	Specifies the object name representing your database manager instance (or database) in the directory.
dir_obj_path	Any valid character string Default: /.:/subsys/database/	Specifies the unique name of the database manager instance in the global namespace, which is made up of this value and the value in *dir_obj_name* parameter
dir_type	NONE, DCE Default: NONE	Specifies whether or not DCE directory services is used.
discover	DISABLE, KNOWN, SEARCH Default: SEARCH	Specifies the type of DB2 Discovery requests supported on a client or server. (If this parameter is set to SEARCH, search discovery, in which the DB2 client searches the network for DB2 databases, is supported. If this parameter is set to KNOWN, known discovery, in which the discovery request is issued against the administration server specified by the user, is supported. If this parameter is set to DISABLE, the client or server will not respond to any type of discovery request.)
discover_comm	NULL, TCPIP, NETBIOS Default: NULL	Specifies the communications protocols that clients use to issue search discovery requests, and that servers use to listen for search discovery requests. (Multiple values can be specified by separating each one with a comma.)
discover_inst	ENABLE, DISABLE Default: ENABLE	Specifies whether or not client discovery of an instance is enabled.
dos_rqrioblk	4,096–65,535 Bytes Default: 4,096	Specifies the size of the communication buffer between DOS/Windows applications and their database agents on the database server.
		(continues)

Table 5–2 DB2 Database Manager Instance Configuration Parameters (Continued)		
Parameter	**Value Range / Default**	**Description**
drda_heap_sz	16–60,000 4k pages Default: 128	Specifies the number of 4KB pages of memory to allocate for DB2 Connect and the DRDA Application Server Support Feature.
fcm_num_buffers	128–65,300 buffers Default: 4,096	Specifies the number of 4KB buffers that are to be used for internal communications (messages) among the nodes in an instance.
fed_noauth	YES, NO Default: NO	Specifies whether or not authentication at the instance is to be bypassed (because authentication will happen at the data source). (When *fed_noauth* is set to YES, *authentication* is set to SERVER or SERVER_ENCRYPT, and *federated* is set to YES, then authentication at the instance is bypassed.)
federated	YES, NO Default: NO	Specifies whether or not Federated database object support is enabled (i.e., whether or not applications can submit distributed requests for data being managed by DB2 Family and Oracle database management systems).
fenced_pool	–1, 0–*max_coordagents* Default: *max_coordagents*	Specifies the maximum number of fenced processes that may reside at the database server. (Once this limit is reached, no new fenced requests may be invoked.)
fileserver	Any valid character string Default: NULL	Specifies the name of the NetWare file server where the internetwork address of the DB2 Database Manager is registered.
		(continues)

Table 5–2 DB2 Database Manager Instance Configuration Parameters (Continued)		
Parameter	**Value Range / Default**	**Description**
health_mon	ON, OFF Default: OFF	Specifies whether or not the health of the instance and database objects that have been configured in the Health Center is to be monitored. (When turned on, the DB2 Health Monitor collects information from these objects and takes actions when an object is considered unhealthy. The monitor can be started and stopped dynamically by modifying the switch setting.)
indexrec	ACCESS, RESTART Default: ACCESS	Specifies whether invalid indexes should be recreated when the database is restarted or when they are accessed. This DB2 Database Manager instance configuration parameter is only used if an *indexrec* database configuration parameter is set to SYSTEM.
initfenced_jvm	YES, NO Default: NO	Specifies whether or not each fenced process will load the Java Virtual Machine when started.
instance_memory	AUTOMATIC, 8–524,288 4K pages Default: AUTOMATIC	Specifies the amount of memory that should be reserved for instance management. This includes memory areas that describe the databases on the instance. The memory allocated by this parameter establishes the maximum number of databases that can be active at the same time, and the maximum number of agents that can be active at any given time. (If this parameter is set to AUTOMATIC, DB2 will calculate the amount of instance memory needed for the current configuration.)
intra_parallel	SYSTEM, YES, NO Default: NO	Specifies whether or not the DB2 Database Manager instance can use intrapartition parallelism.
		(continues)

Table 5–2	DB2 Database Manager Instance Configuration Parameters (Continued)	
Parameter	**Value Range / Default**	**Description**
ipx_socket	879E–87A2 Default: 879E	Specifies a well-known socket number that represents the connection end point in a DB2 server's NetWare internetwork address.
java_heap_sz	0–4,096 4k pages Default: 512	Specifies the maximum amount of memory (in pages) that is to be used by the Java™ interpreter. For nonpartitioned database systems, one heap of memory is allocated for the instance; for partitioned database systems, one heap of memory is allocated for each database partition server.
jdk_path	Any valid character string Default: NULL	Specifies the directory where the Java Development Kit 1.1 has been installed. CLASSPATH and other environment variables used by the Java interpreter are computed using the value of this parameter.
keepfenced	YES, NO Default: NO	Specifies whether or not a fenced process is to be kept after a fenced call is completed. (If this parameter is set to NO, a new fenced process is created and destroyed for each fenced invocation; if set to YES, a fenced process is reused for subsequent fenced calls.)
max_connections	−1, 1–*maxagents* Default: −1	Specifies the maximum number of client connections that are allowed for each database partition.
max_conretries	0–100 Default: 5	Specifies the number of connection retries that can be made to a database partition server.
max_coordagents	−1, 0–*maxagents* Default: −1	Specifies the maximum number of coordinating agents that can exist on a node at one time.
		(continues)

Table 5–2 DB2 Database Manager Instance Configuration Parameters (Continued)		
Parameter	Value Range / Default	Description
max_logicalagents	−1, *max_coordagents*– 64,000 Default: −1	Specifies the maximum number of applications that can be connected to the instance. (Typically, each application is assigned a coordinator agent.)
max_querydegree	ANY, 1–32,767 Default: ANY	Specifies the maximum degree of parallelism that is to be used for any SQL statement executing on this instance of the DB2 Database Manager. For a multimode system, this parameter applies to the degree of parallelism used within a single node.
max_time_diff	1–1,440 minutes Default: 60	Specifies the maximum time difference, in minutes, that is permitted among the system clocks of the database partition servers listed in the **db2nodes.cfg** file.
maxagents	1–64,000 Default: 200 (400 on a partitioned database server)	Specifies the maximum number of DB2 Database Manager agents that can exist simultaneously, regardless of which database is being used. (An agent facilitates the operations between the application and the database.)
maxcagents	−1, 1–*max_coordagents* Default: −1	Specifies the maximum number of DB2 Database Manager agents that can be concurrently executing a DB2 Database Manager transaction. This parameter can be set to the same value as the *maxagents* parameter.
maxtotfilop	100–32,768 Default: 16,000	Specifies the maximum number of files that can be open per application. The value specified in this parameter defines the total database and application file handles that can be used by a specific process connected to a database.

(continues)

Table 5–2   DB2 Database Manager Instance Configuration Parameters (Continued)

Parameter	Value Range / Default	Description
min_priv_mem	32–112,000 4K pages Default: 32	Specifies the number of pages that the database server process will reserve as private virtual memory when a DB2 Database Manager instance is started.
mon_heap_sz	0–60,000 4K pages Default: 12, 32, or 56 depending on the operating system used.	Specifies the amount of memory (in 4KB pages) to allocate for database system monitor data. (Database system monitor heap size.)
nname	Any valid character string Default: NULL	Specifies the name of the node or workstation. Database clients use this value to access database server workstations using NetBIOS. If the database server workstation changes the name specified in *nname,* all clients that access the database server workstation must catalog it again and specify the new name.
nodetype	N/A	Read-only; provides information about the DB2 products that you have installed on your machine.
notifylevel	0–4 Default: 3	Specifies the severity level used to determine which messages are written to the notification files. (For Windows NT, notifications are written to the Windows NT event log. For all other operating systems and node types, notifications are written to the notification file called instance.nfy. Notifications can be written by DB2, the Health Monitor, and the Capture and Apply programs, as well as by user applications.)
num_initagents	0–*num_poolagents* Default: 0	Specifies the initial number of agents that are created in the agent pool when the DB2 Database Manager is started.

(continues)

Table 5–2   DB2 Database Manager Instance Configuration Parameters (Continued)

Parameter	Value Range / Default	Description
num_initfenced	0–*fenced_pool* Default: 0	Specifies the initial number of idle fenced processes that are created in the fenced pool at DB2START time.
num_poolagents	–1, 0–maxagents Default: –1	Specifies the size to which the agent pool is allowed to grow.
numdb	1–256 Default: 3 (Windows) or 8 (UNIX)	Specifies the maximum number of local databases that can be active (that is, that can have applications connected to them) at one time.
objectname	Any valid character string Default: NULL	Provides the name of the database manager instance in a IPX/SPX network. (Each server instance registered to a NetWare fileserver must have a unique name.)
priv_mem_thresh	–1, 32–112,000 4K pages Default:1,296	Specifies a threshold below which a server will not release the memory associated with a client when that client's connection is terminated.
query_heap_sz	2–524,288 4K pages Default: 1,000	Specifies the maximum amount of memory (in 4 KB pages) that can be allocated for the query heap. The query heap is used to store each query in the agent's private memory.
release	N/A	Read-only; specifies the release level of the DB2 Database Manager configuration file.
restbufsz	16–524,288 4k pages Default: 1,024	Specifies the size (in 4KB pages) of the buffer that is used for restoring a database (if the buffer size is not specified when the RESTORE utility is invoked).

(continues)

Table 5-2	DB2 Database Manager Instance Configuration Parameters (Continued)	
Parameter	Value Range / Default	Description
resync_interval	1–60,000 seconds Default: 180	Specifies the time interval (in seconds) after which a Transaction Manager (TM), Resource Manager (RM), or Sync Point Manager (SPM) should retry to recover any outstanding in-doubt transactions found in the TM, RM, or SPM. This parameter value is only used when transactions are running in a distributed unit of work (DUOW) environment.
route_obj_name	Any valid character string Default: NULL	Specifies the name of the default routing information object entry that will be used by all client applications attempting to access a DRDA server.
rqrioblk	4,096–65,535 bytes Default: 32,767	Specifies the size (in bytes) of the communication buffer that is used between remote applications and their corresponding database agents on the database server.
sheapthres	250–2,097,152 4k pages Default: 10,000 or 20,000	Specifies the limit on the total amount of memory (in pages) that is to be made available for sorting operations.
spm_log_file_sz	4–1,000 4K pages Default: 256	Specifies the size (in 4KB pages) of the Sync Point Manager (SPM) log file.
spm_log_path	Any valid character string Default: sqllib/spmlog	Specifies the directory where Sync Point Manager (SPM) log files are written.
spm_max_resync	10–256 Default: 20	Specifies the number of simultaneous agents that can perform resynchronization operations.
spm_name	Any valid character string Default: Derived from TCP/IP hostname.	Specifies the name of the Sync Point Manager (SPM) instance that is to be used by the DB2 Database Manager.

(continues)

Table 5-2 DB2 Database Manager Instance Configuration Parameters (Continued)		
Parameter	**Value Range / Default**	**Description**
ss_logon	YES, NO Default: YES	Specifies whether or not a LOGON user ID and password is required before issuing a DB2START or DB2STOP command. (This parameter is only applicable to the OS2 environment.)
start_stop_time	1–1,440 minutes Default: 10	Specifies the time, in minutes, in which all nodes of a partitioned database must respond to DB2START, DB2STOP, and ADD NODE commands.
svcename	Any valid character string Default: NULL	Specifies a service name that represents the DB2 Database Manager instance in a TCP/IP network. This value must be the same as the Connection Service name specified in the services file.
sysadm_group	Any valid character string Default: NULL	Specifies the group name that has System Administrator (SYSADM) authority for the DB2 Database Manager instance.
sysctrl_group	Any valid character string Default: NULL	Specifies the group name that has System Control (SYSCTRL) authority for the DB2 Database Manager instance.
sysmaint_group	Any valid character string Default: NULL	Specifies the group name that has System Maintenance (SYSMAINT) authority for the DB2 Database Manager instance.
tm_database	1ST_CONN, any valid database name Default: 1ST_CONN	Specifies the name of the transaction manager (TM) database for each DB2 Database Manager instance.
tp_mon_name	CICS, MQ, ENCINA, CB, SF, TUXEDO, TOPEND, blank, or any valid character string Default: blank	Specifies the name of the transaction processing (TP) monitor product being used. *(continues)*

Table 5–2	DB2 Database Manager Instance Configuration Parameters (Continued)	
Parameter	**Value Range / Default**	**Description**
tpname	Any valid character string Default: NULL	Specifies the name of the remote transaction program that the database client must use when it issues an allocate request to the DB2 Database Manager instance using the APPC communication protocol.
trust_allclnts	YES, NO, DRDAONLY Default: YES	Specifies whether or not all clients are treated as trusted clients (that is, whether or not a level of security is available at the client that is used to validate users at the client).
trust_clntauth	CLIENT, SERVER Default: CLIENT	Specifies whether or not all users of trusted clients are validated at the client.
udf_mem_sz	128–60,000 4K pages Default: 256	Specifies the amount of memory that is to be allocated and shared between the database process and a fenced User Defined Function (UDF). (For an unfenced process, it specifies the size of the private memory set.)
use_sna_auth	YES, NO Default: NO	Specifies whether or not inbound connections to the server that use the SNA protocol are only authenticated at the SNA layer and not by DB2. (This is only in effect if *authentication* is set to SERVER.)

Adapted from Table 25 and Table 26 on pages 376–382 of the *DB2 Administration Guide—Performance* manual

The contents of a DB2 Database Manager configuration file can be viewed and/or altered using the DBM Configuration dialog, which can be activated by selecting the *Configure Parameters* action from the *Instance* menu found in the Control Center. Figure 5–3 shows the Control Center menu items that must be selected to activate the DBM Configuration dialog; Figure 5–4 shows how the DBM Configuration dialog might look after it has been activated.

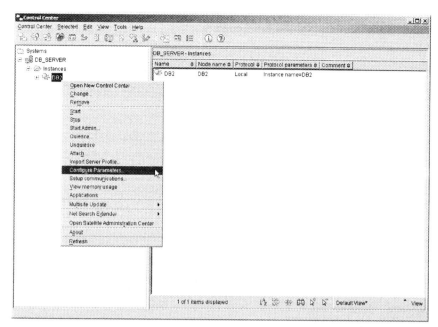

Figure 5-3   Invoking the DBM Configuration dialog from the Control Center.

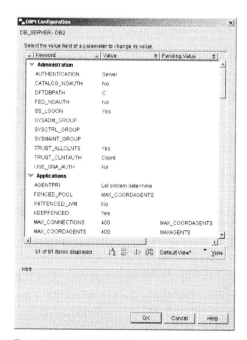

Figure 5-4   The DBM Configuration dialog.

The contents of the DB2 Database Manager configuration file for a particular instance can also be displayed by attaching to the appropriate instance and executing the GET DATABASE MANAGER CONFIGURATION command. The syntax for this command is:

```
GET [DATABASE MANAGER | DB MANAGER | DBM]
[CONFIGURATION | CONFIG | CFG]
<SHOW DETAIL>
```

Thus, if you wanted to view the contents of the DB2 Database Manager configuration file for the current instance, you could do so by executing a GET DATABASE MANAGER CONFIGURATION command that looks like this:

```
GET DBM CFG
```

Similarly, the value assigned to a particular DB2 Database Manager configuration parameter can be changed by attaching to the appropriate instance and executing the UPDATE DATABASE MANAGER CONFIGURATION command. The syntax for this command is:

```
UPDATE [DATABASE MANAGER | DB MANAGER | DBM]
[CONFIGURATION | CONFIG | CFG]
USING [[Parameter] [Value],...]
<IMMEDIATE | DEFERRED>
```

where:

Parameter	Identifies one or more DB2 Database Manager configuration parameters (by keyword) whose values are to be modified. (In many cases, the keyword for a parameter is the same as the parameter name itself.)
Value	Identifies the new value(s) that are to be assigned to the DB2 Database Manager configuration parameter(s) specified.

If the DEFERRED clause is specified with the UPDATE DATABASE MANAGER CONFIGURATION command, changes made to the DB2 Database Manager configuration will not take effect until the DB2 Database Manager instance is stopped and restarted. On the other hand, if the IMMEDIATE clause is specified or if neither clause is used, changes made to the DB2 Database Manager configuration will take effect immediately—provided the configuration parameter(s) specified can be changed dynamically. The DB2 Database Manager configuration parameters that can be changed dynamically are:

➤ *catalog_noauth*

➤ *comm_bandwidth*

➤ *conn_elapse*

➤ *cpuspeed*

➤ *dft_account_str*

➤ *dft_mon_bufpool*

➤ *dft_mon_lock*

➤ *dft_mon_sort*

➤ *dft_mon_stmt*

➤ *dft_mon_table*

➤ *dft_mon_timestamp*

➤ *dft_mon_uow*

➤ *dftdbpath*

➤ *diaglevel*

➤ *diagpath*

➤ *discover_inst*

➤ *fcm_num_buffers*

➤ *fed_noauth*

➤ *health_mon*

➤ *indexrec*

➤ *max_conretries*

➤ *max_querydegree*

➤ *notifylevel*

➤ *start_stop_time*

➤ *use_sna_auth*

Thus, if you wanted to change the value of the *intra_parallel* DB2 Database Manager configuration parameter for the current instance from NO to YES, you could do so by executing an UPDATE DATABASE MANAGER CONFIGURATION command that looks like this:

```
UPDATE DBM CFG USING INTRA_PARALLEL YES
```

Database Configurations

Just as a DB2 Database Manager configuration file is created and initialized whenever a new instance is created, a database configuration file is created and initialized each time a new database is created. Each database configuration file is comprised of 88 different parameters and, just as most DB2 Database Manager instance configuration parameters control the amount of system resources that will be allocated to a single DB2 Database Manager instance, many of the database configuration file parameters control the amount of system resources that will be allocated to the associated database during normal operation. The parameters that make up a database configuration file are shown in Table 5–3.

Table 5–3 DB2 Database Configuration Parameters		
Parameter	**Value Range / Default**	**Description**
app_ctl_heap_sz	0–64,000 4k pages Default: 128	Specifies the maximum size (in 4KB pages) of memory that is to be allocated for the application control heap. The application control heap is used to share information among agents working on behalf of the same application at a node in an MPP or an SMP system.
appgroup_mem_sz	1–1,000,000 4k pages Default: 10,000	Specifies the maximum size of the application group shared memory segment.
applheapsz	16–60,000 4k pages Default: 256	Specifies the number of private memory pages that are to be available for use by the DB2 Database Manager on behalf of a specific agent or subagent.
autorestart	ON, OFF Default: ON	Specifies whether or not the DB2 Database Manager is to automatically issue a RESTART DATABASE command when it is detected that the database is in an inconsistent state (which is the case if the last database connection was disrupted, or if the database was not terminated normally during the previous session). If this parameter is set to ON, a database is restarted automatically if necessary. If this parameter is set to OFF, a database must be restarted manually.
		(continues)

Table 5–3 DB2 Database Configuration Parameters (Continued)		
Parameter	**Value Range / Default**	**Description**
avg_appls	1–*maxappls* Default: 1	Specifies the average number of active applications that normally access the database. The SQL optimizer uses this parameter to help estimate how much buffer pool memory will be available for the chosen access plan at application runtime.
backup_pending	N/A	Read-only; specifies whether or not a database needs to be backed up. If this parameter is set to NO, the database is in a usable state. If this parameter is set to YES, an OFFLINE backup must be performed before the database can be used.
blk_log_dsk_ful	YES, NO Default: NO	Specifies whether or not applications should hang whenever the DB2 Database Manager encounters a log full error. This configuration parameter can be set to prevent disk full errors from being generated when DB2 cannot create a new log file in the active log location.
buffpage	2–524,288 pages Default: 250 (Windows) or 1000 (UNIX)	Specifies the size a buffer pool should be if the CREATE BUFFERPOOL or ALTER BUFFERPOOL statement is executed with the NPAGES parameter set to −1.
catalogcache_sz	−1, 8–524,288 4k pages Default: −1	Specifies the amount of memory (in pages) that is to be used to cache system catalog information.
chngpgs_thresh	5–99% Default: 60	Specifies the percentage of pages stored in a buffer pool that must be modified before the asynchronous page cleaners used by DB2 will be started if they are not already active.
codepage	N/A	Read-only; specifies the code page used by the database.
codeset	N/A	Read-only; specifies the code set used by the database.

(continues)

Table 5–3	DB2 Database Configuration Parameters (Continued)	
Parameter	Value Range / Default	Description
collate_info	N/A	Read-only; specifies the collating sequence used by the database. (This parameter can only be displayed using the GET DATABASE CONFIGURATION API; it cannot be seen using the Command Line Processor or Database Configuration interface.)
copy_protect	YES, NO Default: NO	Specifies whether or not the database is copy protected.
country	N/A	Read-only; specifies the country/territory code used by the database.
database_consistent	N/A	Read-only; specifies whether or not the database is in a consistent state. If this parameter is set to YES, all transactions have been committed or rolled back so that the data is consistent. If this parameter is set to NO, a transaction is pending or some other task is pending on the database.
database_level	N/A	Read-only; identifies the release level of the DB2 Database Manager that can use the database.
database_memory	AUTOMATIC, 0– 4,294,967,295 4K pages Default: AUTOMATIC	Specifies the minimum amount of shared memory that is to be reserved for the database's use. (If this parameter is set to AUTOMATIC, DB2 will calculate the amount of memory needed for the database and allocate it at database activation time.)
dbheap	AUTOMATIC, 32–524,288 4K pages Default: AUTOMATIC	Specifies the size, in pages, of the database heap, which is used to hold control information on all open cursors accessing the database. Both log buffers and catalog cache buffers are allocated from the database heap. (If this parameter is set to AUTOMATIC, DB2 will calculate the amount of memory needed for the database and allocate when the first connection to the database is established.)

(continues)

Table 5–3 DB2 Database Configuration Parameters (Continued)		
Parameter	**Value Range / Default**	**Description**
dft_degree	–1, 1–32,767 Default: 1	Specifies the default value for the CURRENT DEGREE special register and the DEGREE bind option.
dft_extent_sz	2–256 4K pages Default: 32	Specifies the default extent size (in pages) that will be used when new table spaces are created if no extent size is specified.
dft_loadrec_ses	1–30,000 Default: 1	Specifies the default number of load recovery sessions that will be used during the recovery of a table load operation. This parameter is only applicable if roll-forward recovery is enabled.
dft_prefetch_sz	0–32,767 4K pages Default: 16 (Windows) or 32 (UNIX)	Specifies the default prefetch size (in pages) that will be used when new tablespaces are created if no prefetch size is specified.
dft_queryopt	0–9 Default: 5	Specifies the default query optimization class the DB2 Optimizer is to use when compiling SQL queries.
dft_refresh_age	ANY, 0–99,999,999,999,999 Default: 0	Specifies the default value that is to be used for the refresh age of summary tables if the CURRENT REFRESH AGE special register has not been set. (This parameter is used to determine whether summary tables are to be considered when optimizing the processing of dynamic SQL queries.)
dft_sqlmathwarn	YES, NO Default: NO	Specifies whether or not arithmetic errors and retrieval conversion errors are handled as errors or as warnings during SQL statement compilation.
dir_obj_name	Any valid character string Default: NULL	The object name representing your database manager instance (or database) in the directory.
discover_db	ENABLE, DISABLE Default: ENABLE	Specifies whether or not information about a database is to be returned to a client when a discovery request is received at the server.

(continues)

Table 5–3   DB2 Database Configuration Parameters (Continued)

Parameter	Value Range / Default	Description
dl_expint	1–31,536,000 seconds Default: 60	Specifies the interval of time (in seconds) for which the DB2 Data Links Manager file access token generated is valid.
dl_num_copies	0–15 Default: 0	Specifies the number of additional copies of a file to be made in the archive server (such as an TSM server) when a file is linked to the database (DB2 Data Links Manager only).
dl_time_drop	0–365 days Default: 0	Specifies the interval of time (in days) files will be retained on an archive server (such as a TSM server) after a DROP TABLE, DROP DATABASE, or DROP TABLESPACE statement is issued (DB2 Data Links Manager only).
dl_token	MAC0, MAC1 Default: MAC0	Specifies the algorithm used in the generation of DATALINK file access control tokens (DB2 Data Links Manager only).
dl_upper	YES, NO Default: YES	Specifies whether file access control tokens use uppercase letters only, or can contain both uppercase and lowercase letters (DB2 Data Links Manager only).
dl_wt_iexpint	1–31,536,000 Seconds Default: 60	Specifies the interval of time (in seconds) for which the write token generated is valid.
dlchktime	1,000–600,000 milliseconds Default: 10,000	Specifies the frequency at which the DB2 Database Manager checks for deadlocks among all the applications connected to a database.

(continues)

Table 5–3	DB2 Database Configuration Parameters (Continued)	
Parameter	Value Range / Default	Description
dyn_query_mgmt	ENABLE, DISABLE Default: DISABLE	Specifies whether or not queries that exceed thresholds are trapped by DB2 Query Patroller. If this parameter is set to ENABLE and the cost of the dynamic query exceeds the trap threshold for the user or group (as specified in the Query Patroller user profile table), the query will be trapped by DB2 Query Patroller. If this parameter is set to DISABLE, no queries are trapped.
estore_seg_sz	0–1,048,575 4k pages Default: 16,000	Specifies the number of pages to be stored in the extended memory segments of the database.
groupheap_ratio	1–99 % Default: 70	Specifies the percentage of memory (in the application group shared memory set) devoted to the application group heap
indexrec	SYSTEM, ACCESS, RESTART Default: SYSTEM	Specifies whether invalid indexes should be recreated when the database is restarted or when they are accessed. (The value SYSTEM specifies that the value of the DB2 Database Manager configuration parameter *indexrec* is to be used.)
indexsort	YES, NO Default: YES	Indicates whether or not sorting of index keys will occur during index creation.
locklist	4–60,000 4k pages Default: 25, 50 (Windows) or 100 (UNIX)	Specifies the maximum amount of memory (in pages) that is to be allocated and used to hold the lock list.
locktimeout	–1, 0–30,000 Default: –1	Specifies the number of seconds that an application will wait to obtain a lock before timing out. (If this parameter is set to –1, an application will wait forever to acquire a lock.)
log_retain_status	N/A	Read-only; specifies whether or not log files are being retained for use with roll-forward recovery operations.

(continues)

Table 5–3 DB2 Database Configuration Parameters (Continued)		
Parameter	**Value Range / Default**	**Description**
logbufsz	4–4096 4k pages Default: 8	Specifies the amount of memory (in pages) that is to be used to buffer log records before they are written to disk.
logfilsiz	4–262,144 4K pages Default: 250 (Windows) or 1,000 (UNIX)	Specifies the amount of disk storage space (in pages) that is to be allocated to log files that are used for data recovery. This parameter defines the size of each primary and secondary log file.
loghead	N/A	Read-only; specifies the name of the log file that contains the most recent record written to (head) the active log. The next log record written will start at head of the active log file.
logpath	N/A	Read-only; specifies the current path being used to access log files.
logprimary	2–256 Default: 3	Specifies the number of primary log files that will be used for transaction logging.
logretain	RECOVERY, NO Default: NO	Specifies whether or not active log files are to be retained as archived log files for use in roll-forward recovery (also known as archival logging).
logsecond	–1, 0–254 Default: 2	Specifies the number of secondary log files that can be used for transaction logging. (If this parameter is set to –1, infinite active logging will be used.)
max_log	0s–100% Default: 0	This is the maximum active log space consumed by one transaction (as a percent).
maxappls	AUTOMATIC, 1–60,000 Default: AUTOMATIC	Specifies the maximum number of application programs (both local and remote) that can connect to the database at one time. (If this parameter is set to AUTOMATIC, DB2 will dynamically allocate the resources it needs to support new applications.)

(continues)

Table 5–3 DB2 Database Configuration Parameters (Continued)		
Parameter	Value Range / Default	Description
maxfilop	2–32,768 (Windows) 2–1,950 (UNIX) Default: 64	Specifies the maximum number of database files that an application program can have open at one time.
maxlocks	1–100 Default: 22 (Windows) or 10 (UNIX)	Specifies the maximum amount (in percentage) of the lock list that any one application is allowed to use.
min_dec_div_3	YES, NO Default: NO	Specifies whether or not the result of decimal division arithmetic operations is to always have a scale of at least 3.
mincommit	1–25 Default: 1	Specifies the number of COMMIT SQL statements that are to be processed before log records are written to disk.
mirrorlogpath	Any valid character string Default: NULL	Specifies the location where a second copy of primary and secondary log files are to be stored.
multipage_alloc	N/A	Read-only; specifies whether new storage for SMS tablespaces is allocated one page at a time or one extent at a time.
newlogpath	Any valid character string Default: NULL	Specifies a new location to use for storing primary and secondary log files. (Logging will take place after all connections to the database have been terminated.)
num_db_backups	1–32,768 Default: 12	Specifies the number of database backup images to retain for a database. (After the specified number of backups is reached, old backups are marked as expired in the recovery history file.)
num_estore_segs	0–2,147,483,647 Default: 0	Specifies the number of extended storage memory segments available to the database.
num_freqvalues	0–32,767 Default: 10	Specifies the number of "most frequent values" that will be collected when the WITH DISTRIBUTION option is specified with the RUNSTATS command (or function).

(continues)

Table 5–3 DB2 Database Configuration Parameters (Continued)		
Parameter	**Value Range / Default**	**Description**
num_iocleaners	0–255 Default: 1	Specifies the number of asynchronous page cleaners that are to be used by the database.
num_ioservers	1–255 Default: 3	Specifies the number of I/O servers that are to be used by the database. I/O servers are used on behalf of database agents to perform prefetch I/O and asynchronous I/O needed by utilities such as backup and restore.
num_log_span	0–65,535 Default: 0	Number of active log files an active transaction is allowed to span.
num_quantiles	0–32,767 Default: 20	Specifies the number of quantiles (values in a column that satisfy a RANGE predicate) that will be collected when the WITH DISTRIBUTION option is specified with the RUNSTATS command (or function).
numsegs	N/A	Read-only; specifies the number of containers that will be created within the default SMS tablespaces of the database.
overflowlogpath	Any valid character string Default: NULL	Specifies the location where active log files needed for rollback operations are stored.
pckcachesz	–1, 32–64,000 4k pages Default: –1	Specifies the amount of application memory (in pages) that will be used to cache packages.
rec_his_retentn	–1, 0–30,000 days Default: 366	Specifies the number of days that historical information on backups is to be retained.
release	N/A	Read-only; specifies the release level of the database configuration file.
restore_pending	N/A	Read-only; specifies whether or not the database is in "Restore Pending" state.
		(continues)

Table 5–3 DB2 Database Configuration Parameters (Continued)		
Parameter	**Value Range / Default**	**Description**
rollfwd_pending	N/A	Read-only; specifies whether or not a roll-forward recovery procedure needs to be performed on the database. (If this parameter is set to NO, neither the database nor any of its tablespace is in "Roll-forward Pending" state. If this parameter is set to DATABASE, the database needs to be rolled forward before it can be used. If this parameter is set to TABLESPACES, one or more tablespaces in the database needs to be rolled forward.)
seqdetect	YES, NO Default: YES	Specifies whether or not sequential detection for the database is enabled.
sheapthres_shr	250–2,097,152 4k pages Default: *sortheap*	Specifies the maximum amount of memory (in pages) that is to be used at any one time to perform sort operations.
softmax	1–100 * *logprimary* Default: 100	Specifies the maximum percentage of log file space to be consumed before a soft checkpoint is taken.
sortheap	16–524,288 4k pages Default: 256	Specifies the amount of memory (in pages) that is to be available to perform sort operations.
stat_heap_sz	1,096–524,288 4k pages Default: 4384	Specifies the maximum size of the heap space (in pages) that is to be used in creating and collecting all table statistics when distribution statistics are gathered.
stmtheap	128–65,535 4k pages Default: 2048	Specifies the heap size (in pages) that is to be used for compiling SQL statements.
territory	N/A	Read-only; specifies the territory of the database.

(continues)

Table 5–3 DB2 Database Configuration Parameters (Continued)		
Parameter	**Value Range / Default**	**Description**
trackmod	YES, NO Default: NO	Specifies whether or not database modifications are to be tracked so the BACKUP utility can detect which subsets of the database pages must be examined by an incremental backup and potentially included in the backup image.
tsm_mgmtclass	Any valid character string Default: NULL	Specifies how the server should manage backup versions or archive copies of the objects being backed up. The TSM management class is assigned from the TSM administrator.
tsm_nodename	Any valid character string Default: NULL	Specifies the node name associated with the TSM product. (Used to override the default setting.)
tsm_owner	Any valid character string Default: NULL	Specifies the owner associated with the TSM product. (Used to override the default setting.)
tsm_password	Any valid character string Default: NULL	Specifies the password associated with the TSM product. (Used to override the default setting.)
userexit	YES, NO Default: NO	Specifies whether or not a user exit program, which is a program that is used to automatically move log files to and from an archive storage location, is to be invoked as log files are closed or needed for roll-forward recovery. (If this parameter is set to OFF, a user exit function cannot be called. If this parameter is set to ON, a user exit function can be called.)
user_exit_status	N/A	Read-only; specifies whether or not a user exit function can be called to store archive log files.
util_heap_sz	16–524,288 4K pages Default: 5000	Specifies the maximum amount of shared memory that can be used simultaneously by the backup, restore, and load utilities.

Adapted from Table 27 and Table 28 on pages 382–388 of the *DB2 Administration Guide—Performance* manual

The contents of a database configuration file can be viewed and/or altered using the Database Configuration dialog, which can be activated by selecting the *Configure Parameters* action from the *Databases* menu found in the Control Center. Figure 5–5 shows the Control Center menu items that must be selected to activate the Database Configuration dialog; Figure 5–6 shows how the Database Configuration dialog might look after it has been activated.

The contents of the database configuration file for a particular database can also be displayed by executing the GET DATABASE CONFIGURATION command. The syntax for this command is:

```
GET [DATABASE | DB] [CONFIGURATION | CONFIG | CFG]
FOR [DatabaseAlias]
<SHOW DETAIL>
```

where:

> *DatabaseAlias*   Identifies the alias assigned to the database that configuration information is to be displayed for.

Thus, if you wanted to view the contents of the database configuration file for a database named SAMPLE, you could do so by executing a GET DATABASE CONFIGURATION command that looks like this:

```
GET DB CFG FOR SAMPLE
```

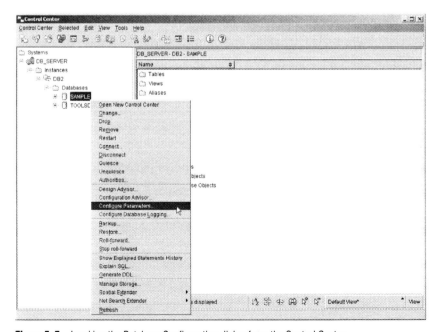

Figure 5–5   Invoking the Database Configuration dialog from the Control Center.

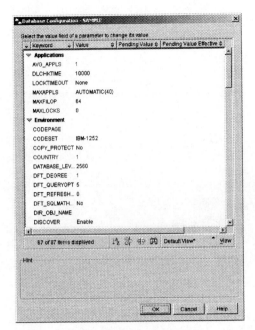

Figure 5–6 The Database Configuration dialog.

Similarly, the value assigned to a particular database configuration parameter can be changed by executing the UPDATE DATABASE CONFIGURATION command. The syntax for this command is:

```
UPDATE [DATABASE | DB]
[CONFIGURATION | CONFIG | CFG]
FOR [DatabaseAlias]
USING [[Parameter] [Value],...]
<IMMEDIATE | DEFERRED>
```

where:

DatabaseAlias	Identifies the alias assigned to the database that configuration information is to be modified for.
Parameter	Identifies one or more database configuration parameters (by keyword) whose values are to be modified. (In many cases, the keyword for a parameter is the same as the parameter name itself.)
Value	Identifies the new value(s) that are to be assigned to the database configuration parameter(s) specified.

If the DEFERRED clause is specified with the UPDATE DATABASE CONFIGURA-TION command, changes made to the database configuration will not take effect until all connections to the database the configuration file is associated with have been terminated and a new connection has been established. On the other hand, if the IMMEDIATE clause is specified or if neither clause is used, changes made to the database configuration will take effect immediately—provided the configuration parameter(s) specified can be changed dynamically. The database configuration parameters that can be changed dynamically are:

➤ *autorestart*

➤ *avg_appls*

➤ *blk_log_dsk_ful*

➤ *catalogcache_sz*

➤ *dbheap*

➤ *dft_degree*

➤ *dft_extent_sz*

➤ *dft_loadrec_ses*

➤ *dft_prefetch_sz*

➤ *dft_queryopt*

➤ *discover_db*

➤ *dl_expint*

➤ *dl_num_copies*

➤ *dl_time_drop*

➤ *dl_token*

➤ *dl_upper*

➤ *dl_wt_iexpint*

➤ *indexrec*

➤ *locklist*

➤ *logsecond*

➤ *maxappls*

➤ *maxfilop*

➤ *maxlocks*

➤ *mincommit*

➤ *num_db_backups*

➤ *num_freqvalues*

➤ *num_quantiles*

➤ *pckcachesz*

➤ *seqdetect*

➤ *sortheap*

➤ *stmtheap*

➤ *tsm_mgmtclass*

➤ *tsm_nodename*

➤ *tsm_owner*

➤ *tsm_password*

➤ *util_heap_sz*

Thus, if you wanted to change the value of the *autorestart* database configuration parameter for a database named SAMPLE from ON to OFF, you could do so by executing an UPDATE DATABASE CONFIGURATION command that looks like this:

```
UPDATE DB CFG FOR SAMPLE USING AUTORESTART OFF
```

The Database System Monitor

With such a broad range of configuration parameters to choose from, deciding which parameters to modify and what modifications to make can be a difficult decision. Often, configuration parameter changes are made to provide greater concurrency and to reduce or eliminate bottlenecks that slow down query response time. Consequently, before you begin making changes to improve database performance, you must identify where performance is suffering, as well as have some idea what needs to be done to improve it. That's where DB2's Database System Monitor comes in.

Along with providing valuable information that should be used when making instance and database configuration modifications, database monitoring is a vital activity that, when performed on a regular basis, provides continuous feedback on the health of a database system. And because database monitoring is such an integral part of database administration, DB2 UDB comes equipped with a monitoring utility that is known as the Database System Monitor.

Although the name "Database System Monitor" suggests that only one monitoring tool is provided, in reality the Database System Monitor is composed of two distinct tools—(a *snapshot monitor* and one or more *event monitors*)—that can be used to capture and return system monitor information. The snapshot monitor allows you to capture a picture of the state of a database (along with all database activity) at a specific point in time, while event monitors capture and log data as specific database events occur. Information collected by both tools is stored in entities that are referred to as *monitor elements* (or *data elements*) and each monitor element used is identified by a unique name and is designed to store a certain type of information. The following are the element types in which monitor elements store data:

> **Counters.** Keeps an accurate count of the number of times an activity or event has occurred. Counter values increase throughout the life of the monitor; often a counter monitor element is resettable.

> **Gauges.** Indicates the current value for an item. Unlike counters, gauge values can go up or down, depending on the amount of database activity (for example, the number of applications currently connected to the database).

> **Water marks.** Indicates the highest (maximum) or lowest (minimum) value an item has seen since monitoring began (for example, the largest number of agents associated with a particular application).

> **Information.** Provides reference-type details of all monitoring activities performed (for example, buffer pool names, database names and aliases, path details, etc.).

> **Timestamps.** Indicates the date and time an activity or event took place (for example, the date and time the first database connection was established). Timestamp values are provided as the number of seconds and microseconds that have elapsed since January 1, 1970.

> **Time.** Indicates the amount of time that was spent performing an activity or event (for example, the amount of time spent performing a sort operation). Time values are provided as the number of seconds and microseconds that have elapsed since the activity or event was started. Some time elements are resettable.

The Database System Monitor utilizes several methods for presenting the data collected. For both snapshot and event monitors you have the option of storing all data collected in files or database tables, viewing it on-screen, or processing it using a custom application. (The Database System Monitor returns monitor data to a client application using a self-describing data stream; with a snapshot monitoring application you call the appropriate snapshot APIs to capture a snapshot and then process the data stream returned. With an event monitoring application, you prepare to receive the data produced via a file or a named pipe, activate the appropriate event monitor, and process the data stream as it is received.)

Because monitoring adds additional processing overhead, the amount of time spent monitoring a system should be limited, and monitoring should always be performed with some purpose in mind.

The Snapshot Monitor

The snapshot monitor is designed to collect information about the state of a DB2 UDB instance and the databases it controls *at a specific point in time* (i.e., at the time the snapshot is taken). Snapshots are useful for determining the status of a database system, and when taken at regular intervals, they can provide valuable information that can be used to observe trends and identify potential problem areas. Snapshots can be taken by executing the snapshot monitor commands from the DB2 Command Line Processor (CLP), by executing the appropriate SQL table functions, or by using the snapshot monitor APIs in a C or C++ application. Furthermore, snapshots can be tailored to return specific types of monitoring data values (for example, a snapshot could be configured to return just information about buffer pools).

 Only users with System Administrator (SYSADM) authority, System Control (SYSC-TRL) authority, or System Maintenance (SYSMAINT) authority are allowed to use the snapshot monitor.

Snapshot Monitor Switches

Often, the collection of system monitor data introduces additional processing overhead. For example, in order to calculate the execution time of SQL statements, the DB2 Database Manager must make a call to the operating system to obtain timestamps before and after every SQL statement is executed. These types of system calls are normally expensive. Another side effect of using the system monitor is an increase in memory consumption. The DB2 Database Manager uses memory to store data collected for every monitor element that is tracked by the system monitor.

To help minimize the overhead involved in collecting system monitor information, a group of switches known as *snapshot monitor switches* can be used to control what information is collected when a snapshot is taken; the type and amount of information collected is determined by the way these snapshot monitor switches have been set. Each snapshot monitor switch has two settings: ON and OFF. When a snapshot monitor switch is set to OFF, monitor elements that fall under that switch's control do not collect information. The opposite is true if the switch is set to ON. (Keep in mind that a considerable amount of monitoring information is not under switch control and will always be collected regardless of how the snapshot monitor switches have been set.) The snapshot monitor switches available, along with a description of the type of information that is collected when each has been set to ON, can be seen in Table 5–4.

Table 5–4	Snapshot Monitor Switches		
Monitor Group	**Monitor Switch**	**DB2 Database Manager Configuration Parameter**	**Information Provided**
Buffer Pools	BUFFERPOOL	*dft_mon_bufferpool*	Amount of buffer pool activity (i.e., number of read and write operations performed and the amount of time taken for each read/write operation).
Locks	LOCK	*dft_mon_lock*	Number of locks held and number of deadlock cycles encountered.
Sorts	SORT	*dft_mon_sort*	Number of sort operations performed, number of heaps used, number of overflows encountered, and sort performance.
SQL Statements	STATEMENT	*dft_mon_stmt*	SQL statement processing start time, SQL statement processing end time, and SQL statement identification.
Tables	TABLE	*dft_mon_table*	Amount of table activity performed such as number of rows read, number of rows written, etc.
Timestamps	TIMESTAMP	*dft_mon_timestamp*	Times and timestamp information.
Transactions (units of work)	UOW	*dft_mon_uow*	Transaction start times, transaction completion times, and transaction completion status.
Adapted from Table 1 on Pages 12–13 of the *DB2 System Monitor Guide and Reference* manual.			

By default, all of the switches shown in Table 5–4 are set to OFF, with the exception of the TIMESTAMP switch, which is set to ON.

Viewing Current Snapshot Monitor Switch Settings

Earlier, we saw that the type and amount of information collected when a snapshot is taken is controlled, to some extent, by the way the snapshot monitor switches have been set. Thus, before you take a snapshot, it is important that you know which snapshot monitor switches have been turned on and which snapshot monitor switches remain off. So how can you find out what the current setting of each snapshot monitor switch available is? The easiest way is by executing the GET MONITOR SWITCHES command from the DB2 Command Line Processor (CLP). The basic syntax for this command is:

```
GET MONITOR SWITCHES
<AT DBPARTITIONNUM [PartitionNum]>
```

where:

>   *PartitonNum*   Identifies the database partition (in a multiparti-
>   tioned database environment) for which the sta-
>   tus of the snapshot monitor switches available is
>   to be obtained and displayed.

So if you wanted to obtain and display the status of the snapshot monitor switches for a single-partition database, you could do so by executing a GET MONITOR SWITCHES command that looks something like this:

```
GET MONITOR SWITCHES
```

And when this command is executed, most likely you will see output that looks something like this:

```
                  Monitor Recording Switches

Switch list for db partition number 0
Buffer Pool Activity Information (BUFFERPOOL) = OFF
Lock Information                       (LOCK) = OFF
Sorting Information                    (SORT) = OFF
SQL Statement Information         (STATEMENT) = OFF
Table Activity Information            (TABLE) = OFF
Take Timestamp Information         (TIMESTAMP) = ON
                             09-15-2003 10:30:00.028810
Unit of Work Information                (UOW) = OFF
```

Upon close examination of this output, you will notice that the TIMESTAMP snapshot monitoring switch has been turned on and that all other switches are off. The timestamp value that follows the TIMESTAMP monitoring switch's state tells you the exact date and time the TIMESTAMP monitoring switch was turned on (which in this case is September 15, 2003, at 10:30 AM).

Changing the State of a Snapshot Monitor Switch

Once you know which snapshot monitor switches have been turned on and which snapshot monitor switches have been turned off, you may find it necessary to change one or more switch settings before you start the monitoring process. Snapshot monitor switch settings can be changed at the instance level by modifying the appropriate DB2 Database Manager configuration parameters (see Table 5–4) with the UPDATE DATABASE MANAGER CONFIGURATION command. (Snapshot monitor switch settings made at the instance level remain persistent across instance restarts.) On the other hand, snapshot monitor switch settings can be changed at the application level by calling the db2MonitorSwitches() API or by executing the UPDATE MONITOR SWITCHES command. The basic syntax for this command is:

```
UPDATE MONITOR SWITCHES USING [[SwitchID] ON | OFF ,...]
```

where:

> SwitchID   Identifies one or more snapshot monitor switches whose state is to be changed. This parameter may contain any or all of the following values: BUFFERPOOL, LOCK, SORT, STATEMENT, TABLE, TIMESTAMP, UOW.

Thus, if you wanted to change the state of the LOCK snapshot monitor switch to ON (at the application level), you could do so by executing an UPDATE MONITOR SWITCHES command that looks like this:

```
UPDATE MONITOR SWITCHES USING LOCKS ON
```

Likewise, if you wanted to change the state of the BUFFERPOOL snapshot monitor switch to OFF, you could do so by executing a UPDATE MONITOR SWITCHES command that looks like this:

```
UPDATE MONITOR SWITCHES USING BUFFERPOOL OFF
```

Setting snapshot monitor switches at the instance level affects all databases under the instance's control (i.e., every application that establishes a connection to a database under the instance's control will inherit the switch settings made in the instance's configuration), while setting monitor switches at the application level only affects the database a single application is interacting with.

Capturing Snapshot Data

As soon as a database is activated or a connection to a database is established, the snapshot monitor begins collecting monitor data. And before the data collected can be viewed, a snapshot must be taken. Snapshots can be taken by embedding the db2GetSnapshot() API in an application program, or by executing the GET SNAPSHOT command. The basic syntax for this command is:

```
GET SNAPSHOT FOR
[[DATABASE MANAGER | DB MANAGER | DBM] |
ALL DATABASES |
ALL APPLICATIONS |
ALL BUFFERPOOLS |
ALL REMOTE_DATABASES |
ALL REMOTE_APPLICATIONS |
ALL ON [DatabaseAlias] |
DATABASE ON [DatabaseAlias] |
APPLICATIONS ON [DatabaseAlias] |
TABLES ON [DatabaseAlias] |
TABLESPACES ON [DatabaseAlias] |
LOCKS ON [DatabaseAlias] |
BUFFERPOOLS ON [DatabaseAlias] |
DYNAMIC SQL ON [DatabaseAlias]]
```

where:

> *DatabaseAlias*   Identifies the alias assigned to the database that snapshot monitor information is to be collected for.

So, if you wanted to take a snapshot that only contained data collected on locks being held by applications interacting with a database named SAMPLE, you could do so by executing a GET SNAPSHOT command that looks like this:

```
GET SNAPSHOT FOR LOCKS ON SAMPLE
```

And when this command is executed, you might see output that looks something like this:

```
              Database Lock Snapshot

    Database name                    = SAMPLE
    Database path                    = C:\DB2\NODE0000\SQL00002\
    Input database alias             = SAMPLE
    Locks held                       = 0
    Applications currently connected = 1
    Agents currently waiting on locks = 0
    Snapshot timestamp               = 09-17-2003 23:37:48.059793

    Application handle               = 6
    Application ID                   = *LOCAL.DB2.00C748033628
    Sequence number                  = 0001
    Application name                 = db2bp.exe
    Authorization ID                 = RSANDERS
    Application status               = Connect Completed
    Status change time               = Not Collected
```

```
Application code page            = 1252
Locks held                       = 0
Total wait time (ms)             = Not Collected
```

While examining the syntax used by the GET SNAPSHOT command, you may have noticed that different types of monitoring data can be captured when a snapshot is taken. This data includes:

DB2 Database Manager data. Information for an active instance is captured.

Database data. Information about all active databases under an instance's control is captured.

Application data. Information about one or more applications is captured.

Buffer pool data. Information about buffer pool activity is captured.

Tablespace data. Information about one or more tablespaces within a database is captured.

Table data. Information about one or more tables within a database is captured.

Lock data. Information about locks being held by applications is captured.

Dynamic SQL data. Point-in-time information about SQL statements being held in the SQL statement cache is captured.

The snapshot monitor switches, together with the GET SNAPSHOT command options available, determine the type and volume of data that will be returned when a snapshot is taken. In fact, if a particular snapshot monitor switch has not been turned on and a snapshot of the monitoring data that is associated with that switch is taken, the monitoring data captured may not contain any values at all. (If you look closely at the previous example, you will see that some values were "Not Collected". That's because when the snapshot of LOCK monitor data was taken, the LOCK snapshot monitor switch was turned off.)

Resetting Snapshot Monitor Counters

Earlier, we saw that one of the element types that monitor elements use to store data is a *counter* and that counters keep a running total of the number of times an activity or event occurs. Thus, counter values increase throughout the life of the monitor. So when exactly does counting begin? Counting typically begins as soon as a snapshot monitor switch is turned on or when connection to a database is established (if instance level monitoring is used, counting begins the first time an application establishes a connection to a database under the instance's control). However, there may be times when it is desirable to reset all counters to zero without turning snapshot monitor switches off and back on and without terminating and reestablishing database connections. By far the easiest way to quickly reset all snapshot monitor counters to zero is by executing the RESET MONITOR command. The basic syntax for this command is:

```
RESET MONITOR ALL
```

or

```
RESET MONITOR FOR [DATABASE | DB] [DatabaseAlias]
```

where:

DatabaseAlias   Identifies the alias assigned to the database that snapshot monitor counters are to be reset for.

Thus, if you wanted to reset the snapshot monitor counters for all databases under an instance's control to zero, you could do so by attaching to that instance and executing a RESET MONITOR command that looks like this:

```
RESET MONITOR ALL
```

On the other hand, if you wanted to reset just the snapshot monitor counters associated with a database named SAMPLE to zero, you could do so by executing a RESET MONITOR command that looks like this:

```
RESET MONITOR FOR DATABASE SAMPLE
```

 You cannot selectively reset counters for a particular monitoring group that is controlled by a snapshot monitor switch using the RESET MONITOR command. To perform this type of operation, you must turn the appropriate snapshot monitor switch off and back on or terminate and reestablish database connections.

Event Monitors

While the snapshot monitor provides a method for recording information about the state of database activity at a given point in time, an event monitor can be used to record information about database activity *when an event or transition occurs*. Thus, event monitors provide a way to collect monitor data when events or activities that cannot be monitored using the snapshot monitor occur. For example, suppose you want to capture monitor data whenever a deadlock cycle occurs. If you are familiar with the concept of deadlocks, you may recall that a special process known as the deadlock detector runs quietly in the background and "wakes up" at predefined intervals to scan the locking system in search of a deadlock cycle. If a deadlock cycle exists, the deadlock detector randomly selects one of the transactions involved in the cycle to roll back and terminate. (The transaction that is rolled back and terminated receives an SQL error code, all locks it had acquired are released, and the remaining transaction(s) are then allowed to proceed.) Information about such a series of events cannot be captured by the snapshot monitor because, in all likelihood, the deadlock cycle will have been broken long before a snapshot can be taken. An event monitor, on the other hand, could be used to capture such information because it would be activated the moment the deadlock cycle was detected.

Unlike the snapshot monitor, which resides in the background and is always available, event monitors are special objects that must be created. Event monitors are created by executing the CREATE EVENT MONITOR SQL statement. The basic syntax for this statement is:

```
CREATE EVENT MONITOR [EventMonName]
FOR [DATABASE |
     BUFFERPOOLS |
     TABLESPACES |
     TABLES |
     DEADLOCKS <WITH DETAIL> |
     CONNECTIONS <WHERE [EventCondition]> |
     STATEMENTS <WHERE [EventCondition]> |
     TRANSACTIONS <WHERE [EventCondition]> , ...]
 WRITE TO [TABLE [GroupName] (TABLE [TableName]) |
          PIPE [PipeName] |
          FILE [DirectoryName]]
 [MANUALSTART | AUTOSTART]
```

where:

EventMonName	Identifies the name to be assigned to the event monitor that is to be created.
EventCondition	Identifies a condition that is used to determine which CONNECTION, STATEMENT, or TRANSACTION events monitor data is to be collected for.
GroupName	Identifies the name assigned to the logical data group for which the target table that all event monitor data collected is to be written to is to be defined.

TableName	Identifies the name assigned to the database table that all event monitor data collected is to be written to.
PipeName	Identifies the name assigned to the named pipe that all event monitor data collected is to be written to.
DirectoryName	Identifies the name assigned to the directory that one or more files containing event monitor data are to be written to.

As you can see by examining the syntax of the CREATE EVENT MONITOR statement, when an event monitor is created the type of event to be monitored must be specified; Table 5–5 lists the event types available, along with the type of information that is collected for each type, and when the data is actually collected.

Table 5–5   DB2 Database Manager-Supplied Default Values

Event Type	Data Collected	When Data Is Collected	Associated Group Name
DATABASE	The values of all database level counters.	When the database is deactivated or when the last application connected to the database disconnects.	DB CONTROL
BUFFERPOOLS	The values of all buffer pool counters, prefetchers, and page cleaners, as well as direct I/O for each buffer pool used.	When the database is deactivated or when the last application connected to the database disconnects.	BUFFERPOOL CONTROL
TABLESPACES	The values of all buffer pool counters, prefetchers, page cleaners, and direct I/O for each tablespace used.	When the database is deactivated or when the last application connected to the database disconnects.	TABLESPACE CONTROL
TABLES	The number of rows read and the number of rows written for each table.	When the database is deactivated or when the last application connected to the database disconnects.	TABLE CONTROL

(continues)

Table 5–5 DB2 Database Manager-Supplied Default Values (Continued)			
DEADLOCKS	Comprehensive information regarding applications involved, including the identification of all SQL statements involved (along with statement text) and a list of locks held by each.	When a deadlock cycle is detected.	CONNHEADER DEADLOCK DLCONN DLLOCK CONTROL
CONNECTIONS	The values of all application level counters.	When an application that is connected to the database disconnects.	CONNHEADER CONN CONTROL
STATEMENTS	Statement start/stop time, amount of CPU used, text of dynamic SQL statements, SQLCA (the return code of the SQL statement), and other metrics such as fetch count. For partitioned databases: amount of CPU used, execution time, table information, and table queue information.	When an SQL statement finishes executing. For partitioned databases: when a subsection of an SQL statement finishes executing.	CONNHEADER STMT SUBSECTION CONTROL
TRANSACTIONS	Transaction start/stop time, previous transaction time, amount of CPU consumed, along with locking and logging metrics. (Transaction records are not generated if database is using two-phase commit processing and an X/Open XA Interface.)	When a transaction is terminated (by a COMMIT or a ROLLBACK statement).	CONNHEADER XACT CONTROL

Adapted from Table 6 on pages 46–47 of the *DB2 System Monitor Guide and Reference* manual.

The location where all monitor data collected is to be written to must be specified as well; output from an event monitor can be written to one or more database tables, one or more external files, or a named pipe. Table event monitors and pipe event monitors stream event records directly to the table or named pipe specified. File event monitors, on the other hand, stream event records to a series of eight-character numbered files that have the extension ".evt" (for example, 00000000.evt, 00000001.evt, 00000002.evt, etc.). The monitor data collected and stored in these files should be considered to be stored as one logical file even though the data is broken up into smaller pieces. In other words, the start of the data stream is the first byte in the file named 00000000.evt; the end of the data stream is the last byte in the file named *nnnnnnnn*.evt).

| If output from an event monitor is to be stored in one or more database tables, all target tables needed are automatically created when the CREATE EVENT MONITOR statement is executed. On the other hand, if output from an event monitor is to be written to one or more external files or a named pipe, the output directory/named pipe specified as the target location for the event monitor does not have to exist when the CREATE EVENT MONITOR statement is executed; however, it must exist and the DB2 Database Manager instance owner must be able to write to it at the time the event monitor is activated. (The application monitoring the named pipe must also have opened the pipe for reading before the event monitor is activated.

Thus, if you wanted to create an event monitor that captures the values of all application-level counters and writes them to a database table named CONN_DATA (that is to be defined in the group for connections) every time an application that is connected to a database terminates its connection, you could do so by executing a CREATE EVENT MONITOR statement that looks something like this:

```
CREATE EVENT MONITOR CONN_EVENTS
FOR CONNECTIONS
WRITE TO TABLE CONN (TABLE CONN_DATA)
```

On the other hand, if you wanted to create an event monitor that captures monitor data for both buffer pool and tablespace events and writes all data collected to a directory named /export/home/BPTS_DATA, you could do so by executing a CREATE EVENT MONITOR statement that looks something like this:

```
CREATE EVENT MONITOR BPTS_EVENTS
FOR BUFFERPOOLS, TABLESPACES
WRITE TO FILE '/export/home/BPTS_DATA'
```

Event monitors can also be created using the Create Event Monitor dialog, which can be activated by selecting the appropriate action from the *Event Monitors* menu found in the Control Center. Figure 5–7 shows the Control Center menu items that must be selected to activate the Create Event Monitor dialog; Figure 5–8 shows how the Create Event Monitor dialog might look after its input fields have been populated.

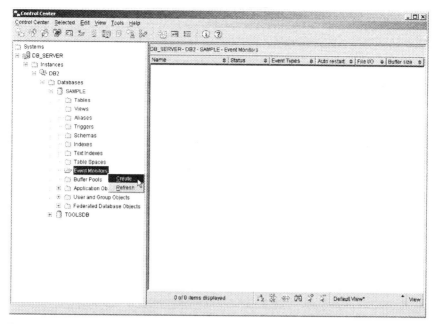

Figure 5–7   Invoking the Create Event Monitor dialog from the Control Center.

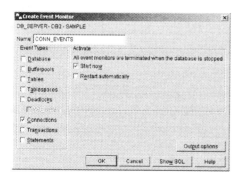

Figure 5–8   The Create Event Monitor dialog.

Only users with System Administrator (SYSADM) authority, System Control (SYSCTRL) authority, System Maintenance (SYSMAINT) authority, or Database Administrator (DBADM) authority are allowed to create and use event monitors.

It is important to note that because event monitors are special database objects that must be created by users that hold the appropriate authorization, they can only be used to collect information for the database in which they have been defined; event monitors cannot be used to collect information at the DB2 Database Manager instance level.

Activating and Deactivating Event Monitors

Like the snapshot monitor, event monitors will begin collecting monitor data as soon as the database they are associated with is activated or a connection to the database is established—provided the AUTOSTART option was specified when the event monitor was created. If the MANUALSTART option was used instead or if neither option was specified (in which case the MANUALSTART option is used by default), an event monitor will not begin collecting data until it is activated. Event monitors are activated (and deactivated) by executing the SET EVENT MONITOR SQL statement. The basic syntax for this statement is:

```
SET EVENT MONITOR [EventMonName]
STATE <=> [MonitorState]
```

where:

EventMonName	Identifies the name assigned to the event monitor whose state is to be altered.
MonitorState	Identifies the state the event monitor is to be placed in. If the event monitor is to be activated (i.e., placed in the active state), the value 1 must be specified for this parameter; if the event monitor is to be deactivated (i.e., placed in the inactive state), the value 0 must be specified for this parameter.

Therefore, if you wanted to activate an event monitor named CONN _EVENTS that was created with the MANUALSTART option specified, you could do so by executing a SET EVENT MONITOR statement that looks like this:

```
SET EVENT MONITOR CONN_EVENTS STATE 1
```

On the other hand, if you wanted to deactivate the CONN_EVENTS event monitor, you could do so by executing a SET EVENT MONITOR statement that looks like this:

```
SET EVENT MONITOR CONN_EVENTS STATE 0
```

Event monitors can also be activated and deactivated by highlighting the appropriate event monitor name shown in the Control Center and selecting the appropriate action from the *Event Monitors* menu. Figure 5–9 shows the Control Center menu item that must be selected to activate (start) an inactive event monitor; Figure 5–10 shows the Control Center menu item that must be selected to deactivate (stop) an active event monitor.

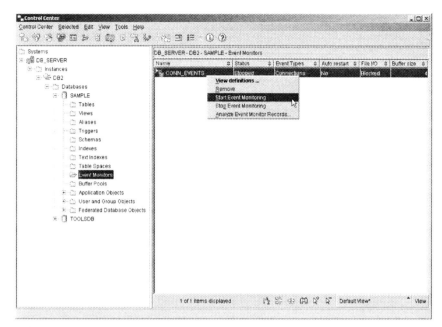

Figure 5–9 Starting an event monitor from the Control Center.

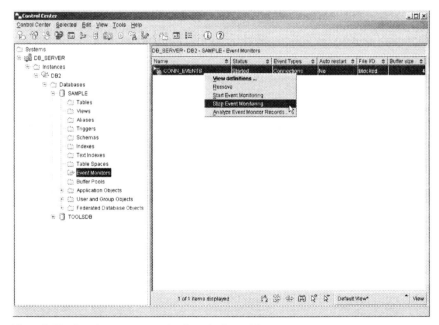

Figure 5–10 Stopping an event monitor from the Control Center.

When an event monitor is activated (started), it sits quietly in the background and waits for one of the events it is associated with to occur; immediately after an event being monitored takes place, the event monitor collects monitor data that is associated with the event that triggered it, and writes all data collected to the event monitor's target location. Thus, the event itself controls when monitor data is collected. Unlike with the snapshot monitor, no special steps are required to capture the monitor data.

Forcing an Event Monitor to Generate Output Prematurely

Because some events do not activate event monitors as frequently as others, it may be desirable to force an event monitor to collect monitor data and write it to its target location *before* a monitor triggering event takes place. In such situations, an event monitor can be made to collect information early by executing the FLUSH EVENT MONITOR SQL statement. The basic syntax for this statement is:

```
FLUSH EVENT MONITOR [EventMonName] <BUFFER>
```

where:

> *EventMonName*   Identifies the name assigned to the event monitor that is to be forced to collect monitor data.

By default, records that are written to an event monitor's target location prematurely are logged in the event monitor log and assigned a "partial record" identifier. However, if the BUFFER option is specified when the FLUSH EVENT MONITOR statement is executed, only monitor data that is present in the event monitor's active internal buffers is written to the event monitor's target location; partial records are not generated.

Thus, if you wanted to force an event monitor named CONN_EVENTS to collect monitor data and write it to its target location immediately, you could do so by executing a FLUSH EVENT MONITOR statement that looks like this:

```
FLUSH EVENT MONITOR CONN_EVENTS
```

It is important to note that when event monitors are flushed, counters are not reset. This means that the event monitor record that would have been generated if the FLUSH EVENT MONITOR statement had not been used to force event monitor data to be written will still be generated when the event monitor is triggered normally.

Viewing Event Monitor Data

Data that has been collected by an event monitor can be viewed in one of two ways: by using a special utility known as the Event Analyzer or by using the Event Monitor Productivity Tool. The Event Analyzer is a graphical user interface (GUI) tool that can be activated by highlighting the desired event monitor shown in the Control Center and selecting the appropriate action from the *Event Monitors* menu. Figure 5–11 shows the Control Center menu items that must be selected to activate the Event Analyzer utility; Figure 5–12 shows how the monitored periods view of the Event Analyzer might look after an event monitor has been activated for two different monitoring sessions.

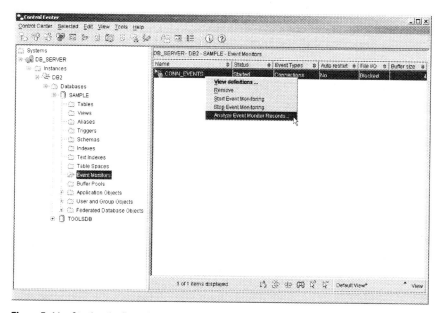

Figure 5–11   Starting the Event Analyzer from the Control Center.

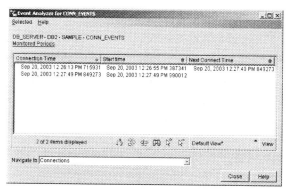

Figure 5–12   The Event Analyzer utility.

Once the Event Analyzer is activated, you can view/analyze the information that was captured for each event that was monitored by selecting the appropriate event from the *Drill down to* menu, which can be displayed by selecting the *Selected* menu item from the Event Analyzer's main menu. Figure 5–13 shows how the *Drill down to* menu would be used to drill down to monitor data that was collected for connection events that took place during one or more monitoring periods; Figure 5–14 shows how the Event Analyzer will display all connection events detected.

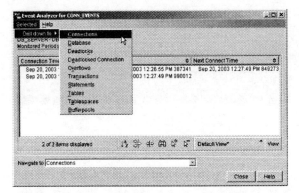

Figure 5–13   Drilling down to specific monitoring events.

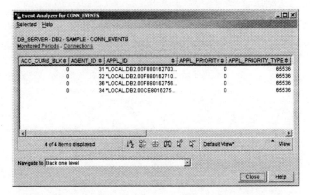

Figure 5–14   Connection events view of the Event Analyzer utility.

Unfortunately, the Event Analyzer can only be used to view event monitor data that was collected and stored in database tables. To view event monitor data that was written to files and named pipes, the Event Monitor Productivity Tool must be used instead. Unlike the Event Analyzer, the Event Monitor Productivity Tool is a text-based tool that is designed to retrieve information from an event monitor data file or named pipe and produce a formatted report. (Event monitor files and named pipes contain a binary stream of logical data groupings that must be formatted before they can be displayed.) The Event Monitor Productivity Tool is activated by executing the `db2evmon` command. The basic syntax for this command is:

```
db2evmon -db [DatabaseAlias] -evm [EventMonName]
```

or

```
db2evmon -path [EventMonTarget]
```

where:

DatabaseAlias	Identifies the alias assigned to the database where the event monitor whose data is to be displayed has been defined.
EventMonName	Identifies the name assigned to the event monitor whose data is to be displayed.
EventMonTarget	Identifies the location (directory or named pipe) where data that has been collected by an event monitor is stored.

Thus, if you wanted to format and display all data collected by an event monitor named CONN_EVENTS that resides in a database named SAMPLE, you could do so by executing a `db2evmon` command statement that looks like this:

```
db2evmon -db SAMPLE -evm CONN_EVENTS
```

Assuming the event monitor CONN_EVENTS was created using the following CREATE EVENT MONITOR statement:

```
CREATE EVENT MONITOR CONN_EVENTS
FOR CONNECTIONS
WRITE TO FILE 'C:\MONDATA'
```

and assuming the event monitor was activated immediately after it was created, the output returned by the command

```
db2evmon -db SAMPLE -evm CONN_EVENTS
```

should look something like this:

```
Reading C:\MONDATA\00000000.EVT ...
--------------------------------------------------------------
                        EVENT LOG HEADER
  Event Monitor name: CONN_EVENTS
  Server Product ID: SQL08010
  Version of event monitor data: 7
```

```
Byte order: LITTLE ENDIAN
Number of nodes in db2 instance: 1
Codepage of database: 1252
Territory code of database: 1
Server instance name: DB2
--------------------------------------------------------------


--------------------------------------------------------------
Database Name: SAMPLE
Database Path: C:\DB2\NODE0000\SQL00002\
First connection timestamp: 09-20-2003 15:50:38.145207
Event Monitor Start time:   09-20-2003 16:01:38.371764
--------------------------------------------------------------

3) Connection Header Event ...
Appl Handle: 66
Appl Id: *LOCAL.DB2.00F880200020
Appl Seq number: 0003
DRDA AS Correlation Token: *LOCAL.DB2.00F880200020
Program Name    : db2bp.exe
Authorization Id: RSANDERS
Execution Id    : RSANDERS
Codepage Id: 1252
Territory code: 1
Client Process Id: 1984
Client Database Alias: SAMPLE
Client Product Id: SQL08010
Client Platform: Unknown
Client Communication Protocol: Local
Client Network Name:
Connect timestamp: 09-20-2003 16:00:18.213902
```

The Health Monitor and the Health Center

Along with the snapshot monitor and event monitors, DB2 UDB Version 8.1 provides two additional tools that are designed to help database administrators monitor DB2 systems under their control. These tools are known as the *Health Monitor* and the *Health Center*. Together, these tools provide a *management by exception* capability that enables administrators to address health issues before they become real problems that adversely affect a system's performance.

The Health Monitor is a server-side tool that constantly monitors the health of a DB2 Database Manager instance without a need for user interaction. Instead, the Health Monitor uses several *health indicators* to evaluate specific aspects of instance and database performance. A health indicator is a system characteristic that the Health Monitor monitors continuously to determine whether or not an object is operating normally; each health indicator has a corresponding set of predefined threshold values and the Health Monitor compares the state of the system against these health-indicator thresholds to see if they have been exceeded. If the Health Monitor finds that a predefined threshold has been exceeded (for example, if the amount of log space available is insufficient), or if it detects an abnormal state for an object (for example, if the instance is down), it will automatically raise an alert.

In most cases, the threshold values provided for a health indicator define boundaries or zones for three different operating states: normal, warning, and alarm. Therefore, there are three types of alerts available: attention, warning, and alarm. Regardless of the type of alert generated, three things can happen whenever an alert is raised:

➤ Alert information can be recorded in the Journal. (All alarm alerts are written to the Journal.)

➤ Alert notifications can be sent via e-mail or pager address to whoever is responsible for the system.

➤ One or more preconfigured actions can be taken (for example, a task can be run).

The Health Center is a GUI tool that is designed to interact with the Health Monitor. Using the Health Center, you can select the instance and database objects that you want to monitor, customize the threshold settings of any health indicator, specify where notifications are to be sent, and what actions should be taken if an alert is issued. The Health Center also allows you to start and stop the Health Monitor, as well as access details about current alerts and obtain a list of recommended actions that describe how to resolve the situation that caused the alert to be generated. Like other GUI tools, the Health Center can be activated by selecting the appropriate action from the *Tools* menu of the Control Center. Figure 5–15 shows the Control Center menu items that must be selected to activate the Health Center; Figure 5–16 shows how the Health Center looks on a Windows 2000 system (in this case, after two warning type alerts have been generated); Figure 5–17 shows the interface that is used to set threshold values for one or more health indicators.

The Health Center and the Control Center are integrated through what are known as *Health Beacons*. Health Beacons provide notifications about new alerts in the Health Center directly to the Control Center. Beacons are implemented on all Control Center windows and notebooks; by clicking on a Health Beacon, control is immediately transferred to the Health Center.

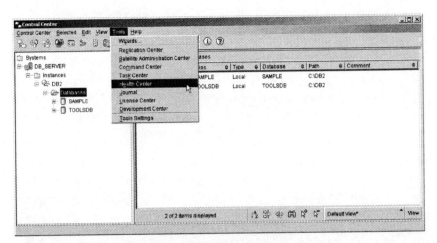

Figure 5–15 Starting the Health Center from the Control Center.

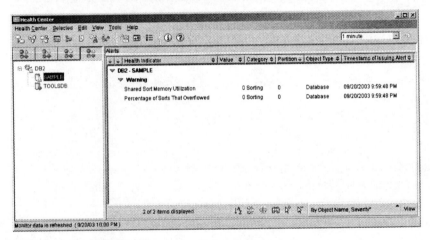

Figure 5–16 The Health Center.

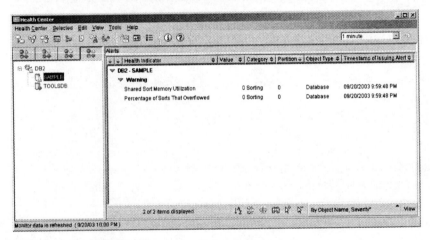

Figure 5–17 The Configure Database Object Health Indicator Settings dialog.

By default, the Health Monitor is disabled when an instance is created. It can be enabled at any time by selecting the appropriate menu item from the Health Center or by setting the *health_mon* DB2 Database Manager configuration parameter to ON.

Monitoring SQL with the Explain Facility

When an SQL statement is submitted to the DB2 database engine for processing, it is analyzed by the DB2 Optimizer to produce what is known as an *access plan*. Each access plan contains detailed information about the strategy that will be used to execute the statement (such as whether or not indexes will be used, what sort methods, if any, are required, what locks are needed, and what join methods, if any, will be used). If the SQL statement is coded in an application, the access plan is generated at precompile time (or at bind time if deferred binding is used) and an executable form of the access plan produced is stored in the system catalog as an object that is known as a *package*. If, however, the statement is submitted from the Command Line Processor or if the statement is a dynamic SQL statement in an application program (i.e., an SQL statement that is constructed at application run time), the access plan is generated at the time the statement is issued and the executable form produced is stored temporarily in memory (in the global package cache) rather than in the system catalog. (If an SQL statement is issued and an executable form of its access plan already exists in the global package cache, the existing access plan is reused and the DB2 Optimizer is not invoked again.)

Why is this important? Because, although the Database System Monitor and the Health Monitor can be used to obtain information about how well (or poorly) some SQL operations perform, they cannot be used to analyze individual SQL statements. To perform this type of analysis, you must be able to capture and view the information stored in an SQL statement's access plan. And in order to capture and view access plan information, you must use the DB2 UDB Explain Facility.

The Explain Facility allows you to capture and view detailed information about the access plan chosen for a particular SQL statement, as well as performance information that can be used to help identify poorly written statements or a weakness in database design. Specifically, Explain data helps you understand how the DB2 Database Manager accesses tables and indexes to satisfy a query. Explain data can also be used to evaluate any performance-tuning action taken. In fact, any time you change some aspect of the DB2 Database Manager, an SQL statement, or the database the statement interacts with, you should collect and examine Explain data to find out what effect, if any, your changes have had on performance.

The Explain Tables

Before Explain information can be captured, a special set of tables, known as the *Explain tables*, must be created. Each Explain table used, along with the information it is designed to hold, can be seen in Table 5–6.

Table 5–6 Explain Tables	
Table Name	**Contents**
EXPLAIN_ARGUMENT	Contains the unique characteristics for each individual operator used, if there are any.
EXPLAIN_INSTANCE	Contains basic information about the source of the SQL statements being explained as well as information about the environment in which the explanation took place. (The EXPLAIN_INSTANCE table is the main control table for all Explain information. Each row of data in the other Explain tables is explicitly linked to one unique row in this table.)
EXPLAIN_OBJECT	Contains information about the data objects that are required by the access plan generated for an SQL statement.
EXPLAIN_OPERATOR	Contains all the operators that are needed by the SQL compiler to satisfy the SQL statement.
EXPLAIN_PREDICATE	Contains information that identifies which predicates are applied by a specific operator.
EXPLAIN_STATEMENT	Contains the text of the SQL statement as it exists for the different levels of Explain information. The original SQL statement as entered by the user is stored in this table along with the version used by the DB2 Optimizer to choose an access plan to satisfy the SQL statement. (The latter version may bear little resemblance to the original, as it may have been rewritten and/or enhanced with additional predicates by the SQL Precompiler.)
EXPLAIN_STREAM	Contains information about the input and output data streams that exist between individual operators and data objects. (The data objects themselves are represented in the EXPLAIN_OBJECT table while the operators involved in a data stream can be found in the EXPLAIN_OPERATOR table.)

Typically, Explain tables are used in a development database to aid in application design, but not in production databases where application code remains fairly static. Because of this, they are not created along with the system catalog tables as part of the database creation process. Instead, Explain tables must be manually created in the database that the Explain Facility is to be used with before the Explain Facility can be used. Fortunately, the process used to create the Explain tables is pretty straightforward: using the Command Line Processor, you establish a connection to the appropriate database and execute a script named EXPLAIN.DDL, which can be found in the "misc" subdirectory of the "sqllib" directory where the DB2 UDB software was initially installed. (Comments in the header of this file provide information on how it is to be executed.)

Collecting Explain Data

The Explain Facility is comprised of several individual tools and not all tools require the same kind of Explain data. Therefore, two different types of Explain data can be collected. They are:

> **Comprehensive Explain Data.** Contains detailed information about an SQL statement's access plan. This information is stored across several different Explain tables.

> **Explain Snapshot Data.** Contains the current internal representation of an SQL statement, along with any related information. This information is stored in the SNAPSHOT column of the EXPLAIN_STATEMENT Explain table.

And, as you might imagine, there are a variety of ways in which both types of Explain data can be collected. The methods available for collecting Explain data include:

➤ Executing the EXPLAIN SQL statement

➤ Setting the CURRENT EXPLAIN MODE special register

➤ Setting the CURRENT EXPLAIN SNAPSHOT special register

➤ Using the EXPLAIN bind option with the PRECOMPILE or BIND command

➤ Using the EXPLSNAP bind option with the PRECOMPILE or BIND command

The EXPLAIN SQL Statement

One way to collect both comprehensive Explain information and Explain snapshot data for a single, dynamic SQL statement is by executing the EXPLAIN SQL statement. The basic syntax for this statement is:

```
EXPLAIN [ALL | PLAN | PLAN SELECTION]
<FOR SNAPSHOT | WITH SNAPSHOT>
FOR [SQLStatement]
```

where:

> *SQLStatement*   Identifies the SQL statement that Explain data
> and/or Explain snapshot data is to be collected
> for. (The statement specified must be a valid
> INSERT, UPDATE, DELETE, SELECT, SELECT INTO,
> VALUES, or VALUES INTO SQL statement.)

If the FOR SNAPSHOT option is specified with the EXPLAIN statement, only Explain snapshot information will be collected for the dynamic SQL statement specified. On the other hand, if the WITH SNAPSHOT option is specified instead, both comprehensive Explain information and Explain snapshot data will be collected for the dynamic SQL statement specified. However, if neither option is used, only comprehensive Explain data will be collected; no Explain snapshot data will be produced.

Thus, if you wanted to collect both comprehensive Explain data and Explain snapshot information for the SQL statement SELECT * FROM DEPARTMENT, you could do so by executing an EXPLAIN statement that looks like this:

```
EXPLAIN ALL WITH SNAPSHOT FOR SELECT * FROM DEPARTMENT
```

On the other hand, if you only wanted to collect Explain snapshot data for the same SQL statement, you could do so by executing an EXPLAIN statement that looks like this:

```
EXPLAIN ALL FOR SNAPSHOT FOR SELECT * FROM DEPARTMENT
```

And finally, if you only wanted to collect comprehensive Explain data for the SQL statement SELECT * FROM DEPARTMENT, you could do so by executing an EXPLAIN statement that looks like this:

```
EXPLAIN ALL FOR SELECT * FROM DEPARTMENT
```

It is important to note that the EXPLAIN statement does not execute the SQL statement specified, nor does it display the Explain information collected. Other Explain Facility tools must be used to view any Explain information collected. (We'll look at those tools shortly.)

The CURRENT EXPLAIN MODE and the CURRENT EXPLAIN SNAPSHOT Special Registers

Although the EXPLAIN SQL statement is useful when you want to collect Explain and/or Explain snapshot information for a single dynamic SQL statement, it can become very time-consuming to use if a large number of SQL statements need to be analyzed. A better way to collect the same information for several dynamic SQL statements is by setting one or both of the special Explain Facility registers provided before a group of dynamic SQL statements are executed. Then, as the statements are prepared for execution, Explain and/or Explain snapshot information is collected for each statement processed. The statements themselves, however, may or may not be executed once Explain and/or Explain snapshot information has been collected.

The two Explain Facility special registers that are used in this manner are the CURRENT EXPLAIN MODE special register and the CURRENT EXPLAIN SNAPSHOT special register. The CURRENT EXPLAIN MODE special register is set using the SET CURRENT EXPLAIN MODE SQL statement and the CURRENT EXPLAIN SNAPSHOT special register is set using the SET CURRENT EXPLAIN SNAPSHOT SQL statement. The basic syntax for the SET CURRENT EXPLAIN MODE SQL statement is:

```
SET CURRENT EXPLAIN MODE <=> [YES | NO | EXPLAIN]
```

while the basic syntax for the SET CURRENT EXPLAIN SNAPSHOT SQL statement is:

```
SET CURRENT EXPLAIN SNAPSHOT <=> [YES | NO | EXPLAIN]
```

As you might imagine, if both the CURRENT EXPLAIN MODE and the CURRENT EXPLAIN SNAPSHOT special registers are set to NO, the Explain Facility is disabled and no Explain data is captured. On the other hand, if either special register is set to EXPLAIN, the Explain Facility is activated and comprehensive Explain information or Explain snapshot data (or both if both special registers have been set) is collected each time a dynamic SQL statement is prepared for execution (the statements themselves are not executed). If either special register is set to YES, the behavior is the same as when either register is set to EXPLAIN with one significant difference; the dynamic SQL statements that Explain information is collected for are executed as soon as the appropriate Explain/Explain snapshot data has been collected. Table 5–7 summarizes the behavior each Explain special register setting has on the Explain Facility and dynamic SQL statement processing.

Table 5–7	Interaction Of Explain Facility Special Register Settings		
EXPLAIN SNAPSHOT Values	**EXPLAIN MODE Values**		
	NO	**YES**	**EXPLAIN**
NO	• Explain Facility is disabled • No Explain data is captured • Dynamic SQL statements are executed	• Explain Facility is enabled • Comprehensive Explain data is collected and written to the Explain tables • Dynamic SQL statements are executed	• Explain Facility is enabled • Comprehensive Explain data is collected and written to the Explain tables • Dynamic SQL statements are not executed
YES	• Explain Facility is enabled • Explain snapshot data is collected and written to the SNAPSHOT column of the EXPLAIN_STATEMENT Explain table • Dynamic SQL statements are executed	• Explain Facility is enabled • Comprehensive Explain data is collected and written to the Explain tables • Explain snapshot data is collected and written to the SNAPSHOT column of the EXPLAIN_STATEMENT Explain table • Dynamic SQL statements are executed	• Explain Facility is enabled • Comprehensive Explain data is collected and written to the Explain tables • Explain snapshot data is collected and written to the SNAPSHOT column of the EXPLAIN_STATEMENT Explain table • Dynamic SQL statements are not executed
EXPLAIN	• Explain Facility is enabled • Explain snapshot data is collected and written to the SNAPSHOT column of the EXPLAIN_STATEMENT Explain table • Dynamic SQL statements are not executed	• Explain Facility is enabled • Comprehensive Explain data is collected and written to the Explain tables • Explain snapshot data is collected and written to the SNAPSHOT column of the EXPLAIN_STATEMENT Explain table • Dynamic SQL statements are not executed	• Explain Facility is enabled • Comprehensive Explain data is collected and written to the Explain tables • Explain snapshot data is collected and written to the SNAPSHOT column of the EXPLAIN_STATEMENT Explain table • Dynamic SQL statements are not executed

Adapted from Table 176 on pages 857–858 of the *DB2 SQL Reference—Volume 1* manual.

The EXPLAIN and EXPLSNAP Bind Options

So far, we have looked at ways in which comprehensive Explain information and Explain snapshot data can be collected for dynamic SQL statements. But often, database applications are comprised of static SQL statements that need to be analyzed as well. So how can you use the Explain Facility to analyze static SQL statements coded in an embedded SQL application? To collect comprehensive Explain information and/or Explain snapshot data for static and/or dynamic SQL statements that have been coded in an embedded SQL application, you rely on the EXPLAIN and EXPLSNAP bind options.

As you might imagine, the EXPLAIN bind option is used to control whether or not comprehensive Explain data is collected for static and/or dynamic SQL statements that have been coded in an embedded SQL application. Likewise, the EXPLSNAP bind option controls whether or not Explain snapshot data is collected. One or both of these options can be specified as part of the PRECOMPILE command that is used to precompile the source code file that contains the embedded SQL statements; if deferred binding is used, these options can be provided with the BIND command that is used to bind the application's bind file to the database.

Both the EXPLAIN option and the EXPLSNAP option can be assigned the value NO, YES, or ALL. If both options are assigned the value NO (for example, EXPLAIN NO EXPLSNAP NO), the Explain Facility is disabled and no Explain data is captured. On the other hand, if either option is assigned the value YES, the Explain Facility is activated and comprehensive Explain information or Explain snapshot data (or both if both options are set) is collected for each static SQL statement found. If either option is assigned the value ALL, the Explain Facility is activated and comprehensive Explain information or Explain snapshot data (or both if both options are set) is collected for every static *and dynamic* SQL statement found, even if the CURRENT EXPLAIN MODE and/or the CURRENT EXPLAIN SNAPSHOT special registers have been set to NO. Table 5–8 summarizes the behavior the EXPLAIN bind option has on the Explain facility and on static and dynamic SQL statement processing when used in conjunction with the EXPLAIN MODE special register; Table 5–9 summarizes the behavior the EXPLSNAP bind option has on the Explain facility and on static and dynamic SQL statement processing when used in conjunction with the EXPLAIN SNAPSHOT special register.

Table 5–8   Interaction of the EXPLAIN Bind Option and the EXPLAIN MODE Special Register

EXPLAIN MODE Special Register Values	EXPLAIN Bind Option Values		
	NO	**YES**	**ALL**
NO	• Explain Facility is disabled • No Explain data is captured	• Explain Facility is enabled • Comprehensive Explain data is collected and written to the Explain tables for static SQL statements	• Explain Facility is enabled • Comprehensive Explain data is collected and written to the Explain tables for both static and dynamic SQL statements
YES	• Explain Facility is enabled • Comprehensive Explain data is collected and written to the Explain tables for dynamic SQL statements	• Explain Facility is enabled • Comprehensive Explain data is collected and written to the Explain tables for both static and dynamic SQL statements	• Explain Facility is enabled • Comprehensive Explain data is collected and written to the Explain tables for both static and dynamic SQL statements
EXPLAIN	• Explain Facility is enabled • Comprehensive Explain data is collected and written to the Explain tables for dynamic SQL statements • Dynamic SQL statements are not executed	• Explain Facility is enabled • Comprehensive Explain data is collected and written to the Explain tables for both static and dynamic SQL statements • Dynamic SQL statements are not executed	• Explain Facility is enabled • Comprehensive Explain data is collected and written to the Explain tables for both static and dynamic SQL statements • Dynamic SQL statements are not executed

Adapted from Table 177 on pages 858–859 of the *DB2 SQL Reference—Volume 1* manual.

Table 5–9	Interaction Of the EXPLAIN Bind Option and the EXPLAIN MODE Special Register		
EXPLAIN SNAPSHOT Special Register Values	**EXPLSNAP Bind Option Values**		
	NO	YES	ALL
NO	• Explain Facility is disabled • No Explain data is captured	• Explain Facility is enabled • Explain snapshot data is collected and written to the SNAPSHOT column of the EXPLAIN_STATEMENT Explain table for static SQL statements	• Explain Facility is enabled • Explain snapshot data is collected and written to the SNAPSHOT column of the EXPLAIN_STATEMENT Explain table for both static and dynamic SQL statements
YES	• Explain Facility is enabled • Explain snapshot data is collected and written to the SNAPSHOT column of the EXPLAIN_STATEMENT Explain table for dynamic SQL statements	• Explain Facility is enabled • Explain snapshot data is collected and written to the SNAPSHOT column of the EXPLAIN_STATEMENT Explain table for both static and dynamic SQL statements	• Explain Facility is enabled • Explain snapshot data is collected and written to the SNAPSHOT column of the EXPLAIN_STATEMENT Explain table for both static and dynamic SQL statements
EXPLAIN	• Explain Facility is enabled • Explain snapshot data is collected and written to the SNAPSHOT column of the EXPLAIN _STATEMENT Explain table for dynamic SQL statements • Dynamic SQL statements are not executed	• Explain Facility is enabled • Explain snapshot data is collected and written to the SNAPSHOT column of the EXPLAIN _STATEMENT Explain table for both static and dynamic SQL statements • Dynamic SQL statements are not executed	• Explain Facility is enabled • Explain snapshot data is collected and written to the SNAPSHOT column of the EXPLAIN _STATEMENT Explain table for both static and dynamic SQL statements • Dynamic SQL statements are not executed

Adapted from Table 178 on pages 859–860 of the *DB2 SQL Reference—Volume 1* manual.

Evaluating Explain Data

So far, we have concentrated on the various ways in which comprehensive Explain and Explain snapshot data can be collected. But once the data is collected, how can it be viewed? To answer this question, we need to take a look at the Explain Facility tools that have been designed specifically for presenting Explain information in a meaningful format. These tools include:

➤ The db2expln tool

➤ The dynexpln tool

➤ The db2exfmt tool

➤ Visual Explain

db2expln

Earlier, we saw that when a source code file containing embedded SQL statements is bound to a database (either as part of the precompile process or during deferred binding), the DB2 Optimizer analyzes each static SQL statement encountered and generates a corresponding access plan, which is then stored in the database in the form of a package. Given the name of the database, the name of the package, the ID of the package creator, and a section number (if the section number 0 is specified, all sections of the package will be processed), the db2expln tool will interpret and describe the access plan information for any package that is stored in a database's system catalog. Since the db2expln tool works directly with a package and not with comprehensive Explain or Explain snapshot data, it is typically used to obtain information about the access plans that have been chosen for packages for which Explain data has not been captured. However, because the db2expln tool can only access information that has been stored in a package, it can only describe the implementation of the final access plan chosen; it cannot provide information on how a particular SQL statement was optimized.

Using additional input parameters, the db2expln tool can also be used to explain dynamic SQL statements (that do not contain parameter markers), much like the dynexpln tool is used.

dynexpln

Like the db2expln tool, the dynexpln tool is designed to describe the final access plan chosen for a particular SQL statement. However, unlike the db2expln tool, which is designed to interact with packages that are associated with static SQL statements, the dynexpln tool is designed to generate and display access plan information for dynamic SQL statements that do not contain parameter markers. When executed, dynexpln creates a static package for the dynamic SQL statements provided (either as an input parameter or within a text file that is provided as an input parameter) and then uses the db2expln tool to describe the access plan(s) stored in it. With DB2 UDB Version 8.1, the functionality of the dynexpln tool is now available with the db2expln tool and the dynexpln tool is only available for backward compatibility.

db2exfmt

Unlike the db2expln tool and the dynexpln tool, the db2exfmt tool is designed to work directly with comprehensive Explain or Explain snapshot data that has been collected and stored in the Explain tables. Given a database name and other qualifying information, the db2exfmt tool will query the Explain tables for information, format the results, and produce a text-based report that can be displayed directly on the terminal or written to an ASCII file.

Visual Explain

Visual Explain is a GUI tool that provides database administrators and application developers with the ability to view a graphical representation of the access plan that has been chosen for a particular SQL statement. In addition, Visual Explain allows you to:

➤ See the database statistics that were used to optimize the SQL statement.

➤ Determine whether or not an index was used to access table data. (If an index was not used, Visual Explain can help you determine which columns might benefit from being indexed.)

➤ View the effects of performance tuning by allowing you to make "before" and "after" comparisons.

➤ Obtain detailed information about each operation that is performed by the access plan, including the estimated cost of each.

However, Visual Explain can only be used to view Explain snapshot data; to view Explain data that has been collected and written to the Explain tables, the db2exfmt tool must be used instead.

Whenever comprehensive Explain and/or Explain snapshot data is collected, information about how and when the data was collected is recorded in the EXPLAIN_INSTANCE Explain table. This information can be viewed at any time using the Explained Statement History dialog. The Explained Statement History dialog is activated by selecting the appropriate action from the *Databases* menu found in the Control Center. Figure 5–18 shows the

Control Center menu items that must be selected to activate the Explained Statement History dialog; Figure 5–19 shows how the Explained Statement History dialog might look when Explain snapshot data has been collected for several SQL statements.

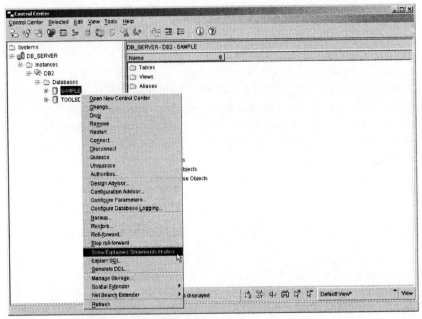

Figure 5–18   Invoking the Explained Statement History dialog from the Control Center.

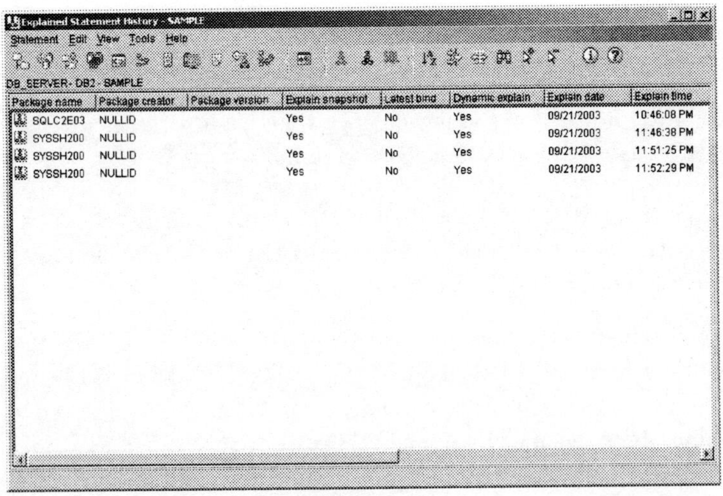

Figure 5–19   The Explained Statement History dialog.

Once the Explained Statement History dialog has been opened, Visual Explain can be used to analyze the Explain snapshot data collected for any record shown by highlighting the desired record and selecting the *Show Access Plan* action from the *Statement* menu. Figure 5–20 shows the menu items that must be selected to activate Visual Explain from the Explained Statement History dialog; Figure 5–21 shows how Visual Explain might look after it has been activated.

Earlier, we saw how the EXPLAIN SQL statement can be used to collect Explain snapshot data for a single dynamic SQL statement. And we just saw how the Explain Statement History dialog can be used to view Visual Explain output for a dynamic SQL statement that Explain snapshot data has been col-

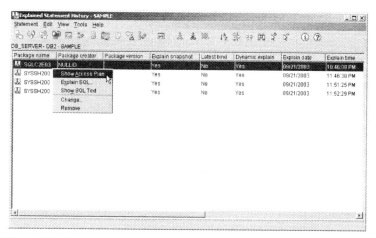

Figure 5–20   Starting Visual Explain from the Explained Statement History dialog.

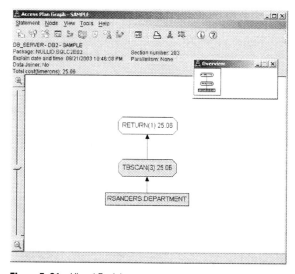

Figure 5–21   Visual Explain.

lected for. What we have not seen is how these two steps can be combined into a single action using the Explain SQL Statement dialog.

Like the Explained Statement History dialog, the Explain SQL Statement dialog is activated by selecting the appropriate action from the *Databases* menu found in the Control Center. Figure 5–22 shows the Control Center menu items that must be selected to activate the Explain SQL Statement dialog; Figure 5–23 shows how the Explain SQL Statement dialog might look after its input fields have been populated.

After the Explain SQL Statement dialog is opened, any dynamic SQL statement can be entered into the *SQL text* entry field. Then, by pressing the "OK"

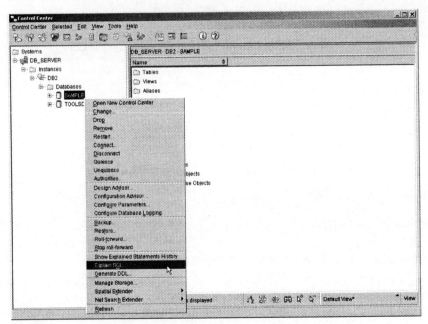

Figure 5–22   Invoking the Explained Statement History dialog from the Control Center.

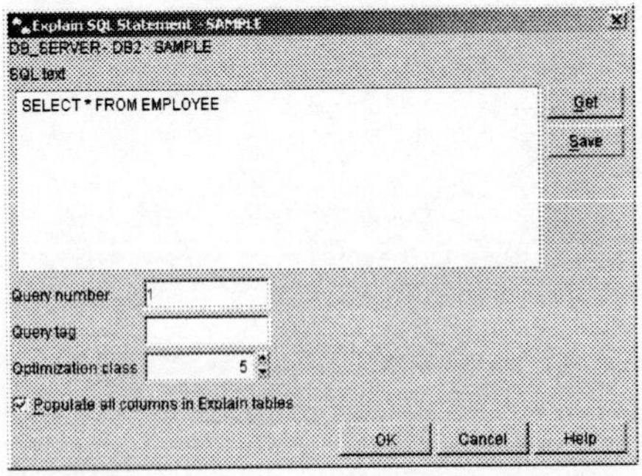

Figure 5–23   The Explained Statement History dialog.

push button located at the bottom of the dialog, Explain snapshot data can be collected for the SQL statement specified. When all processing is complete, control will be transferred to Visual Explain, where a graphical view of the access plan chosen for the SQL statement specified will be presented.

Visual Explain output. As you can see in Figure 5–21, the output provided by Visual Explain consists of a hierarchical graph that represents the various components that are needed to process the access plan that has been chosen for a particular SQL statement. Each component is represented as a graphical object that is known as a *node* and two types of nodes can exist:

Operator. An operator node is used to identify either an action that must be performed on data, or output produced from a table or index.

Operand. An operand node is used to identify an entity on which an operation is performed (for example, a table would be the operand of a table scan operator).

Typically, operand nodes are used to identify tables, indexes, and table queues (table queues are used when intrapartition parallelism is used), which are symbolized in the hierarchical graph by rectangles (tables), diamonds (indexes), and parallelograms (table queues). Operator nodes, on the other hand, are used to identify anything from an insert operation to an index or table scan. Operator nodes, which are symbolized in the hierarchical graph by ovals, indicate how data is accessed, how tables are joined, and other factors such as whether or not a sort operation is to be performed. Table 5–10 lists the more common operators that can appear in an access plan hierarchical graph.

Table 5–10 Common Operators	
Definition	**Description**
DELETE	Deletes rows from a table.
EISCAN	Scans a user-defined index to produce a reduced stream of rows.
FETCH	Fetches columns from a table using a specific record identifier.
FILTER	Filters data by applying one or more predicates to it.
GRPBY	Groups rows by common values of designated columns or functions, and evaluates set functions.
HSJOIN	Represents a hash join, where two or more tables are hashed on the join columns.
INSERT	Inserts rows into a table.
IXAND	ANDs together the row identifiers (RIDs) from two or more index scans.
IXSCAN	Scans an index of a table with optional start/stop conditions, producing an ordered stream of rows.

(continues)

Table 5–10 Common Operators (Continued)	
Definition	Description
MSJOIN	Represents a merge join, where both outer and inner tables must be in join-predicate order.
NLJOIN	Represents a nested loop join that accesses an inner table once for each row of the outer table.
RETURN	Represents the return of data from the query to the user.
RIDSCN	Scans a list of row identifiers (RIDs) obtained from one or more indexes.
SHIP	Retrieves data from a remote database source. Used in the federated system.
SORT	Sorts rows in the order of specified columns, and optionally eliminates duplicate entries.
TBSCAN	Retrieves rows by reading all data directly from the data pages.
TEMP	Stores data in a temporary table to be read back out (possibly multiple times).
TQUEUE	Transfers table data between database agents.
UNION	Concatenates streams of rows from multiple tables.
UNIQUE	Eliminates rows with duplicate values for specified columns.
UPDATE	Updates rows in a table.

Arrows that illustrate how data flows from one node to the next connect all nodes shown in the hierarchical graph and a RETURN operator normally terminates this path. Figure 5–24 shows how the hierarchical graph for an access plan that contains three different operator nodes (IXSCAN, FETCH, and RETURN) and two different operand nodes (a table named RSANDERS.DEPARTMENT and an index named DEPT_NUM) might be displayed in Visual Explain.

Detailed information about each operator node shown in an access plan hierarchical graph is also available and this information can be accessed by placing the mouse pointer over any operator node, right-clicking the mouse button, and selecting the *Show Details* action from the *Node* menu displayed. Figure 5–25 shows the menu items that must be selected to view detailed information about a particular operator node; Figure 5–26 shows how the Operator Details dialog might look after it has been activated.

Likewise, detailed information about the table or index statistics that were used to select the access plan chosen are available for each operand node shown in an access plan hierarchical graph. This information can be accessed by placing the mouse pointer over any operand node, right-clicking the mouse button, and selecting the *Show Statistics* action from the *Node* menu displayed. Figure 5–27 shows the menu items that must be selected to view

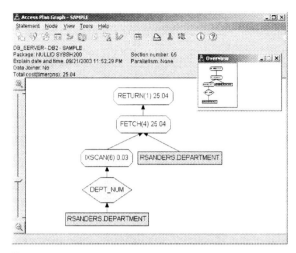

Figure 5–24   A hierarchical graph containing three operator nodes and two operand nodes.

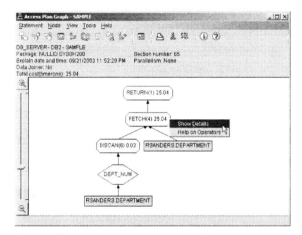

Figure 5–25   Invoking the Operator Details dialog from Visual Explain.

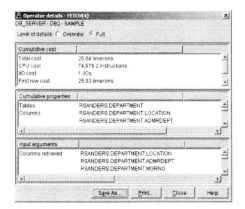

Figure 5–26   The Operator Details dialog.

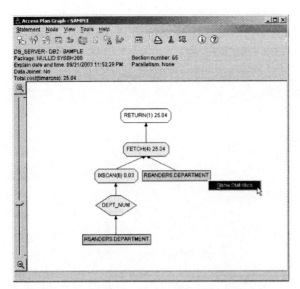

Figure 5–27 Invoking the Table/Index Statistics dialog from Visual Explain.

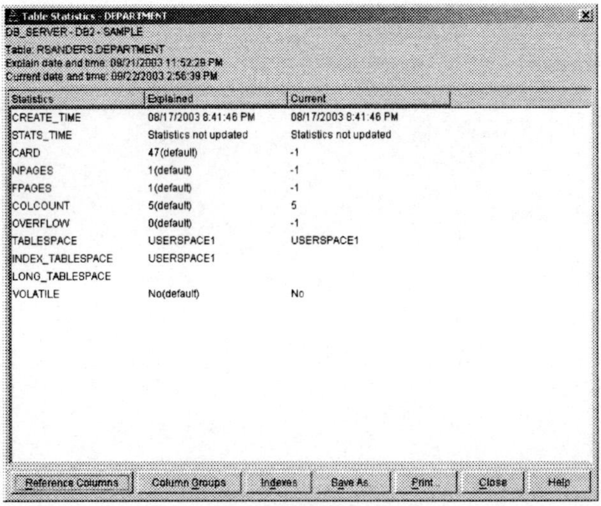

Figure 5–28 The Table/Index Statistics dialog.

detailed information about a particular operand node; Figure 5–28 shows how the Table/Index Statistics dialog might look after it has been activated.

A Quick Comparison of the Tools Used to View Explain Data

As you can see, the various tools that are available for displaying comprehensive Explain information and Explain snapshot data vary greatly both in their complexity in the capabilities they provide. Table 5–11 summarizes the different tools available, and highlights their individual characteristics. To get the most out of the Explain Facility, you should consider your environment and your needs when making a decision on which tool to use.

Table 5–11 Comparison of the Explain Facility Tools Available

Desired Characteristics	Visual Explain	db2exfmt	db2expln	dynexpln
User interface	Graphical	Text-based	Text-based	Text-based
"Quick and dirty" static SQL analysis	No	No	Yes	No
Static SQL supported	Yes	Yes	Yes	No
Dynamic SQL supported	Yes	Yes	Yes	Yes
CLI applications supported	Yes	Yes	No	No
Detailed DB2 Optimizer information available	Yes	Yes	No	No
Suited for analysis of multiple SQL statements	No	Yes	Yes	Yes

Adapted from Table 23 on page 229 of the *DB2 Administration Guide—Performance* manual.

Managing SQL Statement Execution with the DB2 Governor and the DB2 Query Patroller

Although the information collected and displayed by the Explain Facility can be used to optimize the performance of SQL statements that interact with a database, performance can still suffer in environments where large databases are accessed by many different users at one time. To help improve performance in these types of environments, DB2 UDB provides two management tools that allow system and database administrators to monitor and control how SQL statements are executed against a database. The first of these tools, known as the *DB2 Governor,* is used to control what priority users and applications have for executing their SQL statements. The second tool, called the *DB2 Query Patroller,* provides query and resource management for decision support systems by accepting, analyzing, prioritizing, and scheduling all queries that pass through a system.

The DB2 Governor

The DB2 Governor is used to monitor a user's activity and, if required, take appropriate actions. It collects statistics on a regular basis (the frequency used is determined by a configuration parameter) and compares the statistics against a set of predefined rules (which are also stored in the configuration file). Depending on how these rules have been defined, the DB2 Governor may lower the application's priority, or force the application off the database.

So when should the DB2 Governor be used? Ideally, the DB2 Governor is used in large production environments where many different and often complex queries are running against one or more large databases. Such queries can take a very long time to complete, particularly if they are being used for data mining or decision support systems (DSS). By using the DB2 Governor, you can assign a higher priority to queries that need to be finished soon and lower the priority of queries that take up too many resources.

The DB2 Query Patroller

The DB2 Query Patroller is used to provide query and resource management for decision support systems. This tool accepts, analyzes, prioritizes, and can schedule every query that passes through your system. And when a query has completed execution, the DB2 Query Patroller can notify the appropriate user(s) that their query has finished. The Query Patroller will also perform load balancing in partitioned database environments by redirecting work to the appropriate database partitions to ensure that no single database partition is being used too heavily. This functionality is extremely useful in large environments where queries may take several hours to complete or where different departments may have different priorities for usage of a shared system. The Query Patroller is completely server-based; no additional client software is required.

So who should use the DB2 Query Patroller? The DB2 Query Patroller is used primarily by database administrators who are responsible for managing large databases and/or data warehouses. As you might imagine, such systems are usually quite large and have many users running complex queries against them. Without the DB2 Query Patroller, managing all the queries that are being run against such systems can be a difficult job, at best.

Practice Questions

Question 1

Given the following information derived from GET DB CFG FOR DATABASE sample SHOW DETAIL:

Description: Size of database shared memory (4KB)
Parameter: DATABASE_MEMORY
Current Value: AUTOMATIC(7024)
Delayed Value: AUTOMATIC(14048)

Current Value: AUTOMATIC(7024) indicates which of the following?

O A. DB2 determined that 7024 4K pages of memory was needed for the SAMPLE database and allocated the memory for it.

O B. The next time the instance that controls the SAMPLE database is started, DB2 will reserve 7024 4K pages for the database.

O C. The next time the SAMPLE database is activated, DB2 will reserve 7024 4K pages for the database.

O D. DB2 calculated that 7024 4K pages of memory is needed for the current database configuration; a user with SYSCTRL must allocate the memory needed before the database can be used.

Question 2

Assuming the current value for the MAX_CONRETRIES DB2 Database Manager configuration parameter is 5 and the following statement is executed:

    UPDATE DBM CFG USING MAX_CONRETRIES 10 DEFERRED

When will the new setting for the MAX_CONRETRIES DB2 Database Manager configuration parameter take effect?

O A. Immediately after the UPDATE DATABASE MANAGER CONFIGURATION command is executed

O B. The next time the instance is stopped and restarted

O C. When the current value for MAX_CONRETRIES is exceeded

O D. The next time the instance is backed up

Question 3

An application that contains two embedded dynamic SQL statements has been bound to a database. Which of the following can be used to capture explain information for both statements in the application that can be examined with Visual Explain?

○ A. EXPLSNAP ALL and SET CURRENT EXPLAIN MODE EXPLAIN

○ B. EXPLAIN ALL and SET CURRENT EXPLAIN SNAPSHOT ALL

○ C. EXPLSNAP NO and SET CURRENT EXPLAIN SNAPSHOT YES

○ D. EXPLAIN NO and SET CURRENT EXPLAIN MODE YES

Question 4

There are two instances named INST1 and INST2 on the same server. Which command is used to unset the DB2_HASH_JOIN environment/registry variable just for the instance named INST1?

○ A. `db2set -i INST1 DB2_HASH_JOIN = NO`

○ B. `db2set -i INST1 DB2_HASH_JOIN = NULL`

○ C. `db2set -i INST1 DB2_HASH_JOIN =`

○ D. `db2set -g INST1 DB2_HASH_JOIN =`

Question 5

Which two of the following can be used to capture explain snapshot data for SQL statements issued from the Command Line Processor (CLP) in the same session?

❏ A. EXPLAIN PLAN FOR SNAPSHOT FOR <*SQLStatement*>

❏ B. SET CURRENT EXPLAIN MODE EXPLAIN

❏ C. SET CURRENT EXPLAIN SNAPSHOT EXPLAIN

❏ D. EXPLAIN ALL

❏ E. EXPLSNAP ALL

Question 6

Given the following exhibit:

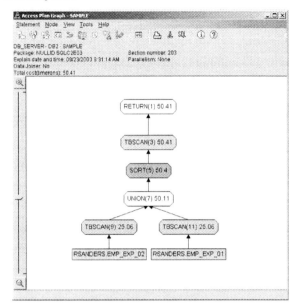

Which operator in the Visual Explain graph shown indicates how data was obtained from table EMP_EXP_02?

○ A. TBSCAN(3)
○ B. TBSCAN(9)
○ C. TBSCAN(11)
○ D. UNION(7)

Question 7

Which of the following event types does not allow a WHERE clause to be used to filter the data returned by an event monitor?

○ A. CONNECTIONS
○ B. STATEMENTS
○ C. TRANSACTIONS
○ D. DATABASE

Question 8

> When a health indicator reaches an alarm threshold, an alert is recorded in which of the following?
>
> ○ A. Journal
> ○ B. Health Monitor
> ○ C. Control Center
> ○ D. Information Center

Question 9

> Which of the following is NOT a valid database snapshot monitor switch?
>
> ○ A. UOW
> ○ B. TIMESTAMP
> ○ C. TABLESPACE
> ○ D. BUFFERPOOL

Question 10

> Given the following command:
>
> ```
> RESTORE DATABASE sample FROM E: WITH 5 BUFFERS
> ```
>
> Which of the following determines the size of the buffers used during the restore operation?
>
> ○ A. 5
> ○ B. DB2RESTSZ registry variable
> ○ C. RESTBUFSZ Database Manager configuration parameter
> ○ D. REST_BUF_SZ Database configuration parameter

Question 11

Given the following exhibit:

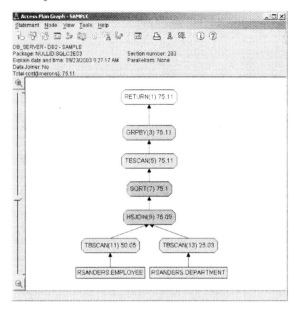

Which of the following describes what takes place in the access plan before a sort operation is performed?

- ○ A. 3 tables are scanned and the data is combined using a union
- ○ B. 2 tables are scanned and the data is combined using a hash join
- ○ C. 3 tables are scanned and the data is combined using a merge join
- ○ D. 2 tables are scanned and the data is combined using a nested loop join

Question 12

Given the following set of commands:

```
UPDATE DBM CFG USING DFT_MON_TABLE ON
UPDATE MONITOR SWITCHES USING LOCK ON
UPDATE MONITOR SWITCHES USING DFT_MON_SORT ON
```

Which of the following snapshot monitor switches will be turned on if the DB2 instance is stopped and restarted?

- ○ A. TABLE
- ○ B. TABLE and LOCK
- ○ C. SORT
- ○ D. LOCK and SORT

Question 13

Which of the following commands will re-initialize the counter for `INSERT` statements executed in the Database System Monitor?

○ A. `RESET MONITOR FOR STATEMENTS`

○ B. `RESET MONITOR ALL`

○ C. `INITIALIZE MONITOR FOR STATEMENTS`

○ D. `INITIALIZE MONITOR ALL`

Question 14

Which two of the following settings enables archival logging?

☐ A. Set the LOGSECOND database parameter to 2

☐ B. Set the ARCHIVELOG database parameter to YES

☐ C. Set the LOGRETAIN database parameter to RECOVERY

☐ D. Set the LOGTYPE database parameter to ARCHIVAL

☐ E. Set the USEREXIT database parameter to YES

Question 15

Which of the following would provide the ability to monitor deadlock activity using db2evmon?

○ A. GET SNAPSHOT FOR DEADLOCKS ON db-name WRITE TO FILE

○ B. GET SNAPSHOT FOR DEADLOCKS ON db-name WRITE TO FILE

○ C. CREATE EVENT MONITOR ev1 FOR DEADLOCKS WRITE TO TABLE

○ D. CREATE EVENT MONITOR ev1 FOR DEADLOCKS WRITE TO FILE

Question 16

Given the following static SQL statements:

```
SELECT col1 FROM tablea WHERE col1 > 100
SELECT col2 FROM tableb ORDER BY col2
```

Which of the following commands can be used to capture explain snapshot information for both statements?

○ A. `bind`

○ B. `db2expln`

○ C. `dynexpln`

○ D. `db2exfmt`

Answers

Question 1

The correct answer is **A**. Any time a configuration parameter is set to AUTOMATIC, DB2 will determine the best value to use for that particular parameter and act accordingly. Four configuration parameters can take advantage of this behavior. They are:

> **instance_memory.** (Instance configuration parameter) When set to AUTOMATIC, DB2 will calculate the amount of instance memory needed for the current configuration.

> **database_memory.** (Database configuration parameter) When set to AUTOMATIC, DB2 will calculate the amount of memory needed for the database and allocate it at database activation time.

> **dbheap.** (Database configuration parameter) When set to AUTO-MATIC, DB2 will calculate the amount of memory needed for the database and allocate when the first connection to the database is established.

> **maxappls.** (Database configuration parameter) When set to AUTO-MATIC, DB2 will dynamically allocate the resources it needs to support new applications.

Question 2

The correct answer is **B**. If the DEFERRED clause is specified with the UPDATE DATABASE MANAGER CONFIGURATION command, changes made to the DB2 Database Manager configuration file will not take effect until the instance is stopped and restarted. If the IMMEDIATE clause is specified or if neither clause is specified, all changes made will take effect immediately.

Question 3

The correct answer is **C**. Only Explain snapshot data can be viewed by Visual Explain and since both EXPLAIN and EXPLSNAP are bind options, their setting has no effect on the application because it has already been bound to the database. (If the application had not been bound, setting the EXPLSNAP bind option to YES or ALL would have caused Explain snapshot data to be collected for the statements when the application was bound.)

Therefore, the CURRENT EXPLAIN SNAPSHOT special register must be used to capture Explain snapshot data for the application and the correct way to set this register is by executing the SQL statement SET CURRENT EXPLAIN SNAPSHOT YES.

Question 4

The correct answer is **C**. You can remove the value of any environment/registry variable by providing just the variable name and the equal sign as input to the db2set command. And the -i option is used with the db2set command to indicate that an instance profile variable is to be displayed, set, or removed. Thus, the correct way to unset the DB2_HASH_JOIN registry variable just for the instance named INST1 is by executing a db2set command that looks like the one shown in answer C.

Question 5

The correct answers are **A** and **C**. One way to collect Explain snapshot data for an SQL statement that is entered using the Command Line Processor is by executing the EXPLAIN SQL statement with the FOR SNAPSHOT option specified (followed by the SQL statement that Explain snapshot data is to be collected for). Another is by setting the value of the CURRENT EXPLAIN SNAPSHOT special register to YES or EXPLAIN, and then executing the desired SQL statements. (If the CURRENT EXPLAIN SNAPSHOT special register is set to EXPLAIN, Explain snapshot data will be collected and the specified statement will not be executed; if the CURRENT EXPLAIN SNAPSHOT special register is set to YES, Explain snapshot data will be collected and the statement will be executed as well.)

Question 6

The correct answer is **B**. The TBSCAN(9) operator indicates that data was retrieved from a table named RSANDERS.EMP_EXP_02 using a table scan operation.

Question 7

The correct answer is **D**. The CREATE EVENT MONITOR statement allows you to specify a WHERE clause when CONNECTIONS, STATEMENTS, and TRANSACTIONS are monitored. However, it does not allow you to specify a WHERE clause when DATABASE, BUFFERPOOLS, TABLESPACES, TABLES, and DEADLOCKS are monitored.

Question 8

The correct answer is **A**. If the Health Monitor determines that a predefined threshold has been exceeded (for example, if the amount of log space available is insufficient), or if it detects an abnormal state for an object (for example, if the instance is down), it will automatically raise an alert. (There are three types of alerts available: attention, warning, and alarm—all alarm alerts are written to the Health Center and the Journal.

Question 9

The correct answer is **C**. The following snapshot monitor switches are available: BUFFERPOOL, LOCK, SORT, STATEMENT, TABLE, TIMESTAMP, and UOW.

Question 10

The correct answer is **C**. The restbufsz DB2 Database Manager configuration parameter is used to specify the size (in 4KB pages) of the buffer that is to be used for restoring a database (if the buffer size is not specified when the RESTORE utility is invoked).

Question 11

The correct answer is **B**. The tables EMPLOYEE and DEPARTMENT are scanned using a table scan operation (TBSCAN(11) and TBSCAN(13), respectively) and the data retrieved is joined using a hash join operation (HSJOIN(9) indicates a hash join operation) before the data is sorted (SORT(7)).

Question 12

The correct answer is **A**. Snapshot monitor switch settings are changed at the instance level by modifying the appropriate DB2 Database Manager configuration parameters (which in this case is the DFT_MON_TABLE parameter) with the UPDATE DATABASE MANAGER CONFIGURATION command. Snapshot monitor switch settings are changed at the application level by executing the

UPDATE MONITOR SWITCHES command. Snapshot monitor switch settings made at the instance level remain persistent across instance restarts.

Question 13

The correct answer is **B**. The easiest way to quickly reset all snapshot monitor counters to zero is by executing the RESET MONITOR command. The basic syntax for this command is RESET MONITOR ALL or RESET MONITOR FOR DATABASE <*DatabaseAlias*>. You cannot selectively reset counters for a particular monitoring group that is controlled by a snapshot monitor switch (in this case STATEMENTS) using the RESET MONITOR command. To perform this type of operation, you must turn the appropriate snapshot monitor switch off and back on or terminate and reestablish database connections.

Question 14

The correct answers are **C** and **E**. When both the *logretain* database configuration parameter and the *userexit* database configuration parameter are set to NO, which is the default, circular logging is used. If the *logretain* parameter is set to RECOVERY and/or the *userexit* parameter is set to YES, archival logging is used instead.

Question 15

The correct answer is **D**. While the snapshot monitor provides a method for recording information about the state of database activity at a given point in time, an event monitor can be used to record information about database activity when an event or transition occurs. Thus, event monitors provide a way to collect monitor data when events or activities that cannot be monitored using the snapshot monitor (such as deadlocks) take place. Therefore, an event monitor must be used. The Event Analyzer can only be used to view event monitor data that was collected and stored in database tables; the Event Monitor Productivity Tool (which is invoked using the db2evmon command) must be used to view event monitor data that was written to files and named pipes.

Question 16

The correct answer is **A**. Both the db2expln tool and the dynexpln tool are designed to describe the final access plan chosen for a particular SQL statement, not to collect explain snapshot data. The db2exfmt tool, on the other hand, is designed to query the explain tables for information (i.e., Explain and/or Explain snapshot data that has already been collected), format the results, and produce a text-based report that can be displayed directly on the terminal or written to an ASCII file. The BIND command, however, is used to bind an application containing embedded SQL to a database and if the EXPL-SNAP YES bind option is used with the BIND command, Explain snapshot data will be collected for the SQL statements coded in the application during the bind process.

DB2 Utilities

*S*eventeen percent (17%) of the DB2 UDB V8.1 for Linux, UNIX, and Windows Database Administration certification exam (Exam 701) and twenty-three percent (23%) of the DB2 UDB V8.1 for Linux, UNIX, and Windows Database Administration certification upgrade exam (Exam 706) is designed to test your ability to perform common database administration tasks using some of the utilities provided with DB2 UDB. The questions that make up this portion of the exam are intended to evaluate the following:

➤ Your ability to use the EXPORT utility to extract data from a database and store it in an external file.

➤ Your ability to use the IMPORT utility to transfer data from an external file to a database table.

➤ Your ability to use the LOAD utility to bulk load data into a database table.

➤ Your knowledge of when to use the IMPORT utility versus when to use the LOAD utility.

➤ Your ability to duplicate and/or migrate databases using db2move and db2look.

➤ Your ability to use the REORKCHK and REORG commands to locate and remove fragmentation in tablespace containers at the table level.

➤ Your ability to use the INSPECT command to check a database for architectural integrity.

➤ Your ability to use the RUNSTATS, REBIND, and FLUSH PACKAGE CACHE commands to ensure that the DB2 Optimizer will always generate the best access plan for a given query, and that applications can take advantage of new access plans immediately.

➤ Your knowledge of the purpose and functionality of the Design Advisor.

This chapter is designed to introduce you to the various database administration utilities that are available with DB2 Universal Database.

 Although basic syntax is presented for most of the DB2 UDB commands and SQL statements covered in this chapter, the actual syntax supported may be much more complex. To view the complete syntax for a specific command or to obtain more information about a particular command, refer to the *IBM DB2 Universal Database, Version 8 Command Reference* product documentation. To view the complete syntax for a specific SQL statement or to obtain more information about a particular statement, refer to the *IBM DB2 Universal Database, Version 8 SQL Reference, Volume 2* product documentation.

Terms you will learn:

Delimited ASCII (DEL)

Non-delimited or fixed-length ASCII (ASC)

Worksheet Format (WSF)

PC Integrated Exchange Format (IXF)

Column delimiters

Row delimiters

Character delimiters

Location method (METHOD L)

Name method (METHOD N)

Position method (METHOD P)

EXPORT

Modifier

LOB Location Specifier (LLS)

IMPORT

CREATE

INSERT

INSERT_UPDATE

REPLACE

REPLACE_CREATE

LOAD

Load phase

Build phase

Delete phase

Index Copy phase

Point of consistency

```
db2move
db2look
REORGCHK
REORG
INSPECT
RUNSTATS
REBIND
FLUSH PACKAGE CACHE
```
Design Advisor (`db2advis`)

Techniques you will master:

Understanding how the EXPORT utility is used to copy specific data from a DB2 UDB database to one or more external files.

Understanding how the IMPORT utility is used to add data stored in one or more external files to a DB2 UDB database.

Understanding how the LOAD utility is used to bulk-load data stored in one or more external files, named pipes, etc., into a DB2 UDB database.

Recognizing the difference between the IMPORT utility and the LOAD utility.

Understanding how and why the REORKCHK and REORG utilities are used.

Understanding how and why the INSPECT utility is used.

Understanding how and why the RUNSTATS, REBIND, and FLUSH PACKAGE CACHE utilities are used.

Understanding how and why the Design Advisor is used.

DB2 UDB's Data Movement Utilities and the File Formats They Support

Although a database usually functions as a self-contained entity, there are times when it becomes necessary to exchange data with "the outside world." However, in order to be able to transfer data between databases and external files, any external file used must be formatted in such a way that it can be processed by any of DB2 UDB's data movement tools available. (A file's format determines how data is physically stored in the file.) The data movement utilities provided by DB2 UDB recognize and support up to four different file formats. They are:

➤ Delimited ASCII (DEL)

➤ Non-delimited or fixed-length ASCII (ASC)

➤ Worksheet Format (WSF)

➤ PC Integrated Exchange Format (IXF)

But just what are these formats, how are they similar, and how do they differ? To answer this question we need to take a closer look at each format supported.

Delimited ASCII (DEL)

The delimited ASCII file format is used extensively in many relational database management systems and software applications to exchange data with a wide variety of application products. With this particular format, data values typically vary in length and a *delimiter*, which is a unique character that is not found in the data values themselves, is used to separate individual values and rows. Actually, delimited ASCII format files typically use three distinct delimiters:

> **Column delimiters.** Column delimiters are characters that are used to mark the beginning and/or end of a data value. (Usually, each value is associated with a particular column, based on its position in the file.) Commas (,) are typically used as the column delimiter for delimited ASCII format files (in fact, such files are sometimes referred to as Comma Separated Variable/Value, or CSV, files and are often given a .csv extension). Vertical bars (|) are also commonly used as column delimiters.

> **Row delimiters.** Row delimiters are characters that are used to mark the end of a single record or row. On UNIX systems, the new line character (0x0A) is typically used as the row delimiter for a delimited ASCII format file; on Windows systems, the carriage return/linefeed characters (0x0D–0x0A) are normally used instead.

> **Character delimiters.** Character delimiters are characters that are used to mark the beginning and end of character data values. Double quotes (") are typically used as character delimiters for delimited ASCII format files.

Typically, when data is written to a delimited ASCII file, rows are streamed into the file, one after another; the appropriate column delimiter is used to separate each column's data values; the appropriate row delimiter is used to separate each individual record (row); and all character/character string values are enclosed with the appropriate character delimiter. Numeric values are represented by their ASCII equivalent—the period character (.) is used to denote the decimal point (if appropriate); real values are represented with scientific notation (E); negative values are preceded by the minus character (–); and positive values may or may not be preceded by the plus character (+)). And because delimited ASCII files are written in ASCII, their contents can be edited with any simple text editor.

Thus, if the comma character was used as the column delimiter, the carriage return/line feed character was used as the row delimiter, and the double quote character was used as the character delimiter, the contents of a delimited ASCII file could look something like this:

```
10,"Headquarters",860,"Corporate","New York"
15,"Research",150,"Eastern","Boston"
20,"Legal",40,"Eastern","Washington"
38,"Support Center 1",80,"Eastern","Atlanta"
42,"Manufacturing",100,"Midwest","Chicago"
51,"Training Center",34,"Midwest","Dallas"
66,"Support Center 2",112,"Western","San Francisco"
84,"Distribution",290,"Western","Denver"
```

Non-Delimited ASCII (ASC)

The non-delimited ASCII file format is also used by a wide variety of software and database applications to exchange data with application products. With this format, data values have a fixed length and the position of each value in the file determines which column and row that value belongs to. (For this reason, non-delimited ASCII files are sometimes referred to as fixed-length ASCII files.)

Typically, when data is written to a non-delimited ASCII file, rows are streamed into the file, one after another; each column's data values are written using a fixed number of bytes, and an appropriate row delimiter is used to separate each individual record (row). On UNIX systems, the new line character (0x0A) typically acts as the row delimiter for non-delimited ASCII format files; on Windows systems, the carriage return/linefeed characters (0x0D–0x0A) act as the row delimiter instead. (If a data value is smaller than the fixed length allotted for a particular column, it is padded with blanks until its length matches the length specified for the column.) As with delimited ASCII format files, numeric values are represented by their ASCII equivalent—the period character (.) is used to denote the decimal point (if appropriate); real values are represented with scientific notation (E); negative values are preceded by the minus character (–); and positive values may or may not be preceded by the plus character (+).

Thus, the contents of a non-delimited ASCII file might look something like this:

```
10Headquarters      860CorporateNew York
15Research          150Eastern  Boston
20Legal              40 Eastern  Washington
38Support Center 180 Eastern  Atlanta
42Manufacturing     100Midwest  Chicago
51Training Center 34 Midwest  Dallas
66Support Center 2112Western   San Francisco
84Distribution      290Western   Denver
```

Like delimited ASCII files, the contents of non-delimited ASCII files can be edited with a simple text editor.

Worksheet Format (WSF)

The worksheet file format is a special file format that is used exclusively by the Lotus 1-2-3 and Lotus Symphony spreadsheet products. Different releases of each of these products incorporate different features into the file formats they use for data storage; however, all releases use a common subset of features and it is this subset that is recognized and used by some of the DB2 UDB data movement utilities available. Worksheet format files cannot be edited with a simple text editor.

PC Integrated Exchange Format (IXF)

The PC Integrated Exchange Format file format is a special file format that is used almost exclusively to move data between different DB2 UDB databases. Typically, when data is written to a PC Integrated Exchange Format file, rows are streamed into the file, one after another, as an unbroken sequence of variable-length records. With this format, character data values are stored in their original ASCII representation (without additional padding) and numeric values are stored either as packed decimal values or as binary values, depending on the data type used to store them in the database. In addition to table data, table definitions and associated index definitions are also stored in PC Integrated Exchange Format files. Thus, tables (along with any corresponding indexes) can be both defined and populated when this particular file format is used. Like worksheet format files, PC Integrated Exchange Format files cannot be edited using a simple text editor.

Extracting Columnar Data from External Files

As you can see, the file format used by an external file determines how data is physically stored in that file. And the way data physically resides in a file determines the method that must be used to extract that file's data values and map it to one or more columns of a table. With DB2 UDB, three methods are used to map data values found in external files to columns in a table. These methods are:

➤ The location method (METHOD L)
➤ The name method (METHOD N)
➤ The position method (METHOD P)

The Location Method

When the location method is used to extract data from an external file, columnar data values are identified by a series of beginning and ending byte positions that, when used together, identify the location of a specific data value within a single row. Each byte position specified is treated as an offset from the beginning of the row (which is byte position 1) and two byte positions are required to extract a single value. Figure 6–1 illustrates how the location method is used to map data values found in an external file to columns in a table.

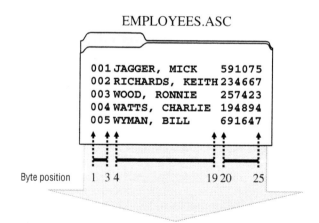

Figure 6–1   Mapping columnar data using the location method.

The location method can only be used to map data values found in external files that use the non-delimited ASCII (ASC) format.

The Name Method

When the name method is used to extract data from an external file, column names are included in the file and columnar data values are identified by the name of the column they are associated with. Figure 6–2 illustrates how the name method is used to map data values found in an external file to columns in a table.

Because DB2 expects column names to be stored in the external file along with the data values themselves when the name method is used, this method can only be used to map data values found in external files that use the PC Integrated Exchange Format (IXF).

The Position Method

When the position method is used to extract data from an external file, columnar data values are identified by their indexed position within a single row; the first data value found is assigned the index position 1, the second

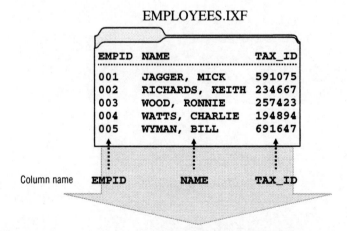

Figure 6–2 Mapping columnar data using the name method.

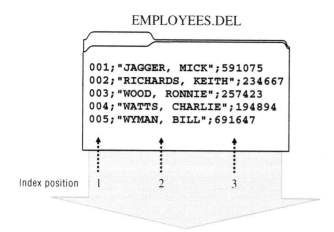

EMPLOYEES.DEL

```
001;"JAGGER, MICK";591075
002;"RICHARDS, KEITH";234667
003;"WOOD, RONNIE";257423
004;"WATTS, CHARLIE";194894
005;"WYMAN, BILL";691647
```

Index position | 1 | 2 | 3

EMPLOYEE TABLE

EMPID	NAME	TAX_ID
001	JAGGER, MICK	591075
002	RICHARDS, KEITH	234667
003	WOOD, RONNIE	257423
004	WATTS, CHARLIE	194894
005	WYMAN, BILL	691647

Figure 6–3   Mapping columnar data using the position method.

data value found is assigned the index position 2, and so on. Figure 6–3 illustrates how the position method is used to map data values found in an external file to columns in a table.

The position method can only be used to map data values found in external files that use either the delimited ASCII (DEL) format or the PC Integrated Exchange Format (IXF).

The DB2 UDB EXPORT Utility

The EXPORT utility is designed to extract data from a DB2 UDB database table or view and externalize it to a file, using the delimited ASCII (DEL) format, worksheet format (WSF), or PC Information Exchange Format (IXF). Such files can then be used to provide data values to other databases (including the database the data was extracted from) and software applications such as spreadsheets and word processors.

One way to invoke the EXPORT utility is by executing the EXPORT command. The basic syntax for this command is:

```
EXPORT TO [FileName] OF [DEL | WSF | IXF]
<LOBS TO [LOBPath ,...]>
<LOBFILE [LOBFileName ,...]>
<MODIFIED BY [Modifier ,...]>
<METHOD N ( [ColumnName ,...] )>
<MESSAGES [MsgFileName]>
[SELECTStatement]
```

where:

FileName	Identifies the name and location of the external file data is to be exported (copied) to.
LOBPath	Identifies one or more locations where large object (LOB) data values are to be stored. (If this option is specified, each LOB value will be stored in its own file at the location specified.)
LOBFileName	Identifies one or more base names that are to be used to name the files that large object (LOB) data values are to be written to. During an export operation, file names are constructed by appending a period (.) and a three-digit sequence number to the current base file name in this list, and then appending the generated file name to the large object data path specified (in *LOBPath*). For example, if the current LOB path is the directory "C:\LOBData" and the current LOB file name is "Value", the LOB files created will be C:\LOBData\Value.001, C:\LOBData\Value.002, and so on.
Modifier	Identifies one or more options that are used to override the default behavior of the EXPORT utility. (Table 6–1 contains a list of valid modifiers.)
ColumnName	Identifies one or more column names that are to be written to the external file data is to be exported to.
MsgFileName	Identifies the name and location of an external file that messages produced by the EXPORT utility are to be written to as the export operation is performed.
SELECTStatement	Identifies a SELECT SQL statement that, when executed, will retrieve data that will be exported to an external file.

Table 6–1 File Type Modifiers Recognized by the EXPORT Command		
Modifier	**Description**	**File Format**
lobsinfile	Indicates that large object (LOB) data values are to be written to their own individual files.	Delimited ASCII (DEL), Worksheet Format (WSF), and PC Integrated Exchange Format (IXF)
chardel*x* where *x* is any valid delimiter character	Identifies a specific character that is to be used as a character delimiter. The default character delimiter is a double quotation mark (") character. The character specified is used in place of the double quotation mark to enclose a character string.	Delimited ASCII (DEL)
codepage=*x* where *x* is any valid code page identifier	Identifies the code page of the data contained in the output data set produced. Character data is converted from the application code page to the code page specified during the export operation.	Delimited ASCII (DEL)
coldel*x* where *x* is any valid delimiter character	Identifies a specific character that is to be used as a column delimiter. The default column delimiter is a comma (,) character. The character specified is used in place of a comma to signal the end of a column.	Delimited ASCII (DEL)
datesiso	Indicates that all date data values are to be exported in ISO format ("YYYY-MM-DD"). By default, the EXPORT utility normally writes • DATE data in "YYYYMMDD" format. • CHAR(*date*) data in "YYYY-MM-DD" format. • TIME data in "HH.MM.SS" format. • TIMESTAMP data in "YYYY-MM-DD-HH.MM.SS.uuuuuu" format.	Delimited ASCII (DEL)
decplusblank	Indicates that positive decimal values are to be prefixed with a blank space instead of a plus sign (+). The default action is to prefix positive decimal values with a plus sign.	Delimited ASCII (DEL)

(continues)

Table 6–1	File Type Modifiers Recognized by the `EXPORT` Command (Continued)	
Modifier	**Description**	**File Format**
decpt*x* where *x* is any valid delimiter character	Identifies a specific character that is to be used as a decimal point character. The default decimal point character is a period (.) character. The character specified is used in place of a period as a decimal point character.	Delimited ASCII (DEL)
dldel*x* where *x* is any valid delimiter character	Identifies a specific character that is to be used as a DATALINK delimiter. The default DATALINK delimiter is a semicolon (;) character. The character specified is used in place of a semicolon as the interfield separator for a DATALINK value. It is needed because a DATALINK value may have more than one subvalue. It is important to note that the character specified as the DATALINK delimiter must not be the same as the character used for the row, column, or character delimiter.	Delimited ASCII (DEL)
nodoubledel	Indicates that double-character delimiters are not to be recognized.	Delimited ASCII (DEL)
1	Indicates that a WSF file that is compatible with Lotus 1-2-3 Release 1 or Lotus 1-2-3 Release 1a is to be created. By default, WSF files that are compatible with Lotus 1-2-3 Release 1 or Lotus 1-2-3 Release 1a are generated unless otherwise specified.	Worksheet Format (WSF)
2	Indicates that a WSF file that is compatible with Lotus Symphony Release 1.0 is to be created.	Worksheet Format (WSF)
3	Indicates that a WSF file that is compatible with Lotus 1-2-3 Version 2 or Lotus Symphony Release 1.1 is to be created.	Worksheet Format (WSF)
4	Indicates that a WSF file containing DBCS characters is to be created.	Worksheet Format (WSF)

Adapted from Table 7 on pages 307–309 of the *IBM DB2 Command Reference* manual.

> **NOTE** If a table whose data is to be exported contains packed character data, that data must be unpacked before it can be written to a PC Integrated Exchange Format (IXF) file. The easiest way to unpack packed character data is to create a view on the table that contains the packed data and export the data using the view—a view will form character data from packed character data automatically.

So, if you wanted to export data stored in a table named DEPARTMENT to an external file named DEPT.DEL that uses the delimited ASCII (DEL) format, you could do so by executing an EXPORT command that looks something like this:

```
EXPORT TO DEPT.DEL OF DEL
MESSAGES EXP_MSGS.TXT
SELECT * FROM DEPARTMENT
```

On the other hand, if you wanted to export data stored in a table named EMPLOYEES to an external file named EMPLOYEES.IXF that uses the PC Integrated Exchange Format (IXF), you could do so by executing an EXPORT command that looks something like this:

```
EXPORT TO EMPLOYEES.IXF OF IXF
MESSAGES EXP_MSGS.TXT
SELECT * FROM EMPLOYEES
```

When data that is to be exported contains large object (LOB) values, by default only the first 32 K (kilobytes) of each LOB value are actually written to the file containing the exported data. As you might imagine, this presents quite a problem if LOB values are greater than 32 K in size—such values will be truncated. By overriding this default behavior (using the *lobsinfile* modifier) and providing the EXPORT utility with one or more locations that LOB data values are to be written to, each LOB value encountered will be stored, in its entirety, in its own individual file (which will be assigned a name that either the user or the EXPORT utility provides). Figure 6–4 illustrates a simple export operation in which LOB values are processed in this manner.

Thus, if you wanted to export data—including LOB data—stored in a table named EMPLOYEES to external files, you could do so by executing an EXPORT command that looks something like this:

```
EXPORT TO C:\DATA\EMPLOYEES.IXF OF IXF
LOBS TO C:\LOB_DATA
MODIFIED BY lobsinfile
MESSAGES EXP_MSGS.TXT
SELECT * FROM EMPLOYEES
```

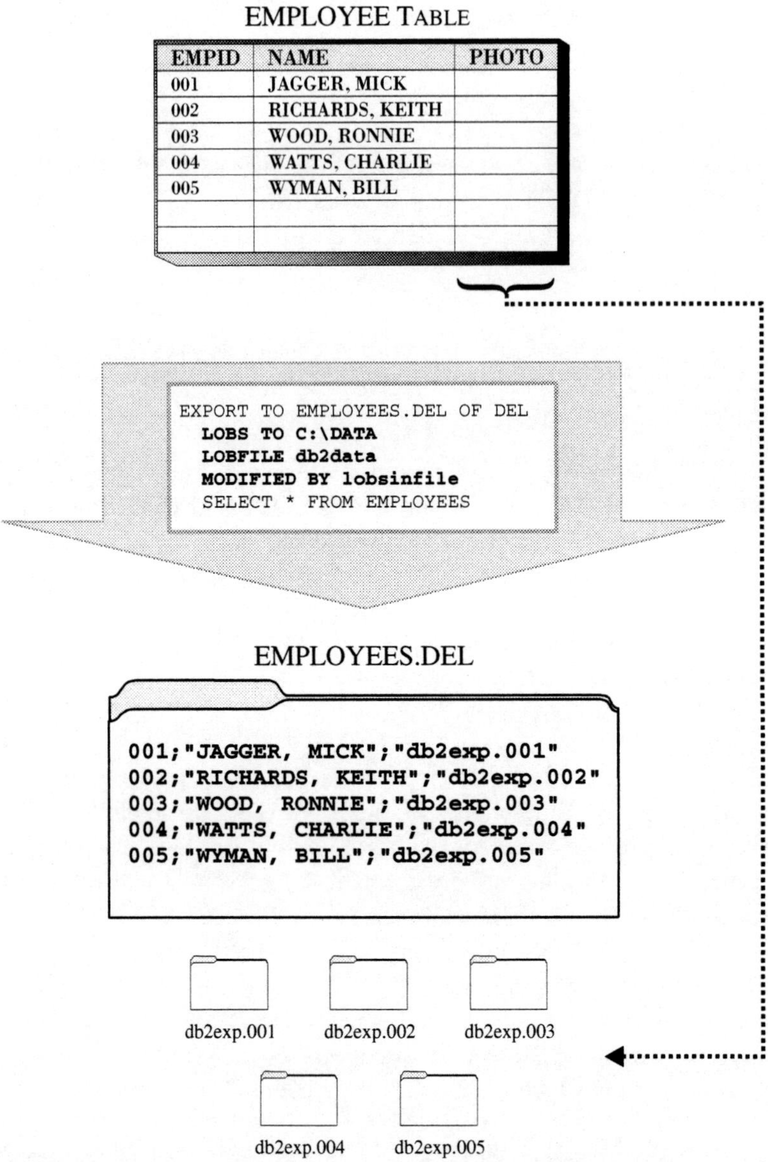

EMPLOYEE TABLE

EMPID	NAME	PHOTO
001	JAGGER, MICK	
002	RICHARDS, KEITH	
003	WOOD, RONNIE	
004	WATTS, CHARLIE	
005	WYMAN, BILL	

```
EXPORT TO EMPLOYEES.DEL OF DEL
   LOBS TO C:\DATA
   LOBFILE db2data
   MODIFIED BY lobsinfile
   SELECT * FROM EMPLOYEES
```

EMPLOYEES.DEL

```
001;"JAGGER, MICK";"db2exp.001"
002;"RICHARDS, KEITH";"db2exp.002"
003;"WOOD, RONNIE";"db2exp.003"
004;"WATTS, CHARLIE";"db2exp.004"
005;"WYMAN, BILL";"db2exp.005"
```

db2exp.001   db2exp.002   db2exp.003

db2exp.004   db2exp.005

Figure 6–4 An EXPORT operation in which LOB values are stored in individual files.

When executed, this command would:

➤ Retrieve all data values stored in the table named EMPLOYEES.

➤ Copy all non-LOB values retrieved from the table named EMPLOYEES to an external file named EMPLOYEES.IXF that uses the PC Integrated Exchange Format (IXF). (This file will reside in a directory named "DATA" that is located on drive C:.)

➤ Copy any LOB values retrieved from the table named EMPLOYEES to their own individual file. (Each file created will reside in a directory named "LOB_DATA" that is located on drive C:.)

➤ Record all messages produced by the EXPORT utility to a file named EXP_MSGS.TXT (which will reside in the current working directory).

When LOB values are exported using the *lobsinfile* modifier, a LOB Location Specifier (LLS) is generated and stored, along with all other non-LOB data values, in the external data file produced. The LLS is a string value that provides specific information about a LOB data value that has been stored in its own file; the LLS string value has the format *Filename.ext.nnn.mmm/* where:

FileName.ext	Identifies the name of the file that contains the LOB data value. During an export operation, file names are constructed by appending a period (.) and a three-digit sequence number to the appropriate base file name. For example, if the base file name is "Value," the LOB files created will be Value.001, Value.002, and so on.
nnn	Identifies the offset within the file, in bytes, where the LOB data value begins.
mmm	Identifies the length, in bytes, of the LOB value.

For example, an LLS value of "empresume.001.323.5131/" indicates that the LOB value can be found in the file empresume.001, that the actual LOB data begins at an offset of 323 bytes in the file, and that the value is 5,131 bytes long.

Data stored in a DB2 UDB database can also be exported to an external file using the Export Table dialog, which can be activated by selecting the appropriate action from the *Tables* or *Views* menu found in the Control Center. Figure 6–5 shows the Control Center menu items that must be selected to activate the Export Table dialog; Figure 6–6 shows how the Export Table dialog might look after its input fields have been populated.

It is important to note that regardless of whether you use the EXPORT command or the Export Table dialog to export data, a database connection must be established before the EXPORT utility is invoked.

Only users with System Administrator (SYSADM) authority, Database Administrator (DBADMN) authority, CONTROL privilege on all tables and/or views referenced, or SELECT privilege on all tables and/or views referenced are allowed to export data using the EXPORT utility.

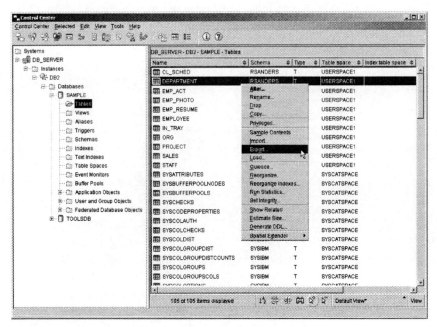

Figure 6–5   Invoking the Export Table dialog from the Control Center.

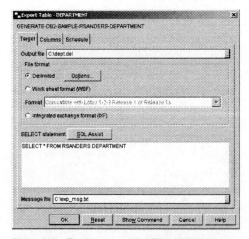

Figure 6–6   The first page of the Export Table dialog.

The DB2 UDB IMPORT Utility

Just as there are times when it is beneficial to copy data stored in a table or view to an external file, there can be times when it is advantageous to copy data stored in an external file to a database table or updatable view. One way to copy data stored in an external file to a database table is by using DB2

UDB's IMPORT utility; the IMPORT utility is designed to read data directly from an external file (provided the file is written in a format that is supported by DB2 UDB) and store it in a specific table or updatable view. It is important to note that all operations must be completed and all locks must be released before data can be imported into a table or updateable view. (Operations are completed and locks are released when transactions interacting with the table/view data is to be imported into are terminated with a commit or roll back operation.)

The IMPORT utility can be invoked by executing the IMPORT command. The basic syntax for this command is:

```
IMPORT FROM [FileName] OF [DEL | ASC | WSF | IXF]
<LOBS FROM [LOBPath ,...]>
<MODIFIED BY [Modifier ,...]>
<Method>
<COMMITCOUNT [CommitCount]>
<RESTARTCOUNT [RestartCount]>
<MESSAGES [MsgFileName]>
[CREATE | INSERT | INSERT_UPDATE | REPLACE]
    INTO [TableName] < ( [ColumnName ,...] )>
    <IN [TSName] <INDEX IN [TSName]> <LONG IN [TSName]>>
```

where:

FileName	Identifies the name and location of the external file data is to be imported (copied) from.
LOBPath	Identifies one or more locations where large object (LOB) data values that are to be imported are stored.
Modifier	Identifies one or more options that are used to override the default behavior of the IMPORT utility. (Table 6–2 contains a list of valid modifiers.)
Method	Identifies the method (location, name, or position) that is to be used to extract data values from the source external file(s) specified and map them to one or more columns of the target table/updatable view specified. The syntax used to specify each method varies. (We'll look at the syntax for each method a little later.)
CommitCount	Identifies the number of rows of data (records) that are to be copied to the table/updatable view specified before a commit operation is to be performed.

RestartCount   Identifies the number of rows of data in the external file specified that are to be skipped. This option is typically used when an earlier IMPORT operation failed. By skipping rows that have already been successfully imported into a table/updatable view, one IMPORT operation can essentially continue where another IMPORT operation left off.

MsgFileName   Identifies the name and location of an external file that messages produced by the IMPORT utility are to be written to as the import operation is performed.

TableName   Identifies the name assigned to the table or updatable view that data is to be imported (copied) to. (This cannot be the name of a system catalog table or view.)

ColumnName   Identifies one or more specific columns (by name) that data is to be imported into.

TSName   Identifies the tablespace that the table and its regular data, indexes, and/or long data/large object data is to be stored in if the table specified is to be created. (Regular data, indexes, and long/large object data can only be stored in separate tablespaces if DMS tablespaces are used.)

Table 6–2   File Type Modifiers Recognized by the IMPORT Command

Modifier	Description	File Format
compound=*x* where *x* is any number between 1 and 100	Indicates that nonatomic compound SQL should be used to insert the data read from a file into a table/updatable view and that a specific number of statements (between 1 and 100) are to be included in the compound SQL block. This modifier cannot be used when INSERT_UPDATE mode is used and is incompatible with the following modifiers: usedefaults, identitymissing, identityignore, generatedmissing, and generatedignore.	Delimited ASCII (DEL), non-delimited ASCII (ASC), Worksheet Format (WSF), and PC Integrated Exchange Format (IXF) *(continues)*

Table 6–2 File Type Modifiers Recognized by the IMPORT Command (Continued)		
Modifier	**Description**	**File Format**
generatedignore	Indicates that although data for all generated columns is present in the file being imported, this data should be ignored. Instead, the IMPORT utility should replace all generated data values found with its own generated values. This modifier is incompatible with the generatedmissing modifier.	Delimited ASCII (DEL), non-delimited ASCII (ASC), Worksheet Format (WSF), and PC Integrated Exchange Format (IXF)
generatedmissing	Indicates that data for generated columns is missing from the file being imported and that the IMPORT utility should generate an appropriate value for each missing value encountered. This modifier is incompatible with the generatedignore modifier.	Delimited ASCII (DEL), non-delimited ASCII (ASC), Worksheet Format (WSF), and PC Integrated Exchange Format (IXF)
identityignore	Indicates that although data for all identity columns is present in the file being imported, that this data should be ignored. Instead, the IMPORT utility should replace all identity column data found with its own generated values. This modifier is incompatible with the identitymissing modifier.	Delimited ASCII (DEL), non-delimited ASCII (ASC), Worksheet Format (WSF), and PC Integrated Exchange Format (IXF)
identitymissing	Indicates that data for identity columns is missing from the file being imported and that the IMPORT utility should generate an appropriate value for each missing value encountered. This modifier is incompatible with the identityignore modifier.	Delimited ASCII (DEL), non-delimited ASCII (ASC), Worksheet Format (WSF), and PC Integrated Exchange Format (IXF)
lobsinfile	Indicates that large object (LOB) data values are stored in their own individual files.	Delimited ASCII (DEL), non-delimited ASCII (ASC), Worksheet Format (WSF), and PC Integrated Exchange Format (IXF)

(continues)

	Table 6–2 File Type Modifiers Recognized by the `IMPORT` Command (Continued)	
Modifier	**Description**	**File Format**
no_type_id	Indicates that data for typed tables should be converted to a single non-typed subtable. This modifier is only valid when importing data into a single sub table of a table hierarchy.	Delimited ASCII (DEL), non-delimited ASCII (ASC), Worksheet Format (WSF), and PC Integrated Exchange Format (IXF)
nodefaults	Indicates that if the source column data for a target table column is not provided, and if the target table column is not nullable, default values are not to be imported. If this modifier is not used and a source column data value for one of the target table columns is not provided, one of the following will occur: • If a default value can be found for the column, the default value will be imported. • If the column is nullable, and a default value cannot be found for that column, a NULL value is stored in the column. • If the column is not nullable, and a default value cannot be found, an error is returned, and the IMPORT utility stops processing.	Delimited ASCII (DEL), non-delimited ASCII (ASC), Worksheet Format (WSF), and PC Integrated Exchange Format (IXF)
usedefaults	Indicates that if the source column data for a target table column is not provided, and if the target table column has a defaults constraint, default values are to be generated for the column. If this modifier is not used and a source column data value for one of the target table columns is not provided, one of the following will occur: • If the column is nullable a NULL value is stored in the column. • If the column is not nullable, and a default value cannot be generated, the row is rejected.	Delimited ASCII (DEL), non-delimited ASCII (ASC), Worksheet Format (WSF), and PC Integrated Exchange Format (IXF)

(continues)

Table 6–2 File Type Modifiers Recognized by the IMPORT Command (Continued)		
Modifier	**Description**	**File Format**
codepage=*x* where *x* is any valid code page identifier	Identifies the code page of the data contained in the output data set produced. Character data is converted from the application code page to the code page specified during the import operation.	Delimited ASCII (DEL) and non-delimited ASCII (ASC)
dateformat="*x*" where *x* is any valid combination of date format elements	Identifies how date values stored in the source file are formatted. The following date elements can be used to create the format string provided with this modifier: • YYYY—Year (four digits ranging from 0000–9999) • M—Month (one or two digits ranging from 1–12) • MM—Month (two digits ranging from 1–12; mutually exclusive with M) • D—Day (one or two digits ranging from 1–31) • DD—Day (two digits ranging from 1–31; mutually exclusive with D) • DDD—Day of the year (three digits ranging from 001–366; mutually exclusive with other day or month elements) Examples of valid date format strings include: "D-M-YYYY" "MM.DD.YYYY" "YYYYDDD"	Delimited ASCII (DEL) and non-delimited ASCII (ASC)
implieddecimal	Indicates that the location of an implied decimal point is to be determined by the column definition—the IMPORT utility is not to assume that the decimal point is at the end of the value (default behavior). For example, if this modifier is specified, the value 12345 would be loaded into a DECIMAL(8,2) column as 123.45, *not* as 12345.00.	Delimited ASCII (DEL) and non-delimited ASCII (ASC) *(continues)*

Table 6–2   File Type Modifiers Recognized by the IMPORT Command (Continued)

Modifier	Description	File Format
noeofchar	Indicates that the optional end-of-file character (0x1A) is not to be treated as an end-of-file character; instead, this character should be treated as a normal character if it is encountered.	Delimited ASCII (DEL) and non-delimited ASCII (ASC)
timeformat="*x*" where *x* is any valid combination of time format elements	Identifies how time values stored in the source file are formatted. The following time elements can be used to create the format string provided with this modifier: • H—Hour (one or two digits ranging from 0–12 for a 12-hour system, and 0–24 for a 24 hour system) • HH—Hour (two digits ranging from 0–12 for a 12-hour system, and 0–24 for a 24-hour system; mutually exclusive with H) • M—Minute (one or two digits ranging from 0–59) • MM—Minute (two digits ranging from 0–59; mutually exclusive with M) • S—Second (one or two digits ranging from 0–59) • SS—Second (two digits ranging from 0–59; mutually exclusive with S) • SSSSS—Second of the day after midnight (five digits ranging from 00000–86399; mutually exclusive with other time elements) • TT—Meridian indicator (AM or PM) Examples of valid time format strings include: "HH:MM:SS" "HH.MM TT" "SSSSS"	Delimited ASCII (DEL) and non-delimited ASCII (ASC)

(continues)

Table 6–2 File Type Modifiers Recognized by the IMPORT Command (Continued)		
Modifier	**Description**	**File Format**
timestampformat="*x*" where *x* is any valid combination of date and time format elements	Identifies how timestamp values stored in the source file are formatted. The following date and time elements can be used to create the format string provided with this modifier: • YYYY—Year (four digits ranging from 0000–9999) • M—Month (one or two digits ranging from 1–12) • MM—Month (two digits ranging from 1–12; mutually exclusive with M) • D—Day (one or two digits ranging from 1–31) • DD—Day (two digits ranging from 1–31; mutually exclusive with D) • DDD—Day of the year (three digits ranging from 001–366; mutually exclusive with other day or month elements) • H—Hour (one or two digits ranging from 0–12 for a 12-hour system, and 0–24 for a 24-hour system) • HH—Hour (two digits ranging from 0–12 for a 12-hour system, and 0–24 for a 24-hour system; mutually exclusive with H) • M—Minute (one or two digits ranging from 0–59) • MM—Minute (two digits ranging from 0–59; mutually exclusive with M) • S—Second (one or two digits ranging from 0–59) • SS—Second (two digits ranging from 0–59; mutually exclusive with S) • SSSSS—Second of the day after midnight (five digits ranging from 00000–86399; mutually exclusive with other time elements) • UUUUUU—Microsecond (six digits ranging from 000000–999999)	Delimited ASCII (DEL) and non-delimited ASCII (ASC)

(continues)

Modifier	Description	File Format
	• TT—Meridian indicator (AM or PM) Examples of valid timestamp format strings include: "YYYY/MM/DD HH:MM:SS.UUUUUU"	
chardel*x* where *x* is any valid delimiter character	Identifies a specific character that is to be used as a character delimiter. The default character delimiter is a double quotation mark (") character. The character specified is used in place of the double quotation mark to enclose a character string.	Delimited ASCII (DEL)
coldel*x* where *x* is any valid delimiter character	Identifies a specific character that is to be used as a column delimiter. The default column delimiter is a comma (,) character. The character specified is used in place of a comma to signal the end of a column.	Delimited ASCII (DEL)
datesiso	Indicates that all date data values are to be exported in ISO format ("YYYY-MM-DD"). By default, the IMPORT utility normally writes • DATE data in "YYYYMMDD" format. • CHAR(*date*) data in "YYYY-MM-DD" format. • TIME data in "HH.MM.SS" format. • TIMESTAMP data in "YYYY-MM-DD-HH.MM.SS.uuuuuu" format.	Delimited ASCII (DEL)
decplusblank	Indicates that positive decimal values are to be prefixed with a blank space instead of a plus sign (+). The default action is to prefix positive decimal values with a plus sign.	Delimited ASCII (DEL)
decpt*x* where *x* is any valid delimiter character	Identifies a specific character that is to be used as a decimal point character. The default decimal point character is a period (.) character. The character specified is used in place of a period as a decimal point character.	Delimited ASCII (DEL)

Table 6–2   File Type Modifiers Recognized by the IMPORT Command (Continued)

(continues)

Table 6–2   File Type Modifiers Recognized by the IMPORT Command (Continued)

Modifier	Description	File Format
delprioritychar	Indicates that the priority for evaluating delimiters is to be *character delimiter, record delimiter, column delimiter* rather than *record delimiter, character delimiter, column delimiter* (which is the default). This modifier is typically used with older applications that depend on the other priority.	Delimited ASCII (DEL)
dldel*x* where *x* is any valid delimiter character	Identifies a specific character that is to be used as a DATALINK delimiter. The default DATALINK delimiter is a semicolon (;) character. The character specified is used in place of a semicolon as the interfield separator for a DATALINK value. It is needed because a DATALINK value may have more than one subvalue. It is important to note that the character specified as the DATALINK delimiter must not be the same as the character used for the row, column, or character delimiter.	Delimited ASCII (DEL)
keepblanks	Indicates that all leading and trailing blanks found for each column that has a data type of CHAR, VARCHAR, LONG VARCHAR, or CLOB are to be retained. If this modifier is not specified, all leading and trailing blanks that reside outside character delimiters are removed, and a NULL is inserted into the table for all missing data values found.	Delimited ASCII (DEL)
nodoubledel	Indicates that double character delimiters are not to be recognized.	Delimited ASCII (DEL) *(continues)*

Table 6–2	File Type Modifiers Recognized by the IMPORT Command (Continued)	
Modifier	**Description**	**File Format**
nochecklengths	Indicates that the IMPORT utility is to attempt to import every row in the source file, even if the source data has a column value that exceeds the size of the target column's definition. Such rows can be successfully imported if code page conversion causes the source data to shrink in size. For example, 4-byte EUC data found in a source file could shrink to 2-byte DBCS data in the target table, and require half the space. This option is particularly useful if it is known in advance that the source data will always fit in a column despite mismatched column definitions/sizes.	Non-delimited ASCII (ASC) and PC Integrated Exchange Format (IXF)
nullindchar=*x* where *x* is any valid character	Identifies a specific character that is to be used as a null indicator value. The default null indicator is the letter **Y**. This modifier is case sensitive for EBCDIC data files, except when the character is an English letter. For example, if the null indicator character is specified to be the letter **N**, then the letter **n** is also recognized as a null indicator.	Non-delimited ASCII (ASC)
reclen=*x* where *x* is any number between 1 and 32767	Indicates that a specific number of characters are to be read from the source file for each row found; new-line characters are to be ignored instead of being used to indicate the end of a row.	Non-delimited ASCII (ASC)
striptblanks	Indicates that all leading and trailing blanks found for each column that has a data type of VARCHAR, LONG VARCHAR, VARGRAPHIC, or LONG VARGRAPHIC are to be truncated. This modifier is incompatible with the striptnulls modifier.	Non-delimited ASCII (ASC)

(continues)

Table 6–2   File Type Modifiers Recognized by the IMPORT Command (Continued)

Modifier	Description	File Format
striptnulls	Indicates that all leading and trailing nulls (0x00 characters) found for each column that has a data type of VARCHAR, LONG VARCHAR, VARGRAPHIC, or LONG VARGRAPHIC are to be truncated. This modifier is incompatible with the striptblanks modifier.	Non-delimited ASCII (ASC)
forcein	Indicates that the IMPORT utility is to accept data despite code page mismatches (in other words, to suppress translation between code pages). Fixed-length target columns are checked to verify that they are large enough to hold the data unless the nochecklengths modifier has been specified.	PC Integrated Exchange Format (IXF)
indexixf	Indicates that the IMPORT utility is to drop all indexes currently defined on the existing table, and is to create new indexes using the index definitions stored in the IXF-formatted source file. This modifier can only be used when the contents of a table are being replaced and it cannot be used with a view.	PC Integrated Exchange Format (IXF)
indexschema or indexschema="*x*" where *x* is a valid schema name	Indicates that the IMPORT utility is to assign all indexes created to the schema specified. If this modifier is used and no schema name is provided, all indexes created will be assigned to the default schema for the user ID that is associated with the current database connection. If this modifier is not used, all indexes created will be assigned to the schema identified in the IXF-formatted source file.	PC Integrated Exchange Format (IXF)

Adapted from Table 8 on pages 388–397 of the *IBM DB2 Command Reference* manual.

Earlier we saw that three methods are used to map data values found in external files to columns in a table: the location method, the name method, and the position method. The syntax used to indicate that the location method is to be used to extract data values from the external file specified is:

```
METHOD L ( [ColumnStart] [ColumnEnd] ,... )
    <NULL INDICATORS ( [NullIndColNumber ,...] )>
```

where:

ColumnStart	Identifies the starting position of one or more data values in the non-delimited ASCII (ASC)-formatted file from which values are to be retrieved.
ColumnEnd	Identifies the ending position of one or more data values in the non-delimited ASCII (ASC)-formatted file from which values are to be retrieved.
NullIndColNumber	Identifies the position of one or more data values that are to be treated as null indicator variables for column data values in the non-delimited ASCII (ASC)-formatted file from which values are to be retrieved.

The syntax used to indicate that the name method is to be used to extract data values from the external file specified is:

```
METHOD N ( [ColumnName ,...] )
```

where:

ColumnName	Identifies one or more unique names assigned to columns in the PC Integrated Exchange Format (IXF)-formatted file from which values are to be retrieved.

And the syntax used to indicate that the position method is to be used to extract data values from the external file specified is:

```
METHOD P ( [ColumnPosition ,...] )
```

where:

ColumnPosition	Identifies the indexed position of one or more columns in the delimited ASCII (DEL) or PC Integrated Exchange Format (IXF)-formatted file from which values are to be retrieved.

As you can see, there are five different options available with the IMPORT command that are used to control how the target table data is to be copied to will be altered by the IMPORT operation. These options include:

CREATE. When the CREATE option is used, the target table is created along with all of its associated indexes, then data is imported into the new table. This option also allows you to control what tablespace the new table will be created in. However, this option can only be used when importing data from PC Integrated Exchange Format (IXF)-formatted files.

INSERT. When the INSERT option is used, data is inserted into the target table (which must already exist). Imported data is appended to any data that already exists.

INSERT_UPDATE. When the INSERT_UPDATE option is used, data is either inserted into the target table (which must already exist), or used to update existing rows (if the row being imported has a primary key value that matches that of an existing record). Existing records will only be updated if the target table specified has a primary key defined.

REPLACE. When the REPLACE option is used, any existing data is deleted from the target table (which must already exist); then, the new data is inserted.

REPLACE_CREATE. When the REPLACE_CREATE option is used, any existing data is deleted from the target table if it already exists; then, the new data is inserted. On the other hand, if the target table does not exist, it is created along with all of its associated indexes, then data is imported into the new table. As you might imagine, this option can only be used when importing data from PC Integrated Exchange Format (IXF)-formatted files. (If the target table is a parent table referenced by a foreign key, this option cannot be used.)

So, if you wanted to import data stored in an external file named DEPT.IXF that uses the PC Integrated Exchange Format (IXF) to a new table named DEPARTMENT, you could do so by executing an IMPORT command that looks something like this:

```
IMPORT FROM DEPT.IXF OF IXF
MESSAGES IMP_MSGS.TXT
CREATE INTO DEPARTMENT IN USERSPACE1
```

On the other hand, if you wanted to import data stored in an external file named EMPLOYEES.DEL that uses the delimited ASCII (DEL) format to

an existing table named EMPLOYEES, you could do so by executing an
IMPORT command that looks something like this:

```
IMPORT FROM EMPLOYEES.DEL OF DEL
MESSAGES IMP_MSGS.TXT
REPLACE INTO EMPLOYEES
```

Earlier, we saw that when data that is to be exported contains large object
(LOB) values, by default only the first 32 K (kilobytes) of each LOB value are
actually written to the file containing the exported data. We also saw that this
behavior can be overridden by using the *lobsinfile* modifier and by providing
the EXPORT utility with one or more locations that LOB data values are to
be written to. In this case, each LOB value encountered will be stored, in its
entirety, in its own individual file, which is assigned a name that either the
user or the EXPORT utility provides. As you might imagine, LOB values
that reside in individual files will also be imported (if the *lobsinfile* modifier is
specified) by the IMPORT utility. And because the names and locations of
the files that contain LOB data values are stored in the source data file, this
information does not have to be provided as input to the IMPORT utility in
order for the LOB data values to be retrieved. Figure 6–7 illustrates a simple
import operation in which LOB values reside in their own individual files.

Thus, if you wanted to import data stored in an external file named
EMPLOYEES.IXF that uses the PC Integrated Exchange Format (IXF),
along with LOB data values stored in individual files, to a table named
EMPLOYEES, you could do so by executing an IMPORT command that looks
something like this:

```
IMPORT FROM C:\DATA\EMPLOYEES.IXF OF IXF
LOBS FROM C:\LOB_DATA
MODIFIED BY lobsinfile
MESSAGES IMP_MSGS.TXT
INSERT INTO EMPLOYEES
```

When executed, this command would:

➤ Retrieve all data values stored in an external file named EMPLOY-
EES.IXF that uses the PC Integrated Exchange Format (IXF). (This file
resides in a directory named "DATA" that is located on drive C:.)

➤ Locate all LOB values referenced in the file named EMPLOYEES.IXF
and retrieve each value from their own individual file. (Each file is
expected to reside in a directory named "LOB_DATA" that is located on
drive C:.)

➤ Insert all data values retrieved from both the file named EMPLOY-
EES.IXF and the individual LOB data files into a table named EMPLOY-
EES (which already exists).

➤ Record all messages produced by the IMPORT utility to a file named
IMP_MSGS.TXT (which will reside in the current working directory).

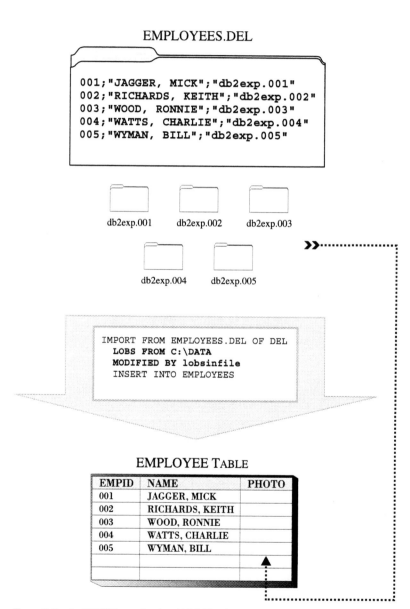

EMPLOYEES.DEL

```
001;"JAGGER, MICK";"db2exp.001"
002;"RICHARDS, KEITH";"db2exp.002"
003;"WOOD, RONNIE";"db2exp.003"
004;"WATTS, CHARLIE";"db2exp.004"
005;"WYMAN, BILL";"db2exp.005"
```

db2exp.001   db2exp.002   db2exp.003

db2exp.004   db2exp.005

```
IMPORT FROM EMPLOYEES.DEL OF DEL
  LOBS FROM C:\DATA
  MODIFIED BY lobsinfile
  INSERT INTO EMPLOYEES
```

EMPLOYEE TABLE

EMPID	NAME	PHOTO
001	JAGGER, MICK	
002	RICHARDS, KEITH	
003	WOOD, RONNIE	
004	WATTS, CHARLIE	
005	WYMAN, BILL	

Figure 6–7   An IMPORT operation in which LOB values are stored in individual files.

Data stored in external files can also be imported using the Import Table dialog, which can be activated by selecting the appropriate action from the *Tables* or *Views* menu found in the Control Center. Figure 6–8 shows the Control Center menu items that must be selected to activate the Import Table dialog; Figure 6–9 shows how the Import Table dialog might look after its input fields have been populated.

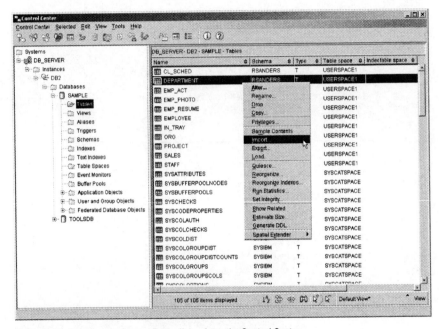

Figure 6–8   Invoking the Import Table dialog from the Control Center.

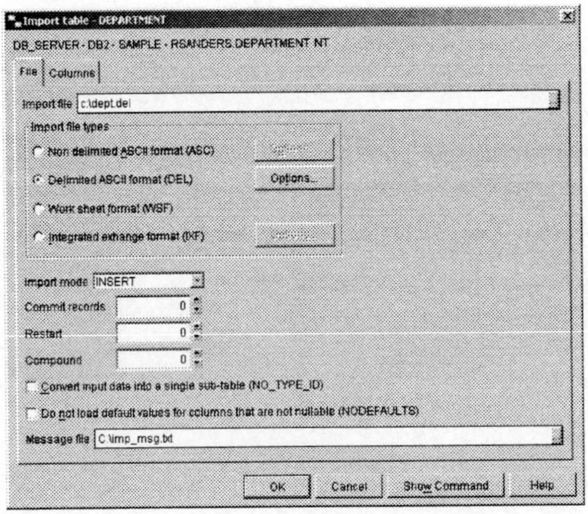

Figure 6–9   The first page of the Import Table dialog.

As with the EXPORT utility, a database connection must be established before the IMPORT utility is invoked.

NOTE Only users with System Administrator (SYSADM) authority, Database Administrator (DBADMN) authority, or CREATETAB on the database *and* either IMPLICIT_SCHEMA privilege on the database or CREATEIN privilege on the schema referenced are allowed to create a new table and import data into it using the CREATE or the REPLACE _CREATE option. Only users with SYSADM authority, DBADMN authority, CONTROL privilege on all tables and/or views referenced, or INSERT *and* SELECT privilege on all tables and/or views referenced are allowed to import data into existing tables using the INSERT option. And only users with SYSADM authority, DBADMN authority, or CONTROL privilege on all tables and/or views referenced are allowed to import data into existing tables using the INSERT_UPDATE, REPLACE, or REPLACE_CREATE option.

The DB2 UDB LOAD Utility

Like the IMPORT utility, the LOAD utility is designed to read data directly from an external file (provided the file is written in a format that is supported by DB2 UDB) and store it in a specific table. However, unlike when the IMPORT utility is used, when the LOAD utility is used, the table that data is to be copied to must already exist in the database before the load operation is initiated. Other differences between the IMPORT utility and the LOAD utility can be seen in Table 6–3.

| **Table 6–3   Differences between the IMPORT Utility and the LOAD Utility** | |
IMPORT Utility	LOAD Utility
Slow when processing large amounts of data.	Significantly faster than the IMPORT utility when processing large amounts of data, because the LOAD utility writes formatted pages directly into the database.
Tables and indexes can be created from IXF format files.	Tables and indexes must exist before data can be loaded into them.
Worksheet Format (WSF)-formatted files are supported.	Worksheet Format (WSF)-formatted files are not supported.
Data can be imported into tables, views, or aliases that refer to tables or views.	Data can only be loaded into tables or aliases that refer to tables—data cannot be loaded into views or aliases that refer to views.
Tablespaces that the table and its indexes reside in remain on-line during processing.	Tablespaces that the table and its indexes reside in are taken off-line during processing.
	(continues)

Table 6–3 Differences between the IMPORT Utility and the LOAD Utility (Continued)	
IMPORT Utility	**LOAD Utility**
All row transactions are recorded in the database's transaction log files.	Minimal logging is performed—row transactions are not recorded in the database's transaction log files.
Triggers can be fired during processing.	Triggers are not fired during processing.
If an import operation is interrupted and a commit frequency value was specified, the table will remain usable and it will contain all rows that were inserted up to the moment the last commit operation was performed. The user has the option of restarting the import operation or leaving the table as it is.	If a load operation was interrupted and a consistency point (commit frequency) value was specified, the table remains in the "Load Pending" state and cannot be used until (1) the load process is restarted and the load operation is completed or (2) the tablespace that the table resides in is restored from a backup image that was created before the load operation was initiated.
The amount of free disk space needed to import data is approximately the size of the largest index being imported plus about 10%. This space is allocated from system temporary tablespaces that have been defined for the database.	The amount of free disk space needed to load data is approximately the size of the sum of all indexes for the table being loaded. This space is temporarily allocated outside the database environment.
All constraint checking is performed during processing.	Only uniqueness checking is performed during processing. All other constraint checking (check constraints, referential integrity constraints, etc.) must be performed after the load operation has completed using the SET INTEGRITY SQL statement.
The keys of each row are inserted into the appropriate index during an import operation.	All keys are sorted during a load operation and the indexes are rebuilt when the load phase of the load operation has completed.
Statistics for the affected table must be manually collected (by issuing the RUNSTATS command) after an import operation is performed.	Statistics for the affected table can be collected and updated during a load operation.
Data can be imported into a host database through DB2 Connect.	Data cannot be loaded into a host database.
Data files to be imported must reside on the same workstation that the import facility is invoked from.	Data files and named pipes that will provide the data to be loaded can reside on the client or the server.

(continues)

Table 6–3 Differences between the IMPORT Utility and the LOAD Utility (Continued)	
IMPORT Utility	**LOAD Utility**
A backup image is not created during an import operation. (Because the IMPORT utility uses SQL inserts, the DB2 Database Manager logs all processing, and no backup images are required to reproduce the import operation in the event a failure occurs.)	A backup image (copy) can be created during a load operation.
The IMPORT utility makes limited use of intrapartition parallelism.	The LOAD utility takes full advantage of intrapartition parallelism on symmetric multiprocessor (SMP) workstations.
Supports hierarchical data.	Does not support hierarchical data.
Numeric data must be stored as character representations.	Numeric data (other than DECIMAL data) can be stored and loaded in either binary form or as character representations. DECIMAL data can be stored and loaded in packed decimal or zoned decimal form or as character representations.
Data conversion between code pages is not performed.	Character data (and numeric data expressed as characters) can be converted from one code page to another during processing.
No FASTPARSE support provided.	FASTPARSE support provided. (FASTPARSE provides reduced data checking of user-supplied data.)
No BINARYNUMERICS support provided.	BINARYNUMERICS support provided.
No PACKEDDECIMAL support provided.	PACKEDDECIMAL support provided.
No ZONEDDECIMAL support provided.	ZONEDDECIMAL support provided.
Cannot override columns defined as GENERATED ALWAYS.	Can override columns defined as GENERATED ALWAYS by using the GENERATEDIGNORE and IDENTITYIGNORE file type modifiers.
No support for importing into materialized query tables.	Support for loading into materialized query tables.

Adapted from Appendix B on pages 309–310 of the *IBM DB2 Data Movement Utilities Guide and Reference* manual.

The most important difference between the IMPORT utility and the LOAD utility is the way in which each utility moves data between an external file and a database table. The IMPORT utility copies data using SQL insert or update operations. As a result, each row processed must be checked for constraint compliance and all activity performed by the IMPORT utility is recorded in the database's transaction log files.

The LOAD utility, on the other hand, inserts data into a table by building data pages consisting of several individual rows of data, and writing those pages directly to the tablespace container(s) the target table uses for data storage. Once all data pages have been constructed and written to the appropriate tablespace container(s), all existing primary and/or unique indexes associated with the target table are rebuilt and all rows that violate primary or unique key constraints defined for the table are deleted (and copied to an exception table, if appropriate). Because pages of data are written instead of individual rows, changes made to the target table are not recorded in the database's transaction log files. As a result, overall performance is typically faster. However, because changes made to a table by the LOAD utility are not logged, if a database failure occurs the data loaded cannot be reloaded by performing a roll-forward recovery operation. To get around this limitation, the LOAD utility can generate a backup copy of all data loaded so it can be quickly reloaded if necessary.

 By default, whenever a LOAD operation is performed on a table, other tables that reside in the same tablespace the table being loaded resides in can be accessed while the LOAD operation is performed. However, there may be times when it is desirable to restrict access to all tablespaces associated with the target table of a LOAD operation. Access to tablespaces associated with the target table of a LOAD operation can be controlled by executing the QUIESCE TABLESPACES FOR TABLE command just before the LOAD operation is initiated and immediately after the LOAD operation completes.

The Four Phases of a LOAD Operation

A complete load operation consists of four distinct phases. These phases are known as:

➤ The Load phase
➤ The Build phase
➤ The Delete phase
➤ The Index Copy phase

The Load phase. Four things happen during the Load phase: data is read from the source file specified and loaded into the appropriate target table, index key values and table statistics are collected, point of consistency information is recorded, and invalid data is placed into dump files. Point of consistency information serves as a checkpoint for the LOAD utility. In the event the load operation is interrupted during execution of the load phase and restarted, the operation will continue from the last consistency point established. As part of updating point of consistency information, the LOAD utility writes a message to the appropriate message file identifying the current number of records that have been successfully loaded. This information can then be used to pick up where the load operation left off if a failure occurs or to monitor the load operation's progress. (The LOAD QUERY command is used to monitor the progress of a load operation.)

The Build phase. During the Build phase, indexes associated with primary and/or unique keys that have been defined for the table that was loaded are updated with the index key values that were collected and sorted during the Load phase. This is also when statistical information about the table and its indexes is updated, if appropriate.

Since the beginning of the Build phase is recorded as a point of consistency, if the load operation is interrupted during execution of the Build phase and restarted, the operation will be restarted at the beginning of the Build phase —the Load phase will not have to be repeated.

The Delete phase. During the Delete phase, all rows that violated primary and/or unique key constraints defined on the target table are removed and copied to an exception table (if appropriate) and a message about each offending row is written to the appropriate message file so it can be modified and manually moved to the target table at some point in the future. These are the only table constraints that are checked. To check loaded data for additional constraint violations, constraint checking should be turned off (with the SET INTEGRITY SQL statement) before the load operation is started, then turned back on and performed immediately (again, with the SET INTEG-RITY SQL statement) after the load operation has completed.

The beginning of the Delete phase is also recorded as a point of consistency. Thus, if a load operation is interrupted during execution of the Delete phase and restarted, the operation will be restarted at the beginning of the Delete phase—the Load phase and the Build phase do not have to be repeated.

The Index Copy phase. During the Index Copy phase, index data is copied from the system temporary tablespace used to the tablespace where the index data is to reside. It is important to note that this phase is only executed if the LOAD command is executed with the ALLOW READ ACCESS and USE [TablespaceName] options specified.

Performing a Load Operation

Now that we have seen how the LOAD utility differs from the IMPORT utility, and how the LOAD utility copies data stored in an external file to a database table, lets look at how the LOAD utility is invoked. The LOAD utility can be invoked by executing the LOAD command. The basic syntax for this command is:

```
LOAD <CLIENT> FROM [FileName OF [DEL | ASC | IXF] |
    PipeName | Device | CursorName OF CURSOR ,...]

<LOBS FROM [LOBPath ,...]>
<MODIFIED BY [Modifier ,...]>
<Method>
<SAVECOUNT [SaveCount]>
<ROWCOUNT [RowCount]>
<WARNINGCOUNT [WarningCount]>
<MESSAGES [MsgFileName]>
<TEMPFILES PATH [TempFilesPath]>
[INSERT | REPLACE | RESTART | TERMINATE]
    INTO [TableName] < ( [ColumnName ,...] )>
<FOR EXCEPTION [ExTableName]>
<STATISTICS
    NO |
    YES |
    <YES> WITH DISTRIBUTION <AND <DETAILED> INDEXES ALL> |
    <YES> [AND | FOR] <DETAILED> INDEXES ALL]>
<NONRECOVERABLE | COPY YES TO [CopyLocation ,...]>
<WITHOUT PROMPTING>
<DATA BUFFER [Size]>
<ALLOW NO ACCESS | ALLOW READ ACCESS <USE [TmpTSName]>>
<CHECK PENDING CASCADE [IMMEDIATE | DEFERRED]>
<INDEXING MODE [AUTOSELECT |
    REBUILD |
    INCREMENTAL |
    DEFERRED>
```

where:

FileName	Identifies the name and location of one or more external files data is to be loaded (copied) from.
PipeName	Identifies the name of one or more named pipes data is to be loaded from.
DeviceName	Identifies the name of one or more devices data is to be loaded from.
CursorName	Identifies the name of one or more cursors data is to be loaded from.
LOBPath	Identifies one or more locations where large object (LOB) data values that are to be loaded are stored.
Modifier	Identifies one or more options that are used to override the default behavior of the LOAD utility. (Table 6–4 contains a list of valid modifiers.)

Method	Identifies the method (location, name, or position) that is to be used to extract data values from the source external file(s) specified and map them to one or more columns of the target table specified. The syntax used to specify each method varies.
SaveCount	Identifies the number of rows of data (records) that are to be copied to the target table specified before the LOAD utility will establish a new point of consistency.
RowCount	Identifies the actual number of rows of data in the external file(s), named pipe(s), device(s), and/or cursor(s) specified that are to be loaded.
WarningCount	Identifies the number of warning conditions the LOAD utility should ignore before terminating the load operation.
MsgFileName	Identifies the name and location of an external file that messages produced by the LOAD utility are to be written to as the load operation is performed.
TempFilesPath	Identifies the location where temporary files that might be needed by the LOAD utility are stored.
TableName	Identifies the name assigned to the table that data is to be loaded into. (This cannot be the name of a system catalog table.)
ColumnName	Identifies one or more specific columns (by name) that data is to be loaded into.
ExTableName	Identifies the name assigned to the table that all rows that violate unique index or primary key constraints defined for the target table specified are to be copied to.
CopyLocation	Identifies the directory or device where a backup copy of all data loaded into the target table is to be stored.
Size	Identifies the number of 4 K (kilobyte) pages that are to be used as buffered storage space for the purpose of transferring data within the LOAD utility.
TmpTSName	Identifies the system temporary tablespace that shadow copies of indexes are to be built in before

they are copied to the appropriate regular tablespace for final storage during the Index Copy phase of a load operation.

Table 6–4   File Type Modifiers Recognized by the LOAD Command

Modifier	Description	File Format
anyorder	Indicates that the preservation of source data order is not required. (This will yield significant performance increases on SMP systems.) This modifier is not supported if SAVECOUNT > 0, since data must be loaded in sequence in order for crash recovery (after a consistency point has been taken) to work properly.	Delimited ASCII (DEL), non-delimited ASCII (ASC), and PC Integrated Exchange Format (IXF)
fastparse	Indicates that reduced syntax checking is to be performed on user-supplied column values. (This can yield significant performance increases.) When this modifier is used, tables are guaranteed to be architecturally correct, and the LOAD utility only performs sufficient data checking to prevent a segmentation violation or trap from occurring.	Delimited ASCII (DEL), non-delimited ASCII (ASC), and PC Integrated Exchange Format (IXF)
generatedignore	Indicates that although data for all generated columns is present in the file being loaded, this data should be ignored. Instead, the LOAD utility should replace all generated data values found with its own generated values. This modifier is incompatible with the generatedmissing modifier.	Delimited ASCII (DEL), non-delimited ASCII (ASC), and PC Integrated Exchange Format (IXF)
generatedmissing	Indicates that data for generated columns is missing from the file being loaded and that the LOAD utility should generate an appropriate value for each missing value encountered. This modifier is incompatible with the generatedignore modifier.	Delimited ASCII (DEL), non-delimited ASCII (ASC), and PC Integrated Exchange Format (IXF)

(continues)

Table 6–4	File Type Modifiers Recognized by the LOAD Command (Continued)	
Modifier	Description	File Format
generatedoverride	Indicates that the LOAD utility is to accept explicit, non-NULL data values for all generated columns in the table (contrary to the normal rules for these types of columns). This modifier is useful when migrating data from another database system, or when loading a table from data that was recovered using the DROPPED TABLE RECOVERY option of the ROLLFORWARD DATABASE command. This modifier is incompatible with the generatedignore and generatedmissing modifiers.	Delimited ASCII (DEL), non-delimited ASCII (ASC), and PC Integrated Exchange Format (IXF)
identityignore	Indicates that although data for all identity columns is present in the file being loaded, that this data should be ignored. Instead, the LOAD utility should replace all identity column data found with its own generated values. This modifier is incompatible with the identitymissing modifier.	Delimited ASCII (DEL), non-delimited ASCII (ASC), and PC Integrated Exchange Format (IXF)
identitymissing	Indicates that data for identity columns is missing from the file being loaded and that the Load utility should generate an appropriate value for each missing value encountered. This modifier is incompatible with the identityignore modifier.	Delimited ASCII (DEL), non-delimited ASCII (ASC), and PC Integrated Exchange Format (IXF)
identityoverride	Indicates that the LOAD utility is to accept explicit, non-NULL data values for all identity columns in the table (contrary to the normal rules for these types of columns). This modifier is useful when migrating data from another database system, or when loading a table from data that was recovered using the DROPPED TABLE RECOVERY option of the ROLLFORWARD DATABASE command.	Delimited ASCII (DEL), non-delimited ASCII (ASC), and PC Integrated Exchange Format (IXF)

(continues)

Modifier	Description	File Format
	Table 6–4 File Type Modifiers Recognized by the LOAD Command (Continued)	
	This modifier should be used only when an identity column that was defined as GENERATED ALWAYS is present in the table that is to be loaded. This modifier is incompatible with the identityignore and identitymissing modifiers.	
indexfreespace=*x* where *x* is a number between 0 and 99 (percent)	Indicates that a percentage of each index page is to be left as free space when loading indexes that are associated with the table being loaded.	Delimited ASCII (DEL), non-delimited ASCII (ASC), and PC Integrated Exchange Format (IXF)
lobsinfile	Indicates that large object (LOB) data values are stored in their own individual files.	Delimited ASCII (DEL), non-delimited ASCII (ASC), and PC Integrated Exchange Format (IXF)
noheader	Indicates that the LOAD utility is to skip the header verification code (applicable only to load operations into tables that reside in a single-node nodegroup) when processing the source data file.	Delimited ASCII (DEL), non-delimited ASCII (ASC), and PC Integrated Exchange Format (IXF)
norowwarnings	Indicates that warning messages about rejected rows are to be suppressed.	Delimited ASCII (DEL), non-delimited ASCII (ASC), and PC Integrated Exchange Format (IXF)
pagefreespace=*x* where *x* is a number between 0 and 100 (percent)	Indicates that a percentage of each data page associated with the table being loaded is to be left as free space.	Delimited ASCII (DEL), non-delimited ASCII (ASC), and PC Integrated Exchange Format (IXF)
subtableconvert	Indicates that the data to be loaded has been exported from a regular table and is to be converted to a single sub table during load processing. This modifier is only valid when loading data into a single subtable.	Delimited ASCII (DEL), non-delimited ASCII (ASC), and PC Integrated Exchange Format (IXF)

(continues)

Table 6-4 File Type Modifiers Recognized by the LOAD Command (Continued)		
Modifier	**Description**	**File Format**
totalfreespace=*x* where *x* is a number between 0 and 100 (percent)	Indicates that a percentage of the total number of data pages used by the table being loaded are to be appended to the end of the table and treated as free space.	Delimited ASCII (DEL), non-delimited ASCII (ASC), and PC Integrated Exchange Format (IXF)
usedefaults	Indicates that if the source column data for a target table column is not provided, and if the target table column has a defaults constraint, default values are to be generated for the column. If this modifier is not used and a source column data value for one of the target table columns is not provided, one of the following will occur: • If the column is nullable a NULL value is stored in the column. • If the column is not nullable, and a default value cannot be generated, the row is rejected.	Delimited ASCII (DEL), non-delimited ASCII (ASC), and PC Integrated Exchange Format (IXF)
codepage=*x* where *x* is any valid code page identifier	Identifies the code page of the data contained in the output data set produced. Character data is converted from the application code page to the code page specified during the load operation.	Delimited ASCII (DEL) and non-delimited ASCII (ASC)
dateformat="*x*" where *x* is any valid combination of date format elements	Identifies how date values stored in the source file are formatted. The following date elements can be used to create the format string provided with this modifier: • YYYY—Year (four digits ranging from 0000–9999) • M—Month (one or two digits ranging from 1–12) • MM—Month (two digits ranging from 1–12; mutually exclusive with M) • D—Day (one or two digits ranging from 1–31) • DD—Day (two digits ranging from 1–31; mutually exclusive with D)	Delimited ASCII (DEL) and non-delimited ASCII (ASC)

(continues)

Modifier	Description	File Format
Table 6–4	**File Type Modifiers Recognized by the LOAD Command (Continued)**	
	• DDD—Day of the year (three digits ranging from 001–366; mutually exclusive with other day or month elements) Examples of valid date format strings include: "D-M-YYYY" "MM.DD.YYYY" "YYYYDDD"	
dumpfile=*x* where *x* is a fully qualified name of a file	Identifies the name and location of an exception file rejected rows are to be written to. The contents of a dump file are written to disk in an asynchronous buffered mode. In the event a load operation fails or is interrupted, the number of records committed to disk cannot be known with certainty, and consistency cannot be guaranteed after a LOAD RESTART. A dump file can only be assumed to be complete for load operations that start and complete in a single pass. This modifier does not support file names with multiple file extensions. For example, dumpfile=/home/DUMP.FILE is acceptable; dumpfile=/home/DUMP.LOAD.FILE is not.	Delimited ASCII (DEL) and non-delimited ASCII (ASC)
implieddecimal	Indicates that the location of an implied decimal point is to be determined by the column definition. The LOAD utility is not to assume that the decimal point is at the end of the value (default behavior). For example, if this modifier is specified, the value 12345 would be loaded into a DECIMAL(8,2) column as 123.45, *not* as 12345.00.	Delimited ASCII (DEL) and non-delimited ASCII (ASC)

(continues)

Table 6–4	File Type Modifiers Recognized by the LOAD Command (Continued)	
Modifier	**Description**	**File Format**
noeofchar	Indicates that the optional end-of-file character (0x1A) is not to be treated as an end-of-file character; instead, this character should be treated as a normal character if it is encountered.	Delimited ASCII (DEL) and non-delimited ASCII (ASC)
timeformat="*x*" where *x* is any valid combination of time format elements	Identifies how time values stored in the source file are formatted. The following time elements can be used to create the format string provided with this modifier: • H—Hour (one or two digits ranging from 0–12 for a 12-hour system, and 0–24 for a 24-hour system) • HH—Hour (two digits ranging from 0–12 for a 12-hour system, and 0–24 for a 24-hour system; mutually exclusive with H) • M—Minute (one or two digits ranging from 0–59) • MM—Minute (two digits ranging from 0–59; mutually exclusive with M) • S—Second (one or two digits ranging from 0–59) • SS—Second (two digits ranging from 0–59; mutually exclusive with S) • SSSSS—Second of the day after midnight (five digits ranging from 00000–86399; mutually exclusive with other time elements) • TT—Meridian indicator (AM or PM) Examples of valid time format strings include: "HH:MM:SS" "HH.MM TT" "SSSSS"	Delimited ASCII (DEL) and non-delimited ASCII (ASC)

(continues)

Table 6-4	File Type Modifiers Recognized by the LOAD Command (Continued)	
Modifier	**Description**	**File Format**
timestampformat="*x*" where *x* is any valid combination of date and time format elements	Identifies how timestamp values stored in the source file are formatted. The following date and time elements can be used to create the format string provided with this modifier: • YYYY—Year (four digits ranging from 0000–9999) • M—Month (one or two digits ranging from 1–12) • MM—Month (two digits ranging from 1–12; mutually exclusive with M) • D—Day (one or two digits ranging from 1–31) • DD—Day (two digits ranging from 1–31; mutually exclusive with D) • DDD—Day of the year (three digits ranging from 001–366; mutually exclusive with other day or month elements) • H—Hour (one or two digits ranging from 0–12 for a 12-hour system, and 0–24 for a 24-hour system) • HH—Hour (two digits ranging from 0–12 for a 12-hour system, and 0–24 for a 24-hour system; mutually exclusive with H) • M—Minute (one or two digits ranging from 0–59) • MM—Minute (two digits ranging from 0–59; mutually exclusive with M) • S—Second (one or two digits ranging from 0–59) • SS—Second (two digits ranging from 0–59; mutually exclusive with S) • SSSSS—Second of the day after midnight (five digits ranging from 0000086399; mutually exclusive with other time elements) • UUUUUU—Microsecond (six digits ranging from 000000–999999)	Delimited ASCII (DEL) and non-delimited ASCII (ASC)

(continues)

Table 6–4	File Type Modifiers Recognized by the LOAD Command (Continued)	
Modifier	**Description**	**File Format**
	• TT—Meridian indicator (AM or PM) Examples of valid timestamp format strings include: "YYYY/MM/DD HH:MM:SS.UUUUUU"	
chardel*x* where *x* is any valid delimiter character	Identifies a specific character that is to be used as a character delimiter. The default character delimiter is a double quotation mark (") character. The character specified is used in place of the double quotation mark to enclose a character string.	Delimited ASCII (DEL)
coldel*x* where *x* is any valid delimiter character	Identifies a specific character that is to be used as a column delimiter. The default column delimiter is a comma (,) character. The character specified is used in place of a comma to signal the end of a column.	Delimited ASCII (DEL)
datesiso	Indicates that all date data values are to be exported in ISO format ("YYYY-MM-DD"). By default, the LOAD utility normally writes • DATE data in "YYYYMMDD" format. • CHAR(*date*) data in "YYYY-MM-DD" format. • TIME data in "HH.MM.SS" format. • TIMESTAMP data in "YYYY-MM-DD-HH.MM.SS.uuuuuu" format.	Delimited ASCII (DEL)
decplusblank	Indicates that positive decimal values are to be prefixed with a blank space instead of a plus sign (+). The default action is to prefix positive decimal values with a plus sign.	Delimited ASCII (DEL)
decpt*x* where *x* is any valid delimiter character	Identifies a specific character that is to be used as a decimal point character. The default decimal point character is a period (.) character. The character specified is used in place of a period as a decimal point character.	Delimited ASCII (DEL)

(continues)

Table 6–4 File Type Modifiers Recognized by the LOAD Command (Continued)		
Modifier	**Description**	**File Format**
delprioritychar	Indicates that the priority for evaluating delimiters is to be *character delimiter, record delimiter, column delimiter* rather than *record delimiter, character delimiter, column delimiter* (which is the default). This modifier is typically used with older applications that depend on the other priority.	Delimited ASCII (DEL)
dldel*x* where *x* is any valid delimiter character	Identifies a specific character that is to be used as a DATALINK delimiter. The default DATALINK delimiter is a semicolon (;) character. The character specified is used in place of a semicolon as the interfield separator for a DATALINK value. It is needed because a DATALINK value may have more than one subvalue. It is important to note that the character specified as the DATALINK delimiter must not be the same as the character used for the row, column, or character delimiter.	Delimited ASCII (DEL)
keepblanks	Indicates that all leading and trailing blanks found for each column that has a data type of CHAR, VARCHAR, LONG VARCHAR, or CLOB are to be retained. If this modifier is not specified, all leading and trailing blanks that reside outside character delimiters are removed, and a NULL is inserted into the table for all missing data values found.	Delimited ASCII (DEL)
nodoubledel	Indicates that double character delimiters are to be ignored.	Delimited ASCII (DEL) *(continues)*

Table 6–4   File Type Modifiers Recognized by the LOAD Command (Continued)

Modifier	Description	File Format
binarynumerics	Indicates that numeric (but not DECIMAL) data is stored in binary format rather than as character representations. When this modifier is used: • No conversion between data types is performed, with the exception of BIGINT, INTEGER, and SMALLINT. • Data lengths must match their target column definitions. • FLOAT values must be in IEEE Floating Point format. • The byte order of the binary data stored in the source file is assumed to be big-endian, regardless of the server platform used. (Little-endian computers [i.e., Intel-based PCs, VAX workstations, etc.] store the least significant byte [LSB[of a multibyte word at the lowest address in a word and the most significant byte [MSB] at the highest address. Big-endian computers [i.e., machines based on the Motorola 68000a series of CPUs—Sun, Macintosh, etc. do the opposite—the MSB is stored at the lowest address and the LSB is stored at the highest address.) • NULLs cannot be present in the data for columns that are affected by this modifier. Blanks (normally interpreted as NULL) are interpreted as a binary value when this modifier is used. • The noeofchar modifier must also be used.	Non-delimited ASCII (ASC)
nochecklengths	Indicates that the LOAD utility is to attempt to load every row found in the source, even if the source data has a column value that exceeds the size of	Non-delimited ASCII (ASC) and PC Integrated Exchange Format (IXF) *(continues)*

Table 6–4 File Type Modifiers Recognized by the LOAD Command (Continued)

Modifier	Description	File Format
	the target column's definition. Such rows can be successfully loaded if code page conversion causes the source data to shrink in size. For example, 4-byte EUC data found in a source file could shrink to 2-byte DBCS data in the target table, and require half the space. This option is particularly useful if it is known in advance that the source data will always fit in a column despite mismatched column definitions/sizes.	
packeddecimal	Indicates that numeric DECIMAL data is stored in packed decimal format rather than as character representations. When this modifier is used: • The byte order of the binary data stored in the source file is assumed to be big-endian, regardless of the server platform used. • NULLs cannot be present in the data for columns that are affected by this modifier. Blanks (normally interpreted as NULL) are interpreted as a binary value when this modifier is used. • The noeofchar modifier must also be used.	Non-delimited ASCII (ASC)
nullindchar=*x* where *x* is any valid character	Identifies a specific character that is to be used as a null indicator value. The default null indicator is the letter **Y**. This modifier is case sensitive for EBCDIC data files, except when the character is an English letter. For example, if the null indicator character is specified to be the letter **N**, then the letter **n** is also recognized as a null indicator.	Non-delimited ASCII (ASC)

(continues)

Table 6-4 File Type Modifiers Recognized by the LOAD Command (Continued)		
Modifier	**Description**	**File Format**
reclen=*x* where *x* is any number between 1 and 32767	Indicates that a specific number of characters are to be read from the source file for each row found; new-line characters are to be ignored instead of being used to indicate the end of a row.	Non-delimited ASCII (ASC)
striptblanks	Indicates that all leading and trailing blanks found for each column that has a data type of VARCHAR, LONG VARCHAR, VARGRAPHIC, or LONG VARGRAPHIC are to be truncated. This modifier is incompatible with the striptnulls modifier.	Non-delimited ASCII (ASC)
striptnulls	Indicates that all leading and trailing nulls (0x00 characters) found for each column that has a data type of VARCHAR, LONG VARCHAR, VARGRAPHIC, or LONG VARGRAPHIC are to be truncated. This modifier is incompatible with the striptblanks modifier.	Non-delimited ASCII (ASC)

zoneddecimal	Indicates that numeric DECIMAL data is stored in zoned decimal format rather than as character representations.
	When this modifier is used:
	• Half-byte sign values can be one of the following:
	    • "+" = 0xC 0xA 0xE 0xF
	    • "−" = 0xD 0xB
	• Supported values for digits are 0x0 to 0x9.
	• Supported values for zones are 0x3 and 0xF.
	• The noeofchar modifier must also be used.
		Non-delimited ASCII (ASC)
		
		(continues)

Table 6–4 File Type Modifiers Recognized by the LOAD Command (Continued)		
Modifier	**Description**	**File Format**
forcein	Indicates that the LOAD utility is to accept data despite code page mismatches (in other words, to suppress translation between code pages). Fixed-length target columns are checked to verify that they are large enough to hold the data unless the nochecklengths modifier has been specified.	PC Integrated Exchange Format (IXF)

Adapted from Table 9 on pages 482–497 of the *IBM DB2 Command Reference* manual.

As with the IMPORT utility, one of three methods can be used to map data values found in external files to columns in a table: the location method, the name method, and the position method. The syntax used to indicate that the location method is to be used to extract data values from the external file specified is:

```
METHOD L ( [ColumnStart] [ColumnEnd] ,... )
   <NULL INDICATORS ( [NullIndColNumber ,...] )>
```

where:

ColumnStart   Identifies the starting position of one or more data values in the non-delimited ASCII (ASC)-formatted file from which values are to be retrieved.

ColumnEnd   Identifies the ending position of one or more data values in the non-delimited ASCII (ASC)-formatted file from which values are to be retrieved.

NullIndColNumber   Identifies the position of one or more data values that are to be treated as null indicator variables for column data values in the non-delimited ASCII (ASC)-formatted file from which values are to be retrieved.

The syntax used to indicate that the name method is to be used to extract data values from the external file specified is:

```
METHOD N ( [ColumnName ,...] )
```

where:

> *ColumnName*   Identifies one or more unique names assigned to columns in the PC Integrated Exchange Format (IXF)-formatted file from which values are to be retrieved.

And the syntax used to indicate that the position method is to be used to extract data values from the external file specified is:

```
METHOD P ( [ColumnPosition ,...] )
```

where:

> *ColumnPosition*   Identifies the indexed position of one or more columns in the delimited ASCII (DEL) or PC Integrated Exchange Format (IXF)-formatted file from which values are to be retrieved.

As you can see, there are four different options available with the LOAD command that control how the table data is to be copied will be affected by the LOAD operation. These options include:

> **INSERT.** When the INSERT option is used, data is appended to the target table (which must already exist).

> **REPLACE.** When the REPLACE option is used, any existing data is deleted from the target table (which must already exist), then the new data is loaded.

> **RESTART.** When the RESTART option is used, any previous load operation that failed or was terminated is continued starting from the last recorded point of consistency. If this option is used, the LOAD command specified must be identical to the load command used to initiate the previous load operation (with the exception of the RESTART option specification).

> **TERMINATE.** When the TERMINATE option is used, the current load operation is terminated and any changes made are backed out if the load operation being terminated was started with the INSERT option. If the load operation being terminated was started with the REPLACE option specified, data in the target table is truncated. (Only a portion of the source data that was to be loaded into the table will actually reside in the table.)

So, if you wanted to load data stored in an external file named DEPT.IXF that uses the PC Integrated Exchange Format (IXF) into an existing table named DEPARTMENT, you could do so by executing a LOAD command that looks something like this:

```
LOAD FROM DEPT.IXF OF IXF
MESSAGES LOAD_MSGS.TXT
INSERT INTO DEPARTMENT
```

On the other hand, if you wanted to load data stored in an external file named SALES.ASC that uses the non-delimited ASCII format (ASC) into an existing table named SALES, replace any existing data in that table, and make a backup copy of all data loaded, you could do so by executing a LOAD command that looks something like this:

```
LOAD FROM SALES.ASC OF ASC
MODIFIED BY reclen=22
METHOD L (1 4, 6 13, 15 22)
MESSAGES LOAD_MSGS.TXT
REPLACE INTO SALES
COPY TO C:\DATABACKUP\SALESDATA
```

And finally, if you wanted to load data stored in an external file named EMPLOYEES.IXF that uses the PC Integrated Exchange Format (IXF), along with LOB data values stored in individual files, to a table named EMPLOYEES, and update the statistics for the EMPLOYEES table and its associated indexes, you could do so by executing a LOAD command that looks something like this:

```
LOAD FROM C:\DATA\EMPLOYEES.IXF OF IXF
LOBS FROM C:\LOB_DATA
MODIFIED BY lobsinfile
MESSAGES LOAD_MSGS.TXT
REPLACE INTO EMPLOYEES
STATISTICS YES WITH DISTRIBUTION INDEXES ALL
```

In this case, you would have to execute the LOAD command with the REPLACE option specified; statistics cannot be collected if the LOAD command is executed with any option other than the REPLACE option specified.

Data can also be loaded into existing tables using the Load Wizard, which can be activated by selecting the appropriate action from the *Tables* menu found in the Control Center. (The Load Wizard cannot be used to load data from named pipes and devices.) Figure 6–10 shows the Control Center menu items that must be selected to activate the Load Wizard; Figure 6–11 shows how the first page of the Load Wizard might look after its input fields have been populated.

Whether you use the LOAD command or the Load Wizard to perform a load operation, a database connection must be established before the LOAD utility is invoked.

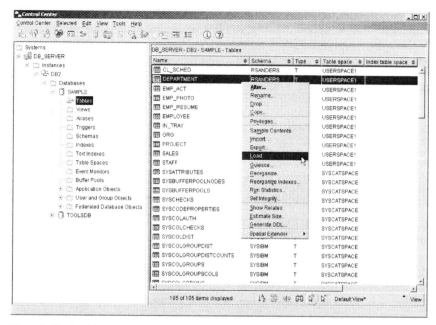

Figure 6–10   Invoking the Load Wizard from the Control Center.

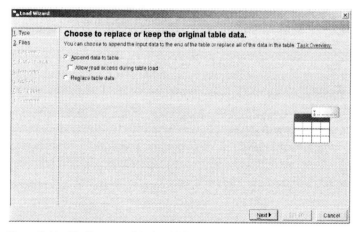

Figure 6–11   The first page of the Load Wizard.

Only users with System Administrator (SYSADM) authority, Database Administrator (DBADMN) authority, or Load (LOAD) authority *and* INSERT privilege on all tables referenced are allowed to load data using the INSERT option (or restart or terminate INSERT load operations). Only users with SYSADM authority, DBADMN authority, or LOAD authority *and* INSERT *and* DELETE privileges on all tables referenced are allowed to load data using the REPLACE option (or restart or terminate REPLACE load operations). And only users with SYSADM authority, DBADMN authority, or INSERT privilege on the exception table used are allowed to perform load operations in which invalid rows are written to an exception table.

db2move and db2look

It's easy to see how the EXPORT utility can be used together with the IMPORT utility or the LOAD utility to copy a table's data from one database to another. But what if you want to copy several tables or an entire database? In this case, data can easily be copied on a table-by-table basis using the EXPORT and IMPORT or LOAD utilities (provided PC Integrated Exchange Format (IXF)-formatted files are used), but a more efficient way to copy an entire DB2 database is by using DB2 UDB's db2move utility. This utility queries the system catalog tables of the specified database and compiles a list of all user tables found. It then exports the contents and table structure of each table found to a PC Integrated Exchange Format (IXF)-formatted file. The set of files produced can then be imported or loaded to another DB2 database on the same system, or they can be transferred to another workstation platform and imported or loaded to a DB2 database residing on that platform.

The db2move utility can be run in one of three modes: EXPORT, IMPORT, or LOAD. When run in EXPORT mode, db2move invokes the EXPORT utility to extract data from one or more tables and externalize it to PC Integrated Exchange Format (IXF)-formatted files. It also produces a file named **db2move.lst** that contains the names of all tables processed, along with the names of the files that each table's data was written to. The db2move utility may also produce one or more message files that contain warning or error messages that were generated as a result of the export operation.

When run in IMPORT mode, db2move invokes the IMPORT utility to recreate each table, and their associated indexes using information stored in PC Integrated Exchange Format (IXF)-formatted files. When run in this mode, the file **db2move.lst** is used to establish a link between the PC Integrated Exchange Format (IXF)-formatted files needed and the tables into which data is to be imported.

When run in LOAD mode, db2move invokes the LOAD utility to populate tables that already exist with data stored in PC Integrated Exchange Format (IXF)-formatted files. (The LOAD mode should never be used to populate an empty database that contains no table definitions.) Again, the file **db2move.lst** is used to establish a link between the IXF-formatted files needed and the tables into which data is to be loaded.

Unfortunately, the db2move utility can only be used to migrate table and index data objects. If the database to be migrated contains other data objects such as aliases, views, triggers, user-defined data types (UDTs), user-defined functions (UDFs), and so on, you must find another way to duplicate those objects in the target database as well. This is where DB2 UDB's db2look utility comes in. This utility can analyze an existing database and produce a set of Data Definition Language (DDL) SQL statements, which can then be used to recreate all of the data objects found in the database that was analyzed. The db2look utility can also examine registry variable and configuration parameter settings found on the source system and generate a set of commands that can be used to duplicate those settings *that have an impact on query optimization* on the target system. (Commands to set every registry variable and configuration parameter available are not generated. Instead, a subset of commands that can be used to set a limited number of registry variables and configuration parameters are produced.)

NOTE To obtain more information about the db2move and db2look utilities, or to see the syntax used to invoke each of these commands, refer to the *IBM DB2 Universal Database, Version 8 Command Reference* product documentation.

Data Maintenance Utilities

The way in which data is physically distributed across tablespace containers can have a significant impact on how applications that access the data perform. And the way data gets distributed is controlled primarily by the insert, update, and delete operations that are performed against tables. For example, a series of insert operations will try to distribute data pages contiguously across tablespace containers. However, a subsequent delete operation may leave empty pages in storage that, for some reason, never get refilled. Or an update operation performed on a variable-length column may cause an entire row to be written to another page because a larger column value no longer allows the record to fit on the original page. In both cases, internal gaps are created in the underlying tablespace containers. Also, when insert and delete operations are performed on a regular basis, semantically related rows can become physically scattered across many different pages. As a consequence, the DB2 Database Manager may have to read more physical pages into memory in order to retrieve the data needed to satisfy a query.

The REORGCHK Utility

As we have just seen, gaps can get created in tablespace containers over the life of a database. So how do you know how much storage space is currently being utilized by data and how much is free, but part of an unusable gap? You can obtain this information by taking advantage of DB2 UDB's REORGCHK utility.

When executed, this utility generates statistics on the database, and analyzes the statistics produced to determine whether or not one or more tables need to be reorganized (which will cause existing internal gaps to be removed).

The REORGCHK utility is invoked by executing the REORGCHK command using the DB2 Command Line Processor. The basic syntax for this command is:

```
REORGCHK
<UPDATE STATISTICS | CURRENT STATISTICS>
<ON TABLE USER |
    ON SCHEMA [SchemaName] |
    ON TABLE [USER | SYSTEM | ALL | [TableName]>
```

where:

SchemaName	Identifies the name assigned to a schema whose objects are to be analyzed to determine whether or not they need to be reorganized.
TableName	Identifies the name assigned to a specific table that is to be analyzed to determine whether or not it needs to be reorganized.

So if you wanted to generate statistics for all tables that reside in the PAYROLL schema and have those statistics analyzed to determine whether or not one or more tables needs to be reorganized, you could do so by executing a REORGCHK command that looks something like this:

```
REORGCHK UPDATE STATISTICS ON SCHEMA PAYROLL
```

And when such a REORGCHK command is executed, output that looks something like the following might be produced:

```
Doing RUNSTATS ....


Table statistics:

F1: 100 * OVERFLOW / CARD < 5
F2: 100 * (Effective Space Utilization of Data Pages) > 70
F3: 100 * (Required Pages / Total Pages) > 80

SCHEMA  NAME         CARD  OV  NP  FP  ACTBLK  TSIZE  F1  F2   F3   REORG
-----------------------------------------------------------------------
PAYROLL EMPLOYEES     32   0   2   2     -     2784   0   68  100  -*-
PAYROLL DEPARTMENT     9   0   1   1     -      549   0   -   100  ---
-----------------------------------------------------------------------

Index statistics:

F4: CLUSTERRATIO or normalized CLUSTERFACTOR > 80
F5: 100 * (KEYS * (ISIZE + 9) + (CARD - KEYS) * 5) /
       ((NLEAF - NUM EMPTY LEAFS) * INDEXPAGESIZE) > 50
F6: (100 - PCTFREE) * ((INDEXPAGESIZE - 96) /
```

```
             (ISIZE + 12)) ** (NLEVELS - 2) * (INDEXPAGESIZE - 96) /
             (KEYS * (ISIZE + 9) + (CARD - KEYS) * 5) < 100
F7:  100 * (NUMRIDS DELETED / (NUMRIDS DELETED + CARD)) < 20
F8:  100 * (NUM EMPTY LEAFS / NLEAF) < 20


SCHEMA NAME        CARD LEAF ELEAF LVLS ISIZE NDEL KEYS  F4 F5 F6 F7 F8 REORG
-------------------------------------------------------------------
Table: PAYROLL.EMPLOYEES
SYSIBM SQL0064200    12   1     0    1   14     0   12 100  -  -  0  0 -----
-------------------------------------------------------------------
```

CLUSTERRATIO or normalized CLUSTERFACTOR (F4) will indicate REORG is
necessary for indexes that are not in the same sequence as the base table.
When multiple indexes are defined on a table, one or more indexes may be
flagged as needing REORG. Specify the most important index for REORG
sequencing.

Tables defined using the ORGANIZE BY clause and the corresponding dimension
indexes have a '*' suffix to their names. The cardinality of a dimension
index is equal to the Active blocks statistic of the table.

 Only users with System Administrator (SYSADM) authority, Database Administrator
(DBADMN) authority, or CONTROL privilege on the table(s) that are to be evaluated
are allowed to use the REORGCHK utility.

Interpreting REORGCHK Output

As you can see, the output generated by the REORGCHK utility is divided into
two sections: table statistics and index statistics. The table statistics section
shows the table statistics produced, along with the formulas that are used to
determine if table reorganization is necessary. If you examine the preceding
sample output, the first thing you will see listed after the "Table statistics"
heading are three formulas named F1, F2, and F3.

➤ Formula F1 works with the number of overflow rows encountered. It will
recommend that a table be reorganized if 5% or more of the total number
of rows in the table are overflow rows. (Overflow rows are rows that have
been moved to new pages because an update operation made them too
large to be stored in the page they were written to originally or because
new columns were added to an existing table.)

➤ Formula F2 works with free/unused space. It will recommend that a table
be reorganized if the table size (TSIZE) is less than or equal to 70% of the
size of the total storage space allocated for that table. In other words, if
more than 30% of the total storage space allocated for the table is unused.

➤ Formula F3 works with free pages. It will recommend that a table be reorganized if 20% or more of the pages for that table are free. (A page is considered free when it does not contain any rows.)

Immediately below these three formulas is a table that contains information about the values that were used to solve the formula equations for each table processed, along with the results. This table contains the following information:

> **SCHEMA.** The name of the schema the table belongs to.
>
> **NAME.** The name of the table that was evaluated to determine whether or not reorganization is necessary.
>
> **CARD.** The number of rows found in the table.
>
> **OV (OVERHEAD).** The number of overflow rows found in the table.
>
> **NP (NPAGES).** The number of pages that currently contain data.
>
> **FP (FPAGES).** The total number of pages that have been allocated for the table.
>
> **ACTBLK.** The total number of active blocks for a multidimensional clustering (MDC) table (the number of blocks of the table that contain data). This field is only applicable to tables that were defined using the ORGANIZE BY clause.
>
> **TSIZE.** The size of the table, in bytes. This value is calculated by multiplying the number of rows found in the table (CARD) by the average row length. The average row length is computed as the sum of the average column lengths (the AVGCOLLEN column in the system catalog table SYSCAT.SYSCOLUMNS) of all columns defined for the table plus 10 bytes for row overhead. For long data and LOB data columns, only the approximate length of the descriptor is used. The actual size of long data and LOB data columns is not included in TSIZE.
>
> **F1.** The results of Formula F1.
>
> **F2.** The results of Formula F2.
>
> **F3.** The results of Formula F3.
>
> **REORG.** A set of indicators that point out whether or not the table needs to be reorganized. Each hyphen (-) displayed in this column indicates that the calculated results were within the set bounds of the corresponding formula, and each asterisk (*) indicates that the calculated results exceeded the set bounds of its corresponding formula. The first - or * corresponds to Formula 1, the second - or * corresponds to Formula 2, and the third - or * corresponds to Formula 3. Table reorganization is suggested when the results of the calculations exceed the bounds set for the formula. For example, the value --- indicates that, since the results of F1, F2, and F3 are within the set bounds of each formula, no table reorganization is necessary. The notation -*- indicates that the results of Formula 2 (F2) suggests

that the table be reorganized, even though the results of F2 and F3 are within their set bounds.

The index statistics section shows information about the index statistics produced, along with the formulas used to determine if index reorganization is necessary. This section is marked by the heading "Index statistics", which is followed by the formulas F4, F5, and F6.

➤ Formula F4 works with the cluster ratio or normalized cluster factor of an index. This ratio identifies the percentage of table data rows that are stored in the same physical sequence as the indexed data for the table. It will recommend that an index be reorganized if the cluster ratio for the index is less than 80%. (Often, the cluster ratio is not optimal for indexes that contain several duplicate keys and a large number of entries.)

➤ Formula F5 works with storage space that has been reserved for index entries. It will recommend that an index be reorganized if 50% or more of the storage space allocated for an index is empty.

➤ Formula F6 measures the usage of the index's pages. It will recommend that an index be reorganized if the actual number of entries found in the index is less than 90% of the number of entries (NLEVELS) the index tree can handle.

➤ Formula F7 measures the number of pseudo-deleted record IDs (RIDs) on non-pseudo-empty pages. (A pseudo-deleted record is a record that has been marked as being deleted even though it has not yet been physically removed.) It will recommend that an index be reorganized if the actual number of pseudo-deleted record IDs (RIDs) found on non-pseudo-empty pages is more than 20%.

➤ Formula F8 measures the number of pseudo-empty leaf pages found. It will recommend that an index be reorganized if the actual number of pseudo-empty leaf pages found in the index is more than 20% of the total number of leaf pages available.

Immediately below these three formulas is a table that contains information about the values that were used to solve the formula equations for each index processed, along with the results. This table contains the following information:

SCHEMA. The name of the schema the index belongs to.

NAME. The name of the index that was evaluated to determine whether or not reorganization is necessary.

CARD. The number of rows found in the base table the index is associated with.

LEAF. The total number of index leafs (pages) that have been allocated for the index.

ELEAF. The number of pseudo-empty index leaf pages found. A pseudo-empty index leaf page is a page on which all the record IDs are marked as deleted, even though they have not yet been physically removed.

LVLS (LEVELS). The total number of levels the index has.

ISIZE. The size of the index, in bytes. This value is calculated by multiplying the number of rows found in the index (CARD) by the average row length. The average row length is computed as the sum of the average column lengths of all columns participating in the index.

NDEL. Number of pseudo-deleted record Ids. A pseudo-deleted RID is a RID that is marked deleted. This statistic reports pseudo-deleted RIDs on leaf pages that are not pseudo-empty. It does not include RIDs marked as deleted on leaf pages where all the RIDs are marked deleted.

KEYS (FULLKEYCARD). The number of unique entries found in the index.

F4. The results of Formula F4.

F5. The results of Formula F5. (The notation +++ indicates that the result exceeds 999, and is invalid, in which case the Reorganize-Check utility should be run again with the UPDATE STATISTICS option specified.)

F6. The results of Formula F6. (The notation +++ indicates that the result exceeds 999, and is invalid, in which case the Reorganize-Check utility should be run again with the UPDATE STATISTICS option specified.)

F7. The results of Formula 7.

F8. The results of Formula 8.

REORG. A set of indicators that point out whether or not the index needs to be reorganized. Each hyphen (-) displayed in this column indicates that the calculated results were within the set bounds of the corresponding formula, and each asterisk (*) indicates that the calculated results exceeded the set bounds of its corresponding formula. The first - or * corresponds to Formula 4, the second - or * corresponds to Formula 5, and so on. Index reorganization is suggested when the results of the calculations exceed the bounds set for the formula. For example, the value ----- indicates that, since the results of F4, F5, F6, F7, and F8 are within the set bounds of each formula, no index reorganization is necessary. The notation -*---

indicates that the results of Formula 5 (F5) suggests that the index be reorganized, even though the results of F4, F6, F7, and F8 are within their set bounds.

The REORG Utility

Upon careful evaluation of the output provided by the REORGCHK utility, you may discover that one or more tables and/or indexes need to be reorganized. If that's the case, you can reorganize them using DB2 UDB's REORG utility. The REORG utility eliminates gaps in tablespace containers by obtaining the data stored in a table and one or more of its associated indexes and rewriting it onto unfragmented, physically contiguous pages in storage. (The REORG utility works much like the way a disk defragmenter works.) The REORG utility can also physically order the data rows of the table to mirror the logical order presented by a particular index, thereby increasing the cluster ratio of the specified index. This behavior has an attractive side effect: if the DB2 Database Manager finds that the data needed to resolve a query is stored in contiguous storage space and already ordered, the overall performance of the query will be improved because the seek time needed to retrieve the data will be shorter. The REORG utility can also be used to convert Type-1 indexes to Type-2 indexes. (Refer to Chapter 4—Database Access for more information on Type-1 and Type-2 indexes.)

The REORG utility can be invoked by executing the REORG command. The basic syntax for this command is:

```
REORG TABLE [TableName]
<INDEX [IndexName]>
<ALLOW READ ACCESS | ALLOW NO ACCESS>
<USE [TmpTSName]>
<INDEXSCAN>
<LONGLOBDATA>
```

or

```
REORG INDEXES ALL FOR TABLE [SourceTableName]
<ALLOW READ ACCESS | ALLOW WRITE ACCESS | ALLOW NO ACCESS>
<CLEANUP ONLY | CLEANUP ONLY PAGES | CLEANUP ONLY ALL |
CONVERT>
```

where:

TableName   Identifies the name assigned to the table whose physical layout is to be reorganized.

IndexName	Identifies the name assigned to the associated index that is to be used to order the data stored in the table that is to be reorganized. (If no index name is specified, the data in the table is reorganized without any regard to order.)
TmpTSName	Identifies the system temporary tablespace where the DB2 Database Manager is to temporarily store a copy of the table to be reorganized. (If no tablespace name is specified, the DB2 Database Manager will store a working copy of the table being reorganized in the same tablespace the table resides in.)
SourceTableName	Identifies the name assigned to the table associated indexes are to be reorganized for.

If the CLEANUP ONLY option is specified, a cleanup operation rather than a full reorganization will be performed. As a result, indexes will not be rebuilt and any pages freed up will only be available for reuse by the indexes defined on the table specified. If the CLEANUP ONLY PAGES option is specified, a cleanup operation that searches for and removes committed pseudo-empty pages from the index tree will be performed. (A committed pseudo empty page is a page in which all keys on the page have been marked as having been deleted and the corresponding delete operations are known to be committed.) If the CLEANUP ONLY ALL option is specified, a cleanup operation that searches for and removes both committed pseudo-empty pages and pseudo-empty deleted keys that reside on pages that are *not* pseudo-empty will be performed.

Thus, if you wanted to reorganize the data for a table named EMPLOYEES and physically order the data to match the order presented by an index named EMPNO_PK, you could do so by executing a REORG command that looks something like this:

```
REORG TABLE EMPLOYEES INDEX EMPNO_PK
```

Tables and indexes can also be reorganized using the Reorganize Table and Reorganize Index dialogs, which can be activated by selecting the appropriate action from the *Tables* menu found in the Control Center. Figure 6–12 shows the Control Center menu items that must be selected in order to activate the Reorganize Table dialog; Figure 6–13 shows how the Reorganize Table dialog might look after its input fields have been populated; Figure 6–14 shows the Control Center menu items that must be selected in order to activate the Reorganize Index dialog; Figure 6–15 shows how the Reorganize Index dialog might look after its input fields have been populated.

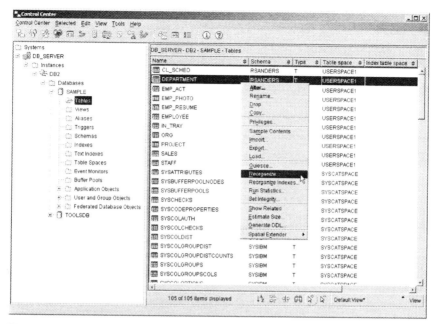

Figure 6–12   Invoking the Reorganize Table dialog from the Control Center.

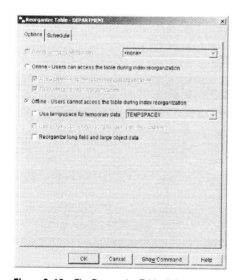

Figure 6–13   The Reorganize Table dialog.

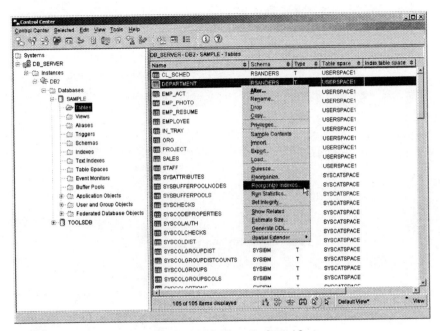

Figure 6–14 Invoking the Reorganize Index dialog from the Control Center.

Figure 6–15 The Reorganize Index dialog.

 Only users with System Administrator (SYSADM) authority, System Control (SYSC-TRL) authority, System Maintenance (SYSMAINT) authority, Database Administrator (DBADMN) authority, or CONTROL privilege on the table/index(es) that are to be reorganized are allowed to use the REORG utility.

The INSPECT Utility

Although the REORGCHK utility can be used to determine whether or not the pages of a database are fragmented to the point that one or more tables and/or indexes need to be reorganized, it cannot be used to check database pages for consistency. That's where the INSPECT utility comes in. The

INSPECT utility inspects tablespaces and tables for architectural integrity by checking the structures of tablespaces and data objects to ensure they are valid and by checking all pages used for consistency. The INSPECT utility is invoked by executing the INSPECT command. The basic syntax for this command is:

```
INSPECT CHECK DATABASE
<BEGIN TBSPACEID [StartTS_ID] <OBJECT ID
[StartObject_ID]>>
<CATALOG TO TABLESPACE CONSISTENCY>
<FOR ERROR STATE ALL>
<LIMIT ERROR TO [ALL |DEFAULT | [ErrorCount]>
RESULTS <KEEP> [FileName]
```

or

```
INSPECT CHECK TABLESPACE
[NAME [TS_Name] | TBSPACEID [TS_ID]]
<BEGIN OBJECTID [StartObject_ID]>
<CATALOG TO TABLESPACE CONSISTENCY>
<FOR ERROR STATE ALL>
<LIMIT ERROR TO [ALL |DEFAULT | [ErrorCount]>
RESULTS <KEEP> [FileName]
```

or

```
INSPECT CHECK TABLE
[NAME [TableName] <SchemaName> |
   TBSPACEID [TS_ID] <OBJECT ID [Object_ID]]
<FOR ERROR STATE ALL>
<LIMIT ERROR TO [ALL |DEFAULT | [ErrorCount]>
RESULTS <KEEP> [FileName]
```

where:

StartTS_ID	Identifies the identification number assigned to the first tablespace in the database that inspection is to begin with. (All tablespaces with identification numbers that are higher than the starting number specified will be inspected along with the tablespace specified.)
StartObject_ID	Identifies the identification number assigned to a specific object (i.e., table, index, view, etc.) within the tablespace specified (in the *StartTS_ID* or *TS_ID* parameter) that inspection is to begin with. (All objects with identification numbers that are

	higher than the starting number specified will be inspected along with the object specified.)
TS_Name	Identifies the name assigned to the tablespace that is to be inspected.
TS_ID	Identifies the identification number assigned to the tablespace that is to be inspected.
TableName	Identifies the name assigned to the table that is to be inspected.
SchemaName	Identifies the name assigned to the schema the table that is to be inspected is associated with.
Object_ID	Identifies the identification number assigned to a specific object (i.e., table, index, view, etc.) within the tablespace specified that is to be inspected.
ErrorCount	Identifies the number of erroneous pages that can be found by the INSPECT utility before the inspection process will terminate. When this limit is reached, the inspection processing will stop.
FileName	Identifies the name of the file that any errors found by the INSPECT utility are to be recorded to. (The actual file will be created in the diagnostic data directory.) If no errors are found, this file will be deleted once the inspection process has completed.

Thus, if you wanted to check the structure of a tablespace named PAYROLL and all of its pages for consistency, and if you wanted to verify that all tables found in the tablespace are listed in the database's system catalog, you could do so by executing an INSPECT command that looks something like this:

```
INSPECT CHECK TABLESPACE
NAME PAYROLL
CATALOG TO TABLESPACE CONSISTENCY
RESULTS InspectResults.txt
```

Only users with System Administrator (SYSADM) authority, System Control (SYSC-TRL) authority, System Maintenance (SYSMAINT) authority, Database Administrator (DBADMN) authority, or CONTROL privilege on the table that is to be inspected are allowed to use the INSPECT utility.

The RUNSTATS Utility

Among other things, the system catalog tables for a database can contain statistical information such as the number of rows stored in a table, the way tables and indexes utilize storage space, and a count of the number of unique values found in a particular column. Such information is used by the DB2 Optimizer when deciding on the best access plan to use to obtain data in response to a query. (Whenever an SQL statement is sent to the DB2 Database Manager for processing, the DB2 Optimizer reads the system catalog tables to determine the size of each table referenced by the statement, the characteristics of the columns that are referenced by the statement, whether or not indexes have been defined for the table(s) that are referenced by the statement, and to obtain other similar information. Using this information, the DB2 Optimizer then determines the best access path to take to satisfy the needs of the SQL statement.) Therefore, if the information needed by the DB2 Optimizer is missing or out of date, it may choose an access plan that will cause the SQL statement to take longer to execute than is necessary. Having valid information available becomes crucial as the complexity of the SQL statement increases. With simple statements, there are usually a limited number of choices available; with complex statements, the number of choices available increases dramatically.

Unfortunately, the information that is used by the DB2 Optimizer is not automatically updated each time changes are made to the database. Instead, this information must be updated periodically by running DB2 UDB's RUNSTATS utility. This utility can be invoked by executing the RUNSTATS command. The basic syntax for this command is:

```
RUNSTATS ON TABLE [TableName]
<FOR <SAMPLED DETAILED | DETAILED>
    INDEXES [IndexName,...] | ALL]>
<ALLOW READ ACCESS | ALLOW WRITE ACCESS>
```

or

```
RUNSTATS ON TABLE [TableName]
<ON ALL COLUMNS |
    ON KEY COLUMNS> |
    ON COLUMNS [ColumnName ,...] |
    ON ALL COLUMNS AND COLUMNS [ColumnName ,...] |
    ON KEY COLUMNS AND COLUMNS [ColumnName ,...]>
<WITH DISTRIBUTION>
<AND <SAMPLED DETAILED | DETAILED>
    INDEXES [IndexName,...] | ALL]>
<ALLOW READ ACCESS | ALLOW WRITE ACCESS>
```

where:

TableName	Identifies the name assigned to the table that statistical information is to be collected for.
IndexName	Identifies the name assigned to one or more associated indexes that statistical information is to be collected for.
ColumnName	Identifies the name assigned to one or more columns that statistical information is to be collected for.

Thus, if you wanted to collect statistics for a table named EMPLOYEES (which resides in a schema named PAYROLL) along with all of its associated indexes and allow read-only access to the table while statistics are being gathered, you could do so by executing a RUNSTATS command that looks something like this:

```
RUNSTATS ON TABLE PAYROLL.EMPLOYEES
FOR INDEXES ALL
ALLOW READ ACCESS
```

On the other hand, if you only wanted to collect basic statistics and distribution statistics are collected for all eligible columns of a table named DEPARTMENT (which resides in a schema named PAYROLL), you could do so by executing a RUNSTATS command that looks something like this:

```
RUNSTATS ON TABLE PAYROLL.DEPARTMENT
ON ALL COLUMNS
WITH DISTRIBUTION
```

(Statistics collection can be done on some columns and not on others. For example, columns with data types such as LONG VARCHAR or CLOB columns are not eligible.)

The RUNSTATS utility does not provide output information other than a success or failure message. To view the results of a RUNSTATS operation, you must examine the contents of the CARD, OVERFLOW, NPAGES, and FPAGES columns of the system catalog table named SYSCAT.TABLES. (If the value of any of these columns is −1, statistical information has not been produced for the object that is identified by that particular row).

Statistical information for tables and indexes can also be collected using the Run Statistics dialog, which can be activated by selecting the appropriate action from the *Tables* menu found in the Control Center. Figure 6–16 shows the Control Center menu items that must be selected in order to activate the Run Statistics dialog; Figure 6–17 shows how the Run Statistics dialog might look after its input fields have been populated.

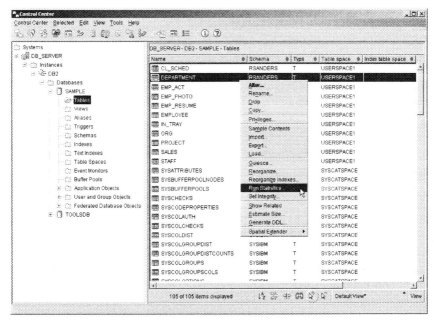

Figure 6–16   Invoking the Run Statistics dialog from the Control Center.

Figure 6–17   The Run Statistics dialog.

Only users with System Administrator (SYSADM) authority, System Control (SYSC-TRL) authority, System Maintenance (SYSMAINT) authority, Database Administrator (DBADMN) authority, or CONTROL privilege on the table/index(es) that statistical information is to be collected for are allowed to use the RUNSTATS utility.

So just how often should the RUNSTATS utility be used to generate statistical information for tables and indexes? Ideally, the RUNSTATS utility should be run immediately after any of the following occur:

➤ A large number of insert, update, or delete operations are performed against a specific table.

➤ An import operation is performed.

➤ A load operation is performed.

➤ One or more columns are added to an existing table.

➤ A new index is created.

It is also a good idea to run the RUNSTATS utility at a regular intervals (for example, once a day on large databases where the volume of activity tends to be high; weekly on smaller systems). And whenever possible, the RUNSTATS utility should be run at a time when the database activity level is relatively low.

A Word about Rebinding

Earlier, we saw that the DB2 Optimizer analyzes the statistical information produced by the RUNSTATS utility to select the best access plan to use to obtain data in response to a query. And because the DB2 Optimizer generates an access plan each time a dynamic SQL statement is prepared for execution, applications using dynamic SQL may see performance improvements immediately after new statistical information has been produced. Unfortunately, that is not the case for applications that use static SQL. That's because the DB2 Optimizer generates access plans for static SQL statements when the package that contains those statements is bound to the database. Therefore, in order for existing packages to take advantage of new statistical information produced by the RUNSTATS utility, they must be rebound to the database so the DB2 Optimizer will evaluate the new information and formulate new access plans (which may or may not perform better than the original access plan used).

The easiest way to rebind an existing package—provided the application source code used to produce the package has not changed—is by executing the REBIND command. The basic syntax for this command is:

```
REBIND <PACKAGE> [PackageName]
<VERSION [Version]>
RESOLVE [ANY | CONSERVATIVE]
```

where:

| *PackageName* | Identifies the name assigned to the package that is to be rebound. |
| *IndexName* | Identifies a specific version of the package that is to be rebound. |

If the RESOLVE CONSERVATIVE clause is specified when the REBIND command is executed, only functions and user-defined data types (UDTs) found in the SQL path that were defined the last time the package was explicitly bound to the database are used for function and UDT resolution. On the other hand, if the RESOLVE ANY clause is specified, all functions and user-defined data types (UDTs) found in the SQL path are considered for function and UDT resolution.

Thus, if you wanted to rebind a package named EMP_MGMT, you could do so by executing a REBIND command that looks something like this:

```
REBIND PACKAGE EMP_MGMT
```

 NOTE   Only users with System Administrator (SYSADM) authority, Database Administrator (DBADMN) authority, or ALTERIN privilege on the schema used to store the package and BINDADD privilege on the package specified are allowed to execute the REBIND command.

Flushing the Package Cache

Because the DB2 Optimizer generates an access plan each time a dynamic SQL statement is prepared for execution, applications that use dynamic SQL can often take advantage of the new statistical information produced by the RUNSTATS utility as soon as it is collected. However, if a dynamic SQL statement is prepared and the corresponding package is placed in memory *before* the new statistical information is collected and if the application that uses the statement is coded such that the statement is prepared once and executed multiple times, that particular statement will not be able to take advantage of the new statistical information produced until it is re-prepared. In most cases, this behavior is acceptable. However, if the new statistical information could result in significant performance gains, you may wish to utilize the new information immediately, as opposed to waiting until the cached package gets rebuilt.

The FLUSH PACKAGE CACHE SQL statement provides database administrators with the ability to remove cached dynamic SQL statement packages from memory (the package cache) by invalidating them. The invalidation of a cached dynamic SQL statement package has no effect on current users of the statement; however, once a package is invalidated, any new requests for the statement the invalidated package was associated with will cause the statement to be reprocessed by the DB2 Optimizer, which in turn will produce a new cached package. The basic syntax for the FLUSH PACKAGE CACHE statement is:

```
FLUSH PACKAGE CACHE DYNAMIC
```

Once this statement is executed, any cached packages associated with dynamic SQL statements that are currently in use will be allowed to continue to exist in the package cache until they are no longer needed by their current user; any new user of the same dynamic SQL statement will force the DB2 Database manager to implicitly prepare the statement, and the new version of the cached dynamic SQL statement will then be executed.

 Only users with System Administrator (SYSADM) authority or Database Administrator (DBADMN) authority are allowed to execute the FLUSH PACKAGE CACHE SQL statement.

The Design Advisor

Up until now, we have looked at how utilities like RUNSTATS and REBIND can be used to update system catalog statistics and force the DB2 Optimizer to use those statistics to provide optimum access plans for applications. But we have not talked about the one factor that can have the greatest influence on access plan selection: the existence (or nonexistence) of appropriate indexes.

So how do you decide when having an index would be beneficial and how do you determine what indexes should exist? If you have a lot of experience with database and database application design, these decisions may be easy to make. On the other hand, if you have relatively little experience in this area or if you want to validate the decisions you have already made, you can turn to DB2 UDB's Design Advisor.

The Design Advisor is a special tool that is designed to identify indexes that would help improve query performance in your database environment. Using current database statistics, the DB2 Optimizer, the Explain facility, and a specific query or set of SQL statements (known as a workload) you provide, the Design Advisor recommends one or more indexes that would improve query/ workload performance. In addition, the indexes recommended for each table, the statistics derived for them, and the data definition language (DDL) statements used to create them can be written to a user-created table named ADVISE_INDEX, if so desired. The Design Advisor is invoked by executing the db2advis command. The basic syntax for this command is:

```
db2advis -d [DatabaseName]
<-w [WorkloadName]>
<-s "[SQLStatement]">
<-i [InFile]>
<-a [UserID] </[Password]>
<-l [DiskLimit]>
<-t "[MaxAdviseTime]">
<-h>
<-p>
<-o [OutFile]>
```

where:

DatabaseName	Identifies the name assigned to the database the Design Advisor is to interact with.
WorkloadName	Identifies the name of a workload that is to be analyzed to determine whether or not new indexes should be created. (This name is used in the ADVISE_WORKLOAD table.)
SQLStatement	Identifies a single SQL statement that is to be analyzed to determine whether or not new indexes should be created.
InFile	Identifies the name assigned to an ASCII format file that contains a set of SQL statements that are to be analyzed to determine whether or not new indexes should be created.
UserID	Identifies the authentication ID (or user ID) that is to be used to establish a connection to the database specified.
Password	Identifies the password that is to be used to establish a connection to the database specified.
DiskLimit	Identifies the maximum amount of storage space, in megabytes, that is available for all indexes in the existing schema.
MaxAdviseTime	Identifies the maximum amount of time in minutes that the Design Advisor will be allowed to conduct an index analysis in. When this time limit is reached, the Design Advisor will stop its analysis.
OutFile	Identifies the name of the file that the DDL needed to create the indexes recommended is to be written to.

If the -h option is specified with the db2advis command, all other options are ignored and help information is displayed; if the -p option is specified, any plans that were generated by the Design Advisor will be stored in the appropriate Explain tables.

Thus, if you wanted to see whether an index would improve the performance of the SQL statement "SELECT DEPTNO FROM DEPARTMENT" and the DDL needed to create each index recommended (if any), you could do so by executing an db2advis command that looks something like this:

```
db2advis -d sample -s "select deptno from department"
```

And when this command is executed, you might see output that looks something like this:

```
execution started at timestamp 2003-08-12-12.44.18.471000
recommending indexes...
Initial set of proposed indexes is ready.
Found maximum set of [1] recommended indexes
Cost of workload with all indexes included [0.026190] timerons
total disk space needed for initial set [    0.009] MB
total disk space constrained to            [  -1.000] MB
   1  indexes in current solution
 [ 25.0306] timerons   (without indexes)
 [  0.0262] timerons   (with current solution)
 [%99.90] improvement


Trying variations of the solution set.
--
--
-- LIST OF RECOMMENDED INDEXES
-- ===========================
-- index[1],     0.009MB
   CREATE INDEX IDX030812124420001 ON "RSANDERS"."DEPARTMENT"
("DEPTNO" DESC) ;
   COMMIT WORK ;
   --RUNSTATS ON TABLE DEPARTMENT FOR INDEX IDX030812124420001 ;
   COMMIT WORK ;
-- ===========================
--
DB2 Workload Performance Advisor tool is finished.
```

A GUI version of the Design Advisor (known as the Design Advisor Wizard) is also available. The Design Advisor Wizard can be activated by selecting the appropriate action from the *Databases* menu found in the Control Center. Figure 6–18 shows the Control Center menu items that must be selected in order to activate the Design Advisor Wizard; Figure 6–19 shows how the first page of the Design Advisor Wizard typically looks after it has been activated.

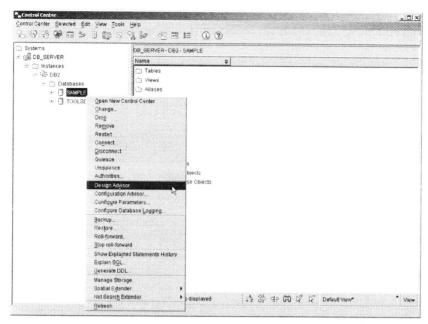

Figure 6–18   Invoking the Design Advisor Wizard from the Control Center.

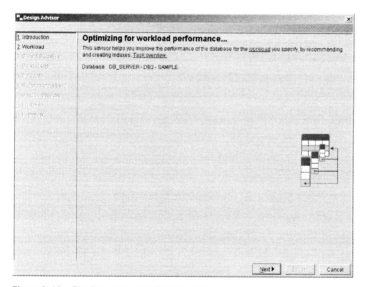

Figure 6–19   The first page of the Design Advisor Wizard.

Practice Questions

Question 1

Given the following statement:

```
EXPORT TO empdata.del OF DEL MODIFIED BY COLDEL; SELECT
* FROM employees
```

Which of the following column delimiters will be used in the output file produced?

- ○ A. , (comma)
- ○ B. | (vertical bar)
- ○ C. ; (semicolon)
- ○ D. (tab)

Question 2

Which of the following can be used as input to the EXPORT command?

- ○ A. Views
- ○ B. Triggers
- ○ C. Indexes
- ○ D. Schemas

Question 3

Given the following statement:

```
IMPORT FROM datafile.del OF DEL MESSAGES IMP_MSGS.TXT
METHOD P (1, 3, 4) INSERT INTO table1
```

Which of the following describes how table and index definitions are affected when data is imported into TABLE1?

- ○ A. Index definitions are changed
- ○ B. Table definitions are changed
- ○ C. Table and index definitions are created
- ○ D. Table and index definitions are not changed

Question 4

Which of the following is NOT a characteristic of the Import utility?

- ○ A. Worksheet Format (WSF) formatted files are supported.
- ○ B. All row transactions are recorded in the database's transaction log files.
- ○ C. System catalog tables can be targets.
- ○ D. Data can be imported into a host database through DB2 Connect.

Question 5

Which of the following options is used to control how many rows of data (records) are to be copied to the target table of a LOAD operation before the Load utility will establish a new point of consistency?

- ○ A. SAVECOUNT
- ○ B. ROWCOUNT
- ○ C. COMMITCOUNT
- ○ D. CHECKPOINT

Question 6

Which two of the following utilities can be used to update the catalog statistics for a table?

- ❏ A. EXPORT
- ❏ B. IMPORT
- ❏ C. LOAD
- ❏ D. REORGCHK
- ❏ E. REORG

Question 7

Which of the following will the REORGCHK command display?

- ○ A. A list of specific tables that need to be organized
- ○ B. A list of specific indexes that need to be organized
- ○ C. A list of specific tables and indexes that need to be reorganized
- ○ D. A list of zero or more tables and indexes that may or may not need to be reorganized

Question 8

Given the following command:

```
db2advis -d testdata -i db2advis.in -l 60 -t 15
```

Which of the following indicates the amount of time that is to be spent analyzing a workload to determine whether performance will be improved if one or more indexes are created?

- ○ A. 60 minutes
- ○ B. 15 minutes
- ○ C. Unlimited
- ○ D. At least 15 minutes, but no more than 60 minutes

Question 9

Which of the following can NOT be exported from a database using db2move?

- ○ A. All tables
- ○ B. All views
- ○ C. All indexes
- ○ D. All data

Question 10

When looking at the system catalog table SYSCAT.TABLES, which of the following columns can be used to tell whether or not a table will benefit from being reorganized?

- ○ A. CARD
- ○ B. NPAGES
- ○ C. FPAGES
- ○ D. OVERFLOW

Question 11

Which of the following authorities/privileges must a user have in order to execute the IMPORT command using the REPLACE_CREATE option?

○ A. SYSCTRL

○ B. SYSMAINT

○ C. CONTROL privilege on each participating table or view

○ D. CREATETAB and IMPLICIT_SCHEMA privilege on the database

Question 12

Which of the following utilities can NOT create a table and place data in it if the table does not already exist?

○ A. LOAD

○ B. INPUT

○ C. IMPORT

○ D. UPLOAD

Question 13

Which of the following is NOT possible with LOAD?

○ A. Table check constraints for data added by LOAD can be enforced with the SET INTEGRITY statement.

○ B. Triggers can be fired as data is loaded into a table.

○ C. Indexes are recreated if appending data to a table automatically during the build phase.

○ D. Loaded data can be captured and stored in files as backup or to be used for replication.

Question 14

Which two of the following commands should always be run after issuing the RUNSTATS command?

- ❑ A. REBIND
- ❑ B. REORGCHK
- ❑ C. INSPECT
- ❑ D. FLUSH PACKAGE CACHE
- ❑ E. DB2ADVIS

Question 15

Which of the following commands will convert all type-1 indexes that have been defined for table TABLE1 to type-2 indexes?

- ○ A. CONVERT INDEXES FOR TABLE table1
- ○ B. REORG INDEXES ALL FOR TABLE table1 CONVERT
- ○ C. REORG TABLE table1 CONVERT ALL INDEXES
- ○ D. REORG INDEXES ALL FOR TABLE table1MAKETYPE2

Question 16

Which of the following commands will report on all errors found in the architectural integrity and page consistency of a database?

- ○ A. INSPECT CHECK DATABASE BEGIN TBSPACEID 0
- ○ B. REORGCHK UPDATE STATISTICS ON TABLE ALL
- ○ C. FORCE PACKAGE CACHE TBSPCID 0 CHECK CONSISTENCY
- ○ D. INSPECT CHECK DATABASE BEGIN TBSPACEID 3 CATALOG
     TO TABLESPACE CONSISTENCY

Answers

Question 1

The correct answer is **C**. By default, the comma character (,) acts as the column delimiter for delimited ASCII files. However, the COLDEL modifier used in the statement (MODIFIED BY COLDEL;) tells the Export utility to use the semicolon character (;) as the column delimiter instead.

Question 2

The correct answer is **A**. Tables, views, and the values of special registers can be used as input to the EXPORT command; essentially any object that can provide data in response to a query can provide input to the EXPORT command.

Question 3

The correct answer is **D**. When data is imported from a delimited ASCII format file, table and index definitions are not affected.

Question 4

The correct answer is **C**. System catalog tables cannot be modified directly by any operation, including an IMPORT operation.

Question 5

The correct answer is **A**. The SAVECOUNT option is used to specify the number of rows of data (records) that are to be copied to the target table of a load operation before the Load utility will establish a new point of consistency. (The point of consistency determines where a failed load operation will resume when it is restarted.)

Question 6

The correct answers are **C** and **D**. The Load utility (when invoked by executing a LOAD ... REPLACE STATISTICS YES command) and the REORGCHK utility (when invoked by executing a REORGCHK UPDATE STATISTICS ...

command) will update the catalog statistics that will be used by the DB2 Optimizer to generate a data access plan. (Note: Catalog statistics cannot be collected if the LOAD command is executed with any option other than the REPLACE option specified.)

Question 7

The correct answer is **D**. The REORGCHK command will return a list of all tables and indexes checked, along with the formulas used, and a set of flags that indicate whether or not the table or index shown might benefit from being reorganized.

Question 8

The correct answer is **B**. The -t option of the db2advis command identifies the maximum amount of time, in minutes, that the Design Advisor will be allowed to conduct an index analysis in (which in this case is 15 minutes). When this time limit is reached, the Design Advisor will stop all processing. (The -l option tells the Design Advisor that the maximum amount of storage space, in megabytes, that is available for all indexes in the existing schema, which in this case is 60 megabytes.)

Question 9

The correct answer is **B**. The db2move utility can only be used to migrate table and index data objects and their data. Data objects such as aliases, views, triggers, user-defined data types (UDTs), user-defined functions (UDFs), and so on, cannot be migrated using db2move (this is where db2look comes in handy).

Question 10

The correct answer is **D**. Overflow rows are rows that have been moved to new pages because an update operation made them too large to be stored in the page they were written to originally or because new columns were added to an existing table. Both result in fragmentation so a high OVERFLOW value indicates that a table will benefit from being reorganized.

Question 11

The correct answer is **D**. Only users with System Administrator (SYSADM) authority, Database Administrator (DBADMN) authority, or CREATETAB on the database *and* either IMPLICIT_SCHEMA privilege on the database or CREATEIN privilege on the schema referenced are allowed to create a new table and import data into it using the CREATE or the REPLACE_CREATE option. Only users with SYSADM authority, DBADMN authority, CONTROL privilege on all tables and/or views referenced, or INSERT *and* SELECT privilege on all tables and/or views referenced are allowed to import data into existing tables using the INSERT option. And only users with SYSADM authority, DBADMN authority, or CONTROL privilege on all tables and/or views referenced are allowed to import data into existing tables using the INSERT_UPDATE, REPLACE, or REPLACE_CREATE option.

Question 12

The correct answer is **A**. The IMPORT utility can create a table and place data into it if the table does not already exist. However, when the LOAD utility is used, the table that data is to be copied to must already exist in the database before the load operation is initiated. (There is no INPUT or UPLOAD utility.)

Question 13

The correct answer is **B**. Triggers are fired by insert, update, and delete operations; since the IMPORT utility inserts data into a table, triggers can be fired. The Load utility, on the other hand, inserts data into a table by building data pages consisting of several individual rows of data, and writing those pages directly to the tablespace container(s) the target table uses for data storage. Therefore, a load operation will not fire triggers.

Question 14

The correct answers are **A** and **D**. In order for existing packages for static SQL applications to take advantage of new statistical information produced by the RUNSTATS utility, they must be rebound to the database and the easiest way to rebind an existing package is by executing the REBIND command. On the other hand, if a dynamic SQL statement is prepared and the corresponding package is placed in memory *before* the new statistical information is collected and if the application that uses the statement is coded such that the statement is prepared once and executed multiple times, that particular statement will not be able to take advantage of the new statistical information produced until it is reprepared. However, if you wish to utilize the new information immediately, as opposed to waiting until the cached package gets rebuilt, you can do so by executing the FLUSH PACKAGE CACHE command.

Question 15

The correct answer is **B**. The correct syntax for the REORG command that will convert all type-1 indexes associated with a table to type-2 indexes is:

```
REORG INDEXES ALL FOR TABLE [TableName] CONVERT
```

Question 16

The correct answer is **A**. The INSPECT utility inspects tablespaces and tables for architectural integrity by checking the structures of tablespaces and data objects to ensure they are valid and by checking all pages used for consistency. The INSPECT utility is invoked by executing the INSPECT command and the basic syntax used to inspect an entire database is:

```
INSPECT CHECK DATABASE
<BEGIN TBSPACEID [StartTS_ID] <OBJECT ID
[StartObject_ID]>>
<CATALOG TO TABLESPACE CONSISTENCY>
<FOR ERROR STATE ALL>
<LIMIT ERROR TO [ALL |DEFAULT | [ErrorCount]>
RESULTS <KEEP> [FileName]
```

7

Backup and Recovery

. . . .

*F*ourteen percent (14%) of the DB2 UDB V8.1 for Linux, UNIX, and Windows Database Administration certification exam (Exam 701) and seventeen percent (17%) of the DB2 UDB V8.1 for Linux, UNIX, and Windows Database Administration certification upgrade exam (Exam 706) exam is designed to evaluate your knowledge of transactions and transaction logging, and to test your ability to backup and restore a database using the various methods of backup and recovery available. The questions that make up this portion of the exam are intended to evaluate the following:

➤ Your knowledge of the various transaction logging features available.

➤ Your knowledge of the types of database recovery available (crash, version, and roll-forward) and your ability to demonstrate when and how each are used.

➤ Your ability to create and use database-level and tablespace-level backup images.

➤ Your ability to create and use full, incremental, and delta backup images.

➤ Your ability to return a damaged or corrupt database to the state it was in at any given point in time.

➤ Your knowledge of how and when invalid indexes are recreated.

➤ Your ability to suspend and resume database I/O and your ability to initialize a split mirror copy of a database.

This chapter is designed to introduce you to the backup and recovery tools that are available with DB2 Universal Database, and to show you how to both backup a database on a regular basis and restore a database if it becomes damaged or corrupted.

Although basic syntax is presented for most of the DB2 UDB commands covered in this chapter, the actual syntax supported may be much more complex. To view the complete syntax for a specific command or to obtain more information about a particular command, refer to the *IBM DB2 Universal Database, Version 8 Command Reference* product documentation.

Terms you will learn:

Transaction

Unit of work

COMMIT

ROLLBACK

Transaction logging

Log buffer

Circular logging

Archival logging

Infinite logging

Log mirroring

Crash recovery

Version recovery

Roll-forward recovery

Transaction failure

Recoverable database

Non-recoverable database

Online backup and recovery

Offline backup and recovery

RESTART

Soft checkpoint

BACKUP

RESTORE

ROLLFORWARD

Recovery History file

LIST HISTORY

PRUNE HISTORY

Redirected restore

SET TABLESPACE CONTAINERS

Invalid index

Split Mirror

Mirroring

Splitting

`SET WRITE`

`db2inidb`

Techniques you will master:

Recognizing the types of transaction logging available and understanding when each is to be used.

Understanding how crash recovery, version recovery, and roll-forward recovery operations are initiated.

Understanding how database-level and tablespace-level backup images are made.

Understanding how full, incremental, and delta backup images are created and used.

Understanding how invalid indexes are recreated.

Understanding how split mirroring is used to backup a database.

Understanding how I/O is suspended and resumed so mirrors can be split, as well as knowing how split mirrors are initialized.

Transactions

A *transaction* (also known as a *unit of work*) is a sequence of one or more SQL operations grouped together as a single unit, usually within an application process. Such a unit is called "atomic" because, like atoms (before fission and fusion were discovered), it is indivisible—either all of its work is carried out or none of its work is carried out. A given transaction can perform any number of SQL operations—from a single operation to many hundreds or even thousands, depending on what is considered a "single step" within your business logic. (It is important to note that the longer a transaction is, the more database concurrency decreases and the more resource locks are acquired; this is usually considered the sign of a poorly written application.)

The initiation and termination of a single transaction defines points of data consistency within a database; either the effects of all operations performed within a transaction are applied to the database and made permanent (committed), or the effects of all operations performed are backed out (rolled back) and the database is returned to the state it was in before the transaction was initiated.

In most cases, transactions are initiated the first time an executable SQL statement is executed after a connection to a database has been made or immediately after a pre-existing transaction has been terminated. Once initiated, transactions can be implicitly terminated, using a feature known as "automatic commit" (in which case, each executable SQL statement is treated as a single transaction, and any changes made by that statement are applied to the database if the statement executes successfully or discarded if the statement fails) or they can be explicitly terminated by executing the COMMIT or the ROLLBACK SQL statement. The basic syntax for these two statements is:

```
COMMIT <WORK>
```

and

```
ROLLBACK <WORK>
```

When the COMMIT statement is used to terminate a transaction, all changes made to the database since the transaction began are made permanent. On the other hand, when the ROLLBACK statement is used, all changes made are backed out and the database is returned to the state it was in just before the transaction began. Figure 7–1 shows the effects of a transaction that was ter-

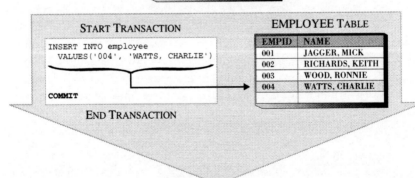

Figure 7–1 Terminating a transaction with the COMMIT SQL statement.

minated with a COMMIT statement; Figure 7–2 shows the effects of a transaction that was terminated with a ROLLBACK statement.

It is important to remember that commit and rollback operations only have an effect on changes that have been made within the transaction they terminate. So in order to evaluate the effects of a series of transactions, you must be able to identify where each transaction begins, as well as when and how each transaction is terminated. Figure 7–3 shows how the effects of a series of transactions can be evaluated.

Changes made by a transaction that have not been committed are usually inaccessible to other users and applications (unless another user or application is using the Uncommitted Read isolation level), and can be backed out with a rollback operation. However, once changes made by a transaction have been committed, they become accessible to all other users and/or applications and can only be removed by executing new SQL statements (within a

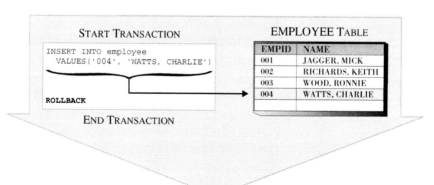

Figure 7–2   Terminating a transaction with the ROLLBACK SQL statement.

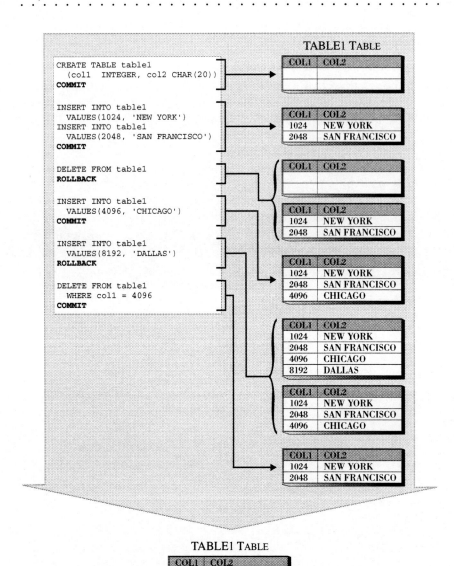

TABLE1 TABLE

COL1	COL2
1024	NEW YORK
2048	SAN FRANCISCO

Figure 7-3 Evaluating the effects of a series of transactions.

new transaction). So what happens if a problem occurs (for example, a power failure occurs or an application abends) before a transaction's changes can be committed? In order to answer that question, we must first look at how data changes are made and at how transaction activity is logged.

Transaction Logging

So just what is transaction logging and how does it work? Transaction logging is simply a process that is used to keep track of changes made to a database (by transactions), *as they are made.* Each time an update or a delete operation is performed, the page containing the record to be updated/deleted is retrieved from storage and copied to the appropriate buffer pool, where it is then modified by the update/delete operation (if a new record is created by an insert operation, that record is created directly in the appropriate buffer pool). Once the record has been modified (or inserted), a record reflecting the modification/insertion is written to the log buffer, which is simply another designated storage area in memory. (The actual amount of memory that is reserved for the log buffer is controlled by the *logbufsiz* database configuration parameter.) If an insert operation is performed, a record containing the new row is written to the log buffer; if a delete operation is performed, a record containing the row's original values is written to the log buffer; and if an update operation is performed, a record containing the row's original values, combined with the row's new values, is written to the log buffer. These kinds of records, along with records that indicate whether the transactions that were responsible for making changes were committed or rolled back, make up the majority of the records stored in the log buffer.

Whenever buffer pool I/O page cleaners are activated, the log buffer becomes full, or a transaction is terminated (by being committed or rolled back), all records stored in the log buffer are immediately written to one or more log files stored on disk. (This is done to minimize the number of log records that might get lost in the event a system failure occurs.) This process is referred to as *write-ahead logging* and it ensures that log records are always flushed to log files before data changes are recorded in the database (i.e., copied to the appropriate tablespace containers for permanent storage). Eventually, all changes made in the buffer pool are recorded in the database, but only after the corresponding log records have been externalized to one or more log files. The modified data pages themselves remain in memory, where they can be quickly accessed if necessary; eventually they will be overwritten. The transaction logging process is illustrated in Figure 7–4.

Because multiple transactions may be working with a database at any given point in time, a single log file may contain log records that belong to several different transactions. Therefore, to keep track of which log records belong to which transactions, every log record is assigned a special "transaction identifier" that ties it to the transaction that created it. By using transaction IDs, log records associated with a particular transaction can be written to one or more log files at any time, without impacting data consistency. Eventually,

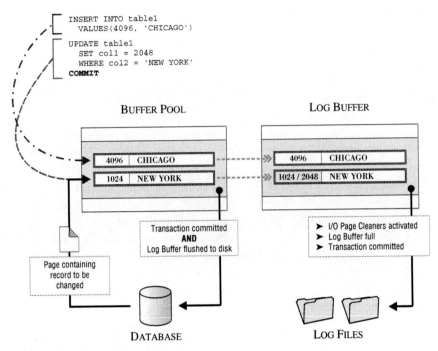

Figure 7-4 The transaction logging process.

the execution of the COMMIT or ROLLBACK statement that terminates the transaction will be logged as well.

Since log records are externalized frequently and since changes made by a particular transaction are only externalized to the database after all log records associated with the transaction have been recorded in one or more log files, the ability to return a database to a consistent state after a failure occurs is guaranteed. When the database is restarted, log records are analyzed and each record that has a corresponding COMMIT record is reapplied to the database; every record that does not have a corresponding COMMIT record is either ignored or backed out (which is why "before" and "after" information is recorded for all update operations).

Logging Strategies

When a database is first created, three log files, known as *primary* log files, are allocated as part of the creation process. On Linux and UNIX platforms, these log files are 1,000 4K (kilobyte) pages in size; on Windows platforms, these log files are 250 4K pages in size. However, the number of primary log files used, along with the amount of data each is capable of holding, is controlled by the *logprimary* and *logfilsiz* parameters in the database's configuration file. The way in which all primary log files created are used is determined by the logging strategy chosen for the database. Two very different strategies, known as *circular logging* and *archival logging*, are available.

Circular Logging

When circular logging is used, records stored in the log buffer are written to primary log files in a circular sequence. Log records are written to the current "active" log file and when that log file becomes full, it is marked as being "unavailable". At that point, DB2 makes the next log file in the sequence the active log file, and begins writing log records to it. And when that log file becomes full, the process is repeated. In the meantime, as transactions are terminated and their effects are externalized to the database, their corresponding log records are released because they are no longer needed. When all records stored in an individual log file are released, that file is marked as being "reusable" and the next time it becomes the active log file, its contents are overwritten with new log records.

Although primary log files are not marked reusable in any particular order (they are marked reusable when they are no longer needed), they must be written to in sequence. So what happens when the logging cycle gets back to a primary log file that is still marked "unavailable"? When this occurs, the DB2 Database Manager will allocate what is known as a *secondary* log file and begin writing records to it. As soon as this secondary log file becomes full, the DB2 Database Manager will poll the primary log file again and if its status is still "unavailable", another secondary log file is allocated and filled. This process will continue until either the desired primary log file becomes "reusable" or the number of secondary log files created matches the number of secondary log files allowed. If the former occurs, the DB2 Database Manager will begin writing log records to the appropriate primary log file and logging will pick up where it left off in the logging sequence. In the meantime, the records stored in the secondary log files are eventually released, and when all connections to the database have been terminated and a new connection is established, all secondary log files are destroyed. On the other hand, if the latter happens, all database activity will stop and the following message will be generated:

SQL0964C The transaction log for the database is full.

By default, up to two secondary log files will be created, if necessary, and their size will be the same as that of each primary log file used. However, the total number of secondary log files allowed is controlled by the *logsecond* parameter in the database configuration file. Circular logging is illustrated in Figure 7–5.

PRIMARY LOG FILES

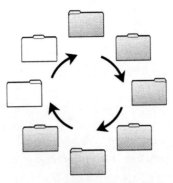

When a primary log file becomes full,
the next file in the sequence is used
(provided it is marked "reusable").

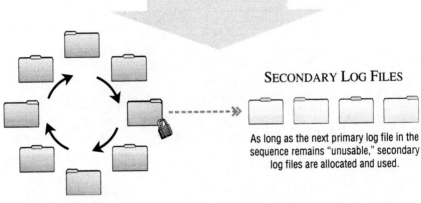

SECONDARY LOG FILES

As long as the next primary log file in the
sequence remains "unusable," secondary
log files are allocated and used.

Figure 7–5 Circular logging.

By default, when a new database is first created, circular logging is the logging strategy used.

Archival Logging

Like circular logging, when archival logging (also known as log retention logging) is used, log records stored in the log buffer are written to the primary log files that have been pre-allocated. However, unlike with circular logging, these log files are never reused. Instead, when all records stored in an individual log file are released, that file is marked as being "archived" rather than as being "reusable" and the only time it is used again is if it is needed to support a roll-forward recovery operation. Each time a primary log file becomes full, another primary log file is allocated so that the desired number of primary log files (as specified by the *logprimary* database configuration parameter) are always available for use. This process continues as long as there is disk space available.

By default, all log records associated with a single transaction must fit within the active log space available (which is determined by the maximum number of primary and secondary log files allowed and the log file size used). Thus, in the event a long running transaction requires more log space than the primary log files provide, one or more secondary log files may be allocated and filled as well. If such a transaction causes the active log space to become full, all database activity will stop and the **SQL0964C** message we saw earlier will be produced.

Because any number of primary log files can exist when archival logging is used, they are classified according to their current state and location. Log files containing records associated with transactions that have not yet been committed or rolled back that reside in the active log directory (or device) are known as *active log files*; log files containing records associated with completed transactions (i.e., transactions that have been externalized to the database) that reside in the active log directory are known as *online archive log files*; and log files containing records that are associated with completed transactions that have been moved to a storage location other than the active log directory are known as *offline archive log files*. Offline archive files can be moved to their storage location either manually or automatically with a user exit program. Archival logging is illustrated in Figure 7–6.

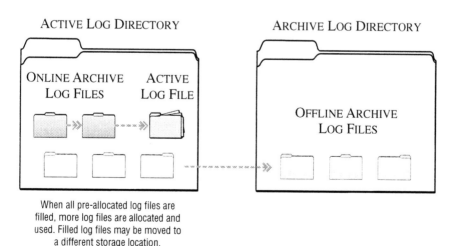

ACTIVE LOG DIRECTORY   ARCHIVE LOG DIRECTORY

ONLINE ARCHIVE   ACTIVE
LOG FILES   LOG FILE

OFFLINE ARCHIVE
LOG FILES

When all pre-allocated log files are
filled, more log files are allocated and
used. Filled log files may be moved to
a different storage location.

Figure 7–6   Archival logging.

Infinite Active Logging. You would think that you could avoid running out of log space simply by configuring a database to use a large number of primary and/or secondary log files if needed. However, the maximum number of log files allowed (primary and secondary combined) is 256 and if the size of your log files is relatively small, you can still run out of log space quickly when transaction workloads become heavy or when transactions run for an inordinate amount of time. Furthermore, you want to avoid allocating a large number of secondary log files if possible because performance is affected each time a log file has to be allocated. Ideally, you want to allocate enough primary log files to handle most situations and you want to use just enough secondary log files to handle peaks in transaction workloads.

If you are concerned about running out of log space and you want to avoid allocating a large number of secondary log files, you can configure a database to perform what is known as *infinite active logging* or *infinite logging*. Infinite active logging allows an active transaction to span all primary logs and one or more archive logs, effectively allowing a transaction to use an infinite number of log files. To enable infinite active logging, you simply set the database configuration parameters *userexit* and *logsecond* to YES and –1, respectively. It is important to note that when the *userexit* database configuration parameter is set to YES, a user-supplied userexit program will be invoked each time a log file is closed and this program can move unneeded log files to another location for permanent storage (thus the risk of running out of log storage space on the server is eliminated).

When the *logsecond* database configuration parameter is set to -1, the *logprimary* and *logfilsiz* configuration parameters are still used to specify how many primary log files DB2 should keep in the active log path as well as with how big each file should be. If DB2 needs to read log data from a log file, but the file is not in the active log path, DB2 will invoke the userexit program provided to retrieve the log file from the archive and copy it to the active log location so that other reads of log data from the same file will be fast. DB2 manages the retrieval, copying, and removal of these log files as required.

NOTE Although infinite active logging can be used to support environments with large jobs that require more log space than you would normally allocate to the primary logs, it does have its tradeoffs. Specifically, rollback operations (both at the savepoint level and at the transaction level) could be very slow due to the need to retrieve log files from the archive storage location. Likewise, crash recovery could be very slow for the same reason.

Log mirroring. With DB2 UDB Version 8.1, you have the ability to configure a database such that the DB2 Database Manager will create and update active log files in two different locations (which is sometimes referred to as dual logging). By storing active log files in one location and mirroring them in another, separate location, database activity can continue if a disk failure or human error causes log files in one location to be destroyed. (Mirroring log files may also aid in database recovery.) To enable log file mirroring, you simply assign the fully qualified name of the mirror log location to the *mirrorlogpath* database configuration parameter. It is important to note that if log mirroring is used, the primary log file location used must be a directory and not a raw device. And ideally, the mirror log file storage location used should be on a physical disk that is separate from the disk used to store primary log files and that does not have a large amount of I/O.

Database Recovery Concepts

Over time, a database can encounter any number of problems, including power interruptions, storage media failure, and application abends. All of these can result in database failure and each failure scenario requires a different recovery action.

The concept of backing up a database is the same as that of backing up any other set of data files: you make a copy of the data and store it on a different medium where it can be accessed in the event the original becomes damaged or destroyed. The simplest way to backup a database is to shut it down to ensure that no further transactions are processed, and then back it up using the BACKUP utility provided with DB2 UDB. Once the backup image has been made, you can rebuild the database if for some reason it becomes damaged or corrupted.

The process of rebuilding a database is known as *recovery* and with DB2 UDB, three types of recovery are available. They are:

➤ Crash recovery
➤ Version recovery
➤ Roll-forward recovery

Crash Recovery

When an event or condition occurs that causes a database and/or the DB2 Database Manager to end abnormally, one or more *transaction failures* may result. Conditions that can cause transaction failure include:

➤ A power failure at the workstation where the DB2 Database Manager is running.
➤ A serious operating system error.

➤ A hardware failure such as memory corruption, disk failure, CPU failure, or network failure.

➤ An application failure.

When a transaction failure takes place, all work done by partially completed transactions that was still in memory is lost. And because some of that work may not have been externalized to the database, the database is left in an inconsistent state (and therefore is unusable). *Crash recovery* is the process that returns such a database to a consistent and usable state. Crash recovery is performed by using information stored in the transaction log files to roll back all incomplete transactions found and complete any committed transactions that were still in memory (but had not yet been externalized to the database) when the transaction failure occurred. Once a database is returned to a consistent and usable state, it has attained what is known as a "point of consistency."

Version Recovery

Version recovery is the process that returns a database to the state it was in at the time a backup image was made. Version recovery is performed by replacing the current version of a database with a previous version, using an image that was created with a backup operation; the entire database is rebuilt using a backup image created earlier. Unfortunately, when a version recovery is performed, all changes that have been made to the database since the backup image was created will be lost. Version recovery can be used to restore an entire database or it can be used to restore individual tablespaces—provided individual tablespace backup images exist.

Roll-Forward Recovery

Roll-forward recovery takes version recovery one step farther by replacing a database or individual tablespaces with a backup image and replaying information stored in transaction log files to return the database/tablespaces to the state they were in at an exact point in time. In order to perform a roll-forward recovery operation, you must have archival logging enabled, you must have a full backup image of the database available, and you must have access to all archived log files (or at least the ones you want to use for recovery) that have been created since the backup image was made. Like version recovery, roll-forward recovery can be applied to an entire database or to individual tablespaces.

Recoverable and Non-recoverable Databases

Although any DB2 UDB database can be recovered from transaction log files (crash recovery) or a backup image (version recovery), whether or not a database is considered *recoverable* is determined by the values of the database's *logretain* and *userexit* configuration parameters; a database is recoverable if the *logretain* parameter is set to RECOVERY and/or the *userexit* parameter is set to YES. (When both of these configuration parameters are set to NO, which is the default, circular logging is used and the database is considered non-recoverable.) A database is considered recoverable when crash recovery, version recovery, *and* roll-forward recovery is possible. A database is considered *non-recoverable* if roll-forward recovery is not supported. Other differences between recoverable and non-recoverable databases are shown in Table 7–1.

Table 7–1 Differences between Recoverable and Non-recoverable Databases	
Recoverable Database	**Non-recoverable Database**
Archive logging is used.	Circular logging is used.
The database can be backed up at any time, regardless of whether or not applications are connected to it and transactions are in progress.	The database can only be backed up when all connections to it have been terminated.
The entire database can be backed up or individual tablespaces can be backed up. Tablespaces can also be restored independently.	The entire database must be backed up; tablespace level backups are not supported.
A damaged database can be returned to the state it was in at any point in time; crash recovery, version recovery, and roll-forward recovery are supported.	A damaged database can only be returned to the state it was in at the time the last backup image was taken; only crash recovery and version recovery are supported.

The decision of whether a database should be recoverable or non-recoverable is based on several factors:

➤ If a database is used to support read-only operations, it can be non-recoverable; since no transactions will be logged, roll-forward recovery is not necessary.

➤ If relatively few changes will be made to a database and if all changes made can be easily recreated, it may be desirable to leave the database non-recoverable.

> If a large amount of changes will be made to a database or if it would be difficult and time-consuming to recreate all changes made, a recoverable database should be used.

Online versus Offline Backup and Recovery

From a backup and recovery perspective, a database is either *online* or *offline*. When a database is offline, other applications and users cannot gain access to it; when a database is online, just the opposite is true. Backup and recovery operations can only be performed against a non-recoverable database after that database has been taken offline. Recoverable databases, on the other hand, can be backed up at any time, regardless of whether the database is offline or online. However, in order to restore a recoverable database (using version recovery and roll-forward recovery), the database must be taken offline. (It is important to note that a recoverable database only has to be taken offline if the entire database is to be restored; individual tablespaces can be restored while the database is online.)

When an online backup operation is performed, roll-forward recovery ensures that *all* changes made while the backup image is being made are captured and can be recreated with a roll-forward recovery operation. Furthermore, online backup operations can be performed against individual tablespaces as well as entire databases. And, unlike when full database version recovery operations are performed, tablespace version recovery operations and tablespace roll-forward recovery operations can be performed while a database remains online. When a tablespace is backed up online, it remains available for use and all simultaneous modifications to the data stored in that tablespace are recorded in the transaction log files. However, when an online restore or online roll-forward recovery operation is performed against a tablespace, the tablespace itself is not available for use until the operation has completed.

Incremental Backup and Recovery

As the size of a database grows, the time and hardware needed to backup and recover the databases also grows substantially. Furthermore, creating full database and tablespace backup images is not always the best approach when dealing with large databases, because the storage requirements for multiple copies of such databases can be enormous. A better alternative is to create one full backup image and several *incremental backup* images as changes are made. An incremental backup is a backup image that only contains pages that have been updated since the previous backup image was made. Along with updated data and index pages, each incremental backup image also contains all of the initial database meta-data (such as database configuration, tablespace definitions, recovery history file, etc.) that is normally found in full backup images.

Two types of incremental backup images are supported: *incremental* and *delta*. An incremental backup image is a copy of all database data that has changed since the most recent, successful, full backup operation has been performed. An incremental backup image is also known as a cumulative backup image, because a series of incremental backups taken over a period of time will have the contents of the previous incremental backup image. The predecessor of an incremental backup image is always the most recent successful full backup of the same object.

A delta backup image is a copy of all database data that has changed since the last successful backup (full, incremental, or delta) of the object in question. A delta backup image is also known as a differential, or noncumulative, backup image; the predecessor of a delta backup image is the most recent successful backup image that contains a copy of each of the objects found in the delta backup image.

The key difference between incremental and delta backup images is their behavior when successive backups are taken of an object that is continually changing over time. Each successive incremental image contains the entire contents of the previous incremental image, plus any data that has changed, or has been added, since the previous full backup image was produced. Delta backup images only contain the pages that have changed since the previous backup image of any type was produced. In either case, database recovery involves restoring the database using the most recent successful full backup image available and applying each incremental backup image produced, in the order in which they were made. (The recovery history file keeps track of which incremental and delta backup images are needed and the order that they were made in.)

Performing a Crash Recovery Operation

Earlier, we saw that whenever transaction processing is interrupted by an unexpected event (such as a power failure), the database the transaction was interacting with at the time is placed in an inconsistent state. Such a database will remain in an inconsistent state and will be unusable until a crash recovery operation returns it to some point of consistency. (An inconsistent database will notify users and applications that it is unusable via a return code and error message that is generated each time an attempt to establish a connection to it is made.)

So just how is a crash recovery operation initiated? One way is by executing the RESTART command from the DB2 Command Line Processor (CLP). The basic syntax for this command is:

```
RESTART [DATABASE | DB] [DatabaseName]
<USER [UserName] <USING [Password]>>
<DROP PENDING TABLESPACES ( [TS_Name], ... )>
<WRITE RESUME>
```

where:

DatabaseName	Identifies the name assigned to the database that is to be returned to a consistent and usable state.
UserName	Identifies the name assigned to a specific user whose authority the crash recovery operation is to be performed under.
Password	Identifies the password that corresponds to the name of the user that the crash recovery operation is to be performed under.
TS_Name	Identifies the name assigned to one or more tablespaces that are to be disabled and placed in "Drop Pending" mode if errors are encountered while trying to return them to a consistent state.

Thus, if you wanted to perform a crash recovery operation on an inconsistent database named SAMPLE, you could do so by executing a RESTART command that looks something like this:

```
RESTART DATABASE SAMPLE
```

 If all database I/O was suspended (using the SET WRITE command) at the time a crash occurred, I/O must be resumed (using the WRITE RESUME option of the RESTART command) as part of the crash recovery process. (We'll look at the SET WRITE command a little later.)

You can also initiate a crash recovery operation for a particular database by selecting the *Restart* action from the *Databases* menu found in the Control Center. Figure 7–7 shows the Control Center menu items that must be selected in order to perform a crash recovery operation on an unusable database.

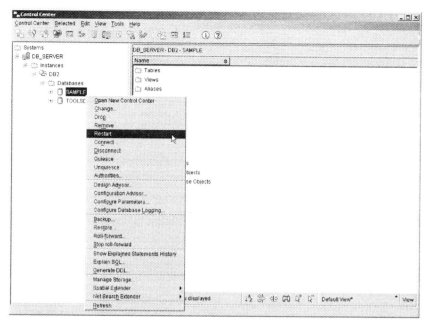

Figure 7–7   Initiating a crash recovery operation from the Control Center.

It is also possible to configure a database in such a way that crash recovery will automatically be performed, if necessary, when an application or user attempts to establish a connection to it. This is done by assigning the value ON to the *autorestart* database configuration parameter. (The DB2 Database Manager checks the state of a database the first time an attempt to establish a connection to the database is made and if it determines that the database is in an inconsistent state, it executes the RESTART command automatically if the *autorestart* database configuration parameter is set to ON.)

Any user can restart an inconsistent database; no authorization checking is performed.

It is important to note that if a crash recovery operation is performed on a recoverable database (i.e., a database that has been configured to support forward recovery operations) and an error occurs during the recovery process that is attributable to an individual tablespace, that tablespace will be taken offline, and will no longer be accessible until it is repaired. This has no effect on crash recovery itself and upon completion of the crash recovery operation, all other tablespaces in the database will be accessible and connections to the database can be established—provided the tablespace that is taken offline is not the tablespace that contains the system catalogs. If the tablespace containing the system catalogs is taken offline, it must be repaired before any connections to the database will be permitted.

A Word about Soft Checkpoints

It was mentioned earlier that crash recovery is performed by using information stored in the transaction log files to roll back all incomplete transactions found and complete any committed transactions that were still in memory (but had not yet been externalized to storage) when the transaction failure occurred. As you might imagine, if the transaction log files for a database are large, it could take quite a while to scan the entire log and check for corresponding rows in the database. However, it's usually not necessary to scan the entire log since records recorded at the beginning of a log file are usually associated with transactions that have been completed and have already been externalized to the database. Furthermore, if these records can be skipped, the amount of time required to recover a crashed database can be greatly reduced.

That's where a mechanism known as the *soft checkpoint* comes in. The DB2 Database Manager uses a log control file to determine which records from a specific log file need to be applied to the database. This log control file is written to disk periodically, and the frequency at which this file is updated is determined by the value of the *softmax* database configuration parameter. Once the log control file is updated the soft checkpoint information stored in it establishes where in a transaction log file crash recovery should begin; all records in a log file that precede the soft checkpoint are assumed to be associated with transactions that have already been written to the database and are ignored.

Backup and Recovery

Although crash recovery can be used to resolve inconsistency problems that result from power interruptions and/or application failures, it cannot be used to handle problems that arise when the storage media being used to hold a database's files becomes corrupted or fails. In order to handle these types of problems, some kind of backup (and recovery) program must be put in place.

A database recovery strategy should include a regular schedule for making database backup images and, in the case of partitioned database systems, include making backup images whenever the system is scaled (i.e., whenever database partition servers are added or dropped). In addition, the strategy used should ensure that all information needed is available when database recovery is necessary and it should include procedures for recovering command scripts, applications, user-defined functions (UDFs), stored procedure code in operating system libraries, and load copies as well as database data. To help with such a strategy, DB2 UDB provides three utilities that are used to facilitate backing up and restoring a database. The utilities are:

- ➤ The BACKUP utility
- ➤ The RESTORE utility
- ➤ The ROLLFORWARD utility

The DB2 UDB BACKUP Utility

The single most important item you can possess that will prevent catastrophic data losses in the event storage media becomes corrupted or fails is a database backup image. A database backup image is essentially a copy of an entire database that includes both its objects and its data. Once created, a backup image can be used at any time to return a database to the exact state it was in at the time the backup image was made (version recovery). A good database recovery strategy should ensure that backup images are created on a regular basis, and that backup copies of critical data are retained in a secure location and on different storage media from that used to store the database itself. Depending on the logging method used (circular or archival), database backup images can be made when a database is offline or while other users and applications are connected to it (online). (In order to backup a database while it is online, archival logging must be used.)

A backup image of a DB2 UDB database (or of a tablespace within a DB2 UDB database) can be created by executing the BACKUP command. The basic syntax for this command is:

```
BACKUP [DATABASE | DB] [DatabaseName]
<USER [UserName] <USING [Password]>>
<TABLESPACE ( [TS_Name],...)
<ONLINE>
<INCREMENTAL <DELTA>>
<TO [Location]>
<WITH [NumBuffers] BUFFERS>
<BUFFER [BufferSize]>
<PARALLELISM [ParallelNum]>
<WITHOUT PROMPTING>
```

where:

DatabaseName	Identifies the name assigned to the database that a backup image is to be created for.
UserName	Identifies the name assigned to a specific user whose authority the backup operation is to be performed under.
Password	Identifies the password that corresponds to the name of the user that the backup operation is to be performed under.
TS_Name	Identifies the name assigned to one or more specific tablespaces that are to be backed up.
Location	Identifies the directory or device where the backup image created is to be stored. (If no location is specified, the current location is used as the default.)
NumBuffers	Identifies the number of buffers that are to be used to perform the backup operation. (By default, two buffers are used if this option is not specified.)
BufferSize	Identifies the size, in pages, that each buffer used to perform the backup operation will be. (By default, the size of each buffer used by the BACKUP utility is determined by the value of the *backbufsz* DB2 Database Manager configuration parameter.)
ParallelNum	Identifies the number of tablespaces that can be read in parallel during a backup operation.

If the INCREMENTAL option is specified, an incremental backup image will be produced. An incremental backup image is a copy of all data that has changed since the last successful, full backup image was produced. Likewise, if the DELTA option is specified, a delta backup image will be produced. A delta backup image is a copy of all data that has changed since the last successful backup image of any type (full, incremental, or delta) was produced.

Thus, if you wanted to create a backup image of a database named SAMPLE and store the image created in a directory named BACKUPS on logical disk drive E:, you could do so by executing a BACKUP command that looks something like this:

```
BACKUP DATABASE SAMPLE
USER DB2ADMIN USING IBMDB2
TO E:\BACKUPS
```

On the other hand, if you wanted to create an incremental backup image of a tablespace named TBSP1 and store the image created in a directory named BACKUPS on logical disk drive E: while the database it is associated with (named SAMPLE) remains online, you could do so by executing a BACKUP command that looks something like this:

```
BACKUP DATABASE SAMPLE
USER DB2ADMIN USING IBMDB2
TABLESPACE (TBSP1) ONLINE INCREMENTAL TO E:\BACKUPS
```

Keep in mind that tablespace backup images can only be created if archival logging is being used; if circular logging is used instead, tablespace backups are not supported.

You can also create a backup image of a database or one or more tablespaces using the Backup Wizard, which can be activated by selecting the *Backup* action from the *Databases* menu found in the Control Center. Figure 7–8 shows the Control Center menu items that must be selected to activate the Backup Wizard; Figure 7–9 shows how the first page of the Backup Wizard might look immediately after it is activated.

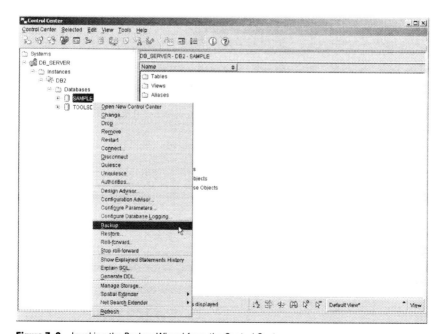

Figure 7–8   Invoking the Backup Wizard from the Control Center.

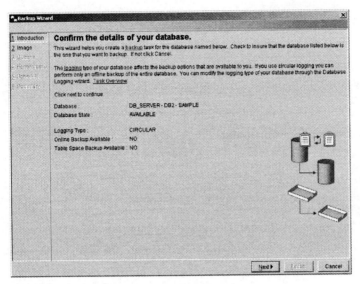

Figure 7–9 The first page of the Backup Wizard.

 Only users with System Administrator (SYSADM) authority, System Control (SYSC-TRL) authority, or System Maintenance (SYSMAINT) authority are allowed to backup a database or any of its tablespaces.

The Recovery History File

In Chapter 3—Data Placement, we saw that a special file, known as the recovery history file, is created as part of the database creation process. This file is used to log historical information about specific actions that are performed against the database it is associated with. Specifically, records are written to the recovery history file whenever any of the following are performed:

➤ A backup image of any type is created.

➤ A version recovery operation is performed either on the database or on one of its tablespaces.

➤ A table is loaded using the LOAD utility.

➤ A roll-forward recovery operation is performed either on the database or on one of its tablespaces.

➤ A tablespace is altered.

➤ A tablespace is quiesced.

➤ Data in a table is reorganized using the REORG utility.

➤ Statistics for a table are updated using the RUNSTATS utility.

➤ A table is created, renamed, or deleted (dropped).

In addition to identifying the event that was performed, each entry in the recovery history file identifies the date and time the event took place, how the event took place, the tablespaces and tables that were affected, and the location of the backup image created (if the action was a backup operation), along with information on how to access this image. (In a moment, we'll look at how this information is used when a version recovery operation is performed.)

Because the recovery history file sits quietly in the background and the DB2 Database Manager is responsible for managing its contents, a database administrator rarely has to interact with it. However, two commands are available that provide a way to both view the contents of a database's recovery history file and to remove one or more entries stored in it. You can view the contents of a database's recovery history file by executing the LIST HISTORY command from the DB2 Command Line Processor (CLP). The basic syntax for this command is:

```
LIST HISTORY
<BACKUP| ROLLFORWARD| DROPPED TABLE | LOAD |
   CREATE TABLESPACE | ALTER TABLESPACE |
   RENAME TABLESPACE | REORG>
[ALL | SINCE [Timestamp] |
   CONTAINING <SchemaName.>ObjectName]
FOR [DATABASE | DB] [DatabaseName]
```

where:

Timestamp	Identifies a timestamp that is to be used as search criteria when retrieving entries from the recovery history file; only entries with timestamps that are greater than or equal to the timestamp provided are retrieved and displayed.
SchemaName	Identifies the name assigned to the schema that is to be used as search criteria when retrieving entries from the recovery history file; only entries that are associated with the schema name specified are retrieved and displayed.
ObjectName	Identifies the name assigned to an object that is to be used as search criteria when retrieving entries from the recovery history file; only entries that are associated with the object specified are retrieved and displayed.

DatabaseName   Identifies the name assigned to the database that recovery history file information is to be retrieved and displayed for.

So, if you wanted to display all entries found in the recovery history file for a database named SAMPLE, you could do so by executing a `LIST HISTORY` command that looks something like this:

```
LIST HISTORY ALL FOR DATABASE SAMPLE
```

And when such a `LIST HISTORY` command is executed, output that looks something like the following might be produced (assuming the SAMPLE database has been backed up):

```
                List History File for SAMPLE

Number of matching file entries = 1


 Op Obj Timestamp+Sequence Type Dev Earliest Log Current Log  Backup ID
 -- --- ------------------ ---- --- ------------ ------------ ------------
  B  D  20030817204927001   F    D  S0000000.LOG S0000000.LOG
 ---------------------------------------------------------------------
  Contains 2 tablespace(s):

  00001 SYSCATSPACE
  00002 USERSPACE1
 ---------------------------------------------------------------------
   Comment: DB2 BACKUP SAMPLE OFFLINE
   Start Time: 20030817204927
   End Time: 20030817204957
 ---------------------------------------------------------------------
   00001 Location: C:\Backup\SAMPLE.0\DB2\NODE0000\CATN0000\20030817
```

You can delete a recovery history file entry by executing the `PRUNE HISTORY` command. The basic syntax for this command is:

```
PRUNE HISTORY [Timestamp]
<WITH FORCE OPTION>
```

where:

Timestamp   Identifies a timestamp that is to be used as search criterion when removing entries from the recovery history file; only entries with timestamps that are less than or equal to the timestamp provided are deleted, provided they are not part of the most recent restore set.

If the `WITH FORCE OPTION` option is specified, entries with timestamps that are less than or equal to the timestamp specified are deleted regardless of whether or not they are part of the most recent restore set.

Thus, if you wanted to remove all recovery history log file entries that were made prior to and including January 1, 2002, regardless of whether or not they are part of the most recent restore set, you could do so by executing a PRUNE HISTORY command that looks something like this:

```
PRUNE HISTORY 20020101 WITH FORCE OPTION
```

It is important to note that where the LIST HISTORY command requires you to provide the name of the database whose recovery history file is to be queried, the PRUNE HISTORY command requires that you establish a connection to the appropriate database before attempting to remove one or more of its recovery history file entries.

The DB2 UDB RESTORE Utility

Earlier, we saw that version recovery is the process that returns a database to the state it was in at the time a backup image was made. This means that in order for version recovery to be available, at least one backup image must exist and be available. And since the recovery history file contains image location information for each backup image available, it acts as a tracking and verification mechanism during version recovery operations; each backup image contains special information in its header and this information is compared to the records stored in a database's recovery history file to determine whether or not a particular backup image is associated with the database that is to be recovered.

So just how is a recovery operation initiated? The most common way is by executing the RESTORE command. The basic syntax for this command is:

```
RESTORE [DATABASE | DB] [DatabaseName]
<USER [UserName] <USING [Password]>>
<TABLESPACE <ONLINE> |
    TABLESPACE ( [TS_Name] ,... ) <ONLINE> |
    HISTORY FILE <ONLINE>>
<INCREMENTAL <AUTO | AUTOMATIC | ABORT>>
<FROM [SourceLocation]>
<TAKEN AT [Timestamp]>
<TO [TargetLocation]>
<INTO [TargetAlias]> <NEWLOGPATH [LogsLocation]>
<WITH [NumBuffers] BUFFERS>
<BUFFER [BufferSize]>
<REPLACE EXISTING>
<REDIRECT>
<PARALLELISM [ParallelNum]>
<WITHOUT ROLLING FORWARD>
<WITHOUT PROMPTING>
```

or

```
RESTORE [DATABASE | DB] [DatabaseName]
[CONTINUE | ABORT]
```

where:

DatabaseName	Identifies the name assigned to the database that is associated with the backup image that is to be used to perform a recovery operation.
UserName	Identifies the name assigned to a specific user that the recovery operation is to be performed under.
Password	Identifies the password that corresponds to the name of the user that the recovery operation is to be performed under.
TS_Name	Identifies the name assigned to one or more specific tablespaces that are to be restored from a backup image.
SourceLocation	Identifies the directory or device where the backup image to be used is stored.
Timestamp	Identifies a timestamp that is to be used as search criterion when looking for a particular backup image to use for recovery. (If no timestamp is specified there must be only one backup image at the source location specified.)
TargetLocation	Identifies the directory where the database that will be created is to be stored, if the backup image is to be used to create a new database.
TargetAlias	Identifies the alias to be assigned to the new database to be created.
LogsLocation	Identifies the directory or device where log files for the new database are to be stored.
NumBuffers	Identifies the number of buffers that are to be used to perform the recovery operation. (By default, two buffers are used if this option is not specified.)
BufferSize	Identifies the size, in pages, that each buffer used to perform the backup operation will be. (By default, the size of each buffer used by the

RESTORE utility is determined by the value of the *restbufsz* DB2 Database Manager configuration parameter.)

ParallelNum Identifies the number of tablespaces that can be read in parallel during a backup operation.

Thus, if you wanted to restore a database named SAMPLE (which already exists and uses circular logging), using a backup image stored in a directory named BACKUPS on logical disk drive E:, you could do so by executing a RESTORE command that looks something like this:

```
RESTORE DATABASE SAMPLE
USER DB2ADMIN USING IBMDB2
FROM E:\BACKUPS
REPLACE EXISTING
WITHOUT PROMPTING
```

On the other hand, if you wanted to restore just a tablespace named TBSP1 in a database named SAMPLE from an incremental backup image stored in a directory named BACKUPS on logical disk drive E: while the database is online, you could do so by executing a RESTORE command that looks something like this:

```
RESTORE DATABASE SAMPLE
USER DB2ADMIN USING IBMDB2
TABLESPACE (TBSP1) ONLINE
INCREMENTAL
FROM E:\BACKUPS
```

Each full database backup image contains, among other things, a copy of the database's recovery history file. However, when an existing database is restored from a full database backup image, the existing recovery history file is not overwritten. But what if the recovery history file for the database happens to be corrupted? Can the recovery history file be restored as well since a copy exists in the database backup image? The answer is yes. A special form of the RESTORE command can be used to restore *just* the recovery history file from a database backup image. Such a RESTORE command might look something like this:

```
RESTORE DATABASE SAMPLE
USER DB2ADMIN USING IBMDB2
HISTORY FILE
FROM E:\BACKUPS
```

It is also possible to create an entirely new database from a full database backup image, effectively cloning an existing database. Thus, you could create a new database named SAMPLE_2 that is an exact duplicate of a database named SAMPLE, using a backup image stored in a directory named BACK-UPS on logical disk drive E: by executing a RESTORE command that looks something like this:

```
RESTORE DATABASE SAMPLE
USER DB2ADMIN USING IBMDB2
FROM E:\BACKUPS
INTO SAMPLE_2
```

It is important to note that if a backup image is used to create a new database, the recovery history file stored in the backup image will become the recovery history file for the new database.

You can also perform any of the restore/recovery operations just described (along with many others) using the Restore Data Wizard, which can be activated by selecting the *Restore* action from the *Databases* menu found in the Control Center. Figure 7–10 shows the Control Center menu items that must be selected to activate the Restore Data Wizard; Figure 7–11 shows how the first page of the Restore Data Wizard might look immediately after it is activated.

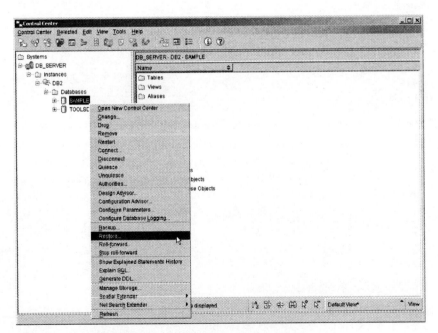

Figure 7–10   Invoking the Restore Data Wizard from the Control Center.

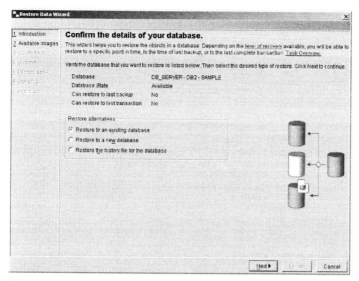

Figure 7–11   The first page of the Restore Data Wizard.

Only users with System Administrator (SYSADM) authority, System Control (SYSC-TRL) authority, or System Maintenance (SYSMAINT) authority are allowed to restore a database or any of its tablespaces from a backup image; only users with SYSADM authority or SYSCTRL authority are allowed to create a new database from a backup image.

Redirected Restore

A full backup image of a database contains, among other things, information about all tablespaces that have been defined for the database, including specific information about each tablespace container being used at the time the backup image was made. During a recovery operation, a check is performed to verify that all tablespace containers referenced by the backup image exist and are accessible. If this check determines that one or more of the tablespace containers needed is no longer available or is no longer accessible, the recovery operation will fail and the database will not be restored. When this happens, any invalid tablespace containers encountered can be redefined at the beginning of the recovery process by performing what is referred to as a *redirected restore* operation.

Redirected restore operations are performed by executing the RESTORE command with the REDIRECT option specified, followed by one or more SET TABLESPACE CONTAINERS commands, followed by the RESTORE command with the CONTINUE option specified. The basic syntax for the SET TABLESPACE CONTAINERS command is:

```
SET TABLESPACE CONTAINERS FOR [TS_ID] USING
[( PATH '[Container]' ,... ) |
   ( [FILE | DEVICE] '[Container]' [ContainerSize] ,... )]
```

where:

TS_ID	Identifies the identification number assigned to the tablespace that new storage containers are to be provided for.
Container	Identifies one or more containers that are to be used to store the data associated with the tablespace specified.
ContainerSize	Identifies the number of pages to be stored in the tablespace container specified.

The steps used to perform a redirected restore operation are as follows:

1. Start the redirected restore operation by executing the RESTORE command with the REDIRECT option specified. (When this option is specified, each invalid tablespace container encountered is flagged, and all tablespaces that reference invalid tablespace containers are placed in the "Restore Pending" state. A list of all tablespaces affected can be obtained by executing the LIST TABLESPACES command.) At some point, you should see a message that looks something like this:

```
SQL1277N Restore has detected that one or more table
space containers are inaccessible, or has set their
state to 'storage must be defined'.
DB20000I The RESTORE DATABASE command completed suc-
cessfully.
```

2. Specify new tablespace containers for each tablespace placed in "Restore Pending" state by executing a SET TABLESPACE CONTAINERS for each appropriate tablespace. (Keep in mind that SMS tablespaces can only use PATH containers, while DMS tablespaces can only use FILE or DEVICE containers.)

3. Complete the redirected restore operation by executing the RESTORE command with the CONTINUE option specified.

To simplify things, all of these steps can be coded in a UNIX shell script or a Windows batch file, which can then be used to perform the redirected restore operation. Such a file might look something like this:

```
db2 "RESTORE DATABASE SAMPLE FROM C:\BACKUPS TO D:\DB_DIR
INTO SAMPLE_2 REDIRECT"
```

```
db2 "SET TABLESPACE CONTAINERS FOR 0 USING
(PATH 'D:\DB_DIR\SYSTEM')"

db2 "SET TABLESPACE CONTAINERS FOR 1 USING
(PATH 'D:\DB_DIR\TEMP')"

db2 "SET TABLESPACE CONTAINERS FOR 2 USING
(PATH 'D:\DB_DIR\USER')"

db2 "RESTORE DATABASE SAMPLE CONTINUE"
```

You can also perform a redirected restore by assigning new tablespace containers to existing tablespaces on the Containers page of the Restore Data Wizard. Figure 7–12 shows how this is used to assist in a redirected restore operation.

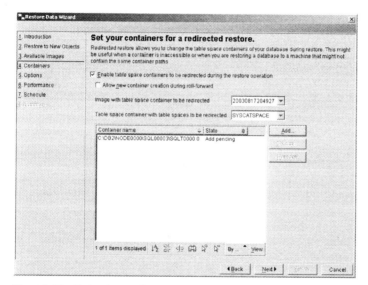

Figure 7–12   Performing a redirected restore using the Containers page of the Restore Data Wizard.

In addition to providing new storage containers for tablespaces when older tablespace containers are inaccessible or are no longer present, a redirected restore can also be used to add new containers to existing SMS tablespaces. (The ALTER TABLESPACE command does not allow you to add new storage containers to existing SMS tablespaces; a redirected restore provides a workaround to this limitation.)

The DB2 UDB ROLLFORWARD Utility

When a backup image is used to restore a damaged or corrupted database, the database can only be returned to the state it was in at the time the backup image was made. Therefore, all changes that were made to the database after the backup image was created will be lost when a recovery operation is performed. To return a database to the state it was in at any given point in time, roll-forward recovery must be used instead. And in order to perform a roll-forward recovery operation, the database must be recoverable (that is, archival logging must be the logging strategy used), you must have a full backup image of the database available, and you must have access to all archived log files that will be needed to perform the roll-forward recovery operation.

Roll-forward recovery starts out as a recovery operation. However, where a recovery operation will leave a non-recoverable database in a "Normal" state, the same operation will leave a recoverable database in "Roll-forward pending" state. (When a recoverable database is restored from a backup image, it is automatically placed in "Roll-forward pending" state unless the WITHOUT ROLLING FORWARD option is used with the RESTORE command; while a database is in "Roll-forward pending state, it cannot be accessed by users and applications.) At that point, the database can either be taken out of "Roll-forward pending" state (in which case all changes made to the database since the backup image used for recovery was made will be lost), or information stored in the database's transaction log files can be replayed to return the database to the state it was in at any given point in time.

Once a database is taken out of "Roll-forward pending" state, it cannot be manually returned to that state again. Therefore, if you discover that a database was taken out of "Roll-forward pending" state prematurely and you need to return it to that state, you must restore the database again using an appropriate backup image.

The process of replaying transactions stored in archived log files is known as "rolling the database forward" and one way to roll a database forward is by executing the ROLLFORWARD command. The basic syntax for this command is:

```
ROLLFORWARD [DATABASE | DB] [DatabaseName]
<USER [UserName] <USING [Password]>>
<TO [PointInTime] <USING LOCAL TIME>
      <AND COMPLETE | AND STOP> |
   TO END OF LOGS <AND COMPLETE | AND STOP> |
   COMPLETE |
   STOP |
   CANCEL |
   QUERY STATUS <USING LOCAL TIME>>
<TABLESPACE ONLINE |
   TABLESPACE <( [TS_Name] ,... )> <ONLINE>>
<OVERFLOW LOG PATH ( [LogDirectory] ,... )>
<RECOVER DROPPED TABLE [TableID] TO [Location]>
```

where:

DatabaseName	Identifies the name assigned to the database that is to be rolled forward.
UserName	Identifies the name assigned to a specific user that the roll-forward operation is to be performed under.
Password	Identifies the password that corresponds to the name of the user that the roll-forward operation is to be performed under.
PointInTime	Identifies a specific point in time, identified by a timestamp value in the form *yyyy-mm-dd-hh.mm.ss.nnnnnn* (year, month, day, hour, minutes, seconds, microseconds) that the database is to be rolled forward to. (Only transactions that took place before and up to the time specified will be reapplied to the database.)
TS_Name	Identifies the name assigned to one or more specific tablespaces that are to be rolled forward.
LogDirectory	Identifies the directory that contains offline archived log files that are to be used to perform the roll-forward operation.
TableID	Identifies a specific table (by ID) that was dropped earlier that is to be recovered as part of the roll-forward operation. (The table ID can be obtained by examining the database's recovery history file.)
Location	Identifies the directory where files containing data that was stored in the table that was dropped are to be written to when the table is recovered as part of the roll-forward operation.

If the AND COMPLETE, AND STOP, COMPLETE, or STOP option is specified, the database will be returned to "Normal" state when the roll-forward operation has completed. Otherwise, the database will remain in "Roll-forward pending state". (When a recoverable database is restored from a backup image, it is automatically placed in "Roll-forward pending" state unless the WITHOUT ROLLING FORWARD option is used with the RESTORE command; while a database is in "Roll-forward pending state, it cannot be accessed by users and applications.)

Thus, if you wanted to perform a roll-forward recovery operation on a database named SAMPLE and take it out of "Roll-forward pending" state, you could do so by executing a ROLLFORWARD command that looks something like this:

```
ROLLFORWARD DATABASE SAMPLE TO END OF LOGS AND STOP
```

On the other hand, if you wanted to perform a roll-forward recovery operation on a database named SAMPLE by reapplying all transactions that were committed at or before 01/01/2003, you could do so by executing a ROLLFORWARD command that looks something like this:

```
ROLLFORWARD DATABASE SAMPLE TO 2003-01-01-00.00.00.0000
AND STOP
```

It is important to note that the time value specified is interpreted as a Coordinated Universal Time (UTC), otherwise known as Greenwich Mean Time (GMT), value. If a ROLLFORWARD command that looks something like this had been executed instead:

```
ROLLFORWARD DATABASE SAMPLE TO 2003-01-01-00.00.00.0000
USING LOCAL TIME AND STOP
```

The time value specified would have been interpreted as a local time value.

You can also initiate a roll-forward recovery operation using the Rollforward Wizard, which can be activated by selecting the *Roll-forward* action from the *Databases* menu found in the Control Center. Figure 7–13 shows the Control Center menu items that must be selected to activate the Rollforward Wizard; Figure 7–14 shows how the first page of the Rollforward Wizard might look immediately after it is activated.

Because a roll-forward recovery operation is typically performed immediately after a database is restored from a backup image, a roll-forward recovery operation can also be initiated by providing the appropriate information on the Roll forward page of the Restore Data Wizard. Figure 7–15 shows how the Roll forward page of the Restore Data Wizard might look after its input fields have been populated.

Only users with System Administrator (SYSADM) authority, System Control (SYSC-TRL) authority, or System Maintenance (SYSMAINT) authority are allowed to perform a roll-forward recovery operation.

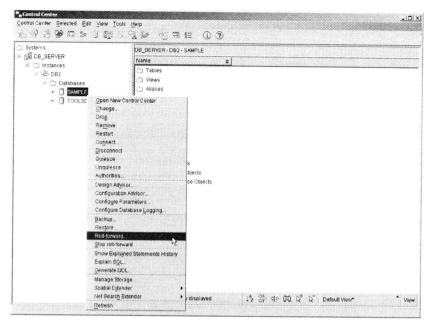

Figure 7–13   Invoking the Rollforward Wizard from the Control Center.

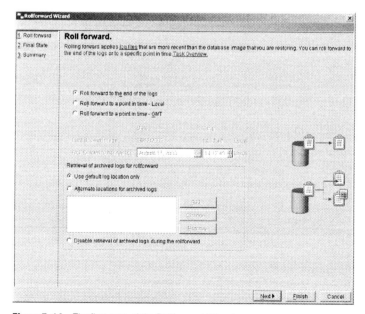

Figure 7–14   The first page of the Rollforward Wizard.

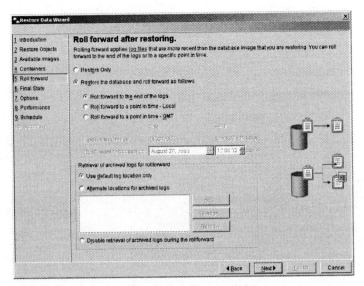

Figure 7–15   The Roll forward page of the Restore Data Wizard.

Rebuilding Invalid Indexes

So far we have looked at ways to recover data in the event the storage media being used to hold a database's files becomes corrupted or fails. But what if only indexes are damaged and a database's data is unaffected (which could be the case if data and indexes are stored in separate DMS tablespaces and only the tablespace container where index data is stored fails)? In this case, the affected indexes are invalidated and can be recovered by being recreated once the faulty media has been replaced.

Whenever the DB2 Database Manager detects that an index is no longer valid, it automatically attempts to rebuild it. However, the point in time at which the DB2 Database Manager attempts to rebuild an invalid index is controlled by the *indexrec* parameter of the database or the DB2 Database Manager configuration file. There are three possible settings for this parameter:

> **SYSTEM.** Invalid indexes are to be rebuilt at the time specified in the *indexrec* parameter of the DB2 Database Manager configuration file. (This setting is only valid for database configuration files.)
>
> **RESTART.** Invalid indexes are to be rebuilt when crash recovery is performed on the database (i.e., when the database is restarted).
>
> **ACCESS.** Invalid indexes are to be rebuilt the first time they are accessed after they have been marked as being invalid.

So when is the best time to rebuild invalid indexes? If the time it takes to perform a crash recovery operation on a database is not a concern, it is better to let the DB2 Database Manager rebuild invalid indexes while it is returning a database to a consistent state; the time needed to restart a database will be longer due to the index recreation process, but normal processing will not be affected. On the other hand, if indexes are rebuilt as they are accessed, crash recovery can be performed faster, but users may experience an initial decrease in performance; references made to tables that contain associated invalid indexes will have to wait for the invalid index(es) to be rebuilt. Furthermore, unexpected locks may be acquired and held long after an invalid index has been recreated, especially if the transaction that caused the index recreation to occur is not committed (or rolled back) for quite some time.

Backing Up a Database with Split Mirroring

It was mentioned earlier that, as databases increase in size and as heavy usage demands require databases to be available 24 hours a day, seven days a week, the time and hardware needed to backup and restore a database can increase substantially. Backing up an entire database or several tablespaces of a large database can put a strain on system resources, require a considerable amount of additional storage space (to hold the backup images), and can reduce the availability of the database system (particularly if the system has to be taken off line in order to be backed up). Therefore, a popular alternative to creating and maintaining backup images of such databases is to use what is known as a *split mirror*.

A split mirror is an "instantaneous" copy of a database that is made by mirroring the disk(s) that contain the database's data, and splitting the mirror when a backup copy of the database is required. *Mirroring* is the process of writing all database data to two separate disks (or disk subsystems) simultaneously; one disk/subsystem holds the database data while the other holds an exact copy (known as a *mirror*) of the primary disk/subsystem being used. *Splitting* a mirror simply involves separating the primary and secondary copies of the database from each other. Split mirroring provides the following advantages:

➤ The overhead required to create backup images of the database is eliminated

➤ Entire systems can be cloned very quickly

➤ Provides a fast implementation of idle standby failover.

To further enhance split mirroring, DB2 UDB provides a way to temporarily suspend (and later resume) all database I/O so that a mirror can be split without having to take a database offline. The command that provides this functionality is the SET WRITE command and the syntax for this command is:

```
SET WRITE [SUSPEND | RESUME] FOR [DATABASE | DB]
```

Thus, if you wanted to temporarily suspend all I/O for a database, you would do so by establishing a connection to that database and executing a SET WRITE command that looks like this:

```
SET WRITE SUSPEND FOR DATABASE
```

When executed, the SET WRITE SUSPEND FOR DATABASE command causes the DB2 Database Manager to suspend all write operations to tablespace containers and log files that are associated with the current database. (The suspension of writes to tablespaces and log files is intended to prevent partial page writes from occurring until the suspension is removed.) All database operations, apart from online backup and restore operations, will function normally while database writes are suspended. That's because read-only transactions are not suspended and are able to continue working with the suspended database, provided they do not request a resource that is being held by the suspended I/O process. Furthermore, applications can continue to process insert, update, and delete operations using data that has been cached in the database's buffer pool(s). However, new pages cannot be read into the buffer pool(s) and no new database connections can be established.

I/O for a suspended database can be resumed at any time by executing a SET WRITE command that looks like this:

```
SET WRITE RESUME FOR DATABASE
```

When executed, the SET WRITE RESUME FOR DATABASE command causes the DB2 Database Manager to lift all write suspensions and to allow write operations to tablespace containers and log files that are associated with the current database to continue.

Database I/O must be resumed from the same connection from which it was suspended.

Initializing a Split Mirror with `db2inidb`

Before a split mirror copy of a DB2 UDB database can be used, it must first be initialized; a split mirror database copy is initialized by executing the system command `db2inidb`. The syntax for this command is:

```
db2inidb [DatabaseAlias]
AS [SNAPSHOT | MIRROR | STANDBY]
<RELOCATE USING [ConfigFile]>
```

where:

DatabaseAlias   Identifies the alias assigned to the database the split mirror copy that is to be initialized references.

ConfigFile   Indicates that the database files contained in the split mirror copy are to be relocated according to information stored in the configuration file specified.

As you can see, a split mirror database copy can be initialized in one of three ways:

SNAPSHOT. The split mirror copy of the database will be initialized as a clone of the primary database. (It will be a working copy that has its own transaction log files.)

MIRROR. The split mirror copy of the database will be initialized as a backup image that can be used to restore the primary database.

STANDBY. The split mirror copy of the database will be initialized and placed in roll-forward pending state so that it can be continuously synchronized with the primary database. (New logs from the primary database can be retrieved and applied to the copy of the database at any time.) The standby copy of the database can then be used in place of the primary database if, for some reason, the primary database goes down.

Thus, if you wanted to initialize a split mirror copy of a database named SAMPLE and make it a backup image that can be used to restore the primary database, you could do so by executing a `db2inidb` command that looks like this:

```
db2inidb SAMPLE AS MIRROR
```

(The split mirror copy of the SAMPLE database used could have been created while the database was online by temporarily suspending I/O with the SET WRITE command, making the split mirror copy of the database using an appropriate non-DB2 UDB utility, and resuming I/O as soon as the split mirror copy was successfully created.)

Practice Questions

Question 1

Which of the following is the primary purpose for using infinite logging?

- ○ A. Eliminate the need to archive log files as they become full.
- ○ B. Eliminate the need to specify the number of primary log files used.
- ○ C. Eliminate the need to specify the size of all log files used.
- ○ D. Support large transactions whose logging activity would normally exceed the space provided by primary and secondary log files.

Question 2

Which of the following is NOT supported when LOGRETAIN is set to RECOVERY and USEREXIT is OFF?

- ○ A. Circular logging
- ○ B. Archival logging
- ○ C. Roll-forward recovery
- ○ D. Crash recovery

Question 3

When attempting to connect to a database named SAMPLE, the following message is displayed:

```
SQL1015N The database must be restarted because the
previous session did not conclude normally.
```

In order to correct the situation, which of the following should be performed?

- ○ A. RESTORE DATABASE sample
- ○ B. RESTART DATABASE sample
- ○ C. RECOVER DATABASE sample
- ○ D. RESET DATABASE sample

Question 4

Some of a database's indexes need to be rebuilt. To minimize application response time, which of the following is the correct setting of the INDEXREC database configuration parameter?

○ A. ACCESS
○ B. RESTART
○ C. IMMEDIATE
○ D. DEFERRED

Question 5

The REDIRECT option of the RESTORE command is used to do which of the following?

○ A. Restore a database to a location that is different from its original location.
○ B. Restore a database whose tablespace containers reference invalid drives/devices.
○ C. Restore a database and at the same time, convert all DMS tablespaces to SMS tablespaces.
○ D. Restore a database and at the same time, convert all SMS tablespaces to DMS tablespaces.

Question 6

The following commands have been entered:

```
UPDATE DB CFG FOR sample USING LOGRETAIN YES IMMEDIATE
BACKUP DB sample TO c:\backups
CONNECT TO sample
INSERT INTO department (deptid, deptname) VALUES ('001', 'RESEARCH')
RESTORE DB sample FROM c:\backups
```

Which two of the following commands can be issued to make the SAMPLE database usable?

❏ A. RESTART DB sample
❏ B. ROLLFORWARD DB sample to END OF LOGS
❏ C. ROLLFORWARD DB sample COMPLETE
❏ D. ROLLFORWARD DB sample to END OF LOGS AND STOP
❏ E. ROLLFORWARD DB sample CONTINUE

Question 7

Given the following command:

```
RESTORE DATABASE sample FROM c:\backups
```

Which of the parameters determines how much buffer space will be used to restore the SAMPLE database?

- ○ A. logbufsz
- ○ B. buffpage
- ○ C. restbufsz
- ○ D. util_heap_sz

Question 8

Given that the USEREXIT configuration parameter for a database is set to YES, which of the following configuration parameters must be set to enable infinite logging?

- ○ A. LOGPRIMARY = −1
- ○ B. LOGSECOND = −1
- ○ C. LOGFILSIZ = −1
- ○ D. LOGRETAIN = −1

Question 9

Which combination of database configuration parameters make a database non-recoverable?

- ○ A. LOGRETAIN=RECOVERY; USEREXIT=YES
- ○ B. LOGRETAIN=NO; USEREXIT=YES
- ○ C. LOGRETAIN=RECOVERY; USEREXIT=NO
- ○ D. LOGRETAIN=NO; USEREXIT=NO

Question 10

When does a log file become an off-line archived log file?

- ○ A. When it is moved from the active log directory
- ○ B. When it is no longer needed for crash recovery
- ○ C. When it is full and a new log is being processed
- ○ D. When it becomes full

Question 11

Given the following command:

```
ROLLFORWARD DATABASE sample TO 2003-01-01-00.00.00.0000 AND
STOP
```

How is the time 2003-01-01-00.00.00.0000 interpreted by the `ROLLFORWARD` command?

◯ A. As a local time value

◯ B. As a coordinated universal time (UTC) value

◯ C. As a timestamp value

◯ D. As a world time value

Question 12

Which of the following configuration parameters enables dual logging for a database?

◯ A. newlogpath

◯ B. seconglogpath

◯ C. mirrorlogpath

◯ D. overflowlogpath

Question 13

Which of the following occurs when the command `SET WRITE SUSPEND FOR DATABASE` is issued?

◯ A. All tablespace writes are suspended; all log writes are suspended; and all database operations continue to function normally.

◯ B. All tablespace writes are suspended and all database operations continue to function normally.

◯ C. All tablespace writes are suspended; all log writes are suspended; and all database operations other than online backup and restore operations continue to function normally.

◯ D. All tablespace writes are suspended and all database operations other than online backup and restore operations continue to function normally.

Question 14

An incremental backup image contains which of the following?

- ○ A. A copy of all data and index changes made since the last successful backup (full, incremental, or delta) was made.
- ○ B. A copy of all data and index changes made since the last successful full backup image was made.
- ○ C. A copy of all data, index, and database meta-data that has changed since the last successful backup (full, incremental, or delta) was made.
- ○ D. A copy of all data, index, and database meta-data that has changed since the last successful full backup image was made.

Question 15

Which of the following commands will produce just a list of all backup operations performed on a database named SAMPLE?

- ○ A. LIST HISTORY BACKUP ALL FOR sample
- ○ B. LIST BACKUP HISTORY FOR sample
- ○ C. LIST ALL BACKUP HISTORY FOR sample
- ○ D. LIST RECOVERY FILE BACKUP HISTORY FOR sample

Question 16

An offline database backup that was started for a database named SAMPLE at 1:00 AM local time completed at 2:30 AM local time. Assuming the SAMPLE database is a recoverable database, and that it is now 11:30 AM, which of the following commands must be performed in order to restore the SAMPLE database to the state it was in at 2:30 this morning?

- ○ A. RESTORE DATABASE sample FROM c:\backups
- ○ B. RESTORE DATABASE sample FROM c:\backups ROLLFORWARD TO 02:30.00.000000 USING LOCAL TIME
- ○ C. RESTORE DATABASE sample FROM c:\backups WITHOUT ROLLING FORWARD
- ○ D. RESTORE DATABASE sample FROM c:\backups ROLLFORWARD STOP

Answers

Question 1

The correct answer is **D**. If you are concerned about running out of log space and you want to avoid allocating a large number of secondary log files, you can configure a database to perform infinite logging. To enable infinite logging, you simply set the database configuration parameters *userexit* and *logsecond* to ON and −1, respectively.

Question 2

The correct answer is **A**. If the *logretain* configuration parameter for a database is set to RECOVERY and/or the *userexit* parameter is set to YES, archival logging is used and roll-forward recovery operations can be performed against the database. On the other hand, when both of these configuration parameters are set to NO, which is the default, circular logging is used and roll-forward recovery is not supported. In either case, crash recovery is supported.

Question 3

The correct answer is **B**. Whenever transaction processing is interrupted by an unexpected event (such as a power failure), the database the transaction was interacting with at the time is placed in an inconsistent state. Such a database will remain in an inconsistent state and will be unusable until a crash recovery operation returns it to some point of consistency; an inconsistent database will notify users and applications that it is unusable via a return code and error message that is generated each time an attempt to establish a connection to it is made. In such a case, crash recovery can be initiated by executing the RESTART command. (Had the *autorestart* database configuration parameter been set to ON, a crash recovery operation would have been started automatically when the user attempted to connect to the SAMPLE database and the error message would not have been displayed.)

Question 4

The correct answer is **B**. If the *indexrec* parameter of a database's configuration file is set to RESTART, invalid indexes will be rebuilt, either explicitly or implicitly, when the database is restarted (i.e., when crash recovery is performed on the database) and it will take longer to restart the database. On the other hand, if the *indexrec* parameter is set to ACCESS, invalid indexes will be rebuilt the first time they are accessed (after they have been marked as being invalid) and users may experience a decrease in performance.

Question 5

The correct answer is **B**. The purpose of a redirected restore (which is initiated by executing the RESTORE command with the REDIRECT option specified) is to redefine any invalid tablespace containers encountered at the beginning of the recovery process. (The TO [Location] option of the RESTORE command is used to restore a database to a location that is different from its original location and it's impossible to change tablespace types with a restore operation, or any other operation for that matter.)

Question 6

The correct answers are **C** and **D**. Because the *logretain* database configuration parameter has been set to YES, roll-forward recovery has been enabled for the SAMPLE database. As a result, when the database is restored using the RESTORE command, it will automatically be placed in "Roll-forward pending" state. While the database is in "Roll-forward pending" state, it cannot be accessed by users and applications. And the only way a database can be taken out of "Roll-forward pending" state is by executing the ROLLFORWARD command with either the STOP or the COMPLETE option specified.

Question 7

The correct answer is **C**. If the BUFFER option of the RESTORE command is not used to specify how much buffer space should be reserved for the RESTORE utility, the amount of buffer space used is determined by the value of the *restbufsz* DB2 Database Manager configuration parameter. (Likewise, if the BUFFER option of the BACKUP command is not used to specify how much buffer space should be reserved for the BACKUP utility, the amount of buffer space used is determined by the value of the *backbufsz* DB2 Database Manager configuration parameter.)

Question 8

The correct answer is **B**. Infinite logging is enabled by setting the *userexit* database configuration parameter to YES and the *logsecond* database configuration parameter to –1.

Question 9

The correct answer is **D**. If the *logretain* configuration parameter for a database is set to RECOVERY and/or the *userexit* parameter is set to YES, archival logging is used, roll-forward recovery operations can be performed against the database, and the database is considered to be recoverable. On the other hand, when both of these configuration parameters are set to NO, circular logging is used, roll-forward recovery is not supported, and the database is considered to be non-recoverable.

Question 10

The correct answer is **A**. An online archive log file is a log file that contains records that are associated with completed transactions that resides in the active log directory. As soon as an online archive log file is moved from the active log directory to another storage location, it becomes an offline archive log file.

Question 11

The correct answer is **B**. Unless the ROLLFORWARD command is executed with the USING LOCAL TIME option, all time values are assumed to be Coordinated Universal Time (also referred to as Greenwich Mean Time) values.

Question 12

The correct answer is **C**. To enable log file mirroring (also referred to as dual logging), you simply assign the fully qualified name of the mirror log location to the *mirrorlogpath* database configuration parameter.

Question 13

The correct answer is **C**. When executed, the SET WRITE SUSPEND FOR DATABASE command causes the DB2 Database Manager to suspend all write operations to tablespace containers and log files that are associated with the current database. All database operations, apart from online backup and restore operations, will function normally while database writes are suspended. That's because read-only transactions are not suspended and are able to continue working with the suspended database, provided they do not request a resource that is being held by the suspended I/O process. Furthermore, applications can continue to process insert, update, and delete operations using data that has been cached in the database's buffer pool(s). However, new pages cannot be read into the buffer pool(s) and no new database connections can be established.

Question 14

The correct answer is **D**. An incremental backup is a backup image that only contains pages that have been updated since the previous backup image was made. Along with updated data and index pages, each incremental backup image also contains all of the initial database meta-data (such as database configuration, tablespace definitions, recovery history file, etc.) that is normally found in full backup images.

Question 15

The correct answer is **A**. Information about backup operations is recorded in a database's recovery history file and you can view the contents of a recovery history file by executing the LIST HISTORY command. The proper syntax for listing just backup operation information with the LIST HISTORY command is LIST HISTORY BACKUP ALL FOR [DatabaseName].

Question 16

The correct answer is **C**. When a recoverable database is restored from a backup image, it is automatically placed in "Roll-forward pending" state unless the WITHOUT ROLLING FORWARD option is used with the RESTORE command. Because the backup image was made while the database was offline, no changes were made between 1:00 AM and 2:30 AM. Therefore, by restoring the database from the backup image that was taken at 1:00 AM and by specifying the WITHOUT ROLLING FORWARD option, the database will be returned to the state it was in at 2:30 AM and it will be taken out of "Roll-forward pending" state.

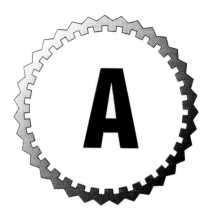

A

DB2 UDB V8.1 for Linux, UNIX, and Windows Database Administration Certification Exam (Exam 701) Objectives

. . . .

*T*he DB2 UDB V8.1 for Linux, UNIX, and Windows Database Administration certification exam (Exam 701) consists of 70 questions, and candidates have 75 minutes to complete the exam. A score of 61% or higher is required to pass this exam.

The primary objectives the DB2 UDB V8.1 for Linux, UNIX, and Windows Database Administration certification exam (Exam 701) is designed to cover are as follows.

DB2 Server Management (19%)

➤ Ability to configure and manage DB2 instances

➤ Knowledge of the DB2 authentication

➤ Knowledge of the DB2 authorizations

➤ Ability to set user and/or group privileges

➤ Knowledge of the DB2 force command

➤ Ability to configure client/server connectivity

➤ Ability to schedule jobs

➤ Ability to configure client/server connectivity using DISCOVERY

➤ Skill in interpreting the Notify log

Data Placement (17%)

➤ Ability to create a database

➤ Skill in discussing the use of schemas

➤ Skill in discussing the various tablespace states

➤ Ability to create and manipulate the various DB2 objects

➤ Ability to create and discuss the characteristics of an SMS tablespace

➤ Ability to create and discuss the characteristics of a DMS tablespace

Data Access (17%)

➤ Ability to create DB2 tasks using the GUI tools

➤ Knowledge of the creation and management of indexes

➤ Ability to create constraints on tables (e.g., RI, Informational, Unique)

➤ Ability to create views on tables

➤ Skill in examining the contents of the System Catalog tables

➤ Ability to use GUI tools to access DB objects

➤ Knowledge of how to enforce data uniqueness

Monitoring DB2 Activity (16%)

➤ Ability to obtain/modify database manager configuration information

➤ Ability to obtain/modify database configuration information

➤ Ability to capture EXPLAIN/VISUAL EXPLAIN information

➤ Skill in analyzing EXPLAIN/VISUAL EXPLAIN information (sortheap, buffpage, degree)

➤ Ability to identify the functions of the DB2 Governor and Query Patroller

➤ Ability to obtain and modify DB2 registry variables

➤ Ability to capture snapshots

➤ Ability to create and activate event monitors

➤ Ability to identify output from the Health Center

DB2 Utilities (17%)

➤ Ability to use EXPORT utility to extract data from a table

➤ Ability to use IMPORT utility to insert data into a table

➤ Ability to use the LOAD utility to insert data into a table

➤ Knowledge to identify when to use IMPORT versus LOAD

➤ Ability to use the REORG, REORGCHK, REBIND, and RUNSTATS utilities

➤ Ability to use DB2Move and DB2Look

➤ Knowledge of the functionality of the DB2 Advisors

➤ Ability to use the DB2 Control Center

Backup and Recovery (14%)

➤ Ability to perform database-level and tablespace-level BACKUP and RESTORE

➤ Knowledge to identify and explain issues on index recreation

➤ Knowledge of database logging

➤ Knowledge of crash recovery

➤ Knowledge of version recovery

➤ Knowledge of roll-forward recovery

DB2 UDB V8.1 for Linux, UNIX, and Windows Database Administration Certification Upgrade Exam (Exam 706) Objectives

The DB2 UDB V8.1 for Linux, UNIX, and Windows Database Administration certification upgrade exam (Exam 706) consists of 30 questions, and candidates have 40 minutes to complete the exam. A score of 55% or higher is required to pass this exam.

The primary objectives the DB2 UDB V8.1 for Linux, UNIX, and Windows Database Administration certification upgrade exam (Exam 706) is designed to cover are as follows.

DB2 Server Management (20%)

➤ Configure DB2 using online configuration parameters

➤ Prepare database for exclusive mode for maintenance

➤ Use of Notify log for system administration

➤ Configure DB2 Administration Server

Data Placement (13%)

➤ Use snapshot monitor to obtain information on a tablespace state

➤ Maintain a DMS tablespace by adding, dropping, or changing the size of a container

➤ Create and manipulate various DB2 objects (buffer pools, new indexing, and temporary tables)

Data Access (13%)

➤ Create and manage indexes to provide better concurrency

➤ Use informational constraints in table definitions

Monitoring DB2 Activity (14%)

➤ Use SQL to access snapshot monitor data

➤ Create and activate event monitors

➤ Configure and use Health Monitor and Health Center to improve database availability

DB2 Utilities (23%)

➤ Use the LOAD utility to insert data into a table online

➤ Use the REORG, REORGCHK, REBIND, and RUNSTATS utilities

➤ Knowledge of the functionality of the DB2 Advisors

➤ Use the DB2 Control Center

➤ Use the inspect utility to determine problems with database

Backup and Recovery (17%)

➤ Configure system for new logging features

➤ Use the roll-forward recovery to different points of time

➤ Use incremental backups to enhance recovery duration

➤ Use DB2 suspend I/O and resume I/O capabilities to enhance recovery and high availability

Index

. . . .

Safari

InformIT

PTR Online